Teach
Yourself
DELPHI™ 3

in 14 days

Teach Yourself
DELPHI™ 3
in 14 days

Dan Osier,
Steve Grobman,
and Steve Batson

SAMS
PUBLISHING

201 West 103rd Street
Indianapolis, Indiana 46290

I would like to dedicate this book to my father James for teaching me right from wrong, and reminding me that anything is possible. —DJO

Thanks to my wife Ashlyn and my beagle Ada for all their support. —SLG

To my beautiful wife Sharon who stands by me when times are tough and supports me in all my dreams and endeavors. To my two beautiful daughters, Alsyssa and Amber, who fill my life with love, laughter, and joy. God has truly blessed me with you all. —STB

Copyright © 1997 by Sams Publishing

FIRST EDITION

International Standard Book Number: 0-672-31114-3

Library of Congress Catalog Card Number: 97-66194

2000   99   98   97   4   3   2   1

Interpretation of the printing code: the rightmost double-digit number is the year of the book's printing; the rightmost single-digit, the number of the book's printing. For example, a printing code of 97-1 shows that the first printing of the book occurred in 1997.

Composed in AGaramond and MCPdigital by Macmillan Computer Publishing

Printed in the United States of America

Trademarks

Publisher and Publisher Richard K. Swadley
Publishing Manager Greg Wiegand
Director of Editorial Services Cindy Morrow
Assistant Marketing Managers Kristina Perry, Rachel Wolfe

Acquisitions Editor
Christopher Denny

Development Editor
Richard W. Alvey, Jr.

Production Editor
Kristi Hart

Indexer
Erika Millen

Technical Reviewers
Peter Dale
Michael Monk
Andrew Kern
David Neff
Anders Ohlsson
Paul Powers
Chris Reed

Editorial Coordinator
Katie Wise

Technical Edit Coordinator
Lynette Quinn

Resource Coordinator
Deborah Frisby

Editorial Assistants
Carol Ackerman
Andi Richter
Rhonda Tinch-Mize

Cover Designer
Tim Amrhein

Book Designer
Gary Adair

Copy Writer
Peter Fuller

Production Team Supervisors
Brad Chinn
Charlotte Clapp

Production
Jena Brandt
Mona Brown
Mark D. Matthews
Ian A. Smith

Overview

Contents

Week 2 At A Glance   243

Day 8   The Visual Component Library   245

Acknowledgments

I would, as always, like to acknowledge the overwhelming contribution of love and support from my wife Diane and my daughter Nathalia. They have made my life more wonderous than I ever thought possible. For the fabulous work of Jim and Darlene, my parents, in being the rutter that kept me on course. And to my friends Lynne Marchi and Greg Kime for making work fun. Life good. —DJO

To all the authors' families and friends for tolerating their mental and physical absence during this effort.

For the fine work of our acquisitions editor, Chris Denny, who hated to hear those six little words, "We have to slip the date."

To Kristi Hart and Rich Alvey for making our scribbling legible and organized for you, the reader.

To PP, Chris Reed, Michael Monk, Peter Dale, David Neff, Andrew Kern, Anders Ohlsson, and Paul Powers at Borland for tech editing the book.

About the Authors

Dan Osier is a Security Product Engineer with Intel Corporation working on encryption and firewall technology. Dan also has worked as a Software Engineer for the Air Force designing real-time aircraft simulations. After receiving his Masters in Software Engineering, Dan taught graduate and undergraduate Computer Science classes at his alma mater. Dan has been writing software since the age of 12, and he had his first contract programming job at the age of 15. In his spare time, Dan enjoys playing classical guitar music and kicking some alien butt in Duke Nukem 3D (Atomic Edition).

Steve Grobman has worked for many years developing a diverse set of computer applications. His works include client/server, Internet, and graphics applications. Steve also is considered an expert in computer networking, data security, simulations, and artificial intelligence.

Steve Batson has worked with computer hardware and software for over 15 years. He gained an electronics background in the United States Air Force where he installed, repaired, and maintained a variety of radio communications equipment. He is currently a Systems Programmer/Analyst for Intel Corporation where he supports e-mail gateways for the company's Information Technology Department. His programming background includes BASIC, C, Assembler, Pascal, Visual Basic, and Delphi. Steve enjoys working with computers at work and as a hobby. He also loves 50s music, Star Trek, and going to the movies.

Tell Sams Publishing What You Think!

As a reader, you are the most important critic and commentator of our books. We value your opinion and want to know what we're doing right, what we could do better, what areas you'd like to see us publish in, and any other words of wisdom you're willing to pass our way. You can help us make strong books that meet your needs and give you the computer guidance you require.

Do you have access to CompuServe or the World Wide Web? Then check out our CompuServe forum by typing GO SAMS at any prompt. If you prefer the World Wide Web, check out our site at http://www.mcp.com.

 NOTE

> If you have a technical question about this book, call the technical support line at (317) 581-3833.

As the publishing manager of the group that created this book, I welcome your comments. You can fax, e-mail, or write me directly to let me know what you did or didn't like about this book—as well as what we can do to make our books stronger. Here's the information:

Fax: (317) 581-4669

E-mail: programming_mgr@sams.mcp.com

Mail: Greg Wiegand
          Sams Publishing
          201 W. 103rd Street
          Indianapolis, IN 46290

Introduction

Teach Yourself Delphi 3 in 14 Days is designed to assist beginners in immersing themselves in the Delphi product. We believe that the best way to learn is through hands-on use. To this end, we strove to make this book as interesting and informative as possible. We hope that as you work through the days, you will do the exercises as well as take the quizzes to help gauge your progress. Good luck and happy programming!

How To Use This Book

This book has been designed as a 14-day teach-yourself training course complete with exercises, chapter quizzes, and examples that you can try out on your own. It is expected that you can complete one chapter each day of the week for two weeks. However, you should work at your own rate. If you think you can complete two or more chapters a day, go for it! Also, if you think that you should spend more than one day on a certain chapter, spend as much time as you need.

Each week begins with a Week At A Glance section. Each day ends with a Q&A section containing questions and answers related to that day's material. There also is a Workshop at the end of the day. A quiz tests your knowledge of the day's concepts, and one or more exercises put your new skills to use. We urge you to complete these sections to reinforce your new knowledge.

 NOTE

> The source code presented in listings throughout the book is available on the Delphi 3 product's CD-ROM.

Who Should Read This Book

This book is for you if you've been wanting to dive into the world of 32-bit programming but didn't know where to begin. This book is written for the beginner—the one who wants to learn what Delphi 3 is all about.

Conventions Used in This Book

This book contains special features to help highlight important concepts and information.

NOTE

A Note presents interesting pieces of information related to the surrounding discussion.

TIP

A Tip offers advice or teaches you an easier way to do something.

WARNING

A Warning advises you about potential problems and helps you steer clear of disaster.

NEW TERM The New Term icon is added to paragraphs in which a new term is defined. The new term also is italicized so you can find it easily.

TYPE The Type icon identifies a Delphi code listing in which you must type some or all of the code yourself. When some or all the code is generated automatically by Delphi, we tell you. All listings are available on the Delphi 3 product's CD-ROM.

ANALYSIS The Analysis icon identifies the explanation and purpose of the listing just presented.

At A Glance

Delphi Basics

On Day 1, you take a look at what Delphi is and how you can benefit from its RAD capabilities. RAD stands for Rapid Application Development. You get your feet wet in Delphi by going through a quick introduction that touches on some basic programming topics common to all programming languages. You also take a whirlwind tour of the IDE, Delphi's integrated development environment.

On Days 2 and 3, you get into some Object Pascal basics to give you the foundation you need to move on. Day 4 addresses some of the concepts involved in object-oriented programming. On Day 5, you learn how to use the Project Manager and to stay organized as you develop applications. Day 6 presents the proper use of the editor and debugger, and you'll be introduced to the Code Insight tool. Day 7 finishes out the first week by presenting some fundamentals of GUI (graphical user interface) design concepts to help you write windows applications that have the familiar standard "look and feel" that you have come to know and love.

Day 1

Welcome to Delphi 3— Is This Visual Pascal?

Day 1 provides you with an overview of Delphi 3 from a philosophical perspective. You gain some insight into where the industry has been and what has driven the development of a tool as unique and powerful as Delphi. You'll breeze through some of the basics and then write a quick application to help you get your Delphi legs. In answer to the question posed in today's title, Delphi 3 *is* Visual Pascal, and much more. Delphi 3 gives you the solid foundation of Borland's Object Pascal plus the visual application-building characteristic of products such as Visual Basic. Delphi offers huge advantages over the competition and can provide some real productivity gains for the programmer. You'll finish out the day by taking a quick look at the IDE (integrated development environment).

Delphi Is RAD, Man!

I may just sound like a gnarly teenager, but Delphi users mean more by RAD than just the fact that Delphi is a great product.

NEW TERM *RAD* stands for *rapid application development.* It's a term coined for a new breed of software development environments. In this new RAD world, programmers use tools that are more intuitive and visual. Looking at a piece of code that generates a window and trying to visualize that window is not as easy as creating the actual window with a couple clicks of your mouse.

In this new world of simpler, more visual interfaces, the first real player to show up was Visual Basic (hereafter referred to as VB). VB brought programming down from a mystical religion (accomplishable only by that guru in the back room you feed Twinkies and Mountain Dew) to something a mere mortal could handle. These new interfaces enable the software developer to "visually" construct the user interface using the mouse, rather than "textually" construct-ing it in code and then having to compile and run the code just to see what it looks like, as illustrated in Figure 1.1. This is sort of like the designers at Lamborghini cutting the body molds for the Diablo without ever making a clay model to see what the end product should look like first!

Figure 1.1.
Delphi enables you to visually build the user interface.

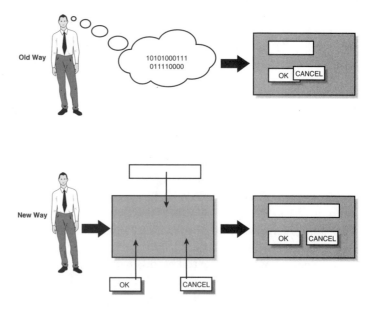

Although VB did well in the market and helped open up the world of programming to us mortals, VB has also had its problems. The language itself did not really promote good design. VB lacked the mechanisms that promote highly structured, compact, and well-refined code.

It lacked the rigor of an object-oriented language (you learn more about this on Day 4, "Object-Oriented Programming and Software Engineering"). VB even promoted bad programming (from our point of view) by enabling developers to hack a quick solution and having "work-arounds" for those pesky but good programming practices we should be observing. All three of this book's authors are good VB programmers (among other things), and we've seen both sides of the fence (the VB/Delphi-OOP fence that is), and we feel we're finally standing back on the right side again.

Delphi is the next step in RAD development environments. It corrects most of the deficiencies found in VB without adding too many new ones. This book describes the strengths and limitations (there aren't many) of Delphi, and it walks you through this new frontier. If you don't have goose bumps yet, you should. It's a great journey you're undertaking, and it will provide substantial rewards.

This Looks Like Visual Basic on Steroids!

This book doesn't assume that you have written code in any other language, but if you have written VB code in the past, you may look at the Delphi 3's development environment and say, "It's VB on steroids!" Well, you're right. The Delphi developers have created a tool that may seem similar to VB at first glance, but it is, in fact, distinctly different (and superior to) the VB environment. The IDE is the portion of Delphi you see when you double-click on the Delphi icon in Windows (which you learn about later in this chapter). Although Delphi 3 bears a visual similarity to VB, the major difference between the two products is the language that exists "behind" the IDE. As stated earlier, the VB language tends to promote rapid program development, rather than good development practices.

Delphi, on the other hand, uses Object Pascal as its foundation language. Borland's Pascal compiler (beginning with Turbo Pascal 1.0) has been one of the fastest compilers in the business. Borland has added object-based extensions to the language to support good programming practices and more efficient code (meaning that you get more done with fewer lines of code). Object Pascal is a true object-based language with a rock solid compiler behind it.

The Benefits of Delphi

Delphi offers real flexibility for the developer. This extends to how your application will be deployed to the user. If you are an individual developer, you most likely will want to give your application to the end user as a single .EXE file. This is the easiest way for an individual developer to keep track of a product. Deploying a single .EXE file also means that you can write simple installation programs. You can implement this option by creating stand-alone .EXE files that do not rely on other files or DLLs to run.

In the corporate development world, a different mindset prevails. Where standards are sought after, Delphi can help there, too. Suppose you are writing Delphi applications for a company of 5,000 users. Every time you deploy a new application, you must send out your huge 1MB .EXE file to each user. This can get to be a nuisance, especially when that 1MB file is sent to all 5,000 machines. Delphi enables you to place standard components into what are called packages. You can take this "package" and place it on each user's computer once. When you write additional applications, you can reference items in that package. In this paradigm, you find that once that large package is on each user's system, you can write whole applications in which the .EXE file is only 200KB, and still get full functionality.

This method of packaging is new to Delphi 3 and is a feature that will help companies deploy these "thin clients" in which a standard package is kept on the target machine all the time. See Day 5, "Applications, Files, and the Project Manager," and Day 14, "Building Internet Applications with Delphi," for more details about packages.

Delphi 3 provides an optimized compiler that generates a fast executable without your having to work harder to optimize the program than you did writing the program in the first place.

Differences Between Delphi 3 and Delphi 2

Although the Delphi 3 IDE may look pretty much the same as the Delphi 2 IDE, there are some major differences between the two under the hood. Here are several key areas of improvement:

- ☐ *Database architecture and connectivity.* The database architecture has been completely restructured to take a multi-tiered approach rather than the traditional client/server design. This enables you to create a very thin client application. Native Access database support (a highly sought-after feature) is provided for helping in the migration of legacy VB apps to Delphi 3. Both of these subjects are discussed on Day 11, "Delphi's Database Architecture."

- ☐ *ActiveX controls.* You can create your own ActiveX controls as well as use a prewritten control in your Delphi project. You build your own ActiveX control on Day 13, "Building VCL and ActiveX Components."

- ☐ *Web applications.* You can create both Web client and Web server applications. This gives Delphi 3 a real lead in the battle for intranet development tools. You build some cool Web stuff on Day 14.

1

- [ ] *Packages.* You now have the freedom to choose between including the runtime library in the executable or having it as a separate DLL (static versus dynamic linking). This feature enables the independent developer to include all information in the .EXE file for ease of distribution, and it lets corporate developers deploy a standard runtime library to all desktops and just release small .EXEs instead. Packages are covered in Bonus Day 15, "Deploying Applications."

- [ ] *Active forms.* You can run your entire Delphi 3 application as an ActiveX control. You literally can run your entire application on a Web page. Think of the possibilities! This topic is covered on Day 13, "Building VCL and ActiveX Components."

- [ ] *IDE editor and debugger enhancements.* Delphi's new editor has several new features, including automatic code completion and a code parameter expert. These are covered on Day 6, "Editor and Debugger."

- [ ] *Thread safe.* Many of the graphics routines have been made thread safe, and so has work on the canvas been made thread safe.

NOTE

> In addition to the ActiveX technology, Delphi 3 enables you to create native Delphi components and reuse them in all your projects. Where ActiveX controls require you to distribute the ActiveX component along with your application, native components require no added files for distributing your applications. You learn how to write your own visual component on Day 13.

What's Up with This Delphi Client/Server?

There are three different versions of Delphi: Delphi Desktop, Delphi Developer, and Delphi Client/Server (hereinafter referred to as the CS Edition). These versions of Delphi offer different levels of connectivity with the outside world. Delphi Desktop enables you to connect to dBASE, Paradox, and Access through the Borland Database Engine. The Developer Edition provides ODBC connectivity (for connecting any data source with an ODBC driver), and the CS Edition comes with SQL Links. The SQL Links product gives you high-speed 32-bit drivers for connecting to SQL server databases such as Sybase and Oracle, as shown in Figure 1.2.

Figure 1.2.
The CS Edition provides native database access.

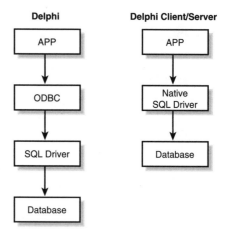

The CS Edition is designed to compete with other client/server application-development products. Its main competitors are PowerBuilder and, of course, Visual Basic Enterprise Edition. These products typically are used in a corporate environment to develop Windows-based front ends for network-based databases.

The Visual Component

Delphi also possesses its own native version of an ActiveX control, called a Visual Component. You write a Visual Component (VC) in Delphi and then add it to the Visual Component Library (VCL). The VCL is a repository of VCs that developers can use to create Delphi applications. All the components in the VCL are displayed on the toolbar so they're easily accessible to the user. The VCL is covered on Day 8, "The Visual Component Library."

The best thing about VCs is that you can construct your own (and you will on Day 13) and then add it to the toolbar. This also promotes code reusability, which is a vital part of high-productivity programming. Constructing VCs is also covered in the Component Writer's Guide help file that accompanies the Delphi 3 product.

Constants and Variables

For those of you who have done no programming before, this section defines a couple basic concepts: constants and variables.

A *constant* in the programming sense is just that—constant. Suppose you decide to use the state tax in your latest program. You could type **0.0775** (7.75 percent) into all the formulas throughout your application. If the tax rate changes, you would have to go back and find every

0.0775 and change it to 0.08 (another new tax—it figures!). This is miserable, not to mention that it's highly likely you could make a typing error in the 40 times you change the entry in your application.

Constants to the rescue! You can define a constant named StateTax, for example, and assign it a value of 0.08, and then use StateTax in those 40 places. Here's an example of the code:

```
Const
StateTax = 0.08;
```

Because constants cannot be changed during program execution, you could not ask the user for the new state tax and then place that user-defined value into StateTax. StateTax must be defined in code, and cannot be changed at runtime.

The idea of a constant is that the name (StateTax) is a direct substitute for 0.08. This means that anywhere you could have used 0.08 in your application, you can now use the constant name. The code may look weird, but it works:

```
YourTax := YourPurchase * StateTax;
```

This line of code brings up the next interesting topic, *variables*. Remember those evil y=mx+b formulas from your algebra classes in school? And remember the teacher saying "It's easy; just solve the equation for y?" You were using variables then, and now you will again. A variable is a placeholder for a value. Whereas constants remain the same throughout the execution of the program, a variable can be changed at any time.

If you define a variable FederalTax as a Single number, that FederalTax variable is now capable of holding one Single number, as in this example:

```
Var
FederalTax : Single;
```

The Single data type is a real number capable of representing a number between the following numbers. This type is big enough for the needs of this example.

$$1.5 \times 10^{-45} \text{ and } 3.4 \times 10^{38}$$

This declaration denotes that you have created a variable called FederalTax and that it is of type Single. Now in your program you can get the user's input and place that input into the FederalTax variable, as illustrated by the following code:

```
FederalTax := Put the user input code here;
```

The great thing about a variable is that you *can* change the value of FederalTax during the program's execution. Variables are a reusable asset and are much more flexible than constants.

There is a dramatic difference between a constant and a variable, not only in functionality but also in the use of each within the compiler. Because a constant is a substitute for a value, when you compile your application, Delphi goes out and simply unsubstitutes all instances of StateTax and replaces them with 0.08. This is done only in the executable that Delphi generates, and your source code is not altered. A variable is handled quite differently. Because the value of a variable can change during the program's execution, the application must allocate a place in memory where the value of that variable can be stored. It must have a memory location in which to store FederalTax to remember it from one minute to the next and to hold the new value of FederalTax when it is changed during the program's execution. Constants and variables are discussed in more depth on Day 2.

Procedures and Functions

When you first start writing programs, you probably will write code that executes sequentially from beginning to end, in a straight path. You might want to consider changing that mindset.

Suppose you need to write a program that displays a "hello world" message on the screen three separate times. To write this program, you probably would write something similar to Listing 1.1, which presents the program in pseudo code just to give you an idea of how it would work.

NEW TERM *Pseudo code* is an English-like interpretation of events that simulate or imitate the code. Listing 1.1 uses it to show the general form of a program without using the actual Object Pascal code.

TYPE   **Listing 1.1. A simple onscreen message.**

```
program Hello;

begin
    create the window
    write "HELLO" to the window
    destroy the window
    create the window
    write "HELLO" to the window
    destroy the window

    create the window
    write "HELLO" to the window
    destroy the window
end.
```

ANALYSIS This program writes HELLO to the screen three separate times. In case you didn't notice, the program repeated itself a little. The program duplicates the same bit of code three times. This means that the programmer has three times as many chances to make mistakes typing the code. There must be a better way, and there is.

Procedures

NEW TERM A *procedure* is nothing more than a logical grouping of program statements into a single program block. That block of code can then be activated by executing a procedure call. Here's the English version of what I just said: If you take those three lines of code and put a wrapper around them, give a name to that wrapper, and then, when you want to call those lines of code, you simply call that code block by using the name you gave it. Look at the example in Listing 1.2.

TYPE **Listing 1.2. A simple procedure.**

```
procedure SayHello;

begin
    create the window
    write "HELLO" to the window
    destroy the window
end;
```

ANALYSIS The lines of code are now in the procedure SayHello (our wrapper). Whenever you want to open a window, print HELLO to the screen, and destroy the window, you just call SayHello. Listing 1.3 shows what your new program could look like.

TYPE **Listing 1.3. The finished program (using a procedure).**

```
program Hello;

procedure SayHello;
   begin
      create the window
      write "HELLO" to the window
      destroy the window
   end;
begin
      SayHello;
      SayHello;
      SayHello
End {Program Hello}.
```

ANALYSIS As you can see, you can create the procedure SayHello once and then call it three separate times. Because you type it only once, there is less chance for error in the SayHello procedure. You can also reuse this code by cutting and pasting the SayHello procedure into another application. This concept is illustrated in Figure 1.3.

Figure 1.3.

Reusing procedures and code.

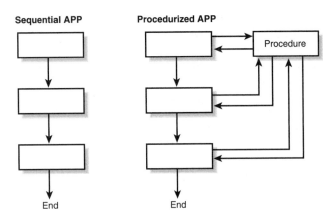

Functions

NEW TERM *Functions* are a slightly different beast. They are procedures that return a single value. Here's an example to illustrate. Take the equation y=cos(6). The cos (cosine) function takes 6 as its operand, calculates the cosine of 6, and then returns that value to the equation. The returned value then is placed into the y variable. These are the same concepts you learned in algebra. The concept of solving for y is a fundamental one. Notice that the cosine function is called from within the mathematical expression—yes, that's right. The great thing about a function is that the function call itself becomes the answer after the function call returns. So, in your expression, the flow of events is as follows:

1. The original equation is i=cos(6)
2. cos(6)
3. The cos(6) function calculates the cosine of 6 and returns .99
4. The equation then is y=cos (with cos=.99)
5. y=.99

Functions are handy because you cannot call a procedure in the middle of an expression. The main reason you can't is a procedure can be set up to return multiple values as a result of the procedure call. Having multiple values in a mathematical expression wouldn't work very well. Functions are the practical alternative because they are designed to return a single value.

Units—Reusable Code

NEW TERM Units are the greatest things since sliced bread! Okay, maybe a close third behind cellular phones and DOOM II. Anyway, *units* are a grouping of related functions and procedures. Just as you can group a series of Pascal statements and wrap them in a procedure or function, you can group those functions and procedures into the next "level" of wrapper, the unit.

Listing 1.4 contains a sample unit that provides three functions, SayHello, SayBye, and SayNothing.

TYPE **Listing 1.4. A simple unit.**

```
unit SayStuff;
begin
procedure SayHello;
   begin
      create the window
      write "HELLO" to the window
      destroy the window
   end;
procedure SayBye;
   begin
      create the window
      write "BYE" to the window
      destroy the window
   end;
procedure SayNothing;
   begin
      create the window
      write "NOTHING" to the window
      destroy the window
   end
end; {of unit SayStuff}
```

ANALYSIS The only difference between this program and the one in Listing 1.3 is that you put three procedures into a common grouping called SayStuff. When you want to reuse this code in your new project, just tell your program to Use SayStuff. If that unit is in your path (in other words, if Delphi can find the SayStuff unit), you can call those three functions. You can create the wheel once and then use it over and over again. This looks pretty good after years of reinventing the wheel every time you write a new program. This is another way in which Delphi (and Object Pascal) promotes software reuse.

The Form

The form is the basis of nearly every Delphi application. You may know the form as a window—the kind of window you see in Word, Paradox, or other Windows-based applications. In Delphi, the form is a foundation on which you place other Delphi components. It's the backdrop of your Windows application. If you do not change the defaults, Delphi assumes that you have a form in every project and displays a blank one every time you start Delphi. You can alter the default desktop by setting options in the dialog box that results from choosing Tools | Options. You can save the position of your windows, as well as which code windows you had open last time. This is done on a project-by-project basis.

You might have seen the form in many of its different roles. Forms can exist both in the modal and modeless state. The modal window is one that stays on top of all other windows and must be closed before you can access other windows. A modeless window is a window that will not stay on top, and will not interfere with the user moving to another task. You'll explore the creation of forms, in all their forms, throughout the book. Forms are the foundation of a Windows application.

What Are Form and Component Properties?

Properties are the attributes a particular object has, as shown in Figure 1.4. A person, for instance, has height, weight, eye color, and a Social Security Number as attributes (among others). In Delphi, all forms and all Visual Components (as well as ActiveX controls) have properties. A form (or window) has a size (height and width), a background color, a border, and some less "visual" attributes, such as a name. You can control the look and feel of these objects by changing or manipulating their attributes or properties.

Figure 1.4.
Everything has properties.

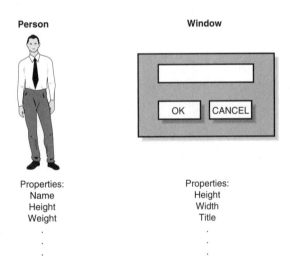

Consider an example of a Delphi visual component that controls a virtual reality headset. This headset would be similar to the ones found in many arcades today. This headset visual component would have some quite interesting properties. A refresh rate (just like a computer monitor), a screen resolution (maybe different for each eye to correct for your 20/50 vision, and so on. Then, while you ran your newly written video game (DOOM VI), the program could constantly adjust the headset to the conditions of the game by changing the properties of the headset VC object. You'll work with properties a lot in this book and will come to see how useful they are.

A Simple Delphi Application

To start you on your way to being a Delphi developer, this section shows you how to construct your first Delphi application. It assumes you already have installed Delphi on your Windows 95 system. Follow these steps:

1. Run Delphi by selecting the Delphi 3 icon from the Start | Programs | Delphi 3 menu.

2. After Delphi starts, you should see a blank form titled FORM1. If this does not appear, you must select File | New Application from the Delphi main menu bar.

3. Choose the Standard tab from the Component Palette, which is the floating toolbar at the upper-right area of the screen.

4. Click on the Button control.

5. Click on the middle of the form. A button should appear there.

6. Double-click on the button. At this point, a code window should appear with the cursor sitting between on a blank line between a begin and end line of code.

7. Type the following line of code on the blank line:

```
Canvas.TextOut(20, 20, 'Delphi 3 makes Windows programming a breeze');
```

   This completes the creation of your first Delphi application.

8. To compile and run your application, press the F9 key or choose Run | Run from the Delphi menu.

When you run the application, you should see a window (that ever-present form you heard about). The button you placed on the form should be there. Click it, and the phrase you entered in the Canvas.TextOut should be displayed in the window.

That is all the more difficult it is to create a working Delphi application. When you are done looking at your newly created application as it runs, press the close button in the upper-right corner of the window (the button with the × on it).

You now can exit Delphi by choosing File | Exit. Answer No when Delphi asks if you wish to save changes to your project.

Overview of the Delphi 3 IDE

Now it's time to learn about the Delphi environment. The goal of the remainder of this chapter is to familiarize you with Delphi's Integrated Development Environment (IDE). It also explains how to customize the IDE for your personal tastes and helps you organize your desktop and programming style.

NEW TERM IDE, Integrated Development Environment, is an environment that provides all the tools necessary to design, run, and test an application, and the tools are well connected to ease program development. In Delphi 3, the IDE consists of a code editor, debugger, toolbar, image editor, and database tools, all of which operate in an integrated fashion. This integration gives the developer a set of tools that operate in harmony, and compliment one another. The result is faster and more error-free development of complex applications.

The Basics

The first step in learning about IDE is to start Delphi. When Delphi is finished loading, your desktop should look similar to the one in Figure 1.5.

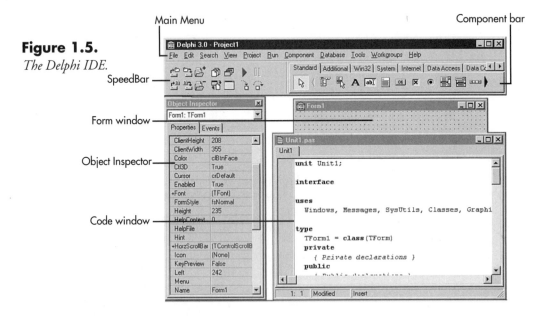

Figure 1.5.
The Delphi IDE.

If you do not have a window labeled Form1 in the middle of your screen, choose File | New Application from the Delphi menu bar. The IDE is composed of several major pieces, and the Delphi menu bar is divided into two major pieces.

SpeedBar

The *SpeedBar*, shown in Figure 1.6, is designed to help you get to your most-used functions easily and quickly. The default setup gives you what Borland considers to be the 14 most used items. These items are also available from the Delphi menu, and are put on the SpeedBar only

to facilitate your access to them. Each item is covered in detail later in the section titled "Delphi Menu Structure."

Figure 1.6.

The Delphi SpeedBar.

SpeedBar

Component Palette

The Component Palette is the "visual inventory" of your Visual Component Library (VCL). It enables you to categorize visual components into groups that make sense. By default, the components are grouped based on functionality; that is, all the data-access components are grouped together, and so on. These groups or *pages* are denoted with labeled tabs. The eight default pages are

Standard
Additional
Win95
Data Access
Data Controls
Win 3.1
Dialogs
System
QReport
ActiveX
Samples

Each tab contains following icon, which is called the *pointer button*:

This pointer button always is present on the left end of the Component Palette regardless of what component page you've selected, but it will be described just once, here. It is usually in the enabled state. When this button is enabled, you can navigate among the forms and windows in order to manipulate the Delphi environment. When you select an item from one of the component pages, you find the pointer button is disabled. This means you have entered a state in which Delphi thinks you are going to place a component onto a form. After you select a component, placing that component onto a form is as simple as clicking on the form itself.

You also can place the component on the form by double-clicking the component, and it is automatically placed on the form. If you select a component and then change your mind, just press the pointer button. That action cancels your component selection and returns you to the mode in which you can select other components.

The specifics of working with each component are covered in the chapter dedicated to the VCL components, Day 8.

Form

The form is the basis of nearly every Delphi application. You may know the form as a window: the kind of windows you see in Word, Paradox, or other Windows-based applications. In Delphi, the form is a foundation on which you place other Delphi components. It is the backdrop of your Windows application. A typical blank Delphi form is shown in Figure 1.7.

Figure 1.7.
A Delphi Form.

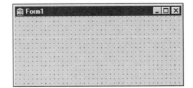

A form in Delphi has the same properties that you would find in any other Windows 95 window. It has a control menu in the upper-right corner of the form, the title bar across the top, and the minimize, maximize, and close (or kill) buttons in the upper-left corner of the form. You can hide these form controls if your form does not require them, or you can disable them on a per-button basis. This enables you to control what the user is capable of doing.

NOTE

> Although most Delphi applications are based on the form, you can use Delphi to write WIN32 DLLs in which a form may not exist. You can also write visual components in which no forms are present. Now, with Delphi 3, you can write your own ActiveX controls and packages that are not based on the form either.

Edit Window

One of the most essential pieces of the Delphi environment is the edit window. The edit window provides the mechanism for the developer (that's you) to input your Delphi code. The Delphi code editor is a great full-featured editor, as shown in Figure 1.8. With color syntax highlighting (which helps you spot those code errors more quickly), Brief-style editor commands (Brief is the programmer's editor, for the purists), and the ability to "undo" from now until the cows come home!

Figure 1.8.
The edit window.

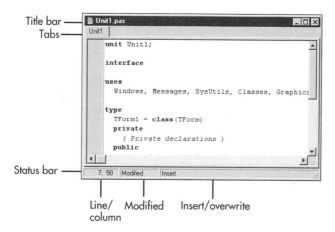

The window's title bar displays the name of file currently being viewed. The tabs along the top of the window indicate the pages that are currently available. Delphi applications can have many source files, and the tabs help you navigate through them.

Along the bottom of the edit window are three other items of interest. The first item on the left is the *line/column indicator*. This helps you figure out where you are in the code. The second item is the *modified* indicator. When you start a new project, the code that Delphi brings up for you is not saved. You must save it yourself. Because this code has changed since the last time it was saved to disk (which in this case is never) the word Modified appears next to the line/column indicator. Modified always appears if the code you see in the editor is not what is on the disk. In this case, there is no code on the disk, and so the modified indicator appears. The third item is the *insert/overwrite* indicator. This is a standard feature of most editors, and it shows you if you are inserting text or overwriting any existing text.

Object Inspector

You will find the Object Inspector essential to your work in Delphi. It provides an easy-to-use interface for changing the properties of a Delphi item, as well as to control the events to which an object reacts.

Properties Tab

The Properties tab of the Object Inspector, shown in Figure 1.9, enables you to look at and modify the properties an object possesses. Click the empty form window, and then observe the attributes present in the Object Inspector's Properties tab. When you see a property with a plus sign next to it, the property has subproperties nested beneath it.

Figure 1.9.

Properties tab of the
Object Inspector.

For example, notice that after you have selected the form, the Object Inspector has a Font property with a plus sign next to it. If you double-click the Font property, it opens and expands into more properties such as Color, Height, Name, and others. This format is a clean, simple, and efficient means for changing an object's attributes.

Events Tab

The Events tab, the other half of the Object Inspector's life, is shown in Figure 1.10. This tab displays all the events to which the selected object can respond. For instance, if you need an application to do something special upon close of the window, you can use the form's OnClose event to do that.

Figure 1.10.

Events tab of the
Object Inspector.

Delphi Menu Structure

The Delphi menu structure gives you access to a rich set of tools that can aid you in more of that RAD development we all need. This section briefly describes all the items on all the menus. The items are explained in detail in the chapters where they apply. Figure 1.11 shows the menu bar upon which all the menus discussed are based.

Figure 1.11.

The main menu bar.

 NOTE

The actual menu items you see depends on the version of Delphi you have. The CS Edition has some extras that are covered in this section. Please refer to your documentation, or call Borland if you need to know the differences among the three versions of Delphi 3.

The File Menu

The File menu is used to open, save, close, and print new or existing projects and files, and to add new forms and units to the open project. It contains several items, as shown in Figure 1.12. These items are described in the following sections.

Figure 1.12.

File menu.

New

Selecting New tells Delphi that you want to create a new object. This object can be any member of the object repository, including a new project. The New Items dialog box appears after making this selection, it enables you to create everything from a new window to an entire Web server. Some of the items in this dialog box are described in greater detail in later days.

New Application

Selecting New Application tells Delphi that you want to create a new project. If you have no project currently open, or the project you have open is up to date (has been saved to disk in its current state), Delphi closes out the current project and creates an entirely new one. This includes creating a new code editor window (with a newly created Unit1.PAS file), new Form object (Form1), and brings up the Object Inspector.

New Form

Selecting New Form tells Delphi you want to create a new form. By default, the form is a blank form (as opposed to one of the special forms in the object repository).

New Data Module

NEW TERM Selecting New Data Module tells Delphi you want to create a new *data module*. A data module is a non-visual form that you can use to house all your data controls. This is important because you need a form from which all the visual forms can get their data. This form serves that purpose.

Open

Selecting Open tells Delphi you want to open an object. The object can be a code module or an entire project. The directory in which Delphi first looks for project is the working directory assigned during Delphi's installation.

ReOpen

Selecting ReOpen displays a list right on the menu, of the last few projects or files you opened, and you can select a file to open from this list. It's a shortcut to choosing File | Open and specifying the filename.

Save

Selecting Save causes Delphi to save the current module you are working on.

1

Save As

Selecting Save As brings up the standard Windows 95 Save dialog box that enables you to save your current module under a new name. You may want to do this if you are going to radically alter a piece of code. (If you are using the client/server version of Delphi, you can also use the PVCS version control software.) This allows you to keep revisions and go back to old code if you make a mistake in the new code.

Save Project As

Selecting Save Project As brings up the standard Windows 95 Save dialog box that enables you to save your current project under a new name. This means that you can save an entire project off to the side for later use.

Save All

Selecting Save All saves everything that is open—project files and all.

Close

Selecting Close closes the currently selected code module or associated form. If you have not saved your module in its current state, Delphi queries you to find out if you want to save your changes.

Close All

Selecting Close All closes the current Delphi project. If you have not saved your project in its current state, Delphi queries you to find out if you want to save your changes.

Use Unit

Selecting Use Unit enables you to put a uses statement into your current code module for the unit you want to use. This is an easy way for you to include units in your code without manually inserting the unit name into the code.

Add to Project

Selecting Add to Project enables you to add an existing unit and its associated form to the Delphi project. When you add a unit to a project, Delphi automatically adds that unit to the uses clause of the project file.

Remove from Project

Selecting Remove from Project enables you to remove an existing unit and its associated form from the Delphi project. When you delete a unit in a project, Delphi automatically deletes that unit from the uses clause of the project file.

Print

Selecting Print enables you to print an item you've selected in Delphi.

If you select a form in Delphi and then select File | Print, Delphi displays the Print Form dialog box, as shown in Figure 1.13. In this dialog box, you specify how you would like the form printed: proportional, fit to page, or no scaling. Press OK to print the form.

Figure 1.13.

Print Form dialog box.

If you select a code window in Delphi and then select File | Print, Delphi displays the Print Selection dialog box, as shown in Figure 1.14. In this dialog box, you specify how you would like the code window printed, such as print line numbers, print selected text only, (assuming you have selected a portion of text), and others.

Figure 1.14.

Print Selection dialog box.

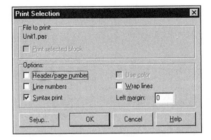

Exit

Selecting Exit, of course, exits the Delphi IDE. If your project has not been saved in its current state, Delphi asks you if you want to save the project before you exit.

The Edit Menu

You use commands on the Edit menu to manipulate text and components at design time. The Edit menu contains several items, as shown in Figure 1.15. These items are described in the following sections.

Figure 1.15.

Edit menu.

UnDelete/Undo

This menu option appears as either UnDelete or Undo depending on the previous action you took. If you just deleted an object or some code using either the Delete key or choosing Edit | Delete, this option appears as UnDelete. UnDelete enables you to restore what you just deleted. If you just added code or components to your project, this option appears as Undo. Undo enables you to undo your last additions (good for those of us who can't make up our minds).

Redo

Redo is the opposite of Undo. Redo backs you out of any number of Undos you have performed.

Cut

Selecting Cut cuts the currently selected item (component(s) on a form or text) to the Clipboard. The selected item(s) are removed from the current form or code unit.

Copy

Selecting Copy copies the currently selected item (component(s) on a form or text) to the Clipboard. The selected item(s) are *not* removed from the current form or code unit.

Paste

Selecting Paste copies the item on the clipboard into the current form or code unit.

Delete

Selecting Delete deletes the currently selected item. There is a reprieve, though; the Undo feature can still undo any mistake you made with the Delete menu selection. Remember that Delete removes the selected item from the form or code unit and does not put it on the clipboard.

Select All

Selecting this menu option selects either all components on the current form or all code in the current unit, depending on which entity you selected prior to choosing Select All.

Align to Grid

Selecting Align to Grid aligns the currently selected component to the grid.

NOTE

> If you have the Snap to Grid option selected in the Options | Environment | Preferences tab, this menu selection is unnecessary. All components placed on the page automatically align themselves to the grid on the form.

Bring to Front

Selecting Bring to Front moves the currently selected component on top of all other components. This is useful when you've placed a number of components on a form and layered them one on top of another. If you do that, you may find one component buried beneath another when it should be on top, and that's what this menu option is for.

Send to Back

This has the opposite effect of the Bring to Front option. Selecting Send to Back moves the currently selected component(s) behind all other components.

  NOTE

> Windowed and non-windowed controls are considered separately. All non-windowed controls are "behind" all windowed controls.

Align

Selecting Align brings up the Alignment dialog box, as shown in Figure 1.16. You can choose from many ways to vertically and horizontally align components on a form. You must select any items you want to align prior to choosing this menu option.

Figure 1.16.

Alignment dialog box.

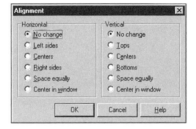

Size

Selecting Size enables you to size a selected component to a specific width and height. Delphi displays the Size dialog box shown in Figure 1.17. If you selected multiple components, you can increase the size of all components to be the size (horizontal, vertical, or both) of the largest selected component on the page, or you can shrink all components to the size of the smallest one.

Figure 1.17.

Size dialog box.

Scale

Have you ever created a form only to realize that all the components on the form are too big or too small? Selecting Scale enables you to proportionally scale the entire contents of the form. Choosing a number over 100 increases the size, and choosing one under 100 decreases the size. Enter the scaling percentage in the edit box and click OK.

Tab Order

Delphi enables you to adjust the tab order for the items in the currently selected form. This is the order in which items will gain focus in your window when the user presses the Tab key to go from field to field in your form. This enables you to control the order in which items are brought into focus and therefore to "lead" the user around the screen.

Selecting Tab Order displays the Edit Tab Order dialog box shown in Figure 1.18, and it includes the names of all the components on the form in a list box. You can visually reorder the items by selecting the item you want to relocate and clicking the up or down arrows to move it to its new position. This is a much better method than having to set a property for each control manually.

Figure 1.18.

Tab Order dialog box.

Creation Order

Selecting Creation Order enables you to control the order in which non-visual components are created. If you are wondering why you should care, the answer is simple. Some of your non-visual components could rely on other non-visual components being present and initialized. If the components are not created in the right order, you have the cart-before-the-horse syndrome.

Lock Controls

Once you design your screen and place your controls, you will probably want to spend some time adjusting properties and events. It is very easy to perform a "mouse-misfire" and end up moving one of your precisely placed controls. Selecting Lock Controls locks all the controls in place on the form. You can click on them to change properties and events without worrying about moving them. A truly handy option!

Add to Interface

Refer to the Delphi online help or manuals for the function of this menu selection.

The Search Menu

The Search menu is used to locate text, errors, objects, units, variables, and symbols in the Code Editor. It contains several items, as shown in Figure 1.19. These items are described in the following sections.

Figure 1.19.

Search menu.

Find

Delphi implements a first-rate find. Selecting Find causes Delphi to display the Find Text dialog box, as shown in Figure 1.20. There you can choose from numerous options in case sensitivity, search direction, and others.

Figure 1.20.

Find Text dialog box.

Find in Files

Selecting Find in Files enables you to search for specific text and then displays each occurrence in a window at the bottom of the Code Editor. The options in the dialog box enable you to search all open files, all files in the current project, and all the files in a particular directory tree.

Replace

Selecting Replace causes Delphi to display the Replace dialog box, which complements the Find dialog box mentioned in a previous section. The difference between the two is that the Replace dialog box has a Replace With edit box, which enables you to replace one piece of text with another.

Search Again

Selecting Search Again repeats the last find you performed using the Find Text dialog box.

Incremental Search

This is one of the neatest options that Borland implemented in their editor. Select Incremental Search, and then start typing characters. As Delphi finds the characters you type, it takes you to the first occurrence of that set of characters. A wonderful tool when you know approximately what you are looking for.

Go to Line Number

Selecting Go to Line Number enables you to enter a line number (only up to the number of lines in your application), and Delphi takes you there immediately.

Find Error

Selecting Find Error enables you to enter the location of your last runtime error. Delphi then compiles your application and stops at the line of code that would be at that location. It's also an easy way to track down runtime errors. This is a feature that has been part of Borland's Pascal for years.

Browse Symbol

Selecting Browse Symbol enables you to actually look at any of the symbols in your application after successfully compiling it. For instance, if you have a form called Form1 in your application, you could type `Form1` into the Browse Symbol dialog box, and Delphi brings up the Object Browser with that symbol loaded.

The View Menu

The commands on the View menu display or hide different elements of the Delphi environment and open windows associated with the integrated debugger, as shown in Figure 1.21. These items are described in the following sections.

Project Manager

Selecting Project Manager brings up the Project Manager window. This is shown and explained in great detail on Day 6.

Figure 1.21.

View menu.

Project Source

Selecting Project Source brings up the project source code in the Code Editor. Under normal circumstances, you don't see the main Delphi routine that starts the Delphi application. It's hidden because it usually is maintained and modified automatically. You can view the source code for this piece, but it is not advisable to change it unless you know what you are doing.

Object Inspector

Selecting Object Inspector brings up the Object Inspector, which you saw in Figures 1.9 and 1.10.

Alignment Palette

Selecting Alignment Palette brings up the Alignment Palette. The Alignment Palette is the visual version of the Alignment dialog box that results from selecting Edit | Align. You simply select the items you want to align, bring up this palette, and select what you want to do. The pictures on the icons show you how the alignment is going to take place. If you are confused about the function of a button, place your cursor over the button, and a hint will pop up that describes the function.

Browser

Selecting Browser brings up a window that enables you to look at the inheritance model and the relationships of objects. This browser is a very powerful mechanism to help you understand the true object foundations of Delphi. It enables you to look at the hierarchy of Delphi's object model.

Breakpoints

Selecting this menu option brings up a Breakpoint List dialog box. It shows you all the current debugger breakpoints that have been set. If you right-click the dialog box, a pop-up menu appears that enables you to add, modify, or delete debugger breakpoints.

Call Stack

Selecting Call Stack brings up the Call Stack dialog box. This dialog box shows you the order in which procedures and functions are being called in your application. You would use this during a debugging session.

Watches

Selecting Watches enables you to view and set watches to look at specific variables or to create expressions based on these variables. When you set a particular watch, you also can specify how the result of your watch will be displayed. Delphi is smart enough to display your watches in their appropriate types (integer displayed as a decimal number and so on).

Threads

Selecting Threads displays a list of the current threads that are running. Because Windows 95 and NT are both multitasking kernels, you can launch several threads from your application to perform many tasks independently.

Modules

Selecting Modules displays the Module List dialog box, which shows all modules in use in the current project.

Component List

Selecting Component List displays the Component List dialog box shown in Figure 1.22. You can search for a component by name, or you can scroll through the list. If you see a component you want to use, simply press the Add To Form button, and that component is placed on your form.

Window List

Sometimes you may have so many windows open at the same time that finding a particular one is difficult. Selecting Window List brings up a dialog box appears that lists all the windows Delphi has open. You can pick the window you would like to see, and Delphi moves that window to the front.

Figure 1.22.

Components dialog box.

Toggle Form/Unit

When you are working on a particular form, you may want to see the code associated with that form, or vice versa. Selecting Toggle Form/Unit toggles you between the form and the unit.

Units

Selecting Units brings up a dialog box that shows all the units in your project. You then can click the unit you want to see, and the code editor displays that unit.

Forms

Selecting Forms brings up a dialog box that shows all the forms in your project. You then can click the form you want to see, and the code editor displays that form.

Type Library

Type Libraries are OLE compound document files that include information about data types, interfaces, member functions, and object classes exposed by an ActiveX control or server. When a Type Library is selected in the Object List Pane, selecting Type Library causes an Attributes page and Uses page to become available.

The Attributes page displays type information about the currently selected Library. The following attributes and flags appear on the Attributes page when a Type Library is selected in the main Object List pane: Name, GUID, Version, LCID, Help File, Help String, and Help Context.

New Edit Window

Selecting New Edit Window opens a new edit window while leaving your current editor window in place. The current unit at the front of your edit window is displayed in the new edit window. This enables you to see two units of code at the same time.

SpeedBar

Selecting SpeedBar makes the SpeedBar visible if it isn't already.

Component Palette

Selecting Component Palette makes the Component Palette visible if it isn't already.

The Project Menu

You use the commands on the Project menu to compile or build your application. You need to have a project open before these menu options are enabled. The Project menu contains several items, as shown in Figure 1.23. These items are described in the following sections.

Figure 1.23.

Project menu.

Add to Project

Selecting Add to Project enables you to add an existing unit and its associated form to the Delphi project. When you add a unit to a project, Delphi automatically adds that unit to the uses clause of the project file. This is the same as File | Add to Project.

Remove from Project

Selecting Remove from Project enables you to remove an existing unit and its associated form from the Delphi project. When you delete a unit in a project, Delphi automatically deletes that unit from the uses clause of the project file. This is the same as File | Remove from Project.

Add To Repository

Selecting Add To Repository adds the current form to the Object Repository. This enables you to reuse forms thereby reducing development time.

Compile

Selecting Compile compiles all the files that have changed in your current project since the last executable you produced.

Build All

Selecting Build All rebuilds all the components, units, forms, regardless of whether it has changed since the last executable you produced.

Syntax Check

Selecting Syntax Check is great way to verify that you used the correct syntax in your Delphi application without having to link it to an executable program.

Information

Selecting Information gives you information about your Delphi compilation and on memory consumption.

Web Deploy

Once you have finished designing an ActiveForm, select Web Deploy to deploy it to your Web server. This is discussed in more detail on Day 14.

Options

Selecting Options up the Project Options dialog, which enables you to set options for the compiler, linker, and directories.

The Run Menu

The Run menu contains commands that provide a way for you to debug your program from within Delphi, as shown in Figure 1.24. These items are described in the following sections.

Run

Selecting Run runs your Delphi application. If a current compilation does not exist, Delphi compiles the application first.

Parameters

Selecting Parameters brings up the Run parameters dialog box, as shown in Figure 1.25. This dialog box enables you to feed command-line parameters to your application.

Figure 1.24.

Run menu.

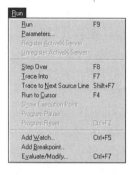

Figure 1.25.

Run parameters dialog box.

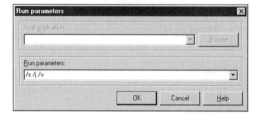

Register ActiveX Server

Selecting this menu option registers your ActiveX server with Windows 95. Doing this enables the ActiveX control to be called up and used by your Web browser or another application. Before a control can be used for the first time, it must be registered. You learn more about this on Day 13.

Un-Register ActiveX Server

Selecting this menu option un-registers your ActiveX server with Windows 95 or NT. This enables you to remove the instance of your ActiveX control from your system. You learn more about this on Day 13.

Step Over

Selecting Step Over executes your application one line of code at a time but executes procedure and function calls as if they were one line of code. This comes in handy if you want to see how your application behaves but don't need to see the internals of each of the procedure and function calls.

Trace Into

Selecting Trace Into executes your application one line of code at a time and executes procedure and function calls one line of code at a time. This comes in handy if you want to see all the gruesome details.

Trace to Next Source Line

Selecting Trace to Next Source Line enables you to see which line of code will be executed next. This is a complementary function to Trace Into.

Run to Cursor

Selecting Run to Cursor executes your application up to the point in the source code where your cursor resides. At that point, you might want to use the Watches window (by choosing View | Watches) to evaluate a variable you had doubts about.

Show Execution Point

Select Show Execution Point if you have closed the edit window and are in the middle of single-stepping through your application in debug mode. This brings you back to an edit window with the cursor on the next line of code that will be executed.

Program Pause

Selecting Program Pause pauses your application so you can use the Watches window to do variable evaluation.

Program Reset

Selecting Program Reset stops a paused program and releases it from memory.

Add Watch

Selecting Add Watch is one way to add a watch to the watch list. The other is to choose View | Watches, right-click on the Watches List window, and choose Add from the pop-up menu.

Add Breakpoint

Selecting Add Breakpoint is one way to add a breakpoint to the breakpoint list. It also toggles on a little red stop sign in your source code showing where the breakpoint is. The other way to accomplish this task is to choose View | Breakpoints, right-click on the Breakpoints List dialog box, and choose Add from the pop-up menu.

Evaluate/Modify

Selecting Evaluate/Modify enables you to modify the value of a variable on the fly in the dialog box. You also can type an expression based on variables from your application, and Delphi will evaluate that expression for you instantly. Now if it would only do calculus...

The Component Menu

You use the Component menu to add as well as configure any ActiveX components in your Delphi application. The Component menu contains several items, as shown in Figure 1.26. These items are described in the following sections.

Figure 1.26.

Component menu.

New Component

Selecting New Component brings up the Component Expert that helps you create a new Delphi component. You learn more about component creation on Day 13.

Install Component

Selecting Install Component enables you to add new Delphi visual components to a new or existing Delphi package.

Import ActiveX Library

Selecting Import ActiveX Library enables you to import an ActiveX control (assuming it already is registered on your system) into a new or existing package within Delphi.

Create Component Template

Create Component Template becomes active when you select more than one component on a form. It enables you to select, for example, a Ttable and a Tdatasource and then combine them in to a single component that can be dropped onto the form at once. This could be a combination of the table, the datasource, a grid, and a dbmemo, or any frequently used combination of components.

Install Packages

Selecting Install Packages enables you to determine which packages are compiled into your application. You can view a list of currently installed components and add, delete, or edit the contents of each package.

Configure Palette

Selecting Configure Palette enables you to add or delete components from the VCL tabs. This gives you the option not to look at components that you don't plan to use in your projects.

The Database Menu

The Database menu contains commands that enable you to create, modify, and view your databases, as shown in Figure 1.27. These items are described in the following sections.

Figure 1.27.

Database menu.

Explore

Selecting Explore starts the Database Explorer. The Explorer enables you to browse database structures. You learn more about this on Day 11.

SQL Monitor

Selecting SQL Monitor starts the SQL Monitor program. The Monitor enables you to see queries going on as they are executed in your application. See Delphi's online help and manuals for the operation of this application.

Form Expert

The Expert assists you in the creation of database entry screens. It works by opening the database you are going to hook to and then helping you design the screens around the data in the files. You learn more about this in Day 11.

The Tools Menu

The Tools menu provides a way to view and change environment settings, to modify the list of programs on the Tools menu, and to modify templates and experts. It contains three items, as shown in Figure 1.28. These items are described in the following sections.

Figure 1.28.
Tools menu.

Environment Options

Selecting Environment Options brings up the Environmental Options dialog box. This dialog box enables you to change the settings for the editor, display, the palette, and the browser. You also can set autosave options so you don't lose your work.

Repository

Selecting Repository brings up the Object Repository dialog box. This dialog box enables you to view the objects that you could have placed here by using Project | Add to Repository. Here you can add and delete them as well.

Configure Tools

Selecting Configure Tools enables you to customize the tools that appear in the Tools menu in Delphi. This provides you with great flexibility to make the Delphi environment work for you.

The WorkGroups Menu

The WorkGroups menu contains several items, as shown in Figure 1.29. These items are described in the following sections. This menu item exists only if you have the Delphi Developer Edition (and have purchased PVCS separately) or if you have the Delphi CS Edition which comes with PVCS.

Figure 1.29.
Workgroups menu.

Browse PVCS Projects

Selecting Browse PVCS Projects brings up the PVCS project window. Here you can browse the files that have previously been checked into the version control system.

Manage Archive Directories

Selecting Manage Archive Directories enables you to manage the directory structure in your PVCS archives. You can create directories to support moving and organizing files.

Add Project1 to Version Control

Selecting this menu option enables you to add the project you are currently working on to the PVCS version control system. Day 5 talks more about project management and the use of PVCS.

Set Data Directories

Selecting Set Data Directories enables you to set your public and private working directories for PVCS.

The Help Menu

The Help menu contains two menu items, as shown in Figure 1.30. These items are described in the following sections.

Figure 1.30.

Help menu.

Help Topics

Selecting Help Topics brings up the main Delphi 3 help file in Windows 95 help format. All search capabilities are in the help engine, so no extra menu selections are needed.

About

Selecting About brings up the About Delphi dialog box, which shows you the version number of the Delphi software. If you want to be amused while this window is open, hold down the Alt key and type **DEVELOPERS**. See what happens.

Customization

To customize Delphi to the way you work, there are several things that you can change in the Speedbar, the Component Palette, and the edit window.

SpeedBar

You can add items to or delete items from the SpeedBar by right-clicking the SpeedBar and selecting Properties from the resulting pop-up menu. This enables you to customize the SpeedBar to suit your personal needs. From this point, you can take the additional items from the SpeedBar Editor and drag them onto the SpeedBar itself. To delete items from the SpeedBar, simply drag an item off the SpeedBar.

Component Palette

You can customize the Component Palette by right-clicking the Component Palette and then choosing Configure from the resulting pop-up menu. This brings up the same dialog box as if you had selected the Options | Environment | Palette tab. This enables you to add, rename, or delete a tab, and to add new components to the Component Palette.

Editor Window

You can customize the edit window by right-clicking on the editor window and choosing Properties from the resulting pop-up menu. Here you can change everything from the syntax and color highlights, to the actual keystrokes the editor uses. The editor supports Brief-style editor commands (Brief is a commercial editor). Changes to keyboard mappings, and smart tabbing are just two of the ways you can make the editor work for you.

Summary

In this chapter, you took the first step toward understanding the Delphi environment. You saw how RAD is more than just a teen slang term, how VBX, ActiveX, and VCs are tools that you can use, and how you can create VCs using Delphi. An overview of constants, variables, functions, and procedures started you on the road to understanding Object Pascal. You were given a primer to the world of event-driven programming and saw how Windows 95 reacts to things around it. Finally, you learned about properties and what they mean to Delphi. The simple application you wrote will become more challenging as the book continues.

As you looked at the Delphi Integrated Development Environment (IDE), you might have wondered why the IDE was presented in a laundry-list style. Here's why. In order for you to fully utilize the Delphi toolset, you need to know what tools are available. As you explore Delphi throughout this book, you'll encounter the different tools and options, and learn how to use them more completely.

After you finish the quiz and exercises for this chapter, you'll be ready to move one to the next chapter and learn about Object Pascal!

Q&A

Q How do I manage all these windows I have open?

A Sometimes I wonder that, too. The best thing to do if you are doing lots of software development is get a big monitor. To us, a 17-inch monitor is the minimum to really stare at all day long (all three of the authors of this book actually have 21-inch monitors (we're called monitor snobs).

Q Why do we need ActiveX controls, as well as visual components?

A The real issue here is extensibility. Delphi is great now, but what happens when we all get our virtual reality headsets? We would like to have a Delphi Visual Component for our VR headset control. By being able to add new functionality to Delphi in the form of toolbar add-ons, we extend the life and usefulness of the product. This concept goes even farther when we start talking about Internet connectivity. Microsoft (and others) is providing new ActiveX controls every day to enhance your programming experience, and Borland is committed to helping you take advantage of it.

Q I bought Delphi Client/Server. I have heard of "similar" products such as PowerBuilder. How is Delphi different?

A Delphi Client/Server is really different in a number of critical ways. The sales brochures can tell you most of it. In my mind, there are two things that really stick out. Object Pascal as the base language really puts Delphi head and shoulders above the rest. If the foundation is solid… Second is the speed. I have seen PowerBuilder applications running, and they seem visually slower. Delphi executables are faster and smaller (generally) than their PowerBuilder equivalents.

Workshop

The Workshop provides two ways for you to affirm what you've learned in this chapter. The Quiz section poses questions to help you solidify your understanding of the material covered. You can find answers to the quiz questions in Appendix A, "Answers to the Quiz Questions." The Exercises section provides you with experience in using what you have learned. Please try to work through all these before continuing to the next day.

Quiz

1. What are two benefits of using a RAD development environment as opposed to a regular compiler?
2. How do native Delphi 3 Visual Controls differ from ActiveX controls?

3. What language is a native Delphi Visual Control written in?

4. What is syntax highlighting?

5. How do you add a new VC, Delphi package, or ActiveX control to the component palette?

Exercises

1. Read the page in the introduction of the *Object Pascal Language Reference Guide* that describes a syntax diagram. Syntax diagrams are important to understand. If you cannot read them, it will be tough for you to look up a particular command or expression syntax to see how it works. The manual described here is on the Delphi CD-ROM, as well as in paper form in some versions of Delphi.

2. Create an application with two buttons and have the text from `button1` overwritten with some new text from `button2` (your new button).

Day **2**

Object Pascal: Part 1

Now that you have seen how Delphi's IDE can help you, let's look at the language that is the foundation of all that you do, Object Pascal. Object Pascal has a long and distinguished heritage starting as Turbo Pascal 1.0. Throughout its evolution, Turbo Pascal has come to be known as one of the richest languages (not to mention fastest compilers) in the business. When Borland later introduced the object-oriented extensions to Turbo Pascal 5.5, a new generation of compiler was born. What you see in Delphi 3 today is the culmination of years of effort to create the perfect language. This chapter presents the fundamentals that make up the language. You continue the study of Object Pascal on Day 3, "Object Pascal: Part 2."

NOTE

IMPORTANT! You must enter the code listings in Days 2 and 3 by following these steps:

1. Start Delphi.

2. If a new project is not automatically opened, choose File | New Project from the Delphi menu bar.

3. Choose Project | Options | Linker, check the Generate Console Application check box, and then press OK. This tells Delphi that the application you are creating is not a windowed application, but a "DOS window" type of application.

4. Choose View | Project Source. The actual master source of the project becomes visible in the editor window. Although you normally do not edit this code, in this case, you will replace this code with your own listing. This is a simple way to create a program.

5. When you run the program, it appears in a window of its own. To close the output window, select Alt+F4, or click the × in the upper-right corner of the output window.

6. There is a trick here. It is important that, when you replace the old source code with your own, you either save the project first with the new name (for example, `MyArrayDemo`), or you do not change the line that says `Program Project1`. The reason is because Delphi likes to be the one to change the program name in the project source file. If you change it and then try to compile, you will get the error `Error in Project 1:Module header is missing or incorrect`. So the trick here is either not to change that program line or to do a File | Save Project As and then type in your new name for the project (for example, `MyArrayDemo`).

A hard copy of the *Object Pascal Reference Manual* comes with most flavors of Delphi (if you don't have a hard copy, it is in the online help). It explains all the concepts covered here, and more. We thought by including Day 2 and Day 3 that this book would provide an overview or *Reader's Digest* version of the reference manual. In learning Object Pascal, a different view or wording can sometimes make the difference between confusion and understanding. Enjoy!

Using the Equal Sign in Pascal

Before getting too far into programming, some of you coming from other programming languages (or no language at all) need to know how Delphi treats the equal sign.

There are two purposes for the equal sign in Delphi. The first is as an assignment operator. For this purpose, Delphi uses := as the assignment operator. An example of this would be y:=mx+b. The way to read this is not this: y equals m times x plus b, but rather this: y takes on the value of the variable m times the variable x, plus the value in variable b. In order for this to work, the variables y, m, x and b must all be assignment compatible. Remember that this is a strongly typed language, and therefore only data types that are assignment compatible can be assigned to each other.

The second way that the equal sign is used in Delphi is for comparison or equivalency. In this case, only the = is used (no colon). An example is comparing two values and acting on the decision made, such as in the following statement:

```
If A=B then WriteLn ('A and B are equal')
```

In this instance, you are not assigning the value in B to the value in A, you are merely wondering whether the two are equal. Another instance of this is in constant declarations, such as in this example:

```
Const
  TaxRate = 0.0075;
```

This example says that the constant TaxRate is equivalent to the numeric value 0.0075. During compile time, the compiler will know to substitute the value 0.0075 wherever it sees a TaxRate constant.

Constants

As briefly mentioned in Day 1, when you first begin programming, you'll find that some of your programs require you to use the same value over and over. An example is a point-of-sale program, which would have the local sales tax rate in it several times. This is not the problem—you simply put 0.075 (7.5 percent) in your application five times. The problem is when the tax rate changes. You have to remember to change it in five places. This also means that you have a high probability of missing a change or mistyping the value.

That's where constants come in. Constants are nothing more than a name for a value you use in your program. In the point-of-sale example, the name TaxRate would be easier to use than the number 0.075. Constants are declared in the const section of your application. Here is the new declaration.

```
const
    TaxRate = 0.075;
```

This constant declaration serves several purposes. First, it makes the number easier to remember. If you see 0.075 in the middle of a code listing, you may not remember what that number represents. Second, it is much easier for someone to maintain your code. The odds are that you (the creator of the application) will not be the maintainer of that code. If someone else goes into your code to change the tax rate (yet another new tax), the TaxRate constant will be much more intuitive than 0.075 in five or more places. So, the two main reasons for using constants are readability and maintainability.

| TIP | Make your variable and constant names be as descriptive as possible. Identifier names can be any length, but only the first 63 characters are recognized. An identifier name's first character must be an underscore or a letter. Subsequent characters must be letters, numbers, or an underscore. |

Constants in Action

Constants can take many forms and encompass many types of data. The following example illustrates a constant with a few different types of data:

```
const
    MyName = 'Joe Smith';
    Age = 32;
    Wage = 6.50;
    Address = '1400 West Third Street';
```

The first constant, MyName, is an example of a string constant. In Delphi, everything between the single quotes, including the spaces, is part of MyName. Age is an example of an integer constant set to the value 32, and Wage is an example of a real constant set to the number 6.50. Address is another example of a string constant.

Let's look at the life span of a constant by considering the point-of-sale example of TaxRate = 0.075 again. In this scenario, when you tell Delphi to compile your application, Delphi looks at your constant declaration of TaxRate = 0.075, and finds every occurrence of TaxRate in your application, and then replaces each one with 0.075. The trick is that Delphi does this only during the compile and does not change your source code. So, you can see that

2

constants are really for your benefit only, not Delphi's. Delphi knows that your constant declarations are simply a big substitution table.

Now that you have seen what a constant is, the following section gives you a look at something that is not so constant.

Variables

You have seen how constants can be useful in replacing a piece of data that you use repeatedly in your application. The problem with a constant is that its value cannot change during the execution of the program. So constants have to remain—constant. Their usefulness is limited to things that will not change. But how many things in this world stay constant, besides death and taxes?

Variables to the rescue! A variable is similar to a constant in that it is a name given to a value, but with one big difference. The value of a variable can change—can vary—during the program's execution. A variable must be defined to be a certain *type*.

You've just learned about three: string, real, and integer. These are some of the data *types* available. The next section describes these and other types of data in Delphi in more detail.

Simple Data Types

The form that data takes plays an important role in how you perceive it. If your friend asks you for the time, you do not tell her 2,345,567 seconds past midnight on 1/1/1970 (this "number of seconds since January 1, 1970" is a UNIX thing). You say 11:30.

Putting data in the proper form can make the difference between understanding and confusion. In the programming sense, the way data is entered and saved has another implication. With a finite amount of memory in a computer, it is essential that you do not waste memory. For instance, if you wanted to store the number 10, you would not place it in a memory location that is big enough to hold the value 1,999,999,999 because that would be wasteful. If you did this many times (mismatched data and where the data is stored), you could use up a lot of memory. To decide how much storage to allocate to the variable, you also need to look at the possible range of values that a variable can have.

Types also relate to another concept. The Object Pascal language is known as a *strongly typed* language, which means Pascal ensures that data of various types can interact with each other in a well-structured way. Strong typing ensures that your Delphi application makes you do the right thing so that you do not try to add your age to your name and place the result in your telephone number. Less rigorous languages make this kind of erroneous programming much easier to do. The joke is, "Strongly typed languages are for people with weak minds." I disagree. Strongly typed languages limit programmers to what they should do, not what they could do.

Delphi supports several simple data types, which are described in detail in the following sections.

☐ Integer data types
☐ Real data types
☐ The Currency data type
☐ Boolean data types
☐ Character data types
☐ String data types

Integer Data Types

Integer data types are used to represent whole numbers (integers, as you learned in math). There are several different integer types, that is, types that are capable of storing an integer value. Table 2.1 lists these types and their ranges.

Table 2.1. Integer data types.

Type	Range of Values	Bytes of Memory Required	Signed (Can hold a negative number)
Byte	0 to 255	1	No
Word	0 to 65535	2	No
ShortInt	−128 to 127	1	Yes
SmallInt	−32768 to 32767	2	Yes
Integer	−2147483648 to 2147483647	4	Yes
Cardinal	0 to 2147483647	4	No
LongInt	−2147483648 to 2147483647	4	Yes

Notice that the different integer types have dramatically different storage capabilities and that everything comes with a price. The amount of memory required goes up with an increase in storage capacity.

2

Memory Sizing and Terminology

This is a good time to mention memory sizing and terminology.

Memory space is counted in bytes. One byte can hold eight bits of information. A bit is a binary 1 or 0. Different data types in Delphi require a different number of bytes in which to store their data. A data type such as the type Byte requires one byte to store its data, and a type such as LongInt requires four bytes to store its data. The lesson here is that nothing comes for free. Each variable you define takes up memory, and there is a limit to that memory.

Integer is one of the generic types in Delphi. *Generic* types are those that are affected by the particular CPU or operating system on which the compiler is implemented. Under a 32-bit operating system such as Windows 95, the generic types take their respective storage capacities based on the OS.

Integers in Action

Let's look at a simple example of how to use an integer type. Listing 2.1 illustrates how to define three variables, Pay, OverTimePay, and TotalPay.

TYPE   Listing 2.1. Simple program using integer types.

```
program MyIntegerDemo;

uses
  Forms;

var
  Pay : Integer;
  OverTimePay : Integer;
  TotalPay : Integer;

begin
  Pay := 500;
  OverTimePay := 100;
  TotalPay := Pay + OverTimePay;
  WriteLn ('The Total Pay is $', TotalPay);
Readln {To keep the window from closing until you press enter}
end.  {MyIntegerDemo}
```

ANALYSIS This program declares three variables of type integer, assigning numeric values to Pay and OverTimePay. It then adds Pay and OverTimePay together and places the resulting value in TotalPay. Lastly, the WriteLn() procedure displays the output on the screen.

Real Data Types

Real data types are designed to hold a number that has a fractional part. The integer example presented in Listing 2.1 assumed that the paycheck would be in even dollars, which is rarely the case. In the real world, you get paid dollars and cents, and you therefore need data types to mimic the real world. This gets back to our discussion on using the correct data type for the job. You can choose from several varieties of real data types, as shown in Table 2.2.

Table 2.2. Real data types.

Type	Range	Bytes of Memory Required
Real	$\pm2.9*10^{-39}$ to $\pm1.7*10^{38}$	6
Single	$\pm1.5*10^{-45}$ to $3.4*10^{38}$	4
Double	$\pm5.0*10^{-324}$ to $1.7*10^{308}$	8
Extended	$\pm3.4*10^{-4932}$ to $1.1*10^{4392}$	10
Comp	-2^{63} to 2^{63-1}	8

The range of values that variables of these types can hold is staggering. If you can generate a number that overflows $1.1*10^{4392}$, you're a wizard.

NOTE The Comp type is really a big integer, not a real number. The reason it is included in this table is that it is implemented in the same "style" as the floating point types. It is really a 64-bit integer.

Reals in Action

Let's look at an example of using real data types. You can now revise the pay program (from Listing 2.1) to make the scenario more realistic, as shown in Listing 2.2.

TYPE **Listing 2.2. Simple program using real types.**

```
program MyRealDemo;

uses
  Forms;

const
  TaxRate = 0.0075;

var
  Pay : Single;
  OverTimePay : Single;
  GrossPay : Single;
  NetPay : Single;

begin
  Pay := 500.55;
  OverTimePay := 100.10;
  GrossPay := Pay + OverTimePay;
  NetPay := GrossPay - (GrossPay * TaxRate);
  WriteLn ('The Total Gross Pay is $', GrossPay:7:2);
  WriteLn ('The Total Net Pay is $', NetPay:7:2);
Readln {To keep the window from closing until you press enter}
end.  {MyRealDemo}
```

ANALYSIS Now the pay program is more like real life. The GrossPay variable stores just that, the gross pay. NetPay is now the result of GrossPay minus the percentage of taxes defined in TaxRate. Notice that the constant TaxRate is the same as it was in the discussion of constants at the beginning of this day.

When you print a real number (of any type) in a WriteLn() statement, you must add a qualifier that tells Delphi how many digits to print. The :7:2 after GrossPay tells Delphi to print the value of this variable in a field of seven digits, with two digits being to the right of the decimal point. Just for fun, try leaving the qualifier off and see what happens.

TIP

> When possible, use Single or Double data types instead of Real. Reals are slower (they are not a native type for the floating point unit in the processor, so every operation requires conversion) and either use more storage or provide less precision than Single or Double.

The Currency **Data Type**

In most languages, you have to use a Real data type (of one sort or another) for representing monetary values. Delphi provides a Currency type specifically for that purpose. This type is a floating point type that is assignment-compatible with all other floating point types, including the Variant type discussed later in this chapter. The Currency type has a precision of four decimal places and is stored as a 64-bit integer (where the four least significant digits represent the four numbers to the right of the decimal point.

You may be wondering why you should use the Currency type instead of a Real data type. The Currency type provides two main benefits:

☐ The Currency type has a greater precision for holding large numbers.

☐ The Currency type is used in the CurrencyField and other components. It is compatible with database types representing money.

You'll learn more about this type throughout the book.

The Currency **Type in Action**

You can rewrite your program MyRealDemo (refer to Listing 2.2) to use the Currency type for monetary items. It should look like the code in Listing 2.3.

TYPE **Listing 2.3. Simple program using the Currency type.**

```
program MyCurrencyDemo;

uses
  Forms;

const
  TaxRate = 0.0075;

var
  Pay : Currency;
  OverTimePay : Currency;
  GrossPay : Currency;
  NetPay : Currency;

begin
  Pay := 500.55;
  OverTimePay := 100.10;
  GrossPay := Pay + OverTimePay;
  NetPay := GrossPay - (GrossPay * TaxRate);
  WriteLn ('The Total Gross Pay is $', GrossPay:7:2);
  WriteLn ('The Total Net Pay is $', NetPay:7:2);
Readln {To keep the window from closing until you press enter}
end.  {MyRealDemo}
```

2

ANALYSIS This program is a revised version of Listing 2.2, and it uses the Currency type. As you can see, the change was simple enough. You simply changed the type of all the variables to Currency. When you print the values in the WriteLn() statements, you still use the place formatters :7:2 to make the printout neat and correct.

Boolean Data Types

Boolean data types are one of simplest and most used types around. Variables of this type represent a logical quantity, for example, TRUE and FALSE. Knowing this, you may wonder why Table 2.3 lists five Boolean types, not two. The answer is "compatibility." In some instances, Windows requires a Boolean value that is one word in size. Instances such as these are when other Boolean types can be of use.

Table 2.3 Boolean data types.

Type	Range	Bytes of Memory Required
Boolean	Preferred one-byte Boolean	1
ByteBool	Byte-sized Boolean	1
Bool	Word-sized Boolean	2
WordBool	Word-sized Boolean	2
LongBool	Double word-sized Boolean	4

The Boolean types are useful whenever you have a situation that can be addressed by only two responses, such as YES or NO, TRUE or FALSE, ON or OFF. Any of these situations can be represented with a variable of the Boolean type.

Variables of type Boolean can accept the and, or, and not operators. This gives you additional flexibility as a developer.

NOTE

> If you use a ByteBool, WordBool, or LongBool in a place where a Boolean type is required, Delphi generates code so that all non-zero values of variables of this type are converted to -1 (TRUE). This is done to maintain compatibility with Visual Basic. FALSE is still 0. And if you use a Boolean type, the TRUE value for it will still be 1 (as in previous versions of Delphi). Because there are two values for TRUE (depending on the Boolean type you use), bounds checking has been turned off for these types.

Booleans in Action

Listing 2.4 is a sample program that illustrates various aspects of Boolean variables.

TYPE **Listing 2.4. Simple program using Boolean types.**

```
program MyBooleanDemo;

uses
  Forms;

var
  OKtoGo : Boolean;
  MyFlag  : Boolean;

begin
  OKtoGo := FALSE;
  MyFlag := not OKtoGo;

  WriteLn ('OKtoGo flag is set to ', OKtoGo);
  WriteLn ('MyFlag is set to ', MyFlag);
  WriteLn ('These two flags logically or''ed is  ', OKtoGo or MyFlag);
  WriteLn ('These two flags logically and''d is  ', OKtoGo and MyFlag);
Readln {To keep the window from closing until you press enter}
end. {MyBooleanDemo}
```

ANALYSIS Listing 2.4 shows how to create two variables, OKtoGo and MyFlag, both of type Boolean. These variables are then assigned a value; OKtoGo is set to FALSE, and MyFlag is set to the opposite of OKtoGo, TRUE. The output shows the user the value of both variables, and then logically ors and ands them (on-the-fly in the WriteLn() statement) on the way to the screen. Although this example is fairly simple, it illustrates the use of the Boolean type in a real application. You'll use this type much more in the coming days.

Character Data Types

The character data types are probably familiar to those of you who have programmed in C or C++. This class of data types was designed to store only one character. A character is one byte long. If you do your math, you will see that 2^8 (one byte) is 256 different characters that could be stored in a variable of type Char. There are ASCII characters from 0 to 255 (computer stuff usually begins counting at zero, not one).

One of the things that is new for Delphi 3 is the addition (or really the redefinition) of the character types. Type Char is now the equivalent of the type ANSIChar. ANSIChar is still an 8-bit ANSI character. A third character type, WideChar, gives you a full 16-bit character type.

These three different character types are provided for the sake of compatibility. Delphi 3 supports the Unicode standard, as shown in Table 2.4. The WideChar data type is the result of that support. A Unicode character uses all 16 bits of the WideChar type. If you place a normal ANSIChar value into a variable of type WideChar, the high-order byte will be zero, and the ANSI character is stored in the low-order byte. Although Windows NT is fully Unicode compliant, Windows 95 is not. If you are writing applications that are going to be used on both, be sure to use the SizeOf() function, and do not assume that characters are only eight bits.

NOTE

> As of the printing of this book, Borland has defined the Char data type to be equivalent to the ANSIChar type. Borland has suggested that in the future the Char data type might be switched to be equivalent to the WideChar type. This would mean that all programs that use the Char data type would default to being Unicode compliant—an added bonus with no work for you.

Table 2.4. Character data types.

Character Type	Size in Bytes	What It Can Hold
ANSIChar	1	One ANSI character
WideChar	2	One Unicode character
Char	1	Currently equal to ANSIChar. In future versions of Delphi, it may be equal to WideChar.

Unicode Compliance

You may have noticed that many things in Delphi are equal to the ANSI definitions now but are poised to move to their Unicode equivalent. As the industry moves away from Windows 3.1, and as Windows 95 and Windows NT eventually merge into one product (Microsoft's prediction), the world of 32-bit NT will arrive. When that happens, software developers will need a development environment that supports Unicode in all its glory. By that time (if not earlier), all the data types in Delphi will be Unicode compliant. It all fits pretty well, doesn't it?

Character Types in Action

For a sample of how the character type works, look at the code in Listing 2.5.

TYPE   **Listing 2.5. Simple program using the `Char` type.**

```
program MyCharDemo;

uses
  Forms;

var
  Answer : Char;
  Question : Char;

begin
  Question := 'A';
  Answer := 'B';
  WriteLn ('Question is ', Question);
  WriteLn ('Answer is ', Answer);

  Answer := Question;
  Question := #66;

  WriteLn ('Question now is ', Question);
  WriteLn ('Answer now is ', Answer);

  Readln {To keep the window from closing until you press enter}

end. {MyCharDemo}
```

ANALYSIS   There are several points of interest in this listing. After declaring two variables of type `Char`, Answer and Question, each of them is assigned a value. The assignment statement assigned the literal character A to Question, and the literal character B to Answer. After writing those out to the screen, the program pulls a fast one. It then assigns the value in the Question variable to Answer. You can do this because both variables are of the same type.

The piece of this that may look funny is the following line:

```
Question :=#66;
```

Remember that a variable of type `Char` can hold one only character. If you look up ASCII character 66, you'll find the letter B. You can use the # sign to tell Delphi that you wish to use the decimal representation of a character instead of the character itself.

2

String Data Types

String data types tend to be a little more useful than the Char data type. The String data type in Delphi used to be a concatenation of up to 255 individual characters. Another term for this is an array of characters. Delphi is quite different in how it handles strings. Table 2.5 lists the four string types available in Delphi.

Table 2.5. String data types.

Type	Length	Element It Holds	Null Terminated
ShortString	255	ANSIChar	No
AnsiString	up to ~3 GB	ANSIChar	Yes
String	either 255 or up to ~3 GB	ANSIChar	Yes or No
WideString	up to ~1.5 GB	WideChar	Yes

Delphi contains long string support. This support is enabled by using the $H+ compiler directive. This directive is on by default. When you use this directive, a variable of the String data type in Delphi can hold a string of nearly unlimited length (about 3 GB).

Once again, Borland has given developers the option to remain compatible with Delphi 1.0 or move ahead. The type String is by default ($H+ on) equal to the type AnsiString. The AnsiString type is a null-terminated string that is dynamically allocated. The real benefit of a variable of this type is the dynamic allocation of that variable. As you place longer strings into this variable, Delphi reallocates the memory for that string. If you plan to change the length of your string significantly, you can also use the SetLength() function to allocate the appropriate memory required for your variable. The other advantage of using the AnsiString type is that it is already null terminated. This means you do not have to use the old StrPCopy() type commands to convert between Pascal style (a string of fixed length) and null-terminated strings.

You may ask, "Why null-terminated strings?" The answer is "compatibility." In most of the calls to system routines, such as the Win32 API, calls need to be passed null-terminated strings. With the old-style Pascal string (now called ShortString), it was not null terminated and required conversion before being used for an API call.

Delphi 3 still maintains compatibility with Delphi 1.0 by offering the ShortString type. This gives you the equivalent of the old type String in Delphi 1.0. You still can define a string of a specific length, even when the $H+ directive is invoked. Consider the following example:

```
{$H+} {Long strings are now turned on}

var
   MyNewString : String; {null terminated, dynamically allocated string}
   MyOldString  : String[20];  {By qualifying the length of
                                ➡this string}
                               {automatically makes MyOldString a
                                ➡type ShortString,}
                               {with a max length of 20 characters.}
```

Delphi 3 VCL components now use the AnsiString type for all properties and events parameters. This simplifies your interactions with VCLs and APIs to make them more uniform in the way they behave. This helps your applications work and play well with others (sort of like kindergarten).

String Types in Action

Let's look at an example of using string data types. Listing 2.6 illustrates the use of a couple of strings.

TYPE   **Listing 2.6. Simple program using string types.**

```
program MyStringDemo;

uses
  Forms;

var
  LastName : String;
  FirstName : String[5];
  NewFirstName : String[30];

begin
  LastName := 'Marchi';
  FirstName := 'Lynne';
  NewFirstName := 'Raquel';

  WriteLn ('First name is ', FirstName);
  WriteLn ('Last name is ', LastName);

  FirstName := NewFirstName;

  WriteLn ('The changed first name is ', FirstName);

Readln {To keep the window from closing until you press enter}
end. {MyStringDemo}
```

ANALYSIS This listing defines a variable LastName of type String. Because it doesn't specify a length, you will get an AnsiString. The variable FirstName is defined as a String of length five (the 5 in the [] bracket denotes the string's length), which is automatically converted to a ShortString[5]. This string now holds a maximum of five characters. And, finally, NewFirstName is defined as a String of length 30, which also is converted to ShortString automatically.

The code has a problem, though. Look at the following line:

```
FirstName := NewFirstName;
```

The output should also tell you something. In the end, when FirstName is written to the screen for the second time, her name is Raque, not Raquel. Why?

The answer is in the definitions of the variables. Remember that FirstName is defined as String[5]. This means that it can hold only five characters. When the contents of NewFirstName (which was eight characters long) were placed them into FirstName (which can hold only five characters), Delphi put as much in as possible and truncated the rest. Remember that computers do what you ask, not what you want. The obvious way of correcting the problem is to define them both of type String and use the AnsiString dynamically allocated capability. These variables then will hold anything you put into them.

The last thing you need to know about String data types is how to empty them, although you probably have figured it out by now. If you wanted to empty the variable NewFirstName, you would write the following line of code:

```
NewFirstName := '';
```

By setting NewFirstName to an empty set of single quotes, you are telling Delphi to set this variable to an empty string.

Data Structures

So far all the types of data presented are used to store a single value, whether it be an integer, real number, or Boolean value. Now you're ready for the big time. Data structures represent a grouping of related data items that resides in memory. This grouping of items can be processed in its individual pieces (or items), although you can also perform many operations on the data structure as a whole. Object Pascal gives you type declarations that enable you to create your own data structures from simple data types. In this section, you'll learn about the following data structures, including how and why they are used and what benefits they provide:

- ☐ Arrays
- ☐ Records
- ☐ Sets

NOTE   A String data type falls into both categories depending on your point of view. If you view the data in the string as one entity, it is a simple data type. If you view the data in the string as an array of characters, it is a data structure. The next section talks about arrays.

One-Dimensional Arrays

Arrays are a wondrous tool. They provide a way for you to associate a single variable name with an entire collection of data. You can move the entire array around in memory, copy it, and so forth—all by referencing a single variable name.

If you wish to process a single element of the array, you identify it by the name of the array and the element being processed. That is, Names[2] would identify the second element of the Names array. The real benefit of the array is reuse. If you are using a single variable and you put a value in it, the old value is overwritten. In the case of an array, you can store each new value in an array element for use later. This preserves the old values as well as the new ones. Each array element is stored in a separate memory location and is unaffected by its neighbor.

As stated earlier, you identify which element of the array you wish to deal with by using the array subscript. This subscript "fingers" the item in the array. Look at the array definition in Listing 2.7.

TYPE   **Listing 2.7. Simple program using a one-dimensional array.**

```
program MyArrayDemo;

Uses
  Forms;

type
  MyArrayType = array [1..5] of Real;

var
  PersonScores : MyArrayType;

begin

  PersonScores[1]:=55.6;
  PersonScores[2]:=79.7;
  PersonScores[3]:=42.2;
  PersonScores[4]:=100.0;
  PersonScores[5]:=34.9;

WriteLn (PersonScores[1]:4:1);
WriteLn (PersonScores[2]:4:1);
WriteLn (PersonScores[3]:4:1);
```

```
WriteLn (PersonScores[4]:4:1);
WriteLn (PersonScores[5]:4:1);

Readln {To keep the window from closing until you press enter}

end. {MyArrayDemo}
```

ANALYSIS This program creates a data type called MyArrayType. Using this data type is no different than using Integer, Real or any of the simple types, except that you created it yourself. The :4:2 qualifier is used because the array items are of type real.

The variable MyArrayType can hold five Real values. The [1..5] part of the type definition means that there will be five elements, numbered from 1 to 5. You may think this is obvious, but you could have an array of five elements labeled [6..10]. Although that would be a little weird, it could be done.

The elements of the array are then loaded with data. Because the array holds Real values, you assign a specific element in the array (array[item]) a real numeric value. Notice how each element of the array was loaded separately. This is necessary because each element is truly independent, although the entire data structure is referenced through one name (PersonScores).

Table 2.6 presents a couple examples of how an array could be used.

Table 2.6. Sample array uses.

Sample Statement	What It Does
WriteLn ('First score is ',PersonScores[1]);	Displays the value of element 1 of the PersonScores array, which has a value of 55.6, in a string of output text on the screen.
Total := PersonScores[2] + PersonScores[5]	Adds the values of elements 2 and 5 (79.7 and 42.2) and places the result in a variable named Total.
Total := Total + PersonScores[4]	Adds element 4 (100.0) to the Total variable.
PersonScores[5]:=PersonScores[3] + PersonScores[1]	Adds element 3 and element 1 of the PersonScores array and places the sum into element 5.

These are just a few examples of how arrays are used. Now it's time to get spatial.

Multidimensional Arrays

The array you used in the previous section was a one-dimensional array. It had one "row" of data with several "columns" in it. You also can define multidimensional arrays, which have multiple rows and columns. Look at a spreadsheet as an example. A spreadsheet is nothing more than a two-dimensional array. The cells can hold data, just like an array.

Think of these as nothing more than a map to get to your data. If you have ever played the board game Battleship, you know that they call out using coordinates such as B-7 and D-3. In an array, the same principle applies. When you define your array type, you need to tell Delphi what the "matrix" looks like. It may be that your array is a grid of three by three cells, for a tic-tac-toe program. See Listing 2.8 to see how you dimension (or define) a two-dimensional array. Think of it as length × width, or length × height, row × column, or anything else that will get you thinking spatially.

TYPE

Listing 2.8. Simple program using a two-dimensional array.

```
program MyTrippyArrayDemo;

uses
  Forms;

type
  SuperArrayType = array [1..3, 1..3] of Char;

var
  SuperArray : SuperArrayType;

begin
SuperArray[1,1] := 'X';
SuperArray[2,2] := 'X';
SuperArray[3,3] := 'X';
SuperArray[3,1] := 'O';
SuperArray[1,3] := 'O';

WriteLn (SuperArray[1,1], ' ', SuperArray[2,1], ' ', SuperArray[3,1]);
WriteLn (SuperArray[1,2], ' ', SuperArray[2,2], ' ', SuperArray[3,2]);
WriteLn (SuperArray[1,3], ' ', SuperArray[2,3], ' ', SuperArray[3,3]);

Readln {To keep the window from closing until you press enter}

end. {MyTrippyArrayDemo}
```

ANALYSIS Judging from the output on your screen, who won the tic-tac-toe game? This program is really not much different from the one-dimensional array program. It still creates a type that defines what the array will look like. The difference is in the array type definition itself, which defines the limits in two dimensions now.

The definition array[1..3, 1..3] of Char means "Please define an array that has dimensions of three cells wide (labeled 1, 2, and 3) by three cells long (labeled 1, 2, and 3), and let each cell hold a piece of data of type Char." With the type defined, you create a variable, SuperArray, of that type. You now can start loading values into the array. Because you have to specify each cell to load into it, you can use the Battleship B-2, D-5 method. You identify the row and column of the array that should be modified. By saying SuperArray[1,1] := 'X', you are saying "Please take the character X and place it into the array SuperArray at row 1, column 1." After you fill several of the cells in the array with Xs and Os, the WriteLn statements display the whole tic-tac-toe board on the screen.

You can, of course, take this many steps further and define arrays of many dimensions. A five- or seven-dimensional array is not out of the question; the definition of the type could be as follows:

```
type
  MegaArrayType = array [1..5, 1..5, 1..5, 1..5, 1..5] of integer;

var
  MegaArray : MegaArrayType;
```

To place a value (in this case an integer value) into our MegaArray, you would simply reference which cell you want the data in, in five dimensions. The following line would work:

```
MegaArray[3,2,4,2,1] := 2;
```

This places the integer value 2 in the cell at row 3, column 2, depth 4, time continuum 2, and cosmic measurement 1. This can get really weird trying to name the many dimensions of an array, but you get the point. Before you fly off into the multidimensional galaxy, remember that memory for all the cells, even the empty ones, is allocated at runtime. This means your MegaArray, all 3,125 cells (that's 5^5 cells) will be allocated. Each one of those 3,125 cells will be given enough space to hold an integer value. If an integer is 4 bytes, that's 12,500 bytes— just for one array. The motto is "Do not forget: use memory wisely."

Records

Another data structure that is ever so useful is the Record data type. Like an array, a record is used to store a group of related information. Unlike in an array, the items in a record do not have to be of the same type. Records are great for storing information about things such as people or places. You can put someone's name, address, phone number, and weight in a record. You then can pass that entire group of information around under one name, similar to an array.

Listing 2.9 illustrates the use of the Record data type.

TYPE Listing 2.9. Simple program using the Record data type.

```
program MyRecordDemo;

uses
  Forms;

type
  PersonRecordType = Record
        Name : String[30];
        PhoneNumber : String[13];
        Age : Integer;
        Sex : Char
  end; {PersonRecordType}

var
  Person : PersonRecordType;

begin
  Person.Name := 'Dan Osier';
  Person.PhoneNumber := '(916)555-1212';
  Person.Age := 32;
  Person.Sex := 'M';

  WriteLn ('The person''s name is ', Person.Name);
  WriteLn ('The person''s Phone number is ', Person.PhoneNumber);
  WriteLn ('The person''s age is ', Person.Age);
  WriteLn ('The person''s sex is ', Person.Sex);

Readln {To keep the window from closing until you press enter}

end. {MyRecordDemo}
```

NOTE

Notice that two single-quote characters are used in succession in the WriteLn statement. In a literal string, two single quotes together mean that an actual single quote is in the string.

ANALYSIS The program starts by defining the Record type. This type is a data structure that consists of several parts. The first line PersonRecordType = Record tells Delphi that the lines of code to follow are items in the Record type definition. Next is a list of the variables (and their types) that will be a part of the record: name is a String of length 30, PhoneNumber is a String of length 13, Age is an Integer, and Sex as a Char type (M or F). The end of the record definition is signified by an end; line.

At this point, you have a `Record` type only. When the variable `Person` is declared (of type `PersonRecordType`), memory is actually allocated for one instance of your `record` type.

After memory is allocated, data is put in the record structure. You cannot say `Person := 'Dan'` because Delphi does not know in what item in `Person` to place the string `'Dan'`. You need to qualify your entry to `Person.Name := 'Dan Osier'`, which tells Delphi what field within the record you wish to access. This *dot notation* (putting a dot or period between the record name and field selector) is fundamental not only to records, but also to the object-oriented programming discussed in Day 7. The next several lines of the program use the dot notation to select and fill up the different fields of the `Person` variable with data.

Once the `Person` variable is loaded, you can extract the data, one field at a time. Notice the `WriteLn()` procedure specifies which field to print. `WriteLn` could not discern which field(s) to print if you simply said `WriteLn (Person);`.

The whole concept of records is a useful one. To make your application easy to write, it is important that you use the data type that best suits the data you want to work with. The record is a natural evolution, storing attributes about a thing, person, or other object.

Brain Buster

Now that you have seen both arrays and records, what if you put them together? You may think this could blow a fuse on your thinking cap, but it's really straightforward. An array holds lots of things that are of the same type, and your `PersonRecordType` is a type, right? Couldn't you define the array to be `array [1..3] of PersonRecordType`? Think about it. An array that holds three records. Yes, it works. Now each of those five records can hold information about a person, such as name, phone number, and so on. The result of this brain teaser is the program in Listing 2.10.

TIP

> There are several lines in Listing 2.10 that are very similar. Instead of typing them all individually, use cut and paste in the editor window and just change the array element number. This will save you some wear and tear.

TYPE **Listing 2.10. Array-record demo program.**

```pascal
program MyArrayRecordDemo;

uses
  Forms;

type
  PersonRecordType = record
        Name : String[30];
        PhoneNumber : String[13];
        Age : Integer;
        Sex : Char
  end; {PersonRecordType}

  MyArrayType = array [1..3] of PersonRecordType;

var
  PersonArray : MyArrayType;

begin

  PersonArray[1].Name := 'Dan Osier';
  PersonArray[1].PhoneNumber := '(916)555-1212';
  PersonArray[1].Age := 32;
  PersonArray[1].Sex := 'M';

  PersonArray[2].Name := 'Susie Smith';
  PersonArray[2].PhoneNumber := '(916)555-9999';
  PersonArray[2].Age := 38;
  PersonArray[2].Sex := 'F';
  PersonArray[3].Name := 'Pat';
  PersonArray[3].PhoneNumber := '(916)555-7766';
  PersonArray[3].Age := 30;
  PersonArray[3].Sex := '?';

  WriteLn ('Person 1 name is ', PersonArray[1].Name);
  WriteLn ('Person 1 phone is ',PersonArray[1].PhoneNumber);
  WriteLn ('Person 1 age is ', PersonArray[1].Age);
  WriteLn ('Person 1 sex is ', PersonArray[1].Sex);

  WriteLn ('Person 2 name is ', PersonArray[2].Name);
  WriteLn ('Person 2 phone is ',PersonArray[2].PhoneNumber);
  WriteLn ('Person 2 age is ', PersonArray[2].Age);
  WriteLn ('Person 2 sex is ', PersonArray[2].Sex);

  WriteLn ('Person 3 name is ', PersonArray[3].Name);
  WriteLn ('Person 3 phone is ', PersonArray[3].PhoneNumber);
  WriteLn ('Person 3 age is ', PersonArray[3].Age);
  WriteLn ('Person 3 sex is ', PersonArray[3].Sex);

  Readln {To keep the window from closing until you press enter}

end. { MyArrayRecordDemo}
```

2

The type declaration section contains the definition of the `PersonRecordType` record, and then that type is used in the `MyArrayType` definition.

WARNING

> You must define something *before* you try to use it. Trying to use the `PersonRecordType` and then defining it later will generate an error at compile time.

2

Look at the `MyArrayType` type definition carefully. Now, the `PersonArray` variable is an array of records. To address `PersonArray`, you must give it the array subscript (the number that identifies which array item you want) and the field identifier within that array subscript that you wish to process or view. Therefore, the statement `PersonArray[3].Name := 'Pat';` says "For the `PersonArray` variable, take the `Name` field within that third array element, and set it equal to the string `'Pat'`.

Brain Buster II

Arrays of records are pretty cool, but how about one more? What about a record with other records inside of it—a record of records. This has some real benefit in certain applications.

As you remember, a record is used to hold a grouping of related data, not necessarily of the same type. One of those components could easily be another record. For example, an employee-tracking application you are creating has information about you as an employee. The record probably contains the standard stuff, as shown in the following lines of code:

```
type
  PersonType = record
    LastName : String[20];
    FirstName : String[10];
    EmployeeNumber : Integer;
  end; {PersonType}
```

Now you need to add the address. Well, the person defined by this record may have a home and work address. A more convenient way to construct the record is by making a universal address record type and reusing it. Here's an example of the type you can create:

```
type
  AddressType = record
    Street : String [50];
    City : String : [20];
    State : String [2];
    ZipCode : String [10]
  end; {AddressType}
```

The nice part about this type is that you can use it in several places. Now your home and work address variables both can be of type AddressType.

Listing 2.11 shows the complete program for loading up me as a sample customer.

Listing 2.11. Record demo program II.

```
program MyRecord2Demo;

uses
  Forms;

type
  AddressType = record
    Street : String [50];
    City : String [20];
    State : String [2];
    ZipCode : String [10]
  end; {AddressType}

  PersonType = record
    LastName : String[20];
    FirstName : String[10];
    EmployeeNumber : Integer;
    HomeAddress : AddressType;
    WorkAddress : AddressType
  end;

var
  Employee : PersonType;

begin

  Employee.LastName := 'Osler';
  Employee.FirstName := 'Don';
  Employee.EmployeeNumber := 16253;

  Employee.HomeAddress.Street := '1313 Your St.';
  Employee.HomeAddress.City := 'MyTown';
  Employee.HomeAddress.State := 'CA';
  Employee.HomeAddress.ZipCode := '95630-0011';

  Employee.WorkAddress.Street := '14 Big Business Road.';
  Employee.WorkAddress.City := 'NoOzone';
  Employee.WorkAddress.State := 'CA';
  Employee.WorkAddress.ZipCode := '95636-2211';

  WriteLn(Employee.LastName);
  WriteLn(Employee.FirstName);
  WriteLn(Employee.EmployeeNumber);

  WriteLn(Employee.HomeAddress.Street);
  WriteLn(Employee.HomeAddress.City);
```

```
WriteLn(Employee.HomeAddress.State);
WriteLn(Employee.HomeAddress.ZipCode);

WriteLn(Employee.WorkAddress.Street);
WriteLn(Employee.WorkAddress.City);
WriteLn(Employee.WorkAddress.State);
WriteLn(Employee.WorkAddress.ZipCode);

Readln {To keep the window from closing until you press enter}

end. {MyRecord2Demo}
```

The PersonType record has two variables, HomeAddress and WorkAddress, that are both record variables of AddressType. Because these are records, you need to specify the entire path to get to the actual variable values. Therefore, specify the variable (Employee), dot, the field (HomeAddress), dot, and—because HomeAddress is also a record—the field within HomeAddress (Street). The result is Employee.HomeAddress.Street, and this points to a single string value! This method may seem long, but it sure is easy to read exactly what another programmer is doing. Now you have loaded up the Employee variable with all the information, including two sets of addresses. To print the information to the screen, you have to retrieve each piece of information separately, and then WriteLn() it to the screen.

Consider how dot notation would work with your home address. You say, "I live in the United States, state of California, city of Sacramento, Fifth Street, number 3423. In this example, the address is constructed from the general to the specific. As you can see, you narrow the scope until you are pointing at only one thing.

The only way you can make this whole thing a little more concise is to use the with clause. The with clause sort of sets a default, such as having an implied "I live in the United States," so that all your searches start in the United States instead of on a world level.

The following statement isn't bad:

```
Employee.WorkAddress.ZipCode := '95636-2211';
```

But, using the with statement is better:

```
with Employee do
  WorkAddress.ZipCode := '95636-2211';
```

Notice that you don't have to specify Employee in front of the WorkAddress.ZipCode line. The with statement implied it. The with only works on the next line of code. "One line?" you say. "Worthless," you think? Not really. If that next line happens to be a begin statement, everything from the begin to its matching end gets the implied with.

The record demo program could benefit from this new idea, as illustrated in Listing 2.12.

TYPE   **Listing 2.12. Record demo program III.**

```
program MyRecord3Demo;

uses
  Forms;

type
  AddressType = record
    Street : String[50];
    City : String[20];
    State : String[2];
    ZipCode : String[10]
  end; {AddressType}

  PersonType = record
    LastName : String[20];
    FirstName : String[10];
    EmployeeNumber : Integer;
    HomeAddress : AddressType;
    WorkAddress : AddressType
  end;

var
  Employee : PersonType;

{The code is the same so far, but now it changes}

begin
 with Employee do
  begin {the with stuff}
    LastName := 'Osler';
    FirstName := 'Don';
    EmployeeNumber := 16253;
  end; {with Employee}

with Employee.HomeAddress do
  begin
    Street := '1313 Your St.';
    City := 'MyTown';
    State := 'CA';
    ZipCode := '95630-0011';
  end; {with Employee.HomeAddress}

with Employee.WorkAddress do
  begin
    Street := '14 Big Business Road.';
    City := 'NoOzone';
    State := 'CA';
    ZipCode := '95636-2211';
  end; {with Employee.WorkAddress}
```

```
 with Employee do
   begin {the with stuff}
     WriteLn(LastName);
     WriteLn(FirstName);
     WriteLn(EmployeeNumber);
   end; {with Employee}

with Employee.HomeAddress do
  begin {the with stuff}
    WriteLn(Street);
    WriteLn(City);
    WriteLn(State);
    WriteLn(ZipCode);
  end; {with Employee.HomeAddress}

with Employee.WorkAddress do
  begin {the with stuff}
    WriteLn(Street);
    WriteLn(City);
    WriteLn(State);
    WriteLn(ZipCode);
  end; {with Employee.WorkAddress}

Readln {To keep the window from closing until you press enter}

end. {MyRecord3Demo}
```

ANALYSIS   Do you see how clean it makes the code? Notice that the with statements also go one level deeper and apply to Employee.HomeAddress instead of just Employee. Using the with statement makes the code the easiest to read. The result is some clean code. Use the with statement auspiciously, and it can improve the readability of your code.

Subranges

When you think of a range, maybe you think of it in a mathematical sense. A range of numbers could be from 1 to 10, 30 to 30,000 or something else. A range of letters could be a to z, or A to F (remember in Delphi that the letter "a" (lowercase) is different from "A" (uppercase) because they are two different ASCII characters).

In Delphi, ranges and subranges mean nearly the same as their counterparts in the real world. When you are writing a program and want to compare input from users to see if they typed a lowercase letter of the alphabet, subranges are your ticket.

NEW TERM   A *subrange* type is a range of values of any of the following types: integer, Boolean, character, or enumerated types. Subranges are useful when you want to limit the number of values a variable can have.

It's easy to construct and use the subrange type. To create a subrange, specify the minimum and maximum values in the range with two periods in between them. Listing 2.13 shows you how subranges can benefit you.

TYPE **Listing 2.13. Demo program using a subrange type.**

```
program MyRangeDemo;

uses
  Forms;

type
  LittleLetter = 'a'..'z';

var
  GoodLetters : LittleLetter;

begin
  GoodLetters := 'b';
  WriteLn(GoodLetters);
Readln {To keep the window from closing until you press enter}
end. {MyRangeDemo}
```

ANALYSIS   This program uses a subrange to define what values are permissible to assign a variable of type LittleLetter. The variable GoodLetters is then created of LittleLetter type. This variable can now hold a single character between a and z.

You may be wondering why you would bother to use subranges. Why not just make GoodLetters a Char type and get it over with? The reason is that Object Pascal has the ability to do range checking. Range checking means that during the execution of your program, when you do an assignment statement such as GoodLetters := 'b';, Pascal checks to see if the value you placed into GoodLetters is legal for its type (or subrange). If the value is out of bounds, a range error occurs. Range checking helps you to quickly detect an error that may have eluded you otherwise. Variables that hold things, such as days of the month (1..31) or months of the year (1..12), are great candidates for a subrange. You can have built-in checking of the values you are passing around your program. As soon as you perform an illegal assignment, your program raises the error. How do you get this, you ask?

For only $49.95 plus tax, you can have this feature—just kidding. It's free with every copy of Delphi. You invoke this feature by putting an {R+} in your code where you want the range checking to start and an optional {R-} where you want it to end. It is also available as a check box in the Compiler tab of the Project Options dialog box.

2

NOTE

> The only rules to defining subranges is that they must be an ordinal type, although only a subset of Integer is okay.
>
> The other rule is that the ordinal value of the first entry needs to be less than the ordinal value of the second entry. So, a subrange of z to a would not do, it would have to be a to z because a has a smaller ordinal place than z does.

2

Sets

Sets are even more fun than subranges. Sets can use subranges in their definitions. A set is a group of elements that you want to associate with a single name and to which you can compare other values for inclusion or exclusion from the set. An example is a set that contains all the possible single-character responses to a Yes/No question. The four responses are y, Y, n, and N. You could create a set that would encompass all four: ['y', 'Y', 'n', 'N']. After you define the set, you can use it to see if something else is in the set or is not in the set.

You look for set inclusion by invoking the in statement. For example, the statement

```
MyInput in ['y', 'Y', 'n', 'N'] then
```

says that if the value of the variable MyInput is one of the items in the set 'y', 'Y', 'n', 'N', this statement evaluates to a Boolean TRUE. If the value in MyInput is not in the set, this statement is FALSE. A set can contain almost anything so long as the set members are of the same ordinal type or of compatible ordinal types.

Not only can sets contain single values, they also can contain subranges. For instance, if you had a telephone simulator, you would want to allow the numbers 0 through 9, and the * and # keys. The set for this would be ['0'..'9', '*', '#']. As the user pressed keys, you could check for inclusion in the set using the in statement. Listing 2.14 illustrates just one of the ways you can use sets.

TYPE **Listing 2.14. Simple program using sets.**

```
program PhoneDemo;

uses
  Forms;

type
  KeysType = set of Char;
var
```

continues

Listing 2.14. continued

```
      Keys : KeysType;
      UserInput : Char;

Begin
  Keys := ['0'..'9', '*', '#'];
  ReadLn(UserInput);
  If UserInput in Keys then
    WriteLn ('That key was OK');
  Readln {To keep the window from closing until you press enter}
end.
```

ANALYSIS This program creates a type called KeysType. Notice that this type is a set of characters. Next, you create a variable based on that type, called Keys. The variable Keys now can hold a set of characters as its data. In the executable portion of the code (after the begin) you set the variable Keys equal to the literal characters 0 through 9, inclusive, as well as the characters * and #. The user's input is read in ReadLn() statement and placed into the UserInput variable that you defined as type Char. An If..Then statement compares the value of the user's input to the values in Keys. If there is a match, the WriteLn() is executed. If there isn't, the WriteLn() is skipped. The program ends with a ReadLn() to keep the DOS window from closing until you press Enter.

Typed Constants

The concept of a typed constant is one unfamiliar to many programmers. Right now you probably think of a constant as just that, constant. The value never changes. Typed constants are better thought of as preinitialized variables. You can define a typed constant and give it a value in a single statement, as illustrated in this example:

```
Const
  Max : Integer  = 88;
  Name : String[10] = 'Dan';
  Digits : Set of '0'..'9';
```

If you thought the constant declaration section was for declaring constants, you might think the placement of these statements is a little confusing. This exception does confuse the convention of putting constants in the Const section of your code. In this case, you make an exception, and it has a beneficial side effect. It means that you can define a variable's type and give it a default value in one statement. The typed constant is initialized only once with the default value, no matter how many times the module containing the declaration is called.

Typed Constants in Action

Using typed constants is easy. Listing 2.15 illustrates how typed constants are used just like variables.

TYPE **Listing 2.15. Typed constant demo program.**

```
program TypedConstantDemo;

uses
  Forms;

const
  MyName : String = 'Dan Osier;

begin
  WriteLn ('My Name is ', MyName);
  MyName:= 'Jim Fischer';
  WriteLn('My new Name is ', MyName);
  Readln {To keep the window from closing until you press enter}

end. {TypedConstantDemo}
```

ANALYSIS This program starts by declaring a typed constant MyName as a String, and give it a value of 'Dan Osier'. First, the value of MyName is printed to show you that the assignment of the typed constant to 'Dan Osier' really worked. Then the value of MyName is changed to 'Jim Fischer' and printed again to show you that the value of a typed constant can be changed during the execution of the program.

Enumerated Types

Enumerated types are one of the things that can really add to the readability of your code. Although you may know what your code does, the next programmer may not. Suppose you are writing a program to control stoplights, and you need to represent the colors red, yellow, and green in your application. You could assign each one of the colors a number, 1 for red, 2 for yellow, and 3 for green. Then, in your application, you could say, if 3 then TurnLight? You know that 3 means green, but what about the poor person who has to change your application after you are famous? Enumerated types are the answer.

Enumerated types enable you to define a group of objects that belong in a set. This is what is known as a user-defined type. An enumerated type is limited to 255 items.

Enumerated Types in Action

Now that you understand the concept of an enumerated type, let's write a program that uses one. Listing 2.16 illustrates using enumerated types.

TYPE   **Listing 2.16. Enumerated type demo program.**

```
program MyEnumeratedDemo;

uses
  Forms;

type
  StopLightColors = (Red, Yellow, Green);

var
  MyLight : StopLightColors;

begin
  MyLight := Red;
  WriteLn ('My light is currently ', Integer(MyLight));
  MyLight :=Green;
  WriteLn('The new light is ', Integer(MyLight));
  Readln {To keep the window from closing until you press enter}
end. {MyEnumeratedDemo}
```

ANALYSIS   This program creates an enumerated type called StopLightColors. This type has its members Red, Yellow, and Green. The variable MyLight is then defined as type StopLightColors. From that point, you can use the variable MyLight and assign any of the three color values to it as you do in the first line of code MyLight := Red;.

Although enumerated types don't benefit the end user at all, they're highly beneficial to developers by making code easier to read and maintain, as you can see in this listing.

The Variant Type

The Variant type is a terrific addition to Delphi. The Variant type can hold an integer, string, or floating-point value, and its use is as varied as its name suggests. The Variant type is a 16-byte structure that holds not only the value, but type information as well. The real value of using the Variant type is in dealing with OLE automation. The flexibility of this type enables an ActiveX object to return a variety of values and data types, and the Variant type can hold them all.

The Variant Type in Action

Listing 2.17 demonstrates how the Variant type can hold many different types of values.

TYPE **Listing 2.17. Simple program using the Variant type.**

```
program MyVariantDemo;

uses
  Forms;

var
   MyInput : Variant;

begin
  MyInput := 3.5555;
  WriteLn (MyInput);

  MyInput := 'Hello, my name is Dan.';
  WriteLn (MyInput);

  MyInput := 4;
  WriteLn (MyInput);
  Readln {To keep the window from closing until you press enter}
end.
```

ANALYSIS This is a simple program that uses a variable called MyInput, which is of type Variant. You first assign MyInput to the numeric value 3.5555, which you normally would put in a real class of variable. The contents of the variable are printed to the screen to prove that MyInput can hold a real value. Next, a string value of 'Hello, my name is Dan.' is placed into MyInput. The contents of MyInput are printed to the screen again to prove that MyInput can hold a string value as well. Last, the value of MyInput is changed to 4, which normally would be stored in an integer class variable. The contents are printed to the screen again to prove the assignment.

The real (no pun intended) value of the Variant data type is its flexibility. You can put just about anything into it. Because Object Pascal is a very strongly typed language (with rigid rules on what types of data go into which variable types), this type gives you a little bit of slack.

Operators

Now that you know about the data types, you need to know how to compare and evaluate variables of those types. Comparisons and evaluations rely on the operators supported by Delphi:

☐ Arithmetic operators

☐ Logical operators

☐ Relational operators

You also learn about the precedence of operators when more than one operator is used in a statement.

Arithmetic Operators

Arithmetic operators enable you to perform binary and unary arithmetic operations. Most Object Pascal operators are binary in that they take two operands. The rest are unary and take only one operand. Binary operators use the usual algebraic form (for example, A + B). A unary operator always precedes its operand (for example, -B). Table 2.7 and Table 2.8 describe the operators for binary and unary operations, respectively, what types are allowed, and what the resulting type is. For example, remember that if you divide an Integer by an Integer, the result is a Real type.

Table 2.7. Binary arithmetic operations.

Operator	Operation	Types Used	Resulting Type
+	Addition	integer	integer
		real	real
–	Subtraction	integer	integer
		real	real
*	Multiplication	integer	integer
		real	real
/	Division	integer	real
		real	real
Div	Integer division	integer	integer
Mod	Remainder	integer	integer

Table 2.8. Unary arithmetic operations.

Operator	Operation	Types Used	Resulting Type
+	Sign identity	integer	integer
		real	real
–	Sign negation	integer	integer
		real	real

Logical Operators

Logical operators are divided into two categories: logical operations and Boolean operations. Logical operations involve shifting or comparing things at a bit level, and Boolean operations involve comparing or manipulating values at a TRUE or FALSE level. Table 2.9 and Table 2.10 describe the operators for logical and Boolean operations, respectively.

Table 2.9. Logical operations.

Operator	Operation	Types Used	Result Types
not	Bitwise negation	integer types	Boolean
and	Bitwise AND	integer types	Boolean
or	Bitwise OR	integer types	Boolean
xor	Bitwise XOR	integer types	Boolean
shl	Operation	integer types	Boolean
shr	Operation	integer types	Boolean

NOTE   If you use the not operator on one of the integer data types, the result will be of the same integer data types. If both operands of an and, or, or xor are integer data types, the resulting type will actually be the common type of the two operands.

Table 2.10. Boolean operations.

Operator	Operation	Types Used	Result Types
not	Negation	Boolean types	Boolean
and	Logical AND	Boolean types	Boolean
or	Logical OR	Boolean types	Boolean
xor	Logical XOR	Boolean types	Boolean

Relational Operators

Relational operators are used to compare the values of two variables. Table 2.11 describes these operators, including what types are allowed, and what the resulting type is. The table includes some types you haven't used yet, but they are covered in future days. For most of the operators, just remember your high school math.

Table 2.11. Relational operations.

Operator	Operation	Types Used	Result Types
=	Equal	Compatible simple, class, class reference, pointer, set, string, or packed string types	Boolean
<>	Not equal to	Compatible simple, class, class reference, pointer, set, string, or packed string types	Boolean
<	Less than	Compatible simple, string, or packed string types, or PChar	Boolean
>	Greater than	Compatible simple, string, or packed string types, or PChar	Boolean
<=	Less than or equal to	Compatible simple, string, or packed string types, or PChar	Boolean
>=	Greater than or equal to	Compatible simple, string, or packed string types, or PChar	Boolean
<=	Subset of	Compatible set types	Boolean
>=	Superset of	Compatible set types	Boolean
in	Member of	Left operand, any ordinal type; right operand, set whose base is compatible with the left operand	Boolean

Note that the =, <=, and >= can be used for some set operations like "subset of." If both of the operands in an expression are literal sets or variables of type set, you can use these operators to check for equality according to the following rules:

If A and B are set operands, their comparisons produce these results:

☐ A = B is True only if A and B contain exactly the same members; otherwise, A <> B.

☐ A <= B is True only if every member of A is also a member of B.

☐ A >= B is True only if every member of B is also a member of A.

Precedence of Operators

Just as in mathematics, you have to know how to evaluate an expression. To do that, you need to know in what order to evaluate the different parts of the expression. The precedence of operators affects the outcome of the code, just as it does in mathematics—the wrong evaluation order produces the wrong result. Table 2.12 lists the operators in the order of their precedence. When more than one operator is listed on a line, the operators are evaluated from left to right.

Table 2.12. Precedence of operators.

Operators	Precedence	Categories
@, not	First	Unary operators
*, /, div, mod, and, shl, shr, as	Second	Multiplication operators
+, -, or, xor	Third	Addition operators
=, <>, >, <, <=, >=, in, is	Fourth	Relational operators

In addition to the order of precedence shown in the table, there are three other key points that will help you out:

☐ An operand between two operators is bound (or attached) to the operator of higher precedence. An example is 8*5-4. Because the 5 is between two operators (the * and the -), the 5 is bound to the *, which is an operator of higher precedence.

☐ An operand between two equal operators is bound to the one on the left. An example is 8-5-4. In this case, the 5 is between two operators of equal precedence (the - and - are the same), so the 5 is bound to the - on the left.

☐ Expressions within parentheses are evaluated prior to being treated as a single operand (work from inside the parentheses out, just as in math). An example is 8*(5-4). In this case, the 5-4 would be evaluated first, then the result is multiplied by 8.

Summary

Today you looked at the first portion of the Object Pascal language. You explored the different data types that are offered and gained a basic understanding of how the language works. The best way for you to become more familiar with Object Pascal is to use it. Look at all the examples provided with Delphi. Open up some of the examples in the Demos directory of your Delphi installation, and read through the source code even if you don't understand everything that is going on. On Day 3, you'll continue learning about Object Pascal and about the structure of a Delphi program.

Q&A

Q Can I convert a variable from one type to another type?

A Yes. There is a concept called variable typecasting that enables you to do this. See Exercise 1 in Day 3.

Q Is Object Pascal the same as the Pascal on other platforms and by other vendors?

A There is an ANSI standard Pascal. Borland has added many enhancements to the standard Pascal that make it much more useful. The benefits of going beyond the ANSI standard outweigh the drawback of being "just" ANSI compliant.

Workshop

The Workshop provides two ways for you to affirm what you've learned in this chapter. The Quiz section poses questions to help you solidify your understanding of the material covered. You can find answers to the quiz questions in Appendix A, "Answers to the Quiz Questions." The Exercises section provides you with experience in using what you have learned. Please try to work through all these before continuing to the next day.

Quiz

1. At a fundamental level, how do constants and variables differ?
2. Why is precedence of operators necessary?
3. What is the advantage of using typed constants?

Exercises

1. To better understand the use of variant types, write an application that uses an `Integer` and `Variant` type. Make sure that you move the `Integer` value into the `Variant` variable. Try writing both values to the screen to see that the `Variant` type really holds other data types (`Integer` in this case).

2. Write a program that uses enumerated types. Try making a type called `FamilyMember` that has all the members of your family as elements. Try inputting ages for each one and then printing the whole thing.

Day 3

Object Pascal: Part 2

In Day 2, "Object Pascal: Part 1," you learned about Delphi's data types and how to use them. Today, you begin to explore how to use some powerful statements in Object Pascal to control the behavior of your application. You also learn how to modularize your application to decrease errors and improve code reliability, how to use pointers, and how to pass parameters.

Control the Flow

The heart of a program stems from the application's capability to make decisions, based on input or other criteria, and then perform a given task or operation. This capability is commonly called *conditional execution*. Object Pascal has two statements that provide this conditional capability.

If...Then...Else

The `If...Then...Else` statement is the most fundamental of the conditional statements. It enables you to pose a question and, based on the answer, perform a given operation or task. If you wanted to take input from the user and then tell the user whether that input is incorrect, how would you do it? First, let's try an example using a standard sequential piece of code, and then you'll get in into a conditional example. Listing 3.1 demonstrates a way to ask the user a question, without the use of conditional code.

TYPE   **Listing 3.1. Simple program with user input.**

```
program IfDemo;

uses
  Forms;

var
  UserInput : Integer;

begin
  Write ('How old are you ?');
  ReadLn (UserInput);
  WriteLn ('Being ', UserInput, ' years old is great!');
  Writeln('Press enter to exit program');
  ReadLn {To keep the window from closing until you press Enter}
end{IfDemo}.
```

ANALYSIS   First, you declare a variable UserInput of type Integer. This is used to store the age of the user upon input. The Write line asks for the user's age. The Write() function is used here instead of WriteLn() because it leaves the cursor at the end of the line. The ReadLn() function line takes input keystrokes from the user until the Enter key is pressed. The input is placed in the UserInput variable, and the execution of the program continues. The WriteLn() at the end lets the user know that being their age is great.

It's functional, but this program has more than a few problems with it. It does no range checking to see whether the age entered is reasonable (that is, negative ages or ages of 130+). You could use the If...Then clause to fix that.

SYNTAX

The syntax of the If...Then clause is as follows:

```
If Expression1 Then Expression2 Else Expression3;
```

The first expression (the If clause) must evaluate to a logical TRUE or FALSE. The second expression (the Then clause) is the action that should be taken if the first expression evaluates to a TRUE. The third expression (the Else clause) is optional and is what should be done if the first expression evaluates to a FALSE.

The English version of the test for the age range is "If the age is either less than 1 or greater than 130, the user is lying; otherwise, tell him his age is great." Listing 3.2 demonstrates how to put that expression into code form.

TYPE **Listing 3.2. Using the If...Then...Else statement.**

```
program IfDemo2;

uses
  Forms;

var
  UserInput : Integer;

begin
  Write ('How old are you ?');
  ReadLn (UserInput);
  If (UserInput < 1) OR (UserInput > 130) Then
    WriteLn ('You are not telling the truth.')
  Else
    WriteLn ('Being ', UserInput, ' years old is great!');
  Writeln('Press Enter to exit program');
  ReadLn {To keep the window from closing until you press Enter}
end{IfDemo2}.
```

ANALYSIS Remember that the first expression includes everything between the If and Then reserved words. The expression

```
(UserInput < 1) or (UserInput > 130)
```

must evaluate to a TRUE or FALSE, and it does. If the age is less than 1, the first part (UserInput < 1) becomes TRUE. If the age is greater than 130, the expression (UserInput > 130) becomes TRUE. With a logical OR between them, if either part of the expression is TRUE, the whole thing evaluates to TRUE. If the first expression evaluates to TRUE, the second expression is executed. If the first expression is FALSE, the third expression (the WriteLn() after the Else statement)is executed. This is a simple but effective example of the basic building blocks.

Case...of

Before the luxury of masked edit controls, if you wanted to limit the user's input of characters, as well as respond to them, you had to analyze every character individually. After each character was entered, the code would check to determine what the character was and how to respond to it. The Case statement is very useful in this regard. The Case statement enables you to compare an input to a predefined set of "cases," and respond accordingly. Look at the code sample in Listing 3.3.

Type **Listing 3.3. Using the** Case **statement.**

```
program CaseDemo;

Uses
  Forms;

var
  UserIn : Char;

begin
  Write('Type in a character followed by the Enter key: ');
  ReadLn (UserIn);
  Case UserIn of
    'a'      : WriteLn ('That is an small a');
    'z', 'Z' : WriteLn ('That is a small or capital Z')
  else
    WriteLn ('That is a character other than an a, z, or Z.');
  end; {case UserIn}
  Writeln('Press Enter to exit program');
  ReadLn {To keep the window from closing until you press EnterEnter}
end{CaseDemo}.
```

ANALYSIS In this example, the user is given a chance to input a character from the keyboard. Then the user's input (now in the UserIn variable) is compared to the first constant. If that constant (the character a) is a match to the data in UserIn, the statement after the colon on that line is executed. At this point, after the statement for the 'a' line has been executed, the rest of the Case statement will not be executed because a match was found.

If the 'a' line is not a match, the next constant line of the Case statement is compared to UserIn. If that line is a match, the statement line associated with that constant is executed, and so on. If no match is found, the else statement will be executed .

NOTE

That statement on the right side of the colon in a Case statement could be either a call to a function or procedure (which you learn about later in this chapter) or a series of statements with a begin and end around them. This provides you with a great amount of flexibility in making the Case statement useful in your application. It is also very important to note that an end statement follows a Case statement as its terminator.

3

TIP   It is wise to use the else as a part of any Case statement to help catch those "what if" sorts of things. This is another way to help bullet-proof your application.

When using the Case statement, here are a few rules you should follow:

- ☐ If you use more than one constant on a comparison line, commas must separate them unless you are denoting a range of values such as (a through z).

- ☐ Because the expression or the constant being compared to the expression must be byte or word-sized ordinal type, you cannot use a String or LongInt type as an argument.

- ☐ The constants you are comparing your expression to (in this case, UserIn) cannot overlap. That means that the following Case statement would not work:

```
program EvilCaseDemo;

uses
   Forms;

var
   UserIn : Char;

begin
   ReadLn (UserIn);
   Case UserIn of
      'a'            : WriteLn ('That is an small a');
      'a', 'z', 'Z' : WriteLn ('That''s a  Z or z, or it
                               ➡could be an a.');
      'Zap'          : WriteLn ('This will not work either')
   else
      WriteLn ('That is a character other than an a, z, or Z.')
   end;
   Writeln('Press Enter to exit program');
   ReadLn {To keep the window from closing until
           ➡you press Enter}
end{EvilCaseDemo}.
```

- ☐ If you try to run this application, you get a duplicate case label error from the compiler. This is good because even if the compiler allowed this program to run, it would not make any sense. In order for the Case statement to run correctly, all the values must be unique. Having a duplicate "a" would give two possible alternatives.

Just for fun, we also added another Case option of Zap. We did this just to show you that because the Case variable is of type Char, a string value will not work either. If you correct the duplicate "a" problem and recompile, you'll find that the compiler gives you another error. It tells you that type Char and type String are incompatible, and rightly so. You cannot mix types in Case statements.

Loops

Sometimes you may want to perform a set of instructions over and over until a certain condition is met. The set of instructions is called a loop. Pascal provides three looping constructs, which are described in detail in the following sections.

Looping Construct	When To Use It
Repeat...Until	Use this construct when you want the loop to execute at least once before testing whether the condition is met.
While...Do	Use this construct when you want to test whether the condition is met before you start executing the loop.
For	Use this construct when you know how many times you want the loop to repeat itself. The conditional part is the number of times to execute.

Repeat...Until

The functionality of Repeat...Until is very straightforward. The statements between the Repeat and the Until are repeated until the condition defined after the reserved word Until evaluates to TRUE. Look the code sample in Listing 3.4.

TYPE   **Listing 3.4. Using the Repeat...Until loop.**

```
program RepeatDemo;

uses
  Forms;

var
  I : Char;

begin
  Repeat
      Write('Enter a value (q or Q to quit): ');
      ReadLn(I);
  Until (I = 'q') or (I = 'Q');
  Writeln('Press Enter to exit program');
  ReadLn {To keep the window from closing Until you press Enter}
end{RepeatDemo}.
```

ANALYSIS   This program continues soliciting characters from the user until the user types either an uppercase "Q" or a lowercase "q". If you're wondering why no begin and end pair is needed around the statements being executed, it's because the Repeat and Until serve as the markers to show which code is being run in the loop.

As you can tell from this listing, the code segment between the Repeat and the Until statements will be executed once prior to checking the condition, in this case (I = 'q') or (I = 'Q'). You must make sure that the code segment can handle one iteration prior to checking its state. If your code cannot be bullet-proofed without that checking, use one of the other looping constructs available.

The other item of interest is how many times this loop will run. The answer is unknown. This loop could run one time or a thousand times depending on the user's input. This is something else to consider when using this statement.

While...Do

The While...Do statement pair has a similar function to Repeat...Until but with a two-fold twist:

☐ The conditional statement is checked prior to entering the loop.

☐ If the condition is FALSE, the loop will not be executed, which is the reverse of the Repeat...Until logic.

This means that the While...Do loop may not be executed at all, unlike the Repeat...Until which is always executed once. Listing 3.4 demonstrates how to use While...Do to accomplish the same task of handling user input as Listing 3.5 did with the Repeat...Until.

TYPE **Listing 3.5. Using the While...Do loop.**

```
program WhileDoDemo;

uses
  Forms;

var
   I: Char;

begin
  While (I <> 'q') AND (I <> 'Q') Do
    begin
      Write('Enter a value: ');
        ReadLn(I);
    end;
  Writeln('Press Enter to exit program');
  ReadLn {To keep the window from closing until you press Enter}
end{WhileDoDemo}.
```

ANALYSIS Notice that you had to reverse the logic from (I = 'q') or (I = 'Q') to (I <> 'q') or (I <> 'Q') in order to get the loop to work. This is due to a fundamental change in logic from "Do this until that" to "While this is TRUE, do that." As with the Repeat loop, there is no way to anticipate the number of times the loop is going to be executed. The execution is all dependent on the user's input.

For...Do

The For...Do loop is one of the simplest of the looping constructs. Use this one when you know how many times you want the loop to be executed. Listing 3.6 demonstrates the use of this loop.

TYPE **Listing 3.6. Using the For...Do loop.**

```
program  ForDemo;

Uses
  Forms;

var
  Count : Integer;

begin
  For Count := 1 to 10 do
    WriteLn ('Hello');
  Writeln('Press Enter to exit program');
  ReadLn {To keep the window from closing until you press Enter}
end{ForDemo}.
```

ANALYSIS This program defines a variable Count of type Integer. The For loop does the following:

☐ The Count variable will hold the current value of the loop.

☐ Count is set initially to the value 1.

☐ The statement after the do is executed once (if that statement is a begin, all the code is executed until a matching end is found).

☐ Count is incremented by one.

☐ If Count is greater than the ending value (10) the loop is complete, and execution continues at the statement *after* the For loop's statement line (in this case, after the WriteLn).

☐ If Count is not greater than the ending value (10), the statement after the do is executed again.

NEW TERM A block of code is a fairly broad term that applies to many different situations in Delphi. The basic definition of a *block* is a section of code in between a begin and end statement. In a larger sense, a block may also refer to an entire procedure or function call, and all the code included in that call. When I talk about blocks, it usually will be in relation to statements that can effect a change or operate on an entire block of code.

When using For...Do, you need to heed the following rules:

- ☐ The variable you are using to hold the current value of the loop (in this case, Count) needs to be "in scope" (which you learn about in the section titled "Visibility and Scope," later in this chapter). Simply put, this means that Count needs to be a valid variable local to the block in which the For loop occurs.

- ☐ The initial value (1) must be smaller than the final value (10). This makes sense because the For is incrementing Count. You cannot use Count as a formal parameter to a procedure. You cannot modify the value of Count within the For loop itself.

- ☐ The control variable Count must be assignment-compatible with the initial and final values (1, 10). Delphi 3 must be able to place these values, and every value in between, into Count.

- ☐ You also must remember that Count is undefined once control leaves the For statement, so do not try to use its current value for anything outside the loop.

There is one other variation of the For loop that enables you to decrement the Count variable. Listing 3.7 demonstrates this variation.

TYPE **Listing 3.7. Using the For...Downto...Do loop.**

```
program  ForDowntoDemo;

Uses
  Forms;

var
  Count : Integer;

begin
  For Count := 10 downto 1 do
    WriteLn ('Hello');
  Writeln('Press Enter to exit program');
  ReadLn {To keep the window from closing until you press Enter}
end{ForDowntoDemo}.
```

ANALYSIS This program is similar to ForDemo (Listing 3.6) except that the to reserved word is replaced by downto, and the initial and final values are reversed. In this For loop, Count starts out as 10 and is decremented by one until it reaches 1, and then the loop ends. Is this fun or what?

Branching

Another capability that must exist in a language such as Object Pascal is the capability to *branch* in the code. Branching is the capability to jump to another piece of code when necessary. Several statements are available that enable you to accomplish this:

- ☐ Goto
- ☐ Break
- ☐ Continue
- ☐ Exit
- ☐ Halt
- ☐ RunError

Goto

The Goto statement enables you to jump ahead in the program from one line to another line that has a specific label. Listing 3.8 demonstrates how to define a label and then use it in a Goto statement.

TYPE **Listing 3.8. Using the Goto statement.**

```
program GotoDemo

Uses
  Forms;

var
 Answer : String;

 label ThePlace;

 begin
   ThePlace : WriteLn ('Hello world');
   WriteLn ('Would you like to run this again?');
   ReadLn (Answer);
   If ((Answer = 'y') OR (Answer 'Y')) then
      Goto ThePlace;
   Writeln('Press Enter to exit program');
   ReadLn {To keep the window from closing until you press Enter}
 end{GotoDemo}.
```

ANALYSIS Before you can use a label in a Goto statement, you must first define it in the code where it will be used. This program defines a label named ThePlace. The label is defined outside the executable code area and after other definitions such as const, var, type, and so on.

The 'Hello There' line will always be executed. The WriteLn asks the user if she wants to run the program again. If the user types **y**, the line Goto ThePlace is executed. Otherwise, the last ReadLn is executed, and when the user presses Enter, the program ends.

NOTE

> The concept of labels is old and has been used widely. I'm sure you could have found other ways to code this program without using Goto. The use of Goto is the subject of a long, on-going argument. Many developers feel that using Goto compensates for bad programming practices and that a rigorous examination of your code would turn up a more graceful way of doing things. Others feel that if you have the tool, use it. My opinion is not any more relevant than your own, so make up your own mind and press on.

Break

Suppose you are in the middle of one those fancy For or While loops and you find a condition for which it is imperative that you exit the loop. The Break statement enables you to cease the execution of the loop entirely. Listing 3.9 demonstrates how this could be done. It's a modified version of the WhileDoDemo program (Listing 3.5).

TYPE **Listing 3.9. Using the Break statement.**

```
program BreakDemo;

uses
  Forms;

var
   I: Char;

begin
   I := ' ';
  While TRUE Do
     begin
       Write('Enter a value: ');
        ReadLn(I);
        If (I = 'q') or (I = 'Q') then
           Break;
     end;
    {The Break will cause execution to end up here!}
    Writeln('Press Enter to exit program');
    ReadLn {To keep the window from closing until you press Enter}
end{BreakDemo}.
```

ANALYSIS This is a strange bit of code, but it does illustrate a point. The While loop will continue forever because the expression evaluates to a TRUE. The only way this loop will end is through the use of the Break statement. So, after reading the user's input with ReadLn, the If statement determines if the user typed **q** or **Q**. If it was a **Q**, the Break statement is invoked. The execution drops to the first line after the block of code on which the Break line was located, and execution of the rest of the application continues.

Continue

There may be times when you're in the middle of executing a loop and you want to end what you're doing in this iteration and start the next iteration. The Continue statement performs this task. When used inside a For, While, or Repeat loop, the Continue statement stops the processing in the current iteration and returns control to the loop itself to continue the next iteration. Listing 3.10 demonstrates how this works.

TYPE **Listing 3.10. Using the Continue statement.**

```
program ContinueDemo;

uses
  Forms;

var
    I     : Char;
    Count : Integer;

begin
  I := ' ';
  For Count := 1 to 10 Do
     begin
       Write('Enter a value: ');
        ReadLn(I);
        WriteLn ('The Count is ',Count);
        If (I = 'q') or (I = 'Q') then
          Continue;
        WriteLn (' This will only be executed if the users
                ➥input is not a q or Q.')
     end;
  Writeln('Press Enter to exit program');
  ReadLn {To keep the window from closing until you press Enter}
end{ContinueDemo}.
```

ANALYSIS This program has a For loop that executes 10 times. The loop gathers a keystroke from the user (that is, the variable I which is a single character). If that keystroke is a **q** or **Q**, the Continue statement is invoked and execution is returned to the For line which increments the variable Count by one and moves on. The WriteLn() statement prints the value of the Count variable as you go so that you can see its progress.

NOTE

> After the control variable (Count) is incremented, it is also tested. You might use both the Break and Continue statements if you encounter an error condition in your loop; use Continue to proceed with the next item or Break to skip the remaining items.

Exit

Use Exit when you want to exit the current block of code. If that block is the main program, Exit causes the program to terminate. If the current block is nested, Exit causes the next outer block to continue with the statement immediately after the statement that passed control to the nested block. If the current block is a procedure or function (you learn about procedures and functions in the "Programs" section later in this chapter), Exit causes the calling block to continue with the statement after the point when the block was called. Listing 3.11 demonstrates how to use the Exit statement.

TYPE   **Listing 3.11. Using the Exit statement.**

```
program ExitDemo;

uses
  Forms;

var
   I: Char;
   Count : Integer;

begin
   Repeat
      Write('Enter a value: ');
      ReadLn(I);
      If  I = 'Q' then
          Exit;
   Until FALSE;
   WriteLn('This line will never get called')
end{ExitDemo}
```

ANALYSIS   Because this program creates an endless loop by setting the Until portion of the loop to FALSE, the loop can never end. The only way for the loop to end is for the user to type **Q** at which time the IF . . . Then evaluates to TRUE and the Exit statement executes. Because the block of code you are in is in the main program, the program ceases.

3

Halt

Halt enables you to halt the execution of your application at will. Wherever you place the Halt statement is where the application ends. Before placing this statement in your application, ask yourself a couple questions:

- ☐ Did I leave any databases or files open? They may get corrupted if I quit here.
- ☐ Did I allocate a bunch of memory that I have not freed, and, therefore, am I wasting memory by quitting now?
- ☐ Did I leave any connections to a server open?
- ☐ Place your concern here!

The point is that you should be careful with such a powerful statement. It could get you in trouble. You might want to use this statement when your application encounters a fatal error condition. Some of the return codes from Windows calls, as well as Delphi calls, let you know that something bad has happened. These could be memory- or disk-related problems. It is up to your discretion to halt the application, rather than exiting gracefully. I recommend that you always try to shut down your application gracefully. Use Halt only as a last resort, and even then think twice. If you halt your application, you might leave files open, memory allocated, and lots of other stuff hanging in the wind. Listing 3.12 presents a simple example of using Halt.

TYPE   **Listing 3.12. Using the Halt statement.**

```
program HaltDemo;

uses
  Forms;

var
   I: Char;
   Count : Integer;

begin
   Repeat
     Write('Enter a value: ');
       ReadLn(I);
       If  I = 'Q' then
           Halt;
   Until FALSE;
   WriteLn('This line will never get called')
end {HaltDemo}.
```

ANALYSIS   In this program, when the user types **Q**, the program quits instantly. It's not a very smooth transition out of the application, but it will do in a pinch. Under normal circumstances (and in a more complex application), you would want to have some code that executes on the way out and cleans up your environment before you leave.

RunError

This is a good one! If you don't like waiting for Delphi 3 to spit out those runtime errors at you, now you can create your own. Anytime during program execution, you can invoke the `RunError` statement with an `Integer` parameter, and it halts the execution of the program and displays the error number you entered as the reason for the program's failure. Listing 3.13 demonstrates how this works.

TYPE **Listing 3.13. Using the `RunError` statement.**

```
program RunErrorDemo;

uses
  Forms;

var
  I: Char;

begin
  Repeat
    Write('Enter a value: ');
    ReadLn(I);
    If  I = 'Q' then
      RunError (240);
  Until FALSE;
  WriteLn('This line will never get called')
end {RunErrorDemo}.
```

ANALYSIS This program generates runtime error 240 every time the user types **Q**. If I have my debugger running, I can see that runtime error coming out. This may come in handy especially if you think your application is not generating enough runtime errors on its own (a little joke). Runtime errors are listed in the Delphi online documentation. By the way, error 240 is not listed as a standard error—it's my own creation. Error values can only go up to 255.

Programs

The first few days of this book have taught you about the structure of a Delphi application using a kind of "baptism by fire" method. You will learn about the details of what files constitute your project and how to manage them in Day 5, "Applications, Files, and the Project Manager." For now, though, you need to know about the internal structure of your application, which is what this section is all about. The programs in this section are revised versions of programs from earlier sections of this chapter—you have been typing them in, haven't you?

The one thing common to all Delphi 3 applications is that each has a segment of code that is the main point from which all the rest of the code branches. That code segment starts with the word program, and is referred to as the main program. This is the point at which your application begins executing. The uses clause usually comes next and is used to include other units of code (which are covered in the section "Units" later in this chapter).

After the uses section comes the declaration section. The reserved words const, type, and var are the statements normally present in this section. Here, global data types, variables, and constants are defined.

Lastly, you have the begin...end pair, with a period behind the end statement. This end with a period signifies the end of the executable code, and there can be only one of these in the main executable. The only other two places an end-with-a-period combination can appear is in a unit, or a DLL.

Listing 3.14 presents an example of what a program code segment looks like.

TYPE **Listing 3.14. The main program section of your code.**

```
program ProgDemo;

uses
   Forms;

const
  Taxes = 7.75;
  Death = TRUE;

begin
  If (Taxes > 0) and Death then

  WriteLn ('R.I.P.');
  Writeln('Press Enter to exit program');
  ReadLn {To keep the window from closing until you press Enter}

end. {ProgDemo}
```

ANALYSIS In case you didn't get the joke, notice there are only two constants: death and taxes. Everything between the begin and end is executed in order from top to bottom, and the program ceases when it reaches the end with the period. Very straightforward, isn't it? Now that you think you have everything under control, let's push on.

Procedures

I believe that the discovery of procedures is greater than the discovery of the light bulb—well, almost. They do provide a serious increase in the quality of your programming life (the procedures, I mean). This section explains how procedures can increase productivity clarity and decrease bugs in your code.

In the throes of programming, you may often overlook the obvious. If you needed to write a program that prints a checkerboard, you might be tempted to write the program in Listing 3.15, which does not use a procedure.

TYPE **Listing 3.15.** `TicTacToePrint` **demo.**

```
program TicTacToePrint;

uses
  Forms;

begin
  WriteLn ('     |   |     ');
  WriteLn ('------------- ');
  WriteLn ('     |   |     ');
  WriteLn ('------------- ');
  WriteLn ('     |   |     ');
  Writeln('Press Enter to exit program');
  ReadLn {To keep the window from closing until you press Enter}
end.
```

NOTE

Due to proportional fonts in Windows, this TicTacToe board may look really lame. I am trying to show a simple example and am really not worried about aesthetics.

ANALYSIS This program admittedly creates a pretty a lame checkerboard, but it is direct, gets the job done, and illustrates the point. Do you see the repetition in this? You are doing the same thing over and over. Now, the concept of a procedure comes into play.

The program in Listing 3.16 is a revised version of Listing 3.16. Look at it, and then we'll talk.

TYPE   **Listing 3.16. Using a procedure.**

```
program CheckerPrint;

uses
  Forms;

{normally any const, var, type and other
 ➥declarations would go here.}

    procedure DoVerticals;
      begin
        WriteLn ('     ¦   ¦     ');
      end;

    procedure DoHorizontals;
      begin
        WriteLn ('------------');
      end;

begin
  DoVerticals;
  DoHorizontals;
  DoVerticals;
  DoHorizontals;
  DoVerticals;
  Writeln('Press Enter to exit program');
  ReadLn {To keep the window from closing until you press Enter}
end.
```

ANALYSIS   This program takes a section (or in this case, a line) of code that is used often, puts a wrapper around it, and gives that wrapper a name. This means you can use that name to access the code inside the wrapper anytime you wish. Two procedures were created to make this possible: one that prints the horizontal lines and one that prints the vertical ones. Notice that the procedures were declared between the reserved word `program`, and the beginning of the executable code (the `begin` statement).

The first thing you do to create a `procedure` is create a procedure heading. The heading consists of the reserved word `procedure` and a unique name for that procedure. In this case, `procedure DoHorizontals;` is the procedure heading. The heading is very similar to the `program TicTacToePrint;` line for your main program. The similarities between the main program and the procedure do not end there. The procedure is sort of a mini-program and has the same format. After the heading, you can have a `const`, `type`, or `var` section, or even another procedure. A procedure can have another procedure nested inside of it. After all this, the procedure, of course, has an executable section marked by the `begin...end` statement pair.

3

Now that you have created this procedure named DoHorizontals, you can call that procedure in your code. When you call that code by its unique name, control will be passed to that procedure. When the procedure is finished executing, the procedure will return control to the line of code *after* the line that called the procedure.

Procedures are a way of modularizing code and making it usable over and over. The other benefit is in code reliability. If you write the same piece of code six times in your application, you have six chances of making mistakes. If you use a procedure, you write the code once, test it once, and then use it repeatedly. You have a lesser chance of making mistakes, and your code quality is better overall.

Parameter Passing

Procedures are of only limited use considering how you've seen them used to this point. A procedure that prints a row of dashes is not very useful. To help increase the worth of procedures, you need to make them more flexible. The best way is to be able to pass additional data into the procedure as you execute it, giving it additional direction or purpose. The way to accomplish this is through the use of parameters.

Listing 3.17 contains a revised version of the DoHorizontals procedure (from Listing 3.17) that includes a parameter which varies the number of times the lines are printed.

Listing 3.17. The DoHorizontals program using a For...Do
TYPE **loop.**

```
procedure DoHorizontals (HowManyTimes : Integer);

var
  Count : Integer;

    begin
      for Count := 1 to HowManyTimes do
        WriteLn ('----------------');
      Writeln('Press Enter to exit program');
    end;
```

ANALYSIS This new procedure allows for some flexibility. It incorporates a variable, HowManyTimes, that is fed into the procedure. The (HowManyTimes : Integer); code is called a *formal parameter list*. This is a laundry list of the data that should be given to this procedure every time it is called, as well as what type(s) that data is. In this case, you want to pass an Integer variable into the procedure that will control the number of times the WriteLn is executed. By giving that variable a name, you are essentially doing a variable definition, not in the var section of the procedure. Now the procedure DoHorizontals has a variable HowManyTimes of type Integer that can be used anywhere within that procedure.

Remember that because this variable was defined inside the DoHorizontals procedure, it can be used only inside that procedure (you learn more about this in the next section, "Visibility and Scope"). As you can see, you then use HowManyTimes as the end count of the for loop that executes the WriteLn as many times as you need. This makes the procedure much more flexible.

Now that you have created a formal parameter list as part of the procedure declaration, you need to change how you call the procedure. You can no longer just say DoHorizontals and off it goes. For every formal parameter you identify, you must supply a matching actual parameter when you make the call. There *must* be a one-to-one mapping between formal and actual parameters. Because your procedure heading was

```
procedure DoHorizontals (HowManyTimes : Integer);
```

you must have one Integer number to pass DoHorizontals when you call it. The program is shown in Listing 3.18.

TYPE Listing 3.18. Using parameters.

```
program ParamDemo;

uses
  Forms;

var
  Number : Integer;

  procedure DoHorizontals (HowManyTimes : Integer);

  var
    Count : Integer;

    begin
      for Count := 1 to HowManyTimes do
        WriteLn ('------------');
      end; {procedure DoHorizontals}

begin
  WriteLn ('How many vertical lines would you like to print :');
  ReadLn(Number);
  DoHorizontals (Number);
  Writeln('Press Enter to exit program');
  ReadLn {To keep the window from closing until you press Enter}
end. {program ParamDemo}
```

ANALYSIS When this program calls the DoHorizontals, it passed along the variable Number. This is called an *actual parameter*. The contents of Number is copied into the procedure DoHorizontals and lands in the locally defined variable HowManyTimes. At that point, the procedure has the data from the global variable Number in HowManyTimes and goes on its way. When DoHorizontals finishes its processing, the data in HowManyTimes disappears because the local variable is destroyed upon exiting the procedure.

When you pass multiple parameters to a procedure, the order is most important. The only way that Delphi 3 can tell the matching of actual to formal parameters is by the order in which they are passed. Here's an example of passing multiple parameters.

```
procedure Junk (Number : Integer; Stuff : String);

begin
   WriteLn ('The number is ', Number);
   WriteLn ('The string is ', Stuff)
end; {procedure Junk}
```

This procedure takes two parameters, one is an Integer value, and the other is a String value. When you call this procedure, you must make the procedure call and pass it an Integer and a String, in that order. The program will not compile otherwise. You would call this procedure as shown in Listing 3.19.

Listing 3.19. JunkDemo **program passing multiple**
TYPE **paramenters.**

```
program JunkDemo;

uses
   Forms;

var
   UsersNumber : Integer;
   UsersString : String;

procedure Junk (Number : Integer; Stuff : String);

begin
   WriteLn ('The number is ', Number);
   WriteLn ('The string is ', Stuff)
end; {procedure Junk}

begin
   Write ('Enter your string :');
   ReadLn (UsersString);
   Write ('Enter the number :');
   ReadLn (UsersNumber);
   Junk (UsersNumber, UsersString);
   Writeln('Press Enter to exit program');
   ReadLn {To keep the window from closing until you press Enter}
end. {program JunkDemo}
```

ANALYSIS This program passes two parameters to Junk in the right order.

You can also pass literal data to the function, as opposed to variable data. An example would be calling Junk(3, 'Hello World'); which would pass the literal data into the local variables for processing. This new line could replace any of the Junk procedure calls in Listing 3.19.

Visibility and Scope

As your applications get broken up into smaller and smaller pieces (through the use of procedures and functions), you need to become aware of how the lives of your variables are affected. With the move to procedures, functions, and units, there is more potential for things to overlap. This complexity means that you need to be aware of two things about variables: visibility and scope. Listing 3.20 uses several variables that will help you understand how variables are seen.

TYPE **Listing 3.20.** VisibleDemo **program showing scope.**

```
program VisibleDemo;

uses
  Forms;

var
  A : Integer;

  procedure Outer;

      var
        B : Integer;

      procedure Inner;

      var
        C : Integer;

      begin
      C := 3;
      B := 8;
      A := 4; {I can see A from the main program declarations}
      end; {procedure Inner}

    begin
      B := 5;
      C := 5; {this would be illegal, I can see only out, not in}
      A := 9 {I can see A from the main program declarations}
    end; {procedure Outer}

  procedure AnotherOne;
```

```
  var
      D : Integer;

  begin
    D := 9;
    A := 55; {I can see A from the main program declarations}
    B := 4; {this would be illegal, I can see only out, not in}
    C := 5; {this would be illegal, I can see only out, not in}
  end; {procedure AnotherOne}

begin
  A:= 1
  {I can not reference any of the local variables in
  ➥any of the procedures
    from here.  None are visible.}
end. {Main program VisibleDemo}
```

 This program has a nested procedure. In order to understand how each of the variables are seen and can be used, let's look at the rules that describe how to accomplish this visibililty and use.

☐ **Rule 1**—Variables are visible (which means you can access them) only in the block in which they are defined.

☐ **Rule 2**—In nested procedures or functions, you can always see from the inside out. This means that procedures which are nested the deepest can see the variables defined in their parent procedure, and it in its parent, and so on.

> You might be asking, "Doesn't Rule 2 directly contradict Rule 1?" The answer is no. This is based on the definition of *block*. Because a nested procedure was defined within its parent's block of code, the visibility is there. And, if that parent is defined within the code block of its parent, the most deeply nested procedure can see all the way out. Just remember that you can always see outward (towards your parents) but not inward.

If you apply these rules to Listing 3.20, you can draw several conclusions.

☐ Because variable C was created in procedure Inner, it is visible only within that procedure.

☐ Because variable B was defined in procedure Outer, it is visible in that procedure, as well as visible to procedure Inner, which is looking "out" from a nested child procedure.

☐ Because variable A was defined in the main body, it is visible to every procedure and function in the main body. It is the parent of all the child procedures. The main body also cannot see any variable in those child procedures, because it cannot look "in," only "out."

☐ Because variable D was defined in procedure Another, it can be seen only by Another because there are no nested child procedures to see it. Another cannot see variable A, a variable in its parent.

Besides the visibility of a variable, you have its scope—in other words, where is it valid to use a variable. The rule here is simple. A variable does not reach beyond the block in which it is defined. Variable C's scope is only within procedure Inner. It literally does not exist outside that procedure. Assignment to variable C outside procedure Inner (for instance, in procedure Outer) would gain you a wonderful compile-time error that would tell you variable C is undefined (in procedure Outer).

This is sometimes referred to as global versus local variables. Global variables are defined in the main program body and are visible to the entire application. Local variables are defined in procedures and functions, and they are visible only to certain portions of the application, depending on that procedure's nesting.

Functions

You may be wondering if there could be anything better than procedures, and the answer is yes, functions. As you see from our previous discussion on procedures, they play an important role in Delphi programming. There is another side to this argument, though. Suppose the world is full of nothing but procedures. Doing math in Delphi would be very interesting to say the least.

The sample procedure that you write next is not supposed to teach you how to write a function, but rather provides an example of life without functions. You'll write and use a procedure that is the equivalent of the Sqr function and then use it in an application. Then you'll see how to write a function that provides the same functionality. If you had a square procedure it would look something like this:

```
procedure Square (The_Number : Integer; var The_Result: Integer);

  begin
    The_Result := The_Number * The_Number
  end;
```

This looks simple enough. To use the new procedure, you would call it as shown in Listing 3.21.

3

TYPE **Listing 3.21. Implementing a new procedure.**

```
program FunctionDemo;

uses
  Forms;

  procedure Square (TheNumber : Integer; var TheResult : Integer);

    begin
      TheResult := TheNumber * TheNumber
    end;

var
  UserInput , TheAnswer : Integer;

begin
  Write ('Enter the number you want to square :');
  ReadLn (UserInput);
  Square (UserInput, TheAnswer);    {Here we called our procedure}
  WriteLn (UserInput, ' squared is equal to ', TheAnswer)
  Writeln('Press Enter to exit program');
  ReadLn {To keep the window from closing until you press Enter}
end. {FunctionDemo}
```

NOTE

> Notice that a var comes before TheResult in the formal parameter list of the Square function call. This shows that you are passing by reference and that the value of the actual parameter (the variable TheAnswer) will be changed after the procedure is done executing.

ANALYSIS

Now this works out okay, but you have to create a separate variable, TheAnswer, just to hold the result of the squaring operation, when all you want to do is print the result immediately after you calculate it. There is a better way, and it involves a function.

A function is similar to a procedure in that you pass parameters to them both, but a function is designed to return a single value. This may not be a big revelation because you've designed procedures that return a single value as well. The difference is that the function returns that single value in the function name itself. The function name becomes a temporary variable in which the function's result is passed back to the calling code.

Here's an example to illustrate the point. In Delphi, there is a Sqr() function that you can use to square a number, and Listing 3.22 demonstrates how to use it. You use Delphi's function first to show you how to call it, then you'll write our own.

Listing 3.22. Function demo program with the `Sqr()` function.

TYPE

```
program FunctionDemo2;

uses
  Forms;

var
   UserInput : Integer;

begin
   Write ('Enter the number you want to square :');
   ReadLn (UserInput);
   WriteLn (UserInput, ' squared is equal to ', Sqr(UserInput));
   Writeln('Press Enter to exit program');
   Readln {To keep the window from closing until you press Enter}
end. { FunctionDemo2}
```

ANALYSIS This program uses the `Sqr()` function and calculates the user's result right in the line that prints the answer. A procedure would not work here for two reasons. First, you do not have a place to put the result from a square procedure, and, second, you cannot call a procedure from within another procedure-call statement.

Here's the `Square()` procedure rewritten as a function:

```
Function Square (TheInput : Real) : Real;

  begin
     Result := TheInput * TheInput
  end;
```

There are two differences between the `Square` procedure implemented in Listing 3.21 and this `Square` function. The first is the function definition line. You pass the user's input into the function through the `TheInput` parameter. You are going to pass the result of the function back through the function name associated with it, like any other variable. The `:Real` at the end of the function definition defines the return type of the function variable `Result`. Notice that in the function itself you have the following line:

```
Result := TheInput * TheInput
```

Before your function can finish, you must assign a value to the variable `Result`. This special variable name is used to pass the result of your function call back to the calling code. `Result` is simply a transport mechanism to get your result back to the calling code. You need to set `Result` equal to a value of type `Real` (remember the `:Real`), before the function ends. Then, when control is returned to the program that called the function, the function name `Square` actually has the function result in it. The function name `Square` remains a temporary variable

3

only in the line of code that called the function in the first place. Once that line of code is done executing, the name Square has no value, and now is referencing a function call that requires parameters and the like.

Listing 3.23 is a modified version of the program in Listing 3.22, and it demonstrates how the function call is of a temporary nature.

TYPE **Listing 3.23. Function demo program showing variable life.**

```
program FunctionDemo3;

uses
  Forms;

    Function Square (TheInput : Integer) : Integer;

      begin
          Square := TheInput * TheInput
      end;

var
   UserInput : Integer;

begin
  Write ('Enter the number you want to square :');
  ReadLn (UserInput);
  WriteLn (UserInput, ' squared is equal to ', Square(UserInput));
  {If we try to print the value of Square out after
    ➥the line that called it
    we will get a compile time error.  This program will not run.}
  WriteLn ('In case you did not get it the value of the
          ➥square is ', Square)
end. { FunctionDemo3}
```

ANALYSIS The second WriteLn in this program will not compile. The word Square has no value at that point and is back to meaning the name of a function. The compile tells you that you are missing parameters for that function call. This does not diminish the value of functions, it just limits their use. You will find functions throughout Delphi 3. Functions are invaluable as tools for doing math, graphics, and other interesting things.

Units

One of the reasons that software development progressed so slowly in the early years (when dinosaurs roamed the earth and programmers used punch cards and paper tape) is that everyone wanted to reinvent the wheel every time they developed a new application. "I have to do it my way." The number of times programmers wrote bubble-sort routines could not be counted because it was so huge (a slight exaggeration). With the advent of new development tools came new ideas.

The unit enables you to write and compile your own bubble-sort routine (maybe along with other routines) into a unit of code. That unit could then be reused and distributed to other developers. Because the unit is compiled, other developers could use my code without seeing the source code and my secret bubble-sort algorithm. Using units, you have to invent that wheel only once, and then you can use it over and over again.

The Format of a Unit

 The *unit* is constructed similarly to a Delphi main program. A unit has the general form:

```
Unit YourNameHere;

    interface
        uses ...

        const ...
        type ...
        var ...
        procedure ...
        function ...

    implementation
        uses ...
        Label ...
        const ...
        type ...
        var ...
        procedure ...
        function ...

    initialization {optional}
        begin
          ...
        end;

    finalization {optional}
        begin
          ...
        end;

end. {end of the unit}
```

The interface section of the unit comes first. Here, you define any variables, constants, types, or other goodies that you want to make available to the project or other units with this unit is their uses statement. All items in the interface section are available to any program that has your unit name in their uses statement. This gives you the option to include predefined structures to help another developer use your unit. The next part of the interface section is the procedure and function headers of all the procedures and functions you have implemented in your unit. This is how Delphi 3 tracks what is available to the application from your unit.

Now that you have made public your intentions (in the interface section), you implement the functions and procedures you described there in the implementation section. In this section, you weave your magic as you implement your super-secret XOR encryption algorithm that will earn you international fame (and maybe a movie deal).

In the implementation section, you place any variables, constants, and so on, that will be used by functions or procedures within this section. The variables you define here cannot be used outside this section. You can also create procedures and functions that are used locally by the procedures and functions you specified in the interface section. As the last item in the implementation section, you implement the functions and procedures that you described in the interface section. The parameter lists must match exactly, or the unit will not compile.

There are two other optional sections you can have in a unit: initialization and finalization. The first is the initialization section, in which you can define variables and such. The problem is that because the interface section has no executable area, you cannot initialize those variables with a value. The initialization section affords you the opportunity to do so. Here, you can initialize your variables, record structures, file variables, and anything else that could use an initial value. This enables you to "prime the pump," as it were. You can also initialize variables in the begin...end block at the end of the unit.

The finalization section is the opposite of the initialization section. It enables you to do some house cleaning prior to shutting the application down. It enables you to close files, deallocate memory, and perform other clean-up activities. Once the initialization section of your unit has been executed, the code in your finalization section is guaranteed to run prior to the application's closing. Another brilliant and necessary stroke is that Delphi 3 executes the finalization of the units used in reverse order from what the initialization code has run. If you initialize the units X, Y, and Z, it makes sense to close them down in Z, Y, and X order. This may be necessary as well; if units have other units in their uses statement, the dependent units will have to wait until their finalization sections have executed.

NOTE

Because the order in which the different pieces are executed in a unit is so important, here's that order again. When your application starts, the initialization section begins executing in order of the unit names in your uses statement in the main program. From that point on, the code in the units is executed as it is called from your main program. When the user ends your application, the finalization section of each unit is called in the opposite order that the initialization sections were in at the beginning of the program.

The following code is an example of a unit you might create to do a couple of simple math functions. The applicability of this unit is in question, but it helps demonstrate the structure and function.

```
Unit MathStuff;

interface
  function AddTwoNumbers (One, Two : Integer) : Integer;

  function SubtractTwoNumbers (One, Two : Integer) : Integer;

 function MultiplyTwoNumbers (One, Two : Integer) : Integer;

  procedure PositiveKarma;

implementation

  function AddTwoNumbers (One, Two : Integer) : Integer;

    begin
       AddTwoNumbers := One + Two
    end;

  function SubtractTwoNumbers (One, Two : Integer) : Integer;

     begin
        SubtractTwoNumbers := One - Two
     end;

  function MultiplyTwoNumbers (One, Two : Integer) : Integer;

     begin
        MultiplyTwoNumbers := One * Two
     end;

   procedure PositiveKarma;
      begin
         WriteLn('You can do it, math is not hard!')
      end;

end. {MathStuff Unit}
```

This simple unit demonstrates the form of a unit. It defines the functions and procedures that are available to the user of the unit in the interface section. In the implementation section, you actually create the items you "advertised" in the interface section. I threw in the PositiveKarma procedure for those of you who hate math. You will see units used extensively in Delphi 3.

To call this unit, you just include it in the uses section of your main program. Listing 3.26 presents an example of calling the MathStuff unit.

3

TYPE **Listing 3.26. Using a unit.**

```
program MathDemo;

Uses
  MathStuff;

var
  A, B : Integer;

begin
  A := 1;
  B := 2;
  WriteLn ('The sum of  ', A, ' and ',  B, ' is ', AddTwoNumbers(A,B));
  Writeln('Press Enter to exit program');
  ReadLn {To keep the window from closing until you press Enter}
end. {program MathDemo}
```

ANALYSIS This program uses one of the MathStuff functions, AddTwoNumbers, to demonstrate the use of units. Once you add that MathStuff unit to your project, you can call the AddTwoNumbers function in that unit. For your general information, you add an existing unit to your project by selecting View | Project Manager, and clicking the Add button. You then can select your unit file from disk, and it will be added into the project. You'll learn more about this in Day 5.

Reusability

The concepts of software reusability and component libraries have come to light in recent years. The unit is a natural extension of this theory of reuse. The unit provides a way for software developers to create a set of library routines and wrap them into a piece of code that can be set aside and used at any time.

The uses statement enables you to include your own units in your application. Delphi 3 provides a standard set of units that perform general functions, such as file I/O, forms, graphics, buttons, and so on. (A full list of standard units is available in Delphi's online help). You'll find several advantages to using the unit model for developing software. Because most of the functionality of an application can be divided into groups or areas, it only makes sense that you have a programming model that supports that concept.

Units also help in the debugging process. If you are having a problem with your self-derived math formula, you would look in your math unit to debug the function, rather than looking through your entire application for the defective math function. The ability to break your program up into pieces enables you to group such things as functions and procedures into units and better organize your project. In a large project involving many people, you may even want to assign a code librarian to keep the latest versions of your units and distribute them to those who need the them.

Distribution Security

I assume that you are writing software (and reading this book) because you have a love of developing software. I also assume that many of you are trying to make money doing it as well. As with authoring books, writing software is creating something from nothing. That creative effort needs to be protected. If you were to come up with an encryption algorithm that could speedily encrypt data, you would more than likely wish to protect that code. You also probably will want to sell that code. This creates a problem—how do you sell your code to other developers without giving them the source code and compromising your algorithm?

Units provide a feature necessary to everyone who wishes to distribute their code and keep it safe from piracy. Delphi units can be compiled into binary files and distributed for use by others. When a unit is compiled, Delphi creates a Delphi compiled unit (DCU) and gives it a .DCU extension. From that point on, you can distribute that .DCU file to others, and they can use that unit in their applications by including it in their uses statement, but they never will see the source code itself. This enables you to develop your code and sell it with more security and peace of mind.

Before developers can use your unit, they must know what functionality it provides. It is necessary for you to detail the functionality in an accompanying document. Many developers simply copy the interface section of the unit and distribute that. Remember that after your unit is compiled, the interface section is not humanly readable. Selling add-on units, DLLs, and VCLs is big business, and there is no reason you cannot play along, too.

NOTE

To date, this concept of distributing units has not worked well between versions of Pascal/Delphi. It usually is necessary to recompile units for every version. For this reason, many developers make their source code available (for a price) along with the compiled unit.

Team Development

Another benefit of breaking your project into units is the ability to assign different developers to create those units. After you have divided the application into math, graphing, and file I/O units, you can assign a developer to create each unit. Assign a developer who is math-wise to do the math unit, a graphics-type developer to the graphics unit, and so on. Most applications are getting too large to be written by a single developer (in a reasonable amount of time). It has become more important than ever to find ways to divide the work among several developers, and get the work done faster, as shown in Figure 3.1.

Figure 3.1.

*The team develop-
ment concept.*

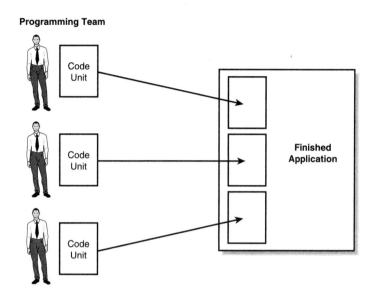

Pointers

The concept of pointers is probably the single most difficult topic for programmers to learn. This section introduces you to pointers, but don't feel badly if you are not a pointer expert by the time you finish reading it. It may take some time working with them before you are comfortable.

When you create data structures in Delphi 3, they are allocated memory. That memory is needed to hold the data in your structure. Many of the data structures (such as records and arrays) can become arbitrarily large. For that reason, as well as others you've learned, allocate only the memory that you are going to use.

A pointer variable is capable of storing the address of a data structure (such as an array or record). This is similar to a looking up something in the white pages of the phone book. You can give other procedures and functions this "pointer" to your data instead of the data itself. If you don't see the immediate benefit of this approach, consider what you would do if your neighbor asked you how to get to the grocery. You wouldn't bring the whole store home to give to your neighbor, but you would provide the neighbor with directions—or a pointer— to the store.

Procedures make extensive use of pointers. You use pointers every time you make a function call and use the var designator in the formal procedure declaration. When you pass parameters using the var designator, this actually passes a pointer to the data into your procedure. That is why, when you change the data in a var parameter variable in your procedure, that data is changed outside your procedure as well. You really are changing the outside data directly, using that "handle" to the data.

There is a real benefit to doing business this way. If you do not use the var designator in the formal parameter list of a procedure call, Delphi 3 has to make a local copy of the data to work on every time you pass something into the procedure. By not using var, you are saying, "Do not touch my original," so it makes a copy. Can you imagine how much memory is used by making copies of 10,000 record arrays? The payback for using pointers is very real.

NOTE

Pointers do not mean that everything is free. Pointers also take resources from the system. To reference the data, Delphi has to dereference a pointer each time. At best, that may double or triple the number of CPU cycles it takes to complete the operation. The rule of thumb is to use only what you need.

Using Pointers

To use a pointer, you must first define one. Consider the simple example of a pointer to a real number shown in Listing 3.25.

TYPE **Listing 3.25. Using pointers to a single variable.**

```
program PointerDemo;

uses
  Forms;

type
  RealPointer = ^Real;

var
  P : RealPointer;

begin
  New (P);
  P^ := 21.6;
  WriteLn (P^ :5:1);
   Dispose (P);
  Writeln('Press Enter to exit program');
   ReadLn {To keep the window from closing until you press Enter}
end.   {PointerDemo}
```

ANALYSIS This program begins by creating a type called RealPointer. RealPointer is a pointer to Real number. The caret ^ denotes "pointing to." Therefore, the line would read in English, "RealPointer is a pointer to a real number." After you define the pointer type, you must create a variable of that type for use. So you create the variable P of type RealPointer. Now, you have a variable that is a pointer to a real number.

Before you begin the execution of the program, you must first allocate memory for P. Right now, P is capable of pointing to a real number but is currently pointing to nothing. By using the New() procedure call, you are having Delphi 3 assign a block of memory capable of holding a Real number and put that memory address into P. Now P is pointing to a memory location that can hold a Real number. The line P^ := 21.6; translates into, "Set the place that P is pointing to equal to 21.6." This is called *dereferencing* a pointer. In other words, you are taking the value 21.6 and placing it into the memory location pointed to by P.

When using the WriteLn to print the value of what is pointed to by P, you again must use the caret to say, "Write to the screen what P is pointing to, and format it in five digits with one digit to the right of the decimal." After you have no more use for P, you must use the Dispose() procedure call to free the memory that P is pointing to and give it back to the free memory pool. Then, you end the program.

You can use pointers also to point to things more complex than just a real number. Listing 3.26 creates a record and uses a pointer to it to access that record's fields.

TYPE **Listing 3.26. Using pointers to data structures.**

```
program PointerDemo2;

uses
  Forms;

type
  PersonType = RECORD
     LastName  : String;
     FirstName : String;
     Age       : Integer
          end; {PersonRecord}

 PersonPointer = ^PersonType;

var
  Person : PersonPointer;

begin
   New (Person);
   Person^.LastName := 'Smith';
   Person^.FirstName := 'James';
   Person^.Age := 35;
```

continues

Listing 3.26. continued

```
    WriteLn ('Well ', Person^.FirstName, ' ', Person^.LastName, ', you are ',
            ➡Person^.Age, ' years old.');
    Dispose (Person);
    Writeln('Press Enter to exit program');
    ReadLn {To keep the window from closing until you press Enter}
end. {PointerDemo2}
```

 This program is very similar to the PointerDemo program (Listing 3.25) in how the pointers are dealt with. The difference is which data structure you are pointing to.

Here, you create a type called PersonType that is a record, consisting of a last name, first name, and an age. Second, you create a PersonPointer type that is a pointer to the record you created earlier. Creating a Person variable is the next step. That variable is of PersonPointer type.

When the execution of the main program begins, you go through the same motions as with the PointerDemo program. Allocation of memory is done with the New() statement. You place values into the record pointed to by Person by using the ^ to dereference the pointer and show which field of the record to place the data in. After assigning values to the record, the results are written to the screen in a string that ends up being similar to "Well James Smith, you are 35 years old." Using the Dispose() statement frees the memory allocated to Person.

The evil reality of it all is that Windows is full of pointers. Many of the ways programs exchange data is by exchanging pointers. In languages such as C++, pointers are it. This has been only a cursory introduction, and many pages could be spent talking about the intricacies of using pointers. Read all the material you can about pointers, and look at examples. Delphi has gone to great lengths to hide as much of the implementation of pointers from you as it could. The hiding of a lot of the underlying complexity (including pointers) enables you to deal with code at a much higher level. The result of this higher level is greater productivity.

Summary

Today you were introduced to the concepts necessary for developing modular programs. You saw how to develop procedures and functions, and learned what they can be used for. You learned about creating loops, branching statements, and visibility and scope issues. I hope this will entice you to study the Delphi documentation for more detailed help in these areas.

Q&A

Q **Why does OP provide constructs such as Goto if it is considered bad programming practice to use them?**

A The subject is not really closed (and probably never will be) on proper use of things such as Goto. The tool will still be there until it is wise to dump it, if ever.

Q **What would happen if a procedure returned execution control to the line of code that called the procedure and not the line after it?**

A It would not work. Every time the procedure finished, it would return control to a line of code that simply called the procedure again. It's like calling the IRS and asking for an audit—not a good idea!

Workshop

The Workshop provides two ways for you to affirm what you've learned in this chapter. The Quiz section poses questions to help you solidify your understanding of the material covered. You can find answers to the quiz questions in Appendix A, "Answers to the Quiz Questions." The Exercises section provides you with experience in using what you have learned. Please try to work through all these before continuing to the next day.

Quiz

1. How many times is the WriteLn() statement executed in the following example?

```
program Quiz4-1;

var
  Count, Count2 : Integer;

begin
  For Count := 1 to 10 do
    For Count2 := 1 to 10 do
        WriteLn ('Hello!');
end.
```
100

2. Which looping construct do you use if you would like to test your conditional prior to entering the processing loop? *WHILE DO*

3. What is the fundamental difference between a procedure and a function? *VAR SENT BACK AS A PART OF NAME*

4. What is the advantage of using pointers in an application, as opposed to passing the real data around instead?

Exercises

1. Write an application that counts to 33, prints the number as it counts, and uses two For loops to do it.

2. Try writing an application that has several units. To get a feel for the uses statement, have your main application use a unit, and have that unit use yet another unit. As long as they compile, the units can be simple.

3. Write a procedure that has several parameters, both passing by reference and passing by value. See how changing the order of the actual parameters (when you call the procedure) can generate different compile-time error messages.

Day **4**

Object-Oriented Programming and Software Engineering

Many of you reading this book may be learning Delphi (or Object Pascal) for the first time. Many of you also may have little or no formal training in software development or software engineering. This lack of training is a significant detriment, because learning to be a good computer scientist involves more than learning the syntax of a particular language such as Delphi.

There are many other aspects of the software field that really bear little connection to the actual act of writing code but are equally important to the act itself. This chapter covers several topics you may not have dealt with before but will affect your career as a software developer. These include the software crisis, software lifecycle, and software engineering.

Now you might be saying, "Come on, I just want to learn Delphi!" To that I answer, "A person who lives with blinders on is soon hit by reality from the side, which he or she cannot see," (an ancient Chinese proverb I just made up). The point here is that if you plan to develop software for money, you have real customers that expect the following to be true:

- [ ] Your software works out of the box.
- [ ] Your software is done on time.
- [ ] Your software is bug free.
- [ ] Your software is inexpensive.

Therefore, you need to read this chapter. Today you learn about the problems inherent in software development, about potential solutions, and how Delphi 3 supports the solutions.

Software Crisis

I know what you're thinking: Crisis, what crisis? There has been a software crisis for so long now that most people think it's normal. People have been programming computers (at least what we think of as computers) for only a handful of decades. But, as anyone who has been around computers can tell you, even a couple of years is a long time in technological terms (think of computer years the way you do dog years). Times and technology change; people don't. The method of programming has changed very little from those early beginnings. Although, rather recently, there has been a large shift in the accepted programming doctrine.

Prior to 1990, when a programmer was given a task, he or she plopped down in a chair in front of a PC and started coding. The tasks were small and the coding was fast. Those were the good old days. It was a time when, if you needed to get something done, you could just sit up all night and get it done. It was a time of thousand-line programs—good programs, too. It was a time when one person could tap along and come up with a million-dollar program! It was, literally, the golden age of programming. But all good things must come to an end, and there is no better example of this than in the arena of programming.

Software Complexity

As computers became more sophisticated, so, too, did their users. The tasks foisted upon programmers became larger and so did the associated coding time. Then a funny thing happened. After a program reached a certain size, the time it took to code turned out to be much longer than expected (based on smaller programs). If a program was twice as long as another program, it was assumed that it would take twice as long to code (we thought the curve was linear). It actually turned out to take more than twice as long (as shown in Figure 4.1). Whether it was the fundamental unfairness of the universe or Murphy's Law, the fact of the matter was that when a program reached a certain size, the human brain couldn't keep track of all the complexity. Complexity was the culprit all right, and there was nothing we could do about it (at least not directly). It was a hard truism to accept, but case after case, program after program, it was proven to be true.

Figure 4.1.

Software size versus complexity.

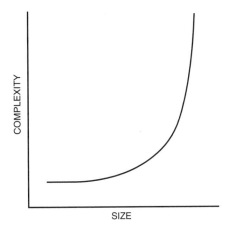

As you may have noticed, there are quite a few very complex programs of the shelves of your local software store. We must have beaten complexity…right? Well, yes and no. Complexity is like the sea, you can't tame it or beat it. You have to ride out complexity, take advantage of calm times, and take shelter in protected harbors when you can. Okay, okay, I've milked that analogy for as much as I can. But the essence is true: You can't beat complexity. How many of those whiz-bang, very complex programs are error free? Very few! A bug is complexity's way of telling you that you haven't beaten it. And just think, we even find bugs in small programs. Only after quite a bit of work, can we say that even the smallest program is truly error free. What hope can we have of putting together a large program that doesn't fall apart at the seams? Well, the trick to beating complexity is to write small "error-free" programs and put them together building a large "error-free" program. Of course, this is easier said than done, but this modular approach helps us manage complexity in programming. Note that I put quotes around "error-free." "Error free" is much the same as "100 percent pure"—for any non-trivial sample, there is no such thing.

The Need To Plan

The obvious thing here is that we figured out that more was needed than just sitting down and coding. We needed to apply scientific analysis to the problem and not just undisciplined artistry (hacking). Like every great battle, there is a battle plan, a set of tactics and weapons to use on the enemy. Software development is no different. You will now learn about the two things that have helped us, not only with the battle but the war. Those two weapons are the software lifecycle and software engineering.

Software Lifecycle

The software lifecycle is a roadmap—a series of steps that should be taken, and taken in order. Using this disciplined approach, the developer can generate a better end product and spend lees time maintaining the product as well. This is not a panacea, but just another tool in the fight against lousy software.

The software lifecycle is broken into six major areas. These areas are shown in Figure 4.2. As you read through these, they will really seem common sense. You would be surprised how many developers skip several steps and go right to the coding, and then skip all the steps after that! Look at each step and consider the implications of each.

Figure 4.2.

The software lifecycle.

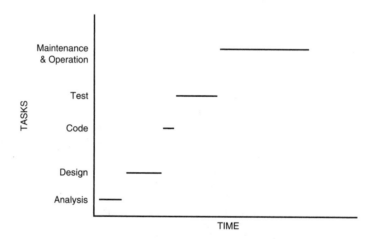

Analysis

During the analysis phase of development, you try to better define the problem at hand. At this point, one thing that needs to be determined is whether a software-based solution is even right. There are many things that can be better accomplished by two columns on a piece of paper rather than a complete software application.

Now you may call me a traitor. No, not really. I am sure that you, too, have seen applications requiring more work from you, to input your data, than the results you get out of the application (a poor return on investment). An application like this is called a "time sucker." It sucks all of your useful time from your body with little return on your investment. You just need to make sure that a computer-based solution will help the problem, not add to it.

During this phase of development, you also need to determine what type of resources you will need to complete the project. It may be just you and your PC and Delphi. For larger projects you may require the assistance of several other developers, technical writers, and the like. At this point you usually do not select a language. This is because you can't possibly know, until you understand the problem and design a solution, which language best supports your solution.

In the big league, the result of this phase of development usually is the creation of a system specification. This specification helps define the system as whole. It maps out the system functions that need to be performed.

In this phase, you also may choose to add some of the customer details. Analysts and designers often take these customer details into account in the analysis portion (unless the customers are insistent upon the details being implemented in a specific manner). In this way, analysts and designers often try to free themselves from having to use possible "poor implementation choices" in their designs. This is sort of like mapping out the bumps in the road so that when you drive down the road, you know where the bumps are and can avoid them.

Requirements

In the requirements phase you take the functions defined in the analysis phase and determine the detailed requirements for each. The system specification is the input to this phase, and the output is a functional software specification. Here you are not designing the complete solution but only the functions the software will perform.

At this point you may want to think of functions in terms of Delphi units, functions, and procedure declarations. If you have decided early on to use the language, using Delphi's syntax for everything helps create a documentation set that is more maintainable and integrated with the solution.

Design

This phase is where all the design details are ironed out. Because you had a good idea from the requirements phase of the functions your software was going to perform, you can take this next step. Here you develop a detailed design of your software solution, including a definition of the relationships among units and a detailed procedural flow.

As you drill down (a term used often with spreadsheets to describe getting to finer and finer levels of detail), you need to figure out and document how everything will work. Things such as screen layouts, button placements, report contents and types are looked at here.

It is important to realize that your customer will not know all the details up front (customers rarely know what they want; they just know *that* they want). This is an iterative process. If this is happening to you, it is a good thing. It means that you and your customer are communicating and getting things out on the table.

One of the benefits of using Delphi as your development language is that during theses phases you can use it as a high-level definition language to show general logic. Because Delphi is a very "English-like" language, it is more self documenting than most other languages. That has been one of the aspects I love most about this language: The ability to read the code from top to bottom and have it read like a book.

Code

Ah, the coding phase! Get that case of Mountain Dew and those Twinkies, and let's get to work. This phase of development starts now and ends...never. Coding exists throughout the rest of the development cycle and continues as you make changes to the code through the rest of the product's lifecycle.

If you have done a good job of designing your software and defining the interfaces for the different modules, the code should literally fall out of this phase. I know what you are saying. Yeah, sure! Well I actually have witnessed the code falling right out of the detailed design document. If you follow the steps with great rigor, the code almost writes itself.

The product from this phase is twofold. The first, of course, is the code itself, but nearly as important is a complete product specification that details the product "as built." This will serve as a tool for testing and may also serve as the basis for the User's Manual.

Test

The real purpose of this phase is to test the "as built" product against the requirements agreed upon in the development specification. Here is where you will know whether you have done a good job at mapping those requirements to reality. There should be mapping of each function in the software to a requirement in the requirements documentation. If there is no requirement for the function, the function should not exist.

NEW TERM Testing usually is done in two steps. The first is *unit testing*. This is where you take individual units of code, write driver stubs for each, and test the functionality (ensure that it returns the proper type of data and does the proper type of calculation, for example) and reliability (check the data range of passed-in parameters and that the return data is valid, for example) of each module. The second step is *integration testing*. Here you put the tested units together and make sure they behave in the manner you assumed they would.

Software testing is an art form in itself. If you are writing a fairly simply application, the testing may be simple. With larger programs, the testing becomes very unwieldy if you don't pay close attention. There are a number of good books on software testing out there, so you will have some good reference material to work with.

4

Maintenance and Operation

So you think you are home free. The product is out the door, and boy are you happy! Just remember that over 30 percent of the effort and money is spent in this phase. Now you will follow this software as it services customers, as they find undocumented features (bugs), and as the software slowly moves to the grave. One thing to remember is that as the product life cycle shortens, the money spent on maintenance will go down. This shortening does happen, as we all start operating in "Internet time," where things move at light speed. You probably also will hear those magic words "If it only did ..." from your customer a few times. This will mean adding new features to your software, as well as revising all the documentation to reflect the change.

Sound dismal? Well the truth is that maintaining a program is not nearly as fun as creating it, but someone has to do it. How do you think that new guy you just hired is going to maintain your application after you become vice president of engineering at your company?

All that wonderful documentation: The user's manual, design document, product specification, and test manual will assist that new lad in getting up to speed on your application. That's right, doing your job right means working yourself out of that job so you can move on to greener pastures. Invention is the spice of life! The discipline to build these pieces using software engineering principles and goals is what got you there.

Where Now?

Now that you know some of the steps necessary to get a disciplined approach down, you need to talk about the next level of consciousness. What you needed in the old days (and some say what's still needed today) was a programming discipline—a set of rules to guide the troubled programmer, help us use the lifecycle process, and refine it with other "rules" to achieve an even more stable environment.

Software Engineering

Enter software engineering. A software engineer is very different from a programmer. A software engineer talks to the intended user and formally writes down what the user needs from the software. He or she then formally writes down what must be done to build this piece of software. Then, and only then, will the software engineer start writing code.

Sounds dull? Sounds like a lot of work? Sounds like it will make very clean, very robust code? Yes, yes, and sometimes (if the software engineer knows what she is doing). It's a lot more fun to sit down in front of the computer and start hacking out code, but for large systems it's a lot more fun down the road to have a working product. At any rate, software engineering is the disciplined approach to programming.

Software Engineering Goals

If you are going to pursue this avenue of disciplined development, you need to have a goal—something you are trying to achieve. If you don't know where the finish line is, it will be hard to win the race. The most straightforward goal of software development is to make the finished product match the requirements specification. You need to break this down into something more manageable, a smaller or more precise set of goals that is both attainable and easy to remember.

Remember that the one thing that is always constant is change. As we discussed earlier, your application will spend the majority of its lifecycle in the maintenance phase. It's important, then, for us to have a set of goals that transcends change. The four generally accepted goals of software engineering are modifiability, efficiency, reliability, and understandability.

Modifiability

In its lifecycle, your software product probably will need to be modified many times. Modifications can be the result of a bug that you or your customer found or a feature request or enhancement that your user(s) requested. Either way, it is important that the work you've done in your well-thought-out design need not perish when you make a change.

You should be able to make changes to your application without wrecking the foundation you built. This goal implies controlled change in which some parts of your application change while others stay the same, and you get the result you sought. This is hard to do. Many languages do not support this very well and are very "touchy" or abrasive to change.

The Object Pascal language, however, is a very readable language. It also provides an environment that enables you to make changes easily. With OP's strong typing, errors are harder to make. These attributes provide an environment that promotes our goal of modifiability. A thought that should always be in your mind when making a change to your application is that you need to make the same change in your documentation. You could (or should) go as far as adding that new user requirement to the requirements document, then trace that requirement through your design document, and finally make the change to the code last. It sounds a little dull, but it will help to make your design more stable.

Efficiency

This is one concept that is very straightforward. Your application should use the available resources optimally. In the days of 64KB computers, we had very little memory to play with, but because operating systems were multitasking, you at least had most of that memory to yourself.

Today, many applications run simultaneously on your PC. This is why it is important that your application be resource friendly and work and play well with others. By *resources*, I am referring to two types, time and space. Your application may have requirements to execute in a given time frame if it is gathering time-sensitive data or live network information. Also, a time requirement could mean that you must leave some CPU cycles for someone else. Your application should be good at sharing that time with other applications. If it is hoarding CPU cycles, look at the `Application.ProcessMessages()` function for help.

The other resource requirement for efficient operation is space. As you probably have noticed, software is getting larger and larger. Most software now comes on a CD-ROM because it is too expensive to supply 40 floppies! Seriously, it is also important that you use disk space efficiently. Just as with anything else, take only what you need, and be frugal.

Reliability

This is probably the most important goal, especially if your application is responsible for a critical function. Applications that operate for long periods of time without human intervention must be stable and be able to recover from problems automatically. Can you imagine an operator of a nuclear power station getting the error `Cannot open configuration file, program terminated` from your application? What a nightmare!

The problem here is that the cost of failure is too high to let you have anything but the highest reliability software. You must design reliability into your software from the ground up. There are many ways to make sure you don't get `numeric overflow` or `invalid record` messages in your applications. Object Pascal's strong typing helps you avoid many of the mistakes you could make with "looser" languages. Also, with things such as range checking turned on, you can avoid other potential problems. Range checking enables you to help validate that the values you think are going into your variables really are. This should help you in the testing phase to iron out any bugs in your software and to make sure that your bullet-proofing is really working.

Understandability

This goal is one that is born from the world of object-oriented programming. For your application to be maintainable, it must be easy to understand. This is a difficult goal in a complex system: to understand all the pieces.

One way in which this goal is attainable is by making sure that your application's design and implementation models the real world. If your application's objects are modeling real-world objects, you can relate the two in your mind more easily. This is why we use object-oriented design in our applications, so we can relate code to the world more easily.

Another way to make your code understandable is by making sure it "works" on a basic readability level. The use of good coding techniques, styles, and commenting adds to the understandability of the end product. The objects in the code should be easily discernible.

Software Engineering Principles

The goals discussed in the previous sections are ones that should apply to any software project. The next question is, "How do you get there?" You must define a set of principles that you stand by and that help you achieve these goals. Here is a set of principles to help guide you.

The Seven Software Engineering Principles

1. Modularity
2. Localization
3. Abstraction
4. Information hiding
5. Confirmability
6. Uniformity
7. Completeness

When I was getting my Master's degree in Software Engineering, one of my professors (Mr. Shepherd) had us memorize these principles for practically all of our tests. It only seems fair that you at least see them. Shepherd—what better name for a teacher guiding his flock through the perils of programming.

These principles are supported in the Delphi class structure. Some are a natural consequence of classes, whereas others must be consciously introduced by the programmer.

Modularity and Localization

Modularity and localization come easily from the class structure. Classes are inherently modular, and localization refers to keeping modules logically organized—each module should be a grouping of logically related code. If you write small autonomous modules when you actually are constructing your code, they are easily transportable to other software projects as well. This is no more evident than in the Object Repository.

The Object Repository holds objects that can be used over and over again. By simply choosing File | New in Delphi, you have access to much work done by others. The key to the success of this paradigm is the modularity of the code and the lack of dependency on outside code.

Abstraction and Information Hiding

Abstraction and information hiding have very good support in the Delphi classes. The private and protected keywords provide two levels of support for hiding information from objects outside a particular class. Abstraction is supported through information hiding and through the interface/implementation nature of class files. You permit only the abstracted nature of the class to be public. The implementation details are hidden.

An example of this is how you work with text files in Delphi. When you open a file, you specify the file you wish to open and specify the mode (mode specifies whether you are opening the file for read or write). Delphi does not demand that you know the exact sector on which the file resides, nor do you need to know which head will read the data off the hard drive's platter. The implementation details of the file system are hidden from you. This enables you to read data equally from either a hard disk, floppy disk, or CD-ROM, even though the physical structures of each storage medium is different.

Confirmability

Confirmability is attained through a combination of strong type checking and the building of testable modules. Type checking is a way for the compiler to confirm that a given variable is used properly. Delphi provides strong typing as part of the language. Testable modules enable you to logically test individual modules for accuracy. Remember, it's a lot easier to build small error-free programs than large error-free programs. All code modules should be submitted to the code repository accompanied by driver programs that test the module. Confirmability implies that you must be able to break your applications down into modules that are testable.

Uniformity and Completeness

Uniformity and completeness fall totally under the domain of the programmer. Code is easier to read and maintain if it is written and commented in a uniform manner. Modules that are complete when originally written do not need to be rewritten or appended when a new need arises—and new needs always arise. Completeness is a lot like error free, it's hard to attain. But, if you're mindful of the need for completeness, you can maximize the adaptability of your code and minimize changes that are needed later. Changes are an open invitation for errors to come into your application.

Every one of the Software Engineering Principles is intended to fight complexity. When you build your classes, keep these principles in mind; they'll help you and your code. Also keep them in mind when you're looking at the Delphi classes. Now and again, you'll find yourself asking why Borland did a such an odd thing in a class. You usually can find the answer in the

Software Engineering Principles (sometimes not—Borland is human, too). The Delphi Class Library is a good example of software engineering. Why Delphi classes? Because using classes is a method of programming in Microsoft Windows that is well founded in software engineering.

Coupling and Cohesion Issues

Part of the benefit to the modular programming approach is that you can extract a module of code from one application and place it into another, and it will work. For example, suppose you have written a Delphi unit that does data encryption. You can provide it with a filename, and it will read that file, encrypt it with a key, and write the file back out to disk.

By writing this unit of code as an independent entity, you can use this in any number of applications simply by calling functions in the unit and getting the results. In order for you to reap this reusability, there are two things that your code must exhibit: strong cohesiveness and loose coupling.

Cohesive means that the internal function of your code modules should be tightly integrated. Strong cohesion is good (sort of a self reliance). The second aspect is coupling. Your modules should be loosely coupled to their neighbors (in other words, either very few or no dependencies). If your unit depends heavily on other units, it isn't portable to other applications without carrying a lot of baggage with it. So, your code should be strongly cohesive and loosely coupled. This is an attainable goal, although you will have to work at it.

Object-Oriented Design (OOD)

Our real-world language has two primary components, nouns (objects) and verbs (operations). In order for your applications to map to reality, your computer language needs the same. Most languages have a large variety of operations you can perform but have a small set of nouns to describe the objects. Delphi provides a very three-dimensional set of nouns that enable you to describe objects.

How would you define an object? This word has been seriously overused. According to Grady Booch, author of *Software Engineering with Ada*, an object is "an entity that has a state; that is, it has some value…the behavior of an object is defined by the actions it suffers and vice versa…every object is actually an instance of some class of objects." That is the first answer, for the first question, of your first quiz, in your first graduate Software Engineering class.

The goal of object-oriented design is that each module on the system represents an object or a class of objects in the real world. Grady Booch said, "A program that implements a model of reality may thus be viewed as a set of objects that interact with one another." You can design a system using this object-oriented mentality by following these steps:

1. Identify the objects and their attributes.
2. Identify the operations that affect each object and the operations that each object must initiate.
3. Establish the visibility of each object in relation to the other objects.
4. Establish the interface for each object.
5. Implement each object.

The Objects

When identifying the objects in your problem space, you usually think in terms of the nouns in your problem. In a heating control system, you would have a heat source, temperature sensor, thermostat, solenoid, or the like. These nouns become the main objects in your system. Objects may be very large and consist of smaller objects. For instance, a car is big object. You would break that down into smaller objects such as the engine, drive train, and body.

The Operations

Here you need to identify the operations that each of the objects you defined earlier perform or have performed on them. For instance, a thermostat can be adjusted, a solenoid can be activated, or a temperature sensor can take a temperature reading. You also would define which operations would come first on an object. A well-designed automobile would start itself when you shift from park to drive.

The Visibility

Here you define the topology of your design. You need a map telling you which objects are seen and can be seen by other objects. In the heating control system, the temperature sensor needs to be seen by the thermostat, but the temperature sensor does not need to see the thermostat.

The Interfaces

Here you define how your objects will interface with other objects. This step is extremely important to designing a system that is truly modular. You need to define exactly how other objects will talk to your object. You might use function or procedure call statements to define the interface for your object. You can do this if, and only if, the language you are using supports a readable format (as Delphi does).

Implement the Objects

In this step, you implement each object in your solution. This means writing the code interfaces for each object. You may opt not to write the complete object code, deferring the code bodies until later. If your object is a complex object (an object made up of smaller objects), you need to decompose your object into its component objects. With each one of these objects, you need to go through the same steps to determine their operations, visibility, and interface. After you create functional skeletons with well-defined interfaces, you can do the body coding anytime.

Using these steps, you can design a system that is cohesive and well thought out. Because Object Pascal has the facilities to let you code the way this method works, so much the better.

Object-Oriented Programming (OOP)

Object-oriented programming has been around for a number of years and has reared its head (bet you thought I was going to say ugly head) in such programming languages as Ada, SmallTalk, C++, Borland Pascal (various versions), and finally in Delphi. This magical term "object" has conjured up such a name for itself that the mere mention of it, especially in the same sentence with the words "software engineer," makes IS managers drool with anticipation.

The reality is just that, reality. We have seen object-oriented code that is far worse than any standard Pascal code could ever be. We have also seen beautiful object-oriented code. OOP is a means to an end, a tool to be used for good or evil.

There are several components in Object Pascal that make it object oriented. This section gives you a look at the basic class definition and a couple other goodies that help Object Pascal take on that object-oriented look.

Classes

Delphi provides a reserved word, *class*, that enables you to define an object. When you create a new project in Delphi, if you look at the declarations in unit1, you will find a class declaration for the form itself. The following code segment shows a sample class declaration. It shows the different sections that are present in a standard declaration.

```
type
  TForm1 = class(TForm)
```

```
public
    { Public declarations }
protected
    { Protected declarations }
private
    { Private declarations }
  end;
```

Here is how to define an object. From the interface section, use your type name (TForm1) and then the base class from which it is derived. All objects must be derived from TObject or one of its child objects.

The public section is reserved for those declarations to which you want the world to have access. There is a private section in which you can declare variables, procedures, and functions that are used within your class only. The protected section gives you the best of both the private and public sections in one. Components declared as protected are accessible only to descendants of the declaring type.

As with private components, you can hide implementation details from end users. However, unlike private components, protected components still are available to programmers who want to derive new objects from your objects without the requirement that the derived objects be declared in the same unit.

Now, create your own data object. You'll store out the bankcard PIN number in the object. The declaration will read as follows:

```
Secret = class(TObject)
  private
    FThe_PIN : Integer;
end;
```

This code not only creates a class called Secret, but it has a private data variable, FThe_PIN, that holds the value of the PIN itself.

Properties

The reserved word property enables you to declare properties. A property definition in a class declares a named attribute for objects of the class and the actions associated with reading and writing the attribute. The attribute you created in the preceding code segment is FThe_PIN. You do not want to allow the programmer to directly affect a change on that value. You want to take input and validate that the change is correct. This is part of the information-hiding principle mentioned earlier.

Use a property called GetThe_PIN to be the go-between in dealing with your value. When you call the property GetThe_PIN, you get the value of FThe_PIN. The difference here is that the variable FThe_PIN is protected from outside modification. Only through the Change_PIN procedure can you modify the value of FThe_PIN. The code segment that would accomplish your objectives is as follows:

```
Secret = class(TObject)
  private
    FThe_PIN : Integer;
  protected
    procedure Change_PIN (New_PIN : Integer);
    property GetThe_PIN : Integer read FThe_PIN write Change_PIN;
  end;
```

Now you can query the value of the PIN number without changing it. Selectors are a necessary part of the object model. If you cannot see the data in an object, it is no good.

> **NEW TERM**   *Selector* is a term used to describe a piece of code that queries the value or state of an object or attribute of an object, but it does not change the state of that object.

Inheritance

> **NEW TERM**   *Inheritance* is one of the most powerful features of an object-oriented language such as Delphi. It enables child classes to take on the properties of their parents. They inherit the fields, properties, methods, and events of their parent class. In addition to having the attributes of its parent, the child class can add new components to those it inherits. This enables you to take a class that has nearly all the fundamental pieces you need and add new objects that customize that class to fit your needs exactly.

If you compile a new project, you can then choose View | Browser and view the entire object base in Delphi, as shown in Figure 4.3. The Inspector pane (the left window) enables you to pick a particular class in your project. You can see by the tree view which classes are parents of the object you selected. By using the Inheritance tab, you can see all descendent and ancestor objects related to the class you selected in the Inspector pane.

Figure 4.3.

The Object Browser.

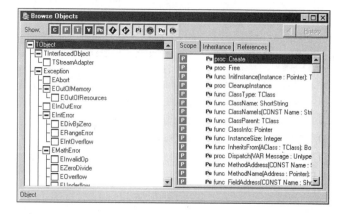

Summary

Okay, maybe OOP won't solve the world's problems, but it can make a contribution toward the common good. The object mentality is a good one, filled with promise of a more organized and orderly world. You've seen how Borland has jumped on the object bandwagon and has provided the foundation for you to grab your OOT (object-oriented trumpet, a little band humor) and do the same.

Today you looked at some of the fundamentals of software engineering, both the principles and the goals of the discipline. You learned about the software lifecycle and should now have a better understanding of your creation's evolution. And, finally, you briefly toured the land of objects.

I realize that this chapter only touches on subjects that are worthy of better consideration, but this book would need to be on CD-ROM to cover all the topics in detail. I hope I have lit the flame of curiosity, and that you will search out other information on these subjects.

I invite you to look at other methods of software development as well. The Recursive Parallel Life Cycle, the Waterfall method, as well as many others, are different ways of dealing with software design problems. These methods appeal to different individuals, as well as apply to different problem spaces. Use the ones that best work for you.

On Day 5, you'll learn about managing your Delphi application from a file perspective, what files make up your Delphi application, and how to use the Delphi 3 environment to organize your project.

4

Q&A

Q Can't we make gains using the software engineering principles with a non-object-oriented language?

A Yes. Anything is possible. The problem is that if your language provides a poor mapping of its structure to the real world, that will be difficult to achieve. Also, maintenance of the code will be equally challenging because the mapping will not be intuitive to the application's maintainers.

Q Can you do object-oriented programming without doing object-oriented design?

A Yes, but again the benefits of using one methodology throughout the product lifecycle bring a sense of uniformity to the process. In the long run, an all-or-nothing approach is better (the all being preferable).

Workshop

The Workshop provides two ways for you to affirm what you've learned in this chapter. The Quiz section poses questions to help you solidify your understanding of the material covered. You can find answers to the quiz questions in Appendix A, "Answers to Quiz Questions." The Exercises section provide you with experience in using what you have learned. Please try to work through all these before continuing to the next day.

Quiz

1. What are the goals of software engineering?
2. How does Object Pascal support information hiding?
3. How does inheritance help Object Pascal succeed at modeling the Windows environment?

Exercise

1. Create your own object called Person that holds information about a person (name, address, and phone number, for example). Then create a property that retrieves the values in Person and a method for changing the values in the Person object.

4

Day 5

Applications, Files, and the Project Manager

Today you learn about the various pieces that make up a Delphi application or, better put, a Delphi project. The Delphi application ultimately will be an executable or group of executables and DLLs. If you use ActiveX controls, they will become part of it as well. ActiveX controls are OLE-based controls that you can write in Delphi, C++, or another language and that you can use in your project. ActiveX controls, however, do not become part of your executable. You'll learn more on ActiveX controls on Day 13, "Creating Your Own Visual and ActiveX Components." That's all fine, but what you really are interested in here are actual files, forms, units, components, resources, and so on, that are built by you or by Delphi.

What Actually Makes Up a Delphi Application?

At first glance, a simple program may look as though it is made up only of a project file and a unit. Actually, several other files are created for you behind the scenes as you work on your program. You may be wondering why you would concern yourself with files created by Delphi. You wouldn't want to accidentally delete or move files that are needed by that new Boss Key...I mean, database front end you have been working so hard on, now would you? In any case, it is a good idea to become familiar with what makes up a Delphi project, where all these extra files that you didn't create came from, and what they all do.

This chapter outlines several important topics, some of which could warrant an entire chapter of their own, but the purpose here is to help you understand the basics of a Delphi project. When you need more detail on a topic than is provided in this chapter, you should refer to the Delphi online help, your Delphi manuals, or elsewhere in this book, as appropriate. In this chapter, I want to give you the big picture in an easily digestible format.

Once you have a good idea of what makes up a Delphi project, you will move on to managing Delphi projects. The Delphi IDE (integrated development environment discussed on Day 1, "Welcome to Delphi 3—Is This Visual Pascal?") has a Project Manager to help you with this task. However, there is more to Delphi project management than just a menu. If you want an organized and well-managed project, you need to give some thought to setting up a directory structure to store your code using appropriate names for the files, forms, components, and variables. The best approach is to organize your projects from the start and keep them that way through their completion.

Projects

A Delphi project consists of forms, units, option settings, resources, and so on. All this information lives in files. Delphi creates many of these files as you build your application. Resources such as bitmaps, icons, and so on, are in files that you obtain from some other source or create with the many tools and resource editors available. In addition, the compiler also creates files. Let's take a quick look at some of these files.

NEW TERM   A Delphi *project* consists of forms, units, option settings, resources, and so on.

Delphi creates the following files as you design your application:

project file (.dpr)   This file is used to keep information about
                                           forms and units. You'll find initialization code
                                           here as well.

unit file (.pas)	This file is used to store code. Some units are associated with forms; some store only functions and procedures. Many of Delphi's functions and procedures are stored in units.
form file (.dfm)	This is a binary file that is created by Delphi to store information about your forms. Each form file has a corresponding unit (.pas) file. For example, myform.pas has a file called myform.dfm associated with it.
project option file (.dfo)	Project option settings are stored in this file.
package info file (.drf)	This is a binary file that is used by Delphi with Packages. The topic of packages is covered later in Bonus Day 15, "Deploying Applications."
resource file (.res)	This binary file contains an icon that the project uses. This file should not be changed or created by the user, Delphi is continually updating or recreating this file.
backup files (.~dp, .~df, .~pa)	These are backup files for the project, form, and unit files, respectively.

The compiler creates this next group of files.

executable file (.exe)	This is your application's executable file. This is a stand-alone executable file that needs nothing else unless you use libraries contained in DLLs, OCXs, and so on.
unit object file (.dcu)	This file is the compiled version of the unit (.pas) files and will be linked into the final executable file.
Dynamic Link Library file (.dll)	This file is created if youdesign your own DLL.

Finally, other Windows files that can be used with Delphi are as follows:

help files (.hlp)	These are standard Windows Help files that can be used with your Delphi application.
image or graphics files (.wmf, .bmp, .ico)	These are commonly used in Windows applications to build attractive and user-friendly applications.

5

NEW TERM The project file (.dpr) itself actually contains Object Pascal code and is the main part of your application that actually gets things started when you execute your application. The funny thing is that you can build an entire Delphi application and never need to look at this file. It is created and modified automatically by Delphi as you build your application. Whatever name you give your project file also will be the name of your executable file. The following code is an example of what a project file would look like if you started a new project and did not change the filenames or form names:

```
program Project1
uses
  Forms,
  Unit1 in 'UNIT1.PAS' {Form1};

{$R *.RES}

begin
    Application.CreateForm(TForm, Form1);
    Application.Run(Form1);
end.
```

NOTE

Notice the word `program` in the first line? This tells Delphi that this is the main program code. It will be replaced with `library` if you are building a DLL.

WARNING

Again, Delphi maintains this file automatically. You typically should not need to modify a project file. I recommend leaving it alone unless you are building a DLL or doing some other advanced programming. However, should you need to get to the project source, you can choose View | Project Source, and the project source will be shown in the Code Editor window. You'll learn more about the editor on Day 6, "Editor and Debugger."

Forms

One of the greatest things about Windows programs is the form. Before I started writing Windows programs, I was using mostly C for DOS-based applications. C is a great and powerful language but not very easy or forgiving when it comes to Windows programming. Then I took a C++ class and a Windows programming class, and I went off to write Windows programs in C/C++. Ouch! I spent hours just trying to create a basic form with a button on the screen and to understand what I had done and how the code worked. The amount of source code involved in C to create just one window is huge.

In C++, it is a little better if you use a development kit such as Borland's OWL (ObjectWindows Library) or Microsoft's MFC (Microsoft Foundation Class), but you still need a good understanding of OOP (object-oriented programming, which is covered on Day 4, "Object-Oriented Programming and Software Engineering") and the language to know what's going on and how to use it all. Delphi basically gives us "mere mortals" a chance to create real Windows programs that blow the socks off programs developed in other visual environments. Delphi programs will run at speeds close or equal to a program written in C++. Delphi does much of the work for you and enables you to focus on the code specific to your application.

NEW TERM As you know, a Windows program is made up of a window or series of windows commonly referred to in Delphi as *forms*. When you start up Delphi, it automatically creates a form for you to use. Forms are used to house your controls, components, and so on.

The Delphi application (as well as most Windows applications) is centered around the form. Although other programs can use the concept of windows or forms, for an application to achieve a true Microsoft Windows likeness, it must comply to Microsoft's guidelines for the layout of its appearance. The information for Delphi forms is stored in two files: the .dfm and the .pas file. The .dfm file actually contains information about your form's appearance, size, location, and so on. This is one of those files that you don't need to worry about or maintain. You just need to be aware of what the .dfm file is used for.

The form's code and the code for its controls are stored in the .pas file, also known as a unit. This is the file you spend most of your time in as you write a Delphi application. Each time you add an event handler for a form or double-click on a control to add code to it, the unit file is updated, and Delphi puts the cursor in the correct spot to add or modify your code. When you add more forms, they also have their own .dfm and .pas files.

Another thing you need to know about forms is that they have properties. These properties can be set to control the appearance and behavior of the form. With these properties, you can change form color, size, location, and whether it is centered, located at the position set at design time, visible, invisible, and more.

A form also has a number of *event handlers* (segments of code you can add to execute when specific form-related events occur). You can include event handlers for events such as a mouse click or form resize.

5

NOTE
For the most part, all the files that make up a Delphi project will be kept synchronized by Delphi as you make updates. You always should use Delphi to change filenames or update the files in order to prevent files getting out of synch. If you don't, you may get errors when you try to load or compile your programs. In other words, if you click on a component and delete it, let Delphi remove the associated code. Don't delete it in the Editor. Delphi cleans up after itself very well.

Units

There are three types of units: unit files associated with forms (the most common), unit files used to store functions and procedures, and unit files used to build components.

NEW TERM *Units* are source code files with the .pas extension. As you work with Delphi, you will become intimately involved with units.

Listing 5.1 contains a basic unit associated with a form. The unit name is on the first line following the word unit. Following the unit header is the interface part, which contains the uses, type, and var clauses. Lastly, the implementation part contains functions and procedures for your controls (event handlers), as well as your own functions, procedures, and code to be used in the unit. The implementation part may also have a uses clause.

TYPE   **Listing 5.1. Unit1, the default unit created by Delphi.**

```
unit Unit1;

interface

uses
  Windows, Messages, SysUtils, Classes, Graphics, Controls, Forms,
  Dialogs;

type
  TForm1 = class(TForm)
    procedure FormCreate(Sender: TObject);
  private
    { Private declarations }
  public
    { Public declarations }
  end;

var
  Form1: TForm1;

implementation
```

```
{$R *.DFM}

procedure TForm1.FormCreate(Sender: TObject);
begin

end;
end.
```

ANALYSIS Believe it or not, this code and the project file code are all you need in Delphi to create an executable that opens a window. It won't do much at this point, but it is a functional Windows program in its simplest form. This code is for discussion purposes only; it is created by Delphi when you create a new Delphi project. If you type it in to the Code Editor without starting a new project, it will not compile.

Look at the names in the uses clause. These are names of other units. If you decide to write a bunch of handy functions and procedures, you could create your own unit, put all your handywork in the unit, and compile it for future use. Each time you wanted to use your home grown unit, you simply would add the name to the uses clause.

Here's a closer look at the parts that make up the unit in Listing 5.1.

unit header	The unit header identifies the code as a unit and is followed by the name that will also be the filename for the unit with an extension of .pas.
interface	This marks the start of the unit interface part that is used to declare variables, types, procedures, and so on. The interface part determines what in this unit is available to other units and parts of the program. The interface portion of the unit ends with the start of the implementation part.
uses	The uses clause tells the compiler which libraries of functions and procedures need to be compiled into the final executable. Delphi automatically puts several of these in for you. If you write your own unit, you need to remember to include the unit name in the uses clause when you need to use functions contained in the unit .
type	The type declaration section is used for creating user-defined types. These types can then be used to define variables.

Visibility specifiers follow the type clause in the interface part and are within a class definition, as shown in Listing 5.1. The following specifiers are used to control how objects appear to other programs and objects:

private	Declarations in this section are treated as public within the module, but they will be unknown and inaccessible outside the unit.
public	Declarations in this section are visible and accessible outside the unit.

5

The following two specifiers are used for creating components and are not used in Listing 5.1. They are covered in detail on Day 13. These specifiers are mentioned here simply to make you aware that they exist in some units.

published   This is used to create components. Published properties are displayed in the Object Inspector to enable you to modify them at design time.

protected   A component's fields, methods, and properties that are declared as protected are accessible to descendants (descendants were discussed on Day 4) of the declaring type (types were discussed on Day 3, "Object Pascal: Part 2").

The four specifiers (private, public, published, and protected) are part of the class definition (again, more on Day 13).

var   This is used to declare variables and object variables. In a form unit, var is used in the interface part (Delphi puts this declaration here for you) to declare the form as an instance of the TForm object. var also is used to declare variables in the implementation part as well as in procedures in functions.

implementation   This is where all the functions and procedures that were declared in the interface part will actually be placed. Any declarations that are made here are private to the unit (not available to other units). You may, however, add a uses clause to the implementation section to provide access to other units.

{$R *.DFM}   In a form unit, Delphi inserts the $R *.DFM entry for you. This is very important because it ties the form to its .dfm file that you heard about earlier. *Do not remove* this from your program, or you will have problems.

The following code block executes when your form is created. You should put any startup code here that needs to be executed when the form starts to load. To create this procedure, use the Object Inspector to view the Events menu for the form, and then double-click the OnCreate event. The Object Inspector is discussed in more detail on Day 8, "The Visual Component Library."

```
procedure TForm1.FormCreate(Sender: TObject);
begin

end;
end.
```

Add, of course, the final end—and notice that it has a period (.) period after it. This signifies the end of the unit.

Finally, there are two additional optional parts you can add to your unit. Please refer to the online help or Delphi manuals for more information about them.

initialization   This part is used to run any code that you might need to run to initialize and prepare for your unit to be run.

finalization   This part enables you to do any cleanup before your unit completely exits.

This concludes the discussion about a unit associated with a form. It is important to keep headings, clauses, and so on, in the correct place. Delphi pretty much takes care of this for you because it creates the unit and code as you make changes to the form. You simply add your code to the correct section as needed.

The remaining two unit types, units associated with a component and units used to store functions and procedures are not covered in this chapter. See the Delphi manuals or online help for more information about unit files for procedures and functions.

The Visual Component Library

The Visual Component Library (VCL) is made up of a rich selection of objects that are written in Delphi's Object Pascal for use as controls (or components) on the Delphi forms. These pre-built components make use of the Windows API as well as provide the code necessary to build your Windows applications with little or no knowledge of how the Windows API actually works. There are two basic types: visible and invisible. Visible components are placed and programmed for the user. Invisible components give special control, or programming interface, to the programmer. An edit box is an example of a visible component, and a timer is an example of an invisible component.

The different categories of components include buttons, list boxes, labels, edit boxes, components that are "data aware," timers, image boxes, selection boxes, and the list goes on. You will come to know and love these components because they are the building blocks of your Delphi application. Each of these components has quite a bit of code associated with it to make it work, and you don't have to write or maintain any of it. You simply drop the components on the form, and they are ready for you to use. Components have properties, events, and methods, all of which enable you to use a component and control the way it behaves. You'll look at the Visual Component Library in much more detail on Day 8.

Optional ActiveX Components

NEW TERM   An *ActiveX control* is a 32-bit, OLE-based, pre-designed Windows control or component that can be used by Delphi or any language with ActiveX support. The ActiveX control mostly likely will have been developed by a third-party vendor or programmer, and created in C++, but Delphi enables you to create them as well (more on ActiveX on Day 13).

Delphi supports ActiveX components. This is both good and bad. On the good side, a ton of third-party controls are on the market and available for you to purchase. You can find controls that will do just about anything you want, from fancy tabs to calendars to full-blown communications controls. The downside to using OCXs or ActiveX controls is that they are not compiled into your executable, and so you must ship them with your application. The important thing to remember here is that if you really need one of these controls and find one that works with Delphi and meets your needs, go for it. The desirable way to add on to your application, however, is with Delphi components. There are a number of vendors producing Delphi components for purchase that you can use in Delphi.

The ActiveX control is the new kid on the block in reusable code or components. ActiveX controls are being supported by most of the visual programming environments today and can be used with Internet- and Web-based applications. ActiveX controls replace the OCX controls supported by Delphi 2. You'll learn more about ActiveX on Day 13.

User-Created Procedures, Functions, and Event Handlers

User-created procedures, functions, and event handlers are an important part to your application. As you build your application, you create forms using the components, but you eventually need to tie them all together with your own code. All those components are pretty useless if you don't have some way to access them for information or instruct them as to what to do. The Object Pascal language behind Delphi has a great selection of tools to help you build your programs. You also will want to write your own routines using Object Pascal. All this code is the "engine" under the fancy exterior. Without the engine, nothing is going to happen.

Graphics Resources

We can't forget about all the good stuff—the graphics! You can't build an attractive application without some pretty graphics. Delphi comes with some sample icons and bitmaps, but you obviously will want to start your own collection as well. When you choose an icon for the program, Delphi stores it in the .res file. Icons aren't the only resources a Delphi program uses. Cursors, bitmaps, and Windows metafiles (.wmf) are also resources.

These all become part of your executable, but they are resources that start outside of your source code. You usually choose the resources you want by setting properties in a component or specifying a filename. This causes the component to load the bitmap, icon, or other graphic. The graphic or resource then is loaded into the project and prepared to be used when you run or compile your application.

Organizing Your Delphi Project

Now that you know what makes up Delphi projects, you should think about organizing and managing them. You may be able to work on simple little programs or projects without much thought about project management, but if you're not careful, it is possible to delete or overwrite files that you didn't want to lose. It also is easy to get confused as to which files go with which project if you aren't organized. So, as you go through the rest of this chapter, you'll learn more about how to start off well organized and how stay that way. It really does not take much effort, and it will save you time and effort later if you know where everything for a project is when you decide to work on it, delete it, back it up, and so forth.

Creating Separate Directories

Let's start off with the basics. I like to create a source directory under the compiler directory. In my case, it is `c:\program files\delphi 3.0\mysource`. Underneath the source directory, I usually like to create a separate directory for each of my projects. This makes it easier to find projects and easier to make backups. It also protects files from being changed accidentally. If you had a project that used a unit called `mainmenu.pas` and you copied another project into the same directory with a `mainmenu.pas`...yep, you guessed it. You just lost your original `mainmenu.pas`. Not fun—I know, because I've done it. Consider the following directory structure:

```
C:\PROGRAM FILES\BORLAND\DELPHI 3.0\
                        |
                    MYSOURCE\
                        |
                    PROJECT1
                        |
                    PROJECT2
```

If you set up a structure like this, projects will be fairly safe from each other. When you choose File | Open or File | Save As, the directory you selected displays. Another benefit to this is that you always know where your updated files and executables go (assuming you have not changed to the wrong directory or set Delphi to put output files someplace else).

This structure also makes backups a breeze. You can use Windows Explorer, File Manager, or a backup utility to back up `c:\program files\borland\Delphi 3.0\mysource` and all its subdirectories.

5

Naming Conventions

Another practice that will help you keep organized (and enable you to look at your Delphi source files and know what they are) is to use some kind of naming convention for your files. In other words, don't use the default names, such as project1.dpr and unit1.pas (this is something most of us are guilty of at some time or another).

Probably the easiest way to break this habit is to immediately do a Project | Save As when you start a new project. Give the unit1.pas and project1.pas files new names when prompted for them. Of course, each time you add a form, you need to give it a new name when you save it. However, if you name all these when you start out, you occasionally can save the project without the need to deal with filenames and so on, and you can enjoy the benefits I've been talking about. If you don't do this, think about how fun it will be if you come back six months later and start wondering what unit1.pas and unit2.pas do in project1.dpr. Of course, if you have a lot of these in various directories, it gets really fun—not!

Actually, a good naming convention should apply not only to your files, but also to forms, components, and variables you use in your application. It is easy to use all the default names for forms and components as you design your application. However, even if you have given the files unique names, you still can end up with a messy project if it gets big enough. Imagine looking over your project and seeing FORM1, FORM2, FORM3 each with its own set of BUTTON1, BUTTON2, BUTTON3, and so on. I think you get the picture. You'll see examples of code like this all the time, including examples in this book. For one form and a few components, it is not a big deal, but as your projects grow, this will cause you to waste time going back to see what a form or component is called or does. If you get in the habit of giving unique and descriptive names to your files, forms, components, and so on, you will save time and frustration.

Let's compare two listings, and you'll see what I am talking about. The first one, Listing 5.2, creates a form on the screen designed to get a user's name. All the filenames, captions, and name properties have been changed from their defaults to something more descriptive and meaningful. The second one, Listing 5.3, is the same code, but it uses all the default names Delphi creates for the unit.

NOTE

Filenames must follow the rules for length and valid characters for the target operating system (for example, Windows 95 or Windows NT). Captions can be up to 255 characters long and must be a valid Pascal string. Names can be up to 63 characters long and must follow the rules that apply to Pascal identifiers (see Delphi's online help for more information on identifiers).

TYPE **Listing 5.2.** Readname, **a unit with descriptive naming.**

```
unit Readname;

interface

uses
  Windows, Messages, SysUtils, Classes, Graphics, Controls, Forms,
  Dialogs;

type
  TGetUserName = class(TForm)
    Button_GetName: TButton;
    Edit_Getname: TEdit;
    procedure FormCreate(Sender: TObject);
    procedure Button_GetNameClick(Sender: TObject);
    procedure Edit_GetnameChange(Sender: TObject);
  private
    { Private declarations }
  public
    { Public declarations }
  end;

var
  GetUserName: TGetUserName;

implementation

{$R *.DFM}

procedure TGetUserName.FormCreate(Sender: TObject);
begin

end;

procedure TGetUserName.Button_GetNameClick(Sender: TObject);
begin

end;

procedure TGetUserName.Edit_GetnameChange(Sender: TObject);
begin

end;

end.
```

5

TYPE   **Listing 5.3. Unit1 uses Delphi's default names.**

```
unit Unit1;

interface

uses
  Windows, Messages, SysUtils, Classes, Graphics, Controls, Forms,
  Dialogs;

type
  TForm1 = class(TForm)
    Button1: TButton;
    Edit1: TEdit;
    procedure FormCreate(Sender: TObject);
    procedure Button1Click(Sender: TObject);
    procedure Edit1Change(Sender: TObject);
  private
    { Private declarations }
  public
    { Public declarations }
  end;

var
  Form1: TForm1;

implementation

{$R *.DFM}

procedure TForm1.FormCreate(Sender: TObject);
begin

end;

procedure TForm1.Button1Click(Sender: TObject);
begin

end;

procedure TForm1.Edit1Change(Sender: TObject);
begin

end;

end.
```

ANALYSIS   The differences should be pretty obvious. Listing 5.2 is much easier to follow because names describe what each item is and what it does (Button_Getname, for example). It is clear that this is a button that is supposed to get a name—much easier to figure out than Button1. With all this information in hand, you are ready to move on to the Project Manager and learn how to manage a Delphi project.

Sample Project

Let's build a small project from the ground up. As you go, you'll learn to put into practice some of the ideas you've been learning about. You'll also be introduced to the Project Manager and other Delphi features you need to know about when working with projects. You'll create a simple Delphi application with two forms that interact with each other.

To get a good start, set up an organized directory structure to work with by following these steps:

First, create the project files:

1. Create a source directory under the Delphi directory (if you don't already have one); for example, `c:\program files\borland\delphi 3.0\mysource`.

2. Create a directory to store your project in. Let's call it Formtalk (`c:\program files\borland\delphi 3.0\mysource\formtalk`). If you are wondering why it is called `Formtalk`, it's because one form talks to another, or in this case it simply updates information on another form.

3. If Delphi is not already running, start it up. Create a new project using File | New, select the Application Icon in the New Items dialog box, which is shown in Figure 5.1, and click OK.

Figure 5.1.

New Items dialog box with the Application icon highlighted.

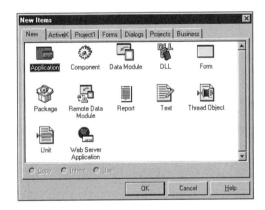

4. Click on the Form Icon or select File | New Form to add a second form to the project.

5. Now you need to change some properties on Form1 and its components so you stay organized. Use the Object Inspector to change the caption property of Form1 to **Input Form** and the form name property to **InputForm**.

6. Using the Object Inspector, change the form caption for the second form (Form2) to **Output Form** and the name property to **OutputForm**. This form will receive the output from the input form when the program is run. Data will be transferred here after data is input and sent by pressing the Send button.

7. Save unit1.pas, but change unit1.pas to the following, as shown in Figure 5.3:

   ```
   c:\program files\borland\delphi 3.0\mysource\formtalk\input.pas
   ```

   This will be the input form that takes information from the user. You then will be prompted to save Unit2; change it's name to **output.pas**.

Figure 5.2.

The File menu with Save Project As selected.

Figure 5.3.

Save Unit As dialog box.

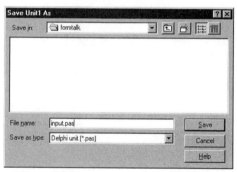

8. To save the project file, choose File | Save Project As (shown previously in Figure 5.2). In the resulting Save Project As dialog box, shown in Figure 5.4, select the directory and filename to save the project file from project1.dpr to the following:

   ```
   c:\program files\borland\delphi3\mysource\formtalk.dpr
   ```

Figure 5.4.

Save Project As dialog box.

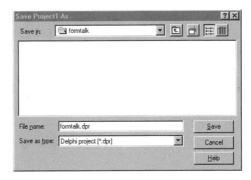

Now, build the form using this procedure:

1. Add an edit box to each of the forms (the VCL tabs and components are covered in more detail on Day 8 and a button to the input form. Next, clear the text property on both edit boxes using the Object Inspector and deleting the text from the text property.

2. Set the name for the edit box in the input form to InText. Set the name for the edit box in the output form to OutText. Set the button caption in the input form to "Send" and its name property to SendText.

3. To make sure both forms come up visible, you need to use the Object Inspector to change the visible property of any forms you add (excluding the first form created when you start a new project) to True.

4. Now, let's add a line of code to the button and make your program functional. Double-click the Send button and add this line of code:

```
OutputForm.OutText.Text:=InputForm.InText.Text;
```

If all went well, you should be able to run the program and test it following these steps:

1. Click on the Run icon or press F9. The following message pops up in a dialog box:

```
Form 'InputForm' references 'OutputForm' declared in 'Output'
which is not in our USES list. Do you wish to add it?
```

2. At this point you should click on Yes.

3. Choose Save All now from the Delphi Toolbar, or select File | Save All. The code was added for you.

4. Run the program again (click on the Run icon or press F9). Your forms should appear on the screen.

5. Test the program by entering text into the Input form's text box, and then press Send. The text you entered should appear in the Output form's text box.

5

Now, let's see what your program's code looks like. Listing 5.4 contains the source code that is created and stored in your project file. Use View | Project Source to show the contents of the project file.

TYPE **Listing 5.4.** `Formtalk`**, the project source listing.**

```
program formtalk;

uses
  Forms,
  input in 'input.pas' {InputForm},
  output in 'output.pas' {OutputForm};

{$R *.RES}

begin
  Application.Initialize;
  Application.CreateForm(TInputForm, InputForm);
  Application.CreateForm(TOutputForm, OutputForm);
  Application.Run;
end.
```

ANALYSIS The uses clause includes the `Forms` unit (which is Delphi's code used to create windows), and the `Input` and `Output` units that contain the code for the forms you created.

After the first `begin`, you see the `Application.Initialize` and `Application.CreateForm` method statements. These methods execute the necessary code to start and create your forms. Simply put, methods are sections of code contained in an object (your form) that object is executed when the method is called, as you have done here. You'll learn more about methods and their use on Day 8.

The final statement, `Application.Run`, actually starts up our application and executes the code associated with your forms (remember, some code is added by Delphi, and some is added by you). Delphi updates the project source for you as you add or delete forms.

Now let's look at the code for the input unit, which is shown in Listing 5.5. Double-click on the Input form to view this code. Notice how nice the code is to read with those descriptive names.

5

TYPE **Listing 5.5.** Input **form unit.**

```
unit input;

interface

uses
  Windows, Messages, SysUtils, Classes, Graphics, Controls, Forms,
  Dialogs,
  StdCtrls;

type
  TInputForm = class(TForm)
    SendText: TButton;
    InText: TEdit;
    procedure SendTextClick(Sender: TObject);
  private
    { Private declarations }
  public
    { Public declarations }
  end;

var
  InputForm: TInputForm;

implementation

uses output;

{$R *.DFM}

procedure TInputForm.SendTextClick(Sender: TObject);
begin
    OutputForm.OutText.Text:=InputForm.InText.Text;
end;

end.
```

ANALYSIS Now look at the code for the Output form in Listing 5.6. As you study the code for the Input and Output forms, you should find it easy to read because you used really descriptive names for files, captions, and names. Imagine a complex project with many forms and controls. The good habits you have been practicing here will help you tremendously with that complex project. It is easier to remember many of the names you create for the various forms and components saving time when you go to look for them in a sea of forms.

The code for this application resides in the Input unit. The uses clause in the Implementation section for the Input unit has a reference to the Output unit. This allows access to the code contained in that unit. The application works by executing the following line of code when the Send button is pressed:

```
OutputForm.OutText.Text:=InputForm.InText.Text;
```

The Output form you created is only text for display that was sent from the Input form. All the code is created by Delphi when you create the form, but you can view its code either by double-clicking on the form or by selecting the Output unit from the View | Units menu option and double-clicking on the Output unit or other unit name in the View Unit Dialog list box.

TYPE **Listing 5.6. Output Form unit.**

```
unit Output;

interface

uses
  Windows, Messages, SysUtils, Classes, Graphics, Controls, Forms,
  Dialogs,
  StdCtrls;

type
  TOutputForm = class(TForm)
    OutText: TEdit;
  private
    { Private declarations }
  public
    { Public declarations }
  end;

var
  OutputForm: TOutputForm;

implementation

{$R *.DFM}

end.
```

ANALYSIS This code was created by Delphi when you created the Output form. Because you use this form only to display data sent by the Input form, it contains no user-created code. You should be familiar with the sections of code used in this unit based on what you learned about units earlier in this chapter.

The Project Manager

Now that you have a project to work with, let's see what the Project Manager and other options in Delphi have to offer. With a project loaded (FormTalk in this case), choose View | Project Manager to pull up the Project Manager, which is shown in Figure 5.5.

Figure 5.5.

Project Manager.

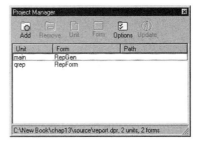

The Project Manager displays the name of each of the units (Input and Output in this case), the form name, and the path (which is empty in this case because you did not set it). Just below the title bar, you have a SpeedMenu with some handy features.

Take a look at the Project Manager SpeedMenu options and their functions. Because most of these options affect the selected unit, make sure that you select the correct one before clicking a button on the toolbar.

Add	Enables you to add a unit file. This is nice because you may have a form you designed for another program that will work well for the current project. You simply add the form to the project. When you click on the Add button, you are presented with the standard file-selection box you've seen many times by now. Simply browse through the directories and select the form file you wish to add.
Remove	Removes the selected unit from the project. The file is not deleted, it's just removed from the project file.
Unit	Takes you to the code for the selected unit.
Form	Displays the form associated with the selected unit.
Options	Takes you to Project Options, which is a tabbed dialog box with several options. You'll learn about this in more detail in the next section, "Project Options."
Update	Synchronizes the forms and units listed in the Project Manager with the project file. This button is disabled unless you have manually changed something in the project file.

WARNING

It is not recommended that you change anything in the project source file unless you are writing a DLL or doing some advanced programming. Delphi will make most changes needed to the project source file for you.

As you can see, the Project Manager enables you to quickly move around in your project, add and remove files, and go to the Project Options dialog box.

In addition to the Project Manager, you can use the File, View, Project, Workgroup (Workgroup is available only if you installed the optional PVCS support, which is not covered, but mentioned briefly at the end of this chapter), and Tools menus. The Delphi SpeedBar enables you to access some project-related functions as you work on your project. With the SpeedBar, you can open create, delete, and close project and related files.

You should be familiar with the IDE at this point, so the next section focuses on those options and features particular to managing the project.

Project Options

The Project Options tabbed dialog box enables you to set many options for your project. This information is saved in the .dfo file you learned about earlier. The Project Options tabbed dialog box has seven tabs, as shown in Figure 5.6: Forms, Application, Compiler, Linker, Directories/Conditionals, VersionInfo and Packages.

Figure 5.6.

The Project Options dialog box with the Forms tab showing.

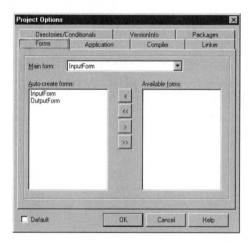

The following sections describe each of these tabs and the options you have available. You'll also check the settings for your Formtalk project.

The Forms Tab

The first tab is the Forms tab (Figure 5.6). This is the active tab when you open the Project Options dialog box. At the top of the tab is the Main form drop-down list. This enables you to select the project's main form. The main form starts up first along with the code in its

OnCreate event. Normally, the first form you create is the main form. For this project, it should be InputForm. If you click on the down arrow of the drop-down box, you see that you could choose OutputForm (which, in this project, is the only other form so far).

Also on the Forms tab are the Auto-create forms and Available forms list boxes. Forms appear in the Auto-create forms list box by default. Available forms are part of your project but will need to be moved to the auto-create section if you want them created on startup. Otherwise, you need to activate them at runtime before they can be used. When a form is added to the Auto-create forms list box, the proper code is added to the project file with a statement such as the following:

```
Application.CreateForm(TInputForm, InputForm);
```

NOTE

> You can't reference a form until it has been created.

To move forms between the two list boxes, you can use the controls (the single- and double-arrow buttons) between the two list boxes. You can also drag and drop to move files between the two boxes or change their order.

If you look at the project you have been working on (Formtalk), InputForm should be the main form, InputForm and OutputForm should both be in the Auto-create forms list box, and the Available forms list box should be empty. Assuming you have the Formtalk project debugged and running, move OutputForm to the Available forms list box.

In the lower-left corner of the tab, you see the Default check box. You use this to set the current options to be the default options for all new projects. You probably don't want to use this when you are working on a specific project unless you want all future projects to use the same settings.

The Application Tab

The Application tab is where you set the application title, help file, and icon, as shown in Figure 5.7. These should all be blank when you come to this tab for the first time. These fields are optional, but fill them in as you read along.

First is the application Title. This is the text that Windows displays with the icon when the application is minimized. In the case of Windows 95 or Windows NT 4.x, it will display on the task bar. If you leave this blank, the application displays the project name (the name you saved the project file as (for example, formtalk.dpr). Add the name **Form Talk Application**, and click OK. This adds the following line to the project source code. You can use View | Project Source to see for yourself.

```
Application.Title := 'Form Talk Application';
```

Figure 5.7.

The Application tab.

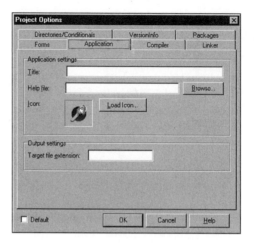

Run the project and minimize it. You should see Form Talk Application as the application title on the Windows 95 Task Bar, as well as to the left of the icon. If you delete the text from the Application Title and run the application, you will notice that it uses the Project Name, `Formtalk` in this case. Make sure you still have `Form Talk Application` in the text box before you move on.

Just below the Title text box, you see the Help file text box with a Browse button to the right of it. You can select a standard Windows Help file to associate with your application. Try it out by following these steps:

1. Click on Browse.

2. Move to the `\program files\borland\Delphi 3.0\help` directory and use the Application Help File dialog box as you would a normal file selection dialog. Depending on what you entered during your Delphi installation, your installed directory names may be different—for example, `\program files\borland\ Delphi 3.0\help`.

3. Select any of the `.hlp` files, (for example, `delphi.hlp`). View the project source code again. Notice that the following line of code has been added:

   ```
   Application.HelpFile := 'c:\program files\borland\Delphi 3.0
   ➥\help\delphi .hlp';
   ```

This doesn't do much for you in your program, but the Help file is attached to the project. If you were to set the proper Help context numbers in the forms and components, pressing F1 would bring up the Delphi Help screen for the Help context set for the selected component or form. The purpose here is only to show you how to set the Help file to be used by the project.

The next item on the tab is an image box that displays the default or selected icon. The Load

Icon button is to its right. The Load Icon button brings up a file-selection box for you to choose the application icon. The application icon is displayed when you minimize the application main form. Click the Choose Icon button, and select the following icon by double-clicking on the filename or clicking the Open button:

```
c:\program files\borland\Delphi 3.0\images\icons\chip.ico
```

Then click OK. This displays a computer chip in the image box.

Run the application again. Minimize it and you should see the new icon (the computer chip) and the title `Form Talk Application`. Choose File | Save All to save the changes.

NOTE

> You are not required to set any of these, but it is recommended because it gives a more finished look to your application. The Default check box is used to set the current options to be the default options for all new projects.

Finally, at the bottom of the tab in the Output Settings, you see the Target File Extension box. Here you can specify the appropriate extension for executables such as .OCX for an ActiveX control.

The Compiler Tab

The Compiler tab, shown in Figure 5.8, is divided into five groups of options: Code generation, Runtime errors, Syntax options, Debugging options, and Messages. Each of these sections includes a number of options that you can toggle on or off. For most projects, the defaults will be fine. You use the Default check box to set the current options to be the default options for all new projects.

> **The Project Options Compiler Tab**
>
> Compiler options found on the Project Options Compiler tab are beyond the scope of this book. However, as an example, notice under the Code generation options that there is an option called Pentium-safe FDIV. This option compiles code that checks for a Pentium processor with the floating-point divide flaw and prevents the flaw from occurring.
>
> If you know your application will not be run on a Pentium system with the flaw, just turn this option off, and your code will be a bit more compact and faster because it doesn't need the extra code or time.

5

I recommend leaving this option on. There probably will be some people out there who won't take Intel up on the free replacement of the flawed unit. You might as well let Delphi protect you from the problem. I point this out simply to give you an idea of the type of control you have with the compiler options because they affect executable size and speed.

For more information about compiler options, consult Delphi's online help or refer to the Delphi manuals.

Figure 5.8.

The Compiler tab.

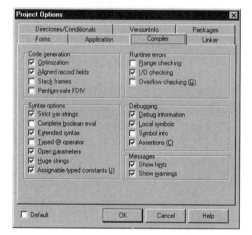

The Linker Tab

The Linker tab, shown in Figure 5.9, includes five groups of options: Map file, Linker output, EXE and DLL options, Memory sizes, and Description. As with the Compiler tab, these options are beyond the scope of this book. Refer to Delphi's online help and the Delphi manuals for more information about linker options. Default options should be fine for most projects. If you make changes to the settings, you can check the Default check box and make the settings the defaults for new projects.

Figure 5.9.

The Linker tab.

The Directories/Conditionals Tab

The Directories/Conditionals tab, shown in Figure 5.10, includes three groups of options: Directories, Conditionals, and Aliases.

Figure 5.10.

*The Directories/
Conditionals tab.*

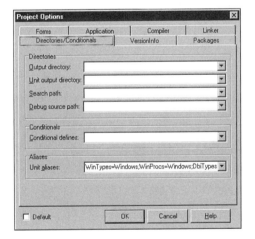

5

The Directories group contains the Output directory and Search path text boxes. Output Directory enables you to specify where you want your compiled executables (.exe) to be placed. Unit output directory enables you to specify where you want the compiled unit files (.dcu) to be placed. I usually leave these items blank and move the tested files to another directory when I am done. When these items are left blank, .exe and .dcu files are stored in the same directory as the source code.

The Search path enables you to specify where to look for .dcu files. When you compile your program, the compiler only looks in the search path defined here, the library search path, and the current directory. You can have multiple search path entries separated by a semicolon (;). Entries are limited to 127 characters. You would use the Search path option if you want your project to use files that are in a directory other than those just mentioned. Keep in mind that you will get an error if the source files can't be found when you try to compile.

You also find the Debug Source Path box here. This box enables you to enter a path were Delphi files can be found in case the files have been moved to a new location since the last compile. Normally, you should not need to change this, but it's here if you need it. For more details on this setting, see Delphi's online help.

In the Conditionals group, the Conditional defines drop-down list box enables you to enter or select from a previous list of compiler conditional directives and symbols. These symbols control how your program compiles, depending on certain conditions. See Delphi's online help or manuals if you need more information about compiler directives and symbols. The check box is used to set the current options to be the default options for all new projects.

The Unit aliases drop-down list in the Aliases group enables you to enter aliases to other units. Notice that the following entry appears in Figure 5.10:

```
WinTypes=Windows;WinProcs=Windows
```

This entry enables backward compatibility to Delphi 1.x source code because the Windows and WinProcs units have been replaced with the Windows unit. Of course, you can add aliases of your own here as well.

TIP	Now that you've learned about the various options for managing your project, look at the File, View, Workgroup, and Tools menus, as well as the various SpeedBar options. You'll find some pretty nice shortcuts there.

The VersionInfo Tab

The VersionInfo tab, shown in Figure 5.11, is used to associate version-specific information such as copyright information with your project. These options are beyond the scope of this book. Refer to Delphi's online help or manuals for more info.

Figure 5.11.

The VersionInfo tab.

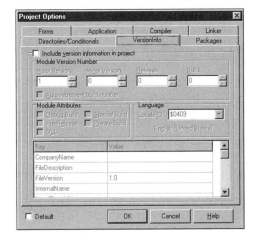

The Packages Tab

The Packages tab enables you to set options for Delphi's support of packages, as shown in Figure 5.12. This is where you can select the required packages for your project, as well as turn on package support. Packages are special runtime DLLs that you can use to significantly decrease the size of your executables. Packages are discussed in more detail on Bonus Day 15.

Figure 5.12.

The Packages tab.

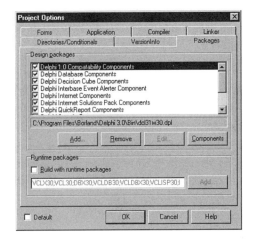

Creating a Project

The remainder of today's lesson is devoted to Delphi's project-related features. You should supplement your reading here with Delphi's online help and manuals. If you are coming from Delphi 1.*x*, you will notice a number of new items, name changes, and new menu locations.

When you start Delphi, you usually are presented with a new blank form and project. The blank form and project are default settings installed with Delphi. These settings can be changed and are described shortly. By now you are familiar with the default form and code, so let's move on and talk about other options you have when creating a new project.

When you choose File | New the New Items dialog box appears, as shown in Figure 5.13. This dialog box contains six tabs: New, ActiveX, Forms, Dialogs, Projects, and Business.

This section gives you only a brief description of these items. If you need more information, please refer to Delphi's online help or manuals.

Figure 5.13.

The New Items dialog box with the New tab showing.

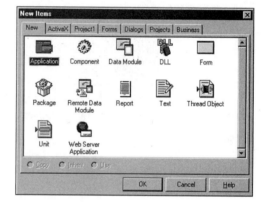

The New Tab

The New tab, shown in Figure 5.13, enables you to create new applications, forms, units, automation objects, text editor objects, components, and DLLs. Click on the icon of your choice and then click OK. If more information is needed for the object you selected, you will be prompted for it by a dialog box.

The ActiveX Tab

The ActiveX tab, shown in Figure 5.14, enables you to create ActiveX-based controls and applications. Click on the icon of your choice. If more information is needed for the object you selected, you will be prompted for it by a dialog box.

Figure 5.14.

The ActiveX tab.

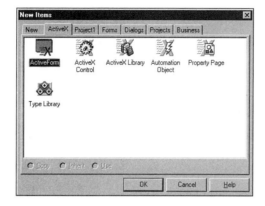

The Forms Tab

The Forms tab, shown in Figure 5.15, enables you to choose the form template to use when creating a new form. You can create your own templates and make them available in this dialog box (more on templates under "Creating and Using Templates" later in today's lesson). Click on the icon of your choice. If more information is needed for the object you selected, you will be prompted for it by a dialog box.

Figure 5.15.

The Forms tab.

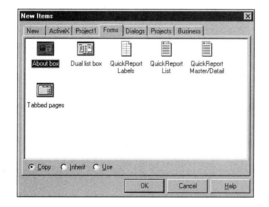

The Dialogs Tab

Like the Forms tab, the Dialogs tab enables you to choose templates with pre-built dialog boxes to use as a basis for your own creations. As with the Forms, you can create your own templates and make them available here (see "Creating and Using Templates" later in today's lesson"). The Dialogs tab is shown in Figure 5.16. Click on the icon of your choice. If more information is needed for the object you selected, you will be prompted for it by a dialog box.

Figure 5.16.

The Dialogs tab.

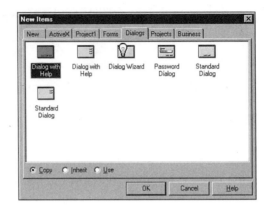

The Projects Tab

The Projects tab, shown in Figure 5.18, enables you to choose a template on which to base your new project. You can save time by using predefined projects that are provided or by creating your own (See "Creating and using Templates" later in today's lesson). Click on the icon of your choice. If more information is needed for the object you selected, you will be prompted for it by a dialog box.

Figure 5.17.

The Projects tab.

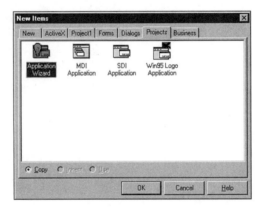

The Business Tab

The Business tab is used to store wizards that simplify common business-realated program-ming tasks. Here you find the Database Form Wizard that helps create database forms from an existing database (see Day 11, "Delphi's Database Architecture"). You also find the QuickReport Wizard and the TeeChart Wizard (see Day 13, "Reports and Charts" as well as the QuickReport and TeeChart documentation files on the CD-ROM for more information).

Figure 5.18.

The Business tab.

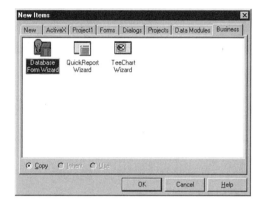

Here's one final note: If you are working on a project, it will be added to the New Items dialog box with its own tab (using the project filename for the tab name). This enables you to see what you have added to the current project as well as to select from it if you need to create a new form or object similar to one already in the project. This tab remains only while the project is loaded.

The Object Repository

In Delphi 1.0 the Gallery was used to store templates and Wizards. The Gallery has been replaced with the Repository in Delphi 2 and continues in Delphi 3. Choose Tools | Repository to access the Object Repository dialog box, as shown in Figure 5.19.

Figure 5.19.

The Object Repository dialog box.

In the Pages list box, you see five selections: Forms, Dialogs, Data Modules, Projects, and Object Repository. Using this dialog box, you can add, delete, and edit selections as well as change defaults that will be used when you create a new form or project. You can create your own pages and objects, and add them to the repository from the Object Repository dialog (for information on adding pages and objects, as well as using the Object Repository, see Delphi's online help).

The Object Repository really enhances your ability to re-use code in Delphi. As you can see, commonly used features are already made available to you, but you can greatly extend your options by creating your own templates and adding them to the Object Repository.

Now you're ready to move on to creating and using templates and Wizards. This will help us tie up some loose ends and get a feel for how all this works.

Wizards and Templates

As you probably know, a Wizard is a program installed with Delphi that takes you through a series of questions and choices to help you build a framework to start with for a complex form or project. A Wizard can be a great time saver. Templates are similar in that they do much of the repetitive work for you, but you don't need to answer questions. You are essentially taking a copy of what you need and inserting it in your new project. Both Wizards and templates show up in the New Items dialog box under the various tabs, so you will have easy access to them. Many of these are included with Delphi, but anything you add using the Repository shows up here as well.

Wizards

There are different types of Wizards, such as the Dialog Wizard that helps you quickly create forms, projects, and so on. To view available Wizards, you can go to the Object Repository and click on each of the selections. When you click on a selection, the objects stored in that section are displayed.

To use a Wizard, choose File | New to open the New Items dialog box. In the New Items dialog box, click on the desired tab and then click on the wizard of your choice. Wizards typically are identified with the word *Wizard* in their names, as in *Dialog Wizard* (these tabs also contain templates). Once the Wizard starts, you are prompted for information. Finally, the Wizard creates a form, project, or object, and you are ready to add your code and changes.

To get an idea how to start a Wizard, choose File | New. In the New Items dialog box, select the Dialogs tab. Click on the Dialog Wizard icon, and the Dialog Wizard appears, as shown in Figure 5.20. At this point you start making your selections and entering information.

Figure 5.20.

The Dialog Wizard.

Creating and Using Templates

A template is just a project, form, or some code framework that has been pre-built and ready for you to use. When you select a template, it is copied into your project where you can add to it as needed. For example, suppose you came up with a really cool application and splash-screen project that you wanted to use for all your programs. You could create a splash-screen template with your logo, colors, and so on. Then all you would need to do to use it in your programs is save it into the Object Repository.

If you want to create your own template, just design your form or application framework as you would any other application or form and set it up however you wish. Once it is set up and tested, you can add the template to the Object Repository as follows:

1. Choose Project | Add To Repository. This brings up the Add To Repository dialog box, as shown in Figure 5.21.

2. Type the title and description, select the page you wish for it to be stored in, type the author's name, and choose an icon.

Figure 5.21.

Add to Repository Dialog.

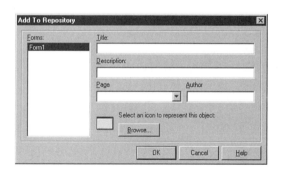

That's all there is to it. Your new template is now available for use. You can find it in the New Items dialog box under the tab that corresponds to the page-selection setting.

To use a template, follow these steps.

1. Choose File | New, and the New Items dialog box appears.
2. Select the tab where the desired template is stored.
3. Click on the icon of the template you want to use.

Every time you start Delphi, choose File | New Application, or choose File | New and select the Application icon from the New tab, you are using a template.

As you become more familiar with Delphi and the types of tasks you want to do, you might want to spend some time creating some commonly used forms and dialogs to convert to templates. As your collection of templates grows, your time spent on routine work will shrink.

Version Control

So far you've learned what makes up a project, how to get organized, how to work with the Delphi Project Manager, and about project-related features. You've even learned how to save a lot of time using Wizards and templates. The next level of project management is version control. It may be fairly simple to keep yourself organized without version control software, but what if you have multiple programmers working on the same project? What if you have multiple flavors of a project that you must support?

A version control system enables you to manage projects in a highly organized and safe manner. For example, if you have a group of programmers working on the same project, a version control system enables you to lock portions of code that you don't want changed. It also enables you to "check out" a portion of code to work on and prevent others from making changes to it until you are finished with it. You can keep archives of previous versions so that you don't lose the ability to revert back to or look at code for a previous version.

Delphi supports Intersolv PVCS Version Manager 5.1 or later, which is included in the Client/Server Edition. Version control features are available from the Workgroups menu.

Explaining how to use the version control system is beyond the scope of this book. Refer to the online help for the version control software for that information. I just wanted you to know that it exists and what some of its benefits are. If you are a lone developer with the regular version of Delphi, you can use smart project management practices by keeping separate directories for each version and a standard set of templates to accomplish pretty much the same effect. If you manage a team of programmers working on the same projects, you should seriously consider using version control software.

Summary

Today you learned about all the various files that make up a Delphi project—both files created at design time and compile time. You learned about forms, units, the VCL, and OCXs as part of your projects, as well as how to include user-created functions, procedures, and event handlers as a part of your project. Resources such as bitmaps, icons, and so on were also covered.

You then moved on to organizing your project by learning how to set up a directory structure that makes it easy to find, maintain, and back up your files. You learned about the Project Manager and how to move about in your project viewing various settings, files, Project source, and so on, as well as how to add and delete files. You learned about the Project Options tabbed dialog boxes, which give you many options about how your project will be compiled.

Next, you learned how to use the Object Repository to choose various Wizards and templates as defaults. You learned how to use Wizards to create forms and projects and to use templates when creating a new form or project. You also learned about how to create your own templates and add them to the Object Repository for use later. Finally, we talked about Delphi's ability to use the Intersolv PVCS Version Manager and what its advantages are.

Q&A

Q Can I create my own Wizards?

A Although I am sure it is possible, Delphi does not provide a way to easily create a Wizard. Wizards are add-on products.

Q Why isn't the PVCS version control system or its Workgroup menu item available from the Delphi IDE menu?

A The PVCS system is an optional product and must be installed separately. To activate it, use Help to search for PVCS, and follow the instructions for activating it.

5

Workshop

The Workshop provides two ways for you to affirm what you've learned in this chapter. The Quiz section poses questions to help you solidify your understanding of the material covered. You can find answers to the quiz questions in Appendix A, "Answers to the Quiz Questions." The Exercise section provides you with experience in using what you have learned. Please try to work through all these before continuing to the next day.

Quiz

1. Which files does Delphi create at design time? At compile time?
2. What are the parts that make up a unit?
3. How do you add a form to a project? How do you delete a form from a project?
4. If you delete a form from the project, does Delphi delete the form file?

Exercise

1. Create a project template that has a main form with File and Help menus. The Help menu should have an About option in it. Also, create an About box form with code in the OK button to remove the form from memory.

Day 6

Editor and Debugger

In earlier days of computer programming, programmers used many different tools to create computer software. These tools included an editor, compiler, linker, and a debugger. These tools often came from different companies, and nothing tied them all together except the programmer. The programming pioneers didn't even have all of these tools, they had to pour over listings of code and examine punch cards. However, today, the IDE (Integrated Development Environment) has all these tools neatly organized into a well-connected package to make life easier. This chapter teaches you how to use all these tools to make your programming tasks easier and more productive. You start with the editor and learn how to take advantage of it, and then you move on to debugging using Delphi's built-in debugger.

The Editor

As you know by now, the Delphi editor pops up when you double-click on a form or control and puts you into a section of code in the Delphi project that relates to what you clicked on, as shown in Figure 6.1. In this way, Delphi builds the application source code for you as you add components and enter your

application-specific code into each segment. Of course, you also can scroll through your
source code to locate, review, or update code in procedures that you've already added.

Figure 6.1.

The Editor.

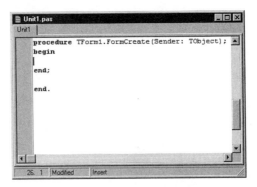

Delphi provides quite a few features that you can take advantage of to make life easier. The
more familiar you are with these features, the quicker and easier you can input and edit your
source code. Here are some of these features:

- [ ] Color syntax highlighting
- [ ] Multiple and group Undo
- [ ] Brief-style editing
- [ ] Keyboard shortcuts or commands
- [ ] Choice of keyboard mapping schemes
- [ ] Code editor SpeedMenu
- [ ] Code error-message box
- [ ] Error highlighting

Along with all this, you can configure colors and behavior to suit your taste. To familiarize
yourself with the editor and some of its features, you'll build a small application that you also
can use to learn about the debugger.

Editor Features and Customization

Before you get started building an application, you should learn about some basic editor
menu options, dialog boxes you can use to customize the editor, and some of the commands
to invoke its features.

Choose Tools | Environment Options, and the Environment Options dialog box appears.
This dialog box contains several tabs, including the Editor, Display, and Colors tabs. These

tabs have several settings that enable you to configure the editor. Let's take a look at each of them.

The Editor Tab

The Editor tab, shown in Figure 6.2, contains several settings that affect the way the editor behaves.

Figure 6.2.

Environment Options Editor tab.

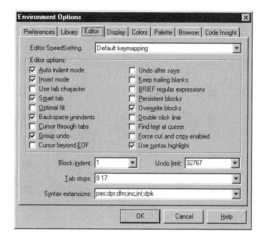

In the Editor SpeedSetting combo box, you can quickly set the keyboard mapping option to one of four choices: Default Keymapping, IDE Classic, Brief emulation, and Epsilon emulation. The basic differences between these four settings is as follows:

Default Keymapping	Auto Indent Mode, Insert Mode, Smart Tab, Backspace Unindents, Group Undo, Overwrite Blocks, and Use Syntax Highlight.
IDE Classic	Auto Indent Mode, Insert Mode, Smart Tab, Backspace Unindents, Cursor Through Tabs, Group Undo, Persistent Blocks, and Use Syntax Highlight.
Brief Emulation	Auto Indent Mode, Insert Mode, Smart Tab, Backspace Unindents, Cursor Through Tabs, Cursor Beyond EOF, Keep Trailing Blanks, BRIEF Regular Expressions, Force Cut And Copy Enabled, and Use Syntax Highlight.
Epsilon Emulation	Auto Indent Mode, Insert Mode, Smart Tab, Backspace Unindents, Cursor Through Tabs, Group Undo, Overwrite Blocks, and Use Syntax Highlight.

6

The Editor Options group has several options that you can enable or disable using check boxes. These settings let you have more control over the editor settings if you don't like what is available in the key mappings just described. You can toggle things such as Auto indent mode and insert mode to syntax highlighting. Also notice that changing between the four key mappings causes various check boxes to become checked or unchecked depending on what you select. For more detailed information, refer to the online help or manuals.

Finally, at the bottom of the dialog box, you have the options to change Block Indent, Undo Limit, Tab Stops, and Syntax extensions.

The default settings on this tab are nicely configured and work well for most situations, so you usually won't need to adjust these.

The Display Tab

The Display tab, shown in Figure 6.3, is divided into groups that enable you to set the following options: Display and file options, Keystroke mapping, margins, and fonts.

Figure 6.3.

Environment Options Display tab.

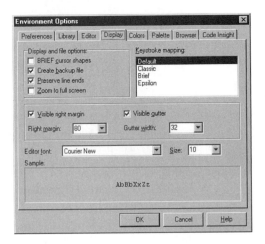

Display and file options enable you to enable/disable BRIEF Cursor Shapes, Create Backup File (when saving editor files), Preserve Line Ends, and Zoom To Full Screen.

Keystroke mapping has the same four editor options as the Editor tab (Default, Classic, Brief, and Epsilon), but these define keystroke settings instead of editor behavior. For example, Ctrl+K+R would read a block from a file in Default or Classic mode, whereas Brief mode uses Alt+R.

The remaining options enable you to configure the margins, gutters, and fonts giving you more flexibility with the appearance of your editor window.

The Colors Tab

The Colors tab, shown in Figure 6.4, provides several options to configure how the various elements in your code will appear in the editor. This is where you configure your syntax highlighting. As with the previous two tabs, there's a speed setting dialog box that enables you to quickly choose from four pre-defined schemes (color, in this case), or you can configure the colors settings to your liking from the various list boxes, check boxes, and so on. You can see the effects of all your changed settings in the sample editor at the bottom of the dialog.

Figure 6.4.

Environment Options Colors tab.

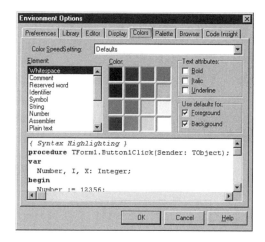

Using the Editor

Now let's put together a very simple application to get a feel for the editor. This isn't anything fancy, just a small application that takes two numbers from the user, adds them when a button is clicked, and displays the results. The form consists of one button, two edit boxes, and four labels.

If you have not done so already, start up Delphi. When Delphi starts, you are presented with a blank project and form by default. You can also get to the same point (if you were working on something else) by choosing File | New and selecting the application icon in the New Items dialog box.

Once you have a new project and form up, use the following steps to build the Addition Application. Follow Figure 6.5 as a guide to lay out the form.

Figure 6.5.

The Addition application.

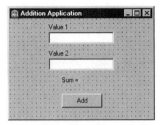

1. On the Delphi Toolbar, select the Standard tab (it should already be selected if you have started up fresh and not selected any of the other tabs).

2. In the Standard tab, click on the icon that looks like a button, and then click on the form. This adds a button to the form, which you can resize and move around the form. Place this button near the bottom of the form.

3. To give the button a useful caption, click once on the button to make sure it is highlighted, and then use the Object Inspector (see Figure 6.6) to change the button's caption property to **Add**.

Figure 6.6.

The Object Inspector.

4. Now, place two labels and two edit boxes on the form just as with the button. The Label icon looks like an "A," and the edit box, as you might imagine, looks like an edit box. From top to bottom, place Label1, Edit1, Label2, and Edit2.

5. As you did for the button, use the Object Inspector for each of the labels to change their captions. Change the caption for Label1 to **Value 1** and the caption for Label2 to **Value 2**.

6. Change the text property for Edit1 and Edit2 to blank by deleting the default text using the Object Inspector.

7. Place two more labels on the form below Edit2. These two labels should be side by side with Label3 on the left and Label4 on the right. Change the caption property for Label3 to **Sum**, and clear the default text in the caption property for Label4.

8. Before you can add code to the button, you need to bring up the code editor. Delphi will create code for the button's OnClick event and pop it up in the editor, as shown in Figure 6.7.

Figure 6.7.

The code editor window showing the code for the button's OnClick *event.*

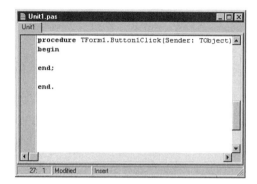

9. Now you need to insert your code for the button (Button1). Edit the code to look like the following:

```
procedure TForm1.Button1Click(Sender: TObject);
Var
   Value1,Value2,Total : integer;
begin
    Value1:=StrToInt(Edit1.Text);
    Value2:=StrToInt(Edit2.Text);
    Label4.Caption:=IntToStr(Value1+Value2);
end;
```

10. To save the project, choose File | Save As. Save the unit to ADDFORM.PAS and the project file to ADD.DPR.

11. Now you can test the application and make sure it works. Press F9 to run the application. If everything went well, your form will pop up and allow you to add numbers to the edit boxes. When you click the Add button, the sum should appear on the form in Label4.

Delphi adds code to the project as you drop your components on the form. In step 9 you added code to Button1. Your complete code listing should like Listing 6.1.

TYPE   **Listing 6.1. The Addition program.**

```
unit addform;

interface

uses
```

continues

Listing 6.1. continued

```
Windows, Messages, SysUtils, Classes, Graphics, Controls, Forms,
Dialogs, StdCtrls;


type
  TForm1 = class(TForm)
    Button1: TButton;
    Edit1: TEdit;
    Edit2: TEdit;
    Label1: TLabel;
    Label2: TLabel;
    Label3: TLabel;
    Label4: TLabel;
    procedure Button1Click(Sender: TObject);
  private
    { Private declarations }
  public
    { Public declarations }
  end;

var
  Form1: TForm1;

implementation

{$R *.DFM}

procedure TForm1.Button1Click(Sender: TObject);
Var
    Value1,Value2,Total : integer;
begin
    Value1:=StrToInt(Edit1.Text);
    Value2:=StrToInt(Edit2.Text);
    Label4.Caption:=IntToStr(Value1+Value2);
end;

end.
```

ANALYSIS The code that makes this application function is the code you placed in the button's OnClick event. It simply takes the text entered by the user in the edit boxes, converts the text—which is in string format—to integer using the StrToInt() function, stores the integers in two variables called Value1 and Value2, adds the two integers, converts the sum back to string format, and places it in the caption of Label4. Delphi has created all the other code.

NOTE

If users enter a value that is not a numeric type, an exception will occur.

As you use the editor, you can use the features discussed earlier, such as the keystrokes that are available for the default editor settings or whatever you may have changed them to. The online help provides details about the keystrokes available in the various editor modes.

You've briefly looked at the various editor options and how to use the editor to enter code. Please refer to Delphi's online help or manuals for more information on using the editor. The purpose here has been to introduce you to what is available. Regardless of which options you set and how you choose to use the editor, you can see that it has a rich selection of features to make your programming experience easier. Along with all of these features, you can of course use all the handy Windows cut and paste features you've come to know and love. Now, let's move on to the final topic regarding the editor, code insight.

Code Insight

This wonderful new feature called Code Insight should excite the beginner as well as the advanced Delphi programmer. If you are just learning Delphi, you often don't remember the syntax for statements such as If, For, While, and so on. The same thing can happen if you are constantly moving between languages: you know what you want to do but sometimes forget the exact syntax of some of the statements. Even if you remember the syntax and you are trying to whip something together, anything Delphi can do for you will help. Code Insight will save you time and typing, prevent typographical errors, and so on. This makes your job that much easier and your time more productive.

Here are three aspects of Code Insight that can help you:

- ☐ Code Template Expert
- ☐ Code Completion Expert
- ☐ Code Parameter Expert

First on the list is the Code Template Expert. Suppose you are typing some code and need to do an If statement. You could type If and then press Ctrl+J, and a pop-up menu would appear giving you a choice of If statement variations. You either can highlight your choice and double-click or press Enter, and the code is completed for you. All you need to do at that point is fill in the blanks. This magic is accomplished through Code Templates. Delphi comes with several common templates ready for you to use. You also have the option of editing, adding, or deleting code templates by choosing Tools | Code Templates, and, in the resulting Code Templates dialog box, using the Add, Edit, or Delete options to make the necessary changes.

6

The Code Completion Expert finishes code for you when you enter a class name followed by a period (.).This can be useful in writing complex components and other applications where some tasks are reused often. A simple example is the TApplication class. You type Application. into the editor window, and a list of the available properties, methods, and events is displayed for you in a list box. Scroll down to the desired choice and double-click on it to add that selection after the class name completing the code for you.

The Code Parameter Expert displays the parameters for functions, procedures, and methods as a ToolTip. So, no more needing to wade through code or online help to find the declarations to know what parameters are expected in what order. To activate the Code Parameter Expert, you simply type the procedure, function, or method, and then the opening parenthesis and a tool tip appears on the screen displaying the parameters. Here is an example:

```
FileOpen(
```

Once the tip appears, you can make your changes and continue.

You're ready now to move on to debugging and some debugging basics. After that, you'll be ready to make a small change to the Addition application to make it function improperly and use Delphi's debugger to quickly spot the problem.

Debugging

As long as people have been alive, there have been insects or "bugs" to pester us. Unlike insects that are part of the food chain and necessary for human survival, a software bug is not desirable or needed. But, no matter how much experience you have and how much care you take when writing software, there always seem to be at least a few bugs in your code.

You may have heard some of the old jokes, "If it compiles, ship it!" or "That's not a bug, it's a feature." Although these are funny, they can also be pretty serious issues. Just because the code compiles and works fine in your initial tests, it may not be bug free. Some bugs are fairly simple to spot and remove, but others are not. Some bugs can be worked around by careful use of the program, whereas others can halt the program and maybe even crash the computer or cause data loss.

So, what can you do to stop these bugs? There are a few things you can do. First, it is important to try to anticipate the types of errors that the user could make that may cause a problem when using your program. Remember, users do not always think like the programmer. With this in mind, you can write your code to handle errors such as missing files, incorrect data formats, and so on. The list of things that can go wrong can be fairly long depending on what your application does.

You can prevent a lot of hassles by handling errors and/or notifying the user about the problem and how to correct it if appropriate. Don't be surprised when the user breaks your application after you spend hours, days, weeks, or even months trying to make it bullet proof. Someone always manages to find something that doesn't work just right or causes problems. If possible, get some beta testers. Let some other programmers and users try the program. Ask them to test all the features and report any problems. You may even want to ask them to try to break it. This will be useful on the prevention side as well as discovering bugs.

As you discover bugs either on your own or from the reports of others, you will need to have a way to find their cause quickly. Sometimes a look at the routines that are running when the bug occurs reveals the problem, but sometimes it isn't that easy to spot. There are basically two types of errors or bugs you will encounter, runtime and logical.

Runtime errors are errors that crept past the compiler but occur when a specific section of code is executed. For example, if you tried to open a file that was not on the disk and provided no method to check for the file or handle the error if it was missing, a runtime error would occur.

Logical errors are errors or flaws in the design of the code that is executing. A good example of this is a routine that goes into a loop waiting for some event to occur that never will. The program would hang. An error like this might be caused if you typed the wrong value to look for in a variable.

There are many different scenarios that can occur within these two error groups, so it is important to keep these in mind as you write code as well as when you debug it. In the next section, you learn how to quickly find and squash these pesky bugs.

Using the Debugger

So what is a debugger? Simply put, a debugger is software that enables you to step through your code one line at a time while at the same time enabling you to examine and modify the values of variables, constants, objects, and so on, as needed. Without a debugger, you would be forced to insert some debugging code to output to the screen, file, or printer, the value of variables, and other information so that you could see what was going on as the program executes. This would be time consuming and could prevent some bugs from occurring if, for example, the bug was a timing-sensitive one. Delphi, thankfully, has a nice debugger as part of the IDE to help you quickly find bugs and correct them. If you are not familiar with debuggers, it may take some practice to get good at debugging your code, but it will pay off in the long run. Let's take a quick tour of the debugger and get ready for a test run.

Setting Debugging Options

First, let's look at the debugging options on the Preferences tab of the Environment Options dialog, as shown in Figure 6.8. You can access this dialog by choosing Tools | Options. There are several settings here, but our concern at this point is the debugging options: Integrated debugging, Step program block, and Break on exception.

Figure 6.8.

The Preferences tab of the Environment Options dialog box.

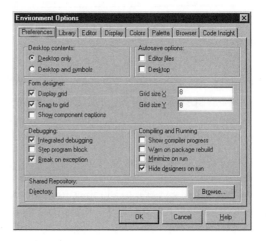

You usually can leave these at their default settings, but here is a brief description of what some of these settings do when checked:

Integrated debugging	Turns on the Integrated Debugger.
Step program block	Stops at the first unit initialization that contains debugging code. (Debugging code is inserted by Delphi at compile time by default.)
Break on exception	Causes the debugger to stop and display information about exceptions that occur.

The Compiler tab of the Project Options dialog box, shown in Figure 6.9, contains other settings you need to be aware of regarding debugging. To access this dialog box, choose Project | Options. The Debugging group has four settings: Debug information, Local symbols, Symbol info, and Assertions.

6

Figure 6.9.

*The Compiler tab of
the Project Options
dialog box.*

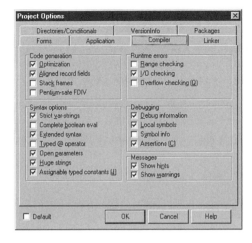

Again, you usually can leave the settings at their defaults, but here is a brief description of what they do when checked:

Debug information   Stores debugging information in the .DCU files of your project when compiled.

Local symbols   Stores symbol information in the .DCU files which enable you to use the integrated or stand-alone debugger to examine or modify the module's local variables.

Symbol info   Enables the generation of symbol reference tables that are stored in the .DCU files.

Assertions   Enables the generation of assertions in a source file. The default is enabled, and you can also use the $C+ and $C- directives in code to turn assertions on or off.

Finally, the Linker tab of the Project Options dialog contains one other setting I want to mention, the Include TDW Debug Info option. This setting must be turned on if you plan to use Turbo Debugger for Windows. When turned on, this option places additional information in the executable. By default, this option is turned off and, for our purposes, you don't need to worry about it.

There is a lot of information regarding debugging, settings, and so on, that could be covered here, but the focus is to get you started using the debugger quickly.

Using Breakpoints

Using the Addition application you created earlier, let's make a few changes (one of which will insert a bug in the application) to illustrate how the debugger works as you step through the application trying to find the bug.

First, you need to move the code that does the addition to its own procedure, and change the code in the button's OnClick event to call the procedure. To do this, add the following procedure in the implementation section:

```
implementation

{$R *.DFM}

procedure TForm1.AddNum;
Var
   Value1,Value2,Total : integer;
begin
     Value1:=StrToInt(Edit1.Text);
     Value1:=StrToInt(Edit2.Text);
     Label4.Caption:=IntToStr(Value1+Value2);
end;
```

Next, add the following line to the button's OnClick event, and remove any of the old code in that event. It should look like the following snippet when you are done:

```
procedure TForm1.Button1Click(Sender: TObject);
begin
     AddNum;
end;
```

Save the file with changes under these new project and unit names: Addform2.pas and Add2.dpr.

Your modified program should look like Listing 6.2. Make sure it is identical because a bug has been inserted.

TYPE   **Listing 6.2. Addition application with a bug.**

```
unit addform2;

interface

uses
   Windows, Messages, SysUtils, Classes, Graphics, Controls,
   Forms, Dialogs,  StdCtrls;

type
   TForm1 = class(TForm)
     Button1: TButton;
     Edit1: TEdit;
```

```
    Edit2: TEdit;
    Label1: TLabel;
    Label2: TLabel;
    Label3: TLabel;
    Label4: TLabel;
    procedure Button1Click(Sender: TObject);
  private
    { Private declarations }
    procedure AddNum;
  public
    { Public declarations }
  end;

var
  Form1: TForm1;

implementation

{$R *.DFM}

procedure TForm1.AddNum;
Var
    Value1,Value2,Total : integer;
begin
    Value1:=StrToInt(Edit1.Text);
    Value1:=StrToInt(Edit2.Text);
    Label4.Caption:=IntToStr(Value1+Value2);
end;

procedure TForm1.Button1Click(Sender: TObject);
begin
    AddNum;
end;

end.
```

Now, run the program and notice the results. Enter two small numbers to add together and press the Add button. The resulting sum should be incorrect. To find out why, let's use the debugger to step through the code and see what happened.

The first thing to do is set a breakpoint. A breakpoint will allow the program to run normally until it encounters the breakpoint, and then the debugger will stop at the line where the breakpoint is set without executing it.

To set a breakpoint, click in the gutter (the gray area to the left of the code in the editor) next to the line for which you want to set the breakpoint, in this case the following line:

```
Value1:=StrToInt(Edit1.Text);
```

The line should be highlighted in red with a big red dot in the gutter, as shown in Figure 6.10 (assuming you're using Delphi's default environment settings).

Figure 6.10.

The code editor showing the gutter.

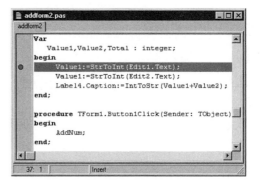

 NOTE   The gutter is visible by default, but it can be disabled in the Environment Options Display tab by unchecking the Visible Gutter option. If the gutter is not visible, click on the first character of the line of code where you want to set the breakpoint, and the line will be highlighted in red.

If you set a breakpoint to a line of code that has been optimized by Delphi, you will get a Warning dialog box stating the condition and asking if you wish to run anyway. This also will occur if you set a breakpoint to a line in the Var declarations. You may also find in some situations that a variable has been optimized, but you need to be able to examine it to debug the program. In that case, choose View | Project Manager, and select the Compiler tab in the Project Options dialog box. There you can disable optimization with the check box in the Code Generation section. See Delphi's online help and manuals for more detail on this.

 NOTE   The gutter is a new feature in Delphi 3 that shows up as a gray area in the left margin of the editor by default. This area highlights lines of code with bullet-style format. It also shows where breakpoints are set and where the current line of execution is when you are stepping through a program using a small arrow. If the gutter is disabled, lines are highlighted.

Run the program again. Type **4** for Value1 and **5** for Value2, and then press the Add button. The code editor should appear showing the location where the breakpoint was set, as shown in Figure 6.11. The breakpoint now has a green check mark in the gutter showing that you have stopped at that breakpoint, and a green right-pointing arrow appears in the gutter showing your location in the code. Your current line should be the breakpoint you set. This line has not been executed yet. In other words, the green arrow points to the next line of execution.

Figure 6.11.

Code editor in debug mode, showing the program stopped at a breakpoint.

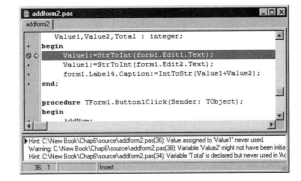

Here's a final note about breakpoints. You can set special breakpoints that will halt execution only if certain conditions occur or on a particular pass through a loop. This can be very helpful if your code fails only under certain conditions or halfway through a very large loop. To set conditions or pass count, you use the Run | Add Breakpoint menu option to access the Edit Breakpoint dialog box. You won't use it here, so no more discussion is presented. Refer to Delphi's online help and manuals for more information.

More Debugging Options

Delphi's Run menu contains some additional debugging options that have corresponding shortcut keystrokes:

Run (F9)	Compiles and executes, or, in debugger mode, continues running from this point.
Step Over (F8)	Executes each line of code, but does not go into functions and procedure calls.
Trace Into (F7)	Enables the debugger to follow the code into a function or procedure call.
Trace to Next Source Line (Shift+F7)	Traces to next executable line.
Run to Cursor (F4)	Runs to the current location of the cursor in the code editor window.
Show Execution Point	Places the cursor at the current execution point.

Now that you have our debugging menu and keystroke options in hand, let's continue and find our problem.

Examining Variable Values with Watches

There are two ways to examine the value stored in variables in Delphi, using watches and using the new feature, ToolTip Expression Evaluation (which is discussed in the next section).

A watch enables you to specify variable names that you wish to monitor and have their values displayed in a small window. To add a watch, you can either press Ctrl+F5 or select Run | Add Watch to access the Watch Properties dialog box, as shown in Figure 6.12. In a watch, you can specify the following: variable names, types, and expressions such as Value1+Value2 or IntToStr(Value1).

Figure 6.12.

Watch Properties dialog box.

In the Watch Properties dialog box, type Value1 in the Expression text box. This creates the Watch List dialog box where your watched variables and their current values will be displayed, as shown in Figure 6.13.

Figure 6.13.

The Watch List dialog box.

If the variable has not been created or assigned yet, various messages are displayed indicating the status of the variable where the value normally would be. The message might say Process not accessible, which means the code that creates these variables either has not started, or it has finished and the variables have been removed from memory. You might also see the message inaccessible here due to optimization (as in Figure 6.13), which usually means the variable hasn't been assigned yet. As the lines of code that deal with the variable you assigned a watch to are executed, the value is displayed in the Watch List dialog box.

In your Addition application, add a watch for the variables `Value2` and `Total`. To do this, access the Watch List dialog box as described earlier, type the variable name you need to watch (for example, `Value2` or `Total`) into the Expression text box, and then click OK. You must do this for each variable separately. Now press F8 (Step Over) twice to step through the rest of the procedure so that you can inspect the variables. What's this, you ask? `Value1` has the number that should have been assigned to `Value2`, `Value2` has a strange number you didn't expect, and `Total` has a message indicating that it was removed by the linker.

Refer to the `AddNum` procedure in Listing 6.2, and you'll see that the value in `Edit2.Text` was assigned to `Value1` when it should have been assigned to `Value2`. This type of error might have occurred after a cut-and-paste operation, and you forgot to go back and change variable names appropriately. This also caused `Value2` never to be initialized using whatever value happened to be in memory at that location when the program was run.

That takes care of `Value1` and `Value2`, but what's the deal with `Total`? In this case, it was never used, and so the linker removed it. This is common when designing a routine—you create variables you initially think you'll need. Then, in the design of the code, you decide to assign the variable directly to its intended location, such as a `label` in this case, and then you forget to go back and remove the unused variable declaration. It doesn't harm anything, but the compiler is letting you know that `Total` isn't used so that you either can use it or delete its declaration.

Status Indicator During Debugging

At this point, you also should notice the list box below the editor. This list box displays errors, warnings, hints, and so on. Scrollbars appear if there are more messages than will fit in the visible range. (Refer back to Figure 6.11.) Here you can find useful information that can help in debugging our code.

For your Addition application example, the first error reads:

```
Hint:...(36):value assigned to 'Value1' never used.
```

The second reads:

```
Warning:...(38): Variable 'Value2' might not have been initialized.
```

The third reads:

```
Hint:...(34): Variable 'Total' is declared but never used in 'AddNum'.
```

Now that you have found some errors using the debugger, you can go change the code to remove the errors and get the program working properly. Make sure to exit the program; you can do this by pressing Ctrl+F2. Go back to the `AddNum` procedure and change `Value1` to `Value2` in the second line after the `begin`. Also, remove the variable `Total` in the declarations.

6

Rerun the program by pressing the F9 Key. After you type in the numbers again: **4** for Value1 and **5** for Value2. The program again will stop at the breakpoint, but the errors will be gone, and the values should be correct as you step through the program. Press F8 to step through the program one line at a time, and watch the values of the variables as you did earlier. This time, all the values should be correct as they are assigned and calculated (for example, Value1=4 and Value2=5).

Examining Variable Values with ToolTip Expression Evaluation

The second way to inspect the values in variables is with a new feature called ToolTip Expression Evaluation. This enables you to place the cursor over variables, objects, parameters, constants, and expressions, and display the currently assigned value in a ToolTip or hint box near the cursor. Hint information also shows up in the hint box. If a value is assigned to the variable, it is displayed in the ToolTip. A hint would appear if the variable had been optimized by the compiler or a variable was never used, such as the variable called Total that you deleted earlier.

This method is much easier and quicker for examination variable values than using the watch method. You should save a lot of time if you are concerned only with a few variables or have a small section of code to debug because you can easily monitor what is going on as you step through a program without setting up a bunch of watch entries.

Debugging a DLL

Delphi 3 has a new debugging feature that will save you many headaches as well as money in your pocket book. You now can debug your Delphi DLLs in Delphi's debugger. When you set a breakpoint in the DLL code and provide the name of a host application (the executable that will call the DLL), Delphi starts the host application after you select Run as you would in any normal debugging session. When the host application calls the DLL, it stops at the breakpoint you defined. It just doesn't get much better than this!

In the past, you either needed separate debugging programs or had to resort to other tricks, such as writing and debugging your DLL functions in a regular Delphi program and then hoping everything was working properly when you transferred it back to the DLL. Although these methods worked, debugging your DLL code in Delphi makes debugging much easier, quicker, and more natural as you get up to speed in the Delphi 3 environment.

Without going into too much detail about debugging or showing you how to write a DLL here, let's take a quick look at actually debugging a DLL in Delphi. First, create the following

6

DLL by choosing File | New and selecting DLL from the New Items dialog box, and then save it as MYMATH.DPR.

Listing 6.3 shows the complete DLL. Except for the exports section and the function declaration and code, the rest of this code is created by Delphi. Modify the code in Delphi so that your program is the same as that shown in Listing 6.3. When you are done, choose Project | Build All.

TYPE **Listing 6.3. Math DLL for the debugging exercise.**

```
library mymath;

{ Important note about DLL memory management: ShareMem must be the
  first unit in your library's USES clause AND your project's (select
  View-Project Source) USES clause if your DLL exports any procedures or
  functions that pass strings as parameters or function results. This
  applies to all strings passed to and from your DLL—even those that
  are nested in records and classes. ShareMem is the interface unit to
  the DELPHIMM.DLL shared memory manager, which must be deployed along
  with your DLL. To avoid using DELPHIMM.DLL, pass string information
  using PChar or ShortString parameters. }

uses
  SysUtils,
  Classes;
function Sqr(Num : integer):integer;export;
begin
    Sqr:=Num*Num;
end;
exports
    Sqr;
begin
end.
```

ANALYSIS This program creates a DLL that has a function in it called Sqr. The function simply squares (multiplies a number by itself) a number and passes the result back to the calling program.

Now, you need to create a program to test the DLL and debug it. Create a new Delphi application by choosing File | New Application. Make your form look like the one shown in Figure 6.14, and make your code the same as that shown in Listing 6.4. Save this as SQRTEST.PAS and TESTSQR.DPR (save these in the same location as the DLL you just created). Choose Project | Build All.

6

Figure 6.14.

TESTSQR *application*
to test the DLL.

Listing 6.4. TESTSQR **application for the DLL debugging**

TYPE   **exercise.**

```
unit sqrtest;

interface

uses
  Windows, Messages, SysUtils, Classes, Graphics, Controls,
  Forms, Dialogs, StdCtrls;


type
  TForm1 = class(TForm)
    Edit1: TEdit;
    Button1: TButton;
    Label1: TLabel;
    Label2: TLabel;
    Label3: TLabel;
    procedure Button1Click(Sender: TObject);
  private
    { Private declarations }
  public
    { Public declarations }
  end;

var
  Form1: TForm1;

function Sqr(Num : integer):integer;far;external 'mymath.dll';
implementation

{$R *.DFM}

procedure TForm1.Button1Click(Sender: TObject);
begin
    Label3.Caption:=IntToStr(Sqr(StrToInt(Edit1.Text)));
end;

end.
```

This code calls the Sqr function in the DLL you created from Listing 6.3. The number entered into Edit1.Text will be passed to the DLL when Sqr is called. The DLL passes the value back with the result to be Label3.Caption.

Once you have compiled these two without error, test the DLL by running TESTSQR.EXE. If all has gone well, when the window pops up (as shown earlier in Figure 6.14), you enter a number in the edit box, and then click the Square button. This should return a squared number. For instance, type 4 and press Square, and 16 will be displayed below the edit box. Once you verify that the program works properly and produces the correct number (16 in this case), exit the program. Now, open the DLL source code again (MYMATH.DPR), and choose Run | Parameters to bring up the Run Parameters dialog box. Fill in the name and path for the host application, in this case TESTSQR.EXE. Now when you choose Run, Delphi will bring up the host application to call the DLL, but it will stop in the DLL at any defined breakpoints. At this point, you debug as you would any normal Delphi application.

It should be clear now that by using Delphi's built-in debugger, you can quickly spot and correct problems in your code. But, what happens when something strange is going on in Windows or in programs that you didn't write? The answer to that question brings us to the final topic of this day, WinSight32, which is covered in the next section.

WinSight32

Although covering WinSight32 here in any detail is beyond the scope of this book, and so are the inner workings of Windows necessary to understand its use, I thought I should briefly mention WinSight32 here just to give you a feel for another tool available to you in Delphi.

WinSight32 is a type of tool known as a *spy*. It provides a means of looking at currently running Windows processes, tracing out child windows and processes, viewing windows messages, and more. If you are having problems with an application (especially one that is passing messages between your application and the Windows system or another application or object), you may want to use WinSight32 to trace the messages flowing between processes. For details about WinSight32, refer to Delphi's online help.

Summary

Today you learned about features and options related to the Delphi editor. You also learned about some new features available in the editor, including Code Insight which enables you to save time entering code correctly by letting Delphi complete the code for you based on the context at the cursor in the code window. You learned how to use the debugger to debug Delphi applications and DLLs by stepping through them a line at a time and by examining

6

the values of variables. Finally, you learned of a separate tool called WinSight32 which enables you to view Windows processes, messages, and so on.

Although you've only scratched the surface of these topics, you should have enough information to start using the editor and debugger to create great Delphi applications. As you need more information on these topics, you are encouraged to read the Delphi online Help and documentation as well as other articles and books on the topic.

Q&A

Q Are there any other keystrokes that work in the editor?

A Yes, if you come from a WordStar background, you're already familiar with pressing Ctrl+Y to delete a line. In fact, if you are like me, this is burned into your brain. Although not obvious in Delphi's online help, some of these keystrokes work in Delphi's default editor settings. However, be careful if you change to Brief or Epsilon and try these; you may be surprised by what happens.

Q When I access the Run Parameters dialog box, the Host Application is grayed out. What am I doing wrong?

A This occurs if you are trying to enter the host application information from code that is not a DLL. You must load the DLL you wish to debug, and you then will be able to enter the information.

Workshop

The Workshop provides two ways for you to affirm what you've learned in this chapter. The Quiz section poses questions to help you solidify your understanding of the material covered. You can find answers to the quiz questions in Appendix A, "Answers to the Quiz Questions." The Exercises section provides you with experience in using what you have learned. Please try to work through all these before continuing to the next day.

Quiz

1. What are the Editor Speed Setting Options for configuring editor behavior?
2. Where do you turn on syntax highlighting?
3. What is the gutter used for?
4. What do you do in Delphi to trace into a DLL with the debugger?

5. What is WinSight32?

6. What are the three features of Code Insight, and what do they do for you?

7. How do you define a watch in the debugger?

8. Besides using a watch, what other way can you monitor the value of variables, objects, and so on as you step through an application with the debugger?

9. When you set a breakpoint, the line where the breakpoint is set is executed before the debugger pauses execution. True or False?

10. If you want to continue normal execution of a program after you have stepped through to your satisfaction, what do you do?

Exercises

1. From the Tools | Environment Options menu, set the options on the Editor and Display tabs to one of the Editor and Keystroke mapping options. Spend some time reading through the online help to learn about the features and keystrokes for the defined options. Do this for at least two of the editor options, one of which is the default setting.

2. Run WinSight32, try the various options and go through its online help.

Day **7**

Designing the GUI

One of the principal benefits of being a Windows user is that most of the applications you use have a similar look and feel. After you have used several (or in my case, several hundred) applications, you'll find that you almost can anticipate where a particular function exists within that new application you just purchased. This goes for everything from the installation (I just stick Disk 1 into the A drive and type **SETUP**, and I rarely read instructions) to the Help menu that always will be the right-most item on the menu bar. You probably have been doing this, too, but not knowing why things were the way they were.

Microsoft has provided design specifications for Windows software in an effort to change the user's paradigm. That shift in focus is from having to learn the nuances of interfacing with your specific application to being productive with your application instead. Microsoft is enforcing these guidelines in what is called the Win95 Logo program. Under this new program, your application must meet Microsoft's logo program criteria before you can place the "Designed for Windows 95" logo on your packaging. When you see that logo on a piece of software or hardware, you can be sure that the product will run well under the Windows 95 environment and is designed properly using the design guidelines. Delphi 3 is designed to help you develop applications that meet the

Windows 95 logo requirements. Borland has given you the tools, but much is still up to you. As you journey through this chapter, I point out some of the ways you can design your application to improve its usability and to help it meet the logo requirements as well.

Why GUI?

NEW TERM *Graphical user interface* (GUI) is a type of display format that enables a user to choose commands, start programs, and view lists of files and other options by pointing to pictorial representations (icons) and menus of items on the screen. Choices generally can be activated with either a keyboard or a mouse. Windows 95 is an example of a GUI.

First off, why do you need graphical user interfaces (GUIs) anyway? The answer is you don't. Users have survived using the command prompt for a number of decades and could have indefinitely. Before you get ruffled, that does not mean, however, that they would be happy doing it! Time and time again, I have seen the transformation of DOS users as I move them (and their computers) to Windows 3.1 or Windows 95 and the light in their eyes as they see the potential there for improved productivity.

GUIs exist because we need them to. I need access to as many as 12 applications on a daily basis (that's on a light day). With only a command prompt, I would spend most of that day starting and shutting down applications and not doing real work. The word for the day here is *productivity*. We can be more productive by having simultaneous access to several applications. Switching between cc:Mail, Delphi 3, WinZip, WinCim, Windows Explorer, and so on, becomes trivial in the Windows environment. I don't have to shut down one application to access another one. What a time saver this is!

Rapid Prototyping and Development

NEW TERM You may have heard the term *rapid prototyping*. This refers to the practice of creating working models of your application's GUI early in the design process.

You then can present this interface to customers and get feedback as to the feel, object placement, and inclusion of features, as well as give customers an overall warm fuzzy because they feel you are catering to their needs. Over the years, several products have emerged to cater to this growing trend. These rapid prototyping tools build "false" front ends with no data processing on the backend. You got the look and feel, but with no "guts." Things have changed.

With the advent of a new generation of rapid-application-development (RAD) tools such as Delphi 3 and Visual Basic, these rapid prototyping tools are no longer necessary. You now can use the RAD tools themselves to create these ghost front ends to show your customer. Nowhere is this concept easier to implement than in Delphi 3. As you saw in Day 5,

"Applications, Files, and the Project Manager," Delphi has provided you with a set of visual components that enable you to create your screens first and then implement the data processing later. You also can include OCXs purchased from third-party vendors in your new front end. Many of these can exist in your application for demo purposes with little or no coding (just drop them onto your window).

NEW TERM *Rapid application development* (RAD) is just what the term implies. Using a set of the latest generation tools (such as Delphi 3), you develop applications quickly with very little turn-around time. These tools enable you to make large leaps in functionality with a small amount of work. An example of using the tools is using the Windows 95 Open and Save common dialog boxes, instead of writing them from scratch. You also can use the OLE container control to embed an Excel spreadsheet into the application, rather than creating the spreadsheet functionality in Delphi itself. Delphi 3 is a prime example of a RAD development environment because it gives you the tools to create great applications in a short period of time and with a minimum of coding.

The disadvantage that has been overcome here is the problem of duplication of effort. When you created your front end using one of those rapid prototyping tools, you had to recode the interface in the tool you were using to generate the real application as soon as your customer approved the interface. What a waste of time. With Delphi 3, you can develop the front end first, get the customer's approval, and then finish the application within the same environment. This is another huge productivity enhancer.

In order for your GUI design to work well, you should consider another item—your GUI development team. You may be working alone now, but as the products you develop get larger and more complex, you will need help. When creating a GUI development team for your product, do not gather up a group of programmers! Programmers are the worst designers because they take for granted many of the things a regular user wouldn't know. Your GUI development team should consist of people from diverse backgrounds. Writers, human interface experts, usability specialists, and computer users of varying skill levels should be involved. I understand that you may not have the access (or the money) to get all these people on your team, but you get the point. Your team is essential for developing a user interface that is usable.

Once your product has been coded, usability testing will show you how good your design is. The best person to test your software is your non-computer-literate mother. Another good candidate is someone who is afraid of computers. The point here is that you should not have the computer whiz sitting next to you at work test your software, unless that's the user base for whom you are constructing the software.

7

Putting the User First

When you are constructing your killer application, it's important to remember the principles upon which Windows 95 was written. Microsoft has seven user-centered design principles that it employs, each of which is described in the following sections:

- ☐ The User Is in Control
- ☐ Directness
- ☐ Consistency
- ☐ Forgiveness
- ☐ Feedback
- ☐ Aesthetics
- ☐ Simplicity

The User Is in Control

None of us likes being controlled by others. We especially do not like being controlled by our computers. The user must always feel in control of what is happening on the screen. Users should always feel they are the ones initiating an action rather than reacting to the computer's whims. If you are going to provide a high degree of automation in your application, ensure that the user has control over that automation process.

Users are individuals. They each have their own preferences and needs. It's important that you provide a way to personalize your application. For example, notice how easy it is to customize the Windows 95 interface. Your ability to change fonts, colors, icons, and so forth, makes Windows a more personal experience. Many of these attributes within Windows are accessible programmatically to you, the developer. Take advantage of these and enable your program to follow the color schemes and font selections of the rest of the system. If you don't, your application will seem rigid and inflexible.

Have you ever looked at how a good application interacts with the user? A good application tells you what it is doing or what "state" or "mode" you are in. If you are in overwrite mode in Microsoft Word, for example, the letters OVR appear on the status bar. Your application should be as interactive as possible. It should be responsive and not leave your user wondering what is going on.

Directness

Enable users to directly manipulate objects in their environment. The phrase "A picture is worth a thousand words" becomes more true every day. It is so much easier to remember what something looks like than it is to remember its command syntax. Countless times I have seen users who recall accomplishing a task by saying, "I drag this thingy and drop it on that thingy, and it prints." Even if *you* don't, this is the way most people think. Try to design your software to be visually intuitive. Let users see how the actions they take affect the objects on-screen.

One of the most direct ways users can interact with a computer is through the use of metaphors. Metaphors are what made the Macintosh such a popular computer and are partially responsible for its success. The concept of a folder makes much more sense than a directory or file. For those of us in the business world, we can comprehend a filing cabinet, folders inside it, and documents inside the folders. This makes perfect sense to us and makes the transfer of these concepts to the computer much easier. Metaphors support the concept of user-recognition rather than user-recollection. Users usually can remember the meaning associated with an object more easily than a command.

Consistency

This is one of the most important aspects of developing a Windows application. Consistency is one of the main reasons why the Windows 95 logo program was developed. If all applications are consistent in how they present data and in the way they interact with the user, the user can spend time accomplishing tasks, not learning the differences in the way your application interacts with them. This consistency extends to several areas you should consider:

☐ Ensure that your application acts very similarly to the Windows operating system. Then users easily can transfer skills they have learned in Windows to your application.

☐ Ensure that your product is consistent within itself. If you support Ctrl+C as your copy shortcut on one screen, do not use a different paradigm on another screen (such as Ctrl+D).

☐ Ensure that your metaphors are consistent. If a Black Hole icon is the same as the Recycle Bin, users may think that they can retrieve documents from the Black Hole icon as well. (Your Black Hole is actually an application that places those files in the same place as your socks that get lost in the dryer.)

7

You'll hear more about consistency later in this chapter along with the use of menus, toolbars, and other common controls.

Forgiveness

I don't know about you, but I spend a great deal of time just exploring new applications, pushing buttons and seeing what happens. In most well-written applications, this very rarely presents a problem. If I am about to perform an action that will format my hard drive, a dialog box would come up and alert me to that fact. I then can press the Cancel button supplied, and nothing is lost.

This is the concept of forgiveness. You need to let users explore your application. All actions the users take need to be reversible or correctable. Users need to be made aware *beforehand* that the actions they are about to perform are destructive. It is also possible for a user to make a mouse-o (a mouse-o is a typo, but done with a mouse). People make mistakes. You must allow for this and require confirmation for all destructive actions, using either the keyboard or mouse, in case they were initiated in error.

 TIP

> You may want to enable your application's user to shut off some of the confirmation for certain actions once they become accustomed to using them. A tabbed options dialog box enabling users to shut off confirmation of customer deletes, file deletes, and so on, may be a useful addition for the professional user of your application.

Feedback

There is nothing most users hate more than a computer that just sits there. You don't know what it is doing, and it's not telling you a thing. This is a cardinal rule: Let your user know what is happening. Provide feedback to the user in a timely fashion. You can use a combination of visual and audio cues to let users know you are aware of them.

It is important that the feedback be displayed near the position at which users are working. If they are inputting data on the top of the screen, do not present an error message at the bottom (unless you have a specific status bar line defined). You can change the cursor shape to indicate a condition (such as the infamous hourglass we all love). Users will not tolerate a dead computer for more than a couple of seconds (would you?).

Aesthetics

Your application also must be visually pleasing to the customer. This means several things. Besides using the system colors for your screens (so your application blends with the environment), the design of the screen itself is extremely important. The placement of objects determines how usable your screen is, as well as the number of items on the screen itself. When possible, use the "seven rule." Give the user only seven choices (plus or minus two). This number of five to nine choices comes from research on how many things the brain can comprehend at one time. With more than nine choices, people tend to get confused and suffer from brain overload. You'll learn more about screen design later in this chapter.

Simplicity

The final design principle is simplicity. Your application should be easy to learn and easy to use. You need to balance two things that work against each other: (1) access to all the functionality and information in the application, and (2) keeping the interface and the use of the product simple. A good application balances these two principles and finds the happy medium.

Try not to be too wordy when creating your screens. When using labels on data-entry fields, put `Last Name` not `The Last Name of the Customer`. Try to use the fewest number of words that communicate the meaning correctly. Microsoft also recommends the concept of progressive disclosure. This means presenting data as needed. For instance in a phone book program, you may show the person's name and phone number on the initial screen, and the user will have to push a button that reveals all other information about that person.

Data-Centered Design

You may already have used an application based on a data-centered design and don't even know it.

NEW TERM   *Data-centered design* refers to the user's ability to act on specific pieces of data without having to bring up external editors or programs. As the user begins to operate on the data (either browsing or editing the data), the appropriate tools become available to the user automatically. This concept comes to life in applications such as Microsoft Word. When you click on a drawing in Word, the drawing toolbar appears at the bottom of the screen with all the tools you need to perform drawing operations.

7

Document-Centered Design

The concept of a document helps to solidify concepts in a user's mind. The document-centric view of things is easy to remember. Now, you may think that documents apply only to word processing-type applications—not so. Many applications make use of a document-centric view of non-word processing items. In some communications packages, file transfers are even referred to as "document transfers."

Which Model Is Right for You?

A topic you need to know about early on is windows management. There are two different application models, the single document interface (SDI) and the multiple document interface (MDI). By choosing File | New, selecting the Projects tab, and then selecting either SDI application or MDI application, you can create a skeleton application. If you haven't dealt with MDI applications, you may not understand the benefits or the conditions under which an MDI application should be used over an SDI application.

In almost all instances, an application can be interfaced to the user through a single, primary window. If additional information needs to be displayed or gathered, a secondary window can be used. A good example of an SDI application is Windows Explorer. Windows Explorer has a single, primary window that reflects nearly all the information needed for its use. When you need to do something such as view a property, a secondary window is brought up. The other benefit of an SDI application is that it is easier for you, the developer, to manage the one-to-one relationship between a screen and the data on it.

An MDI application, on the other hand, has some real benefits, too. Microsoft Word is a good example of an MDI application. An MDI application has a parent window (the primary) and a number of child windows (also called *documents*). There are times when it is more efficient to display information in multiple windows that share interface elements (such as a toolbar or menu bar). The document windows are controlled or clipped by the parent. If you reduce the size of the parent window, the child windows can be hidden from view.

The conditions under which an MDI application should be used are few. First, MDI should be used only when all the child windows will be used to hold identical objects—such as documents or spreadsheets. Don't use MDI if you plan to have different types of child windows (such as documents and spreadsheets together). Don't use an MDI if you want to control which child window is on top by using the "stay on top" property, or if you want to control the size of the children, or if you want to hide and show a child. MDI was designed for a very narrow application niche, such as Word or Excel where the children are all uniform. Trying to make it accommodate anything else will not work, will cause the developer unknown grief, and generally will make life miserable for all. Finally, it should be noted that

Microsoft discourages development of new MDI applications (mainly because so many people have been writing poor MDI applications in previous Windows versions).

Components of a Window

I know this may seem somewhat basic, but a review of the basics helps you focus. A typical window consists of a frame and a title bar that identifies either the name of the application in the window or the name of the item being viewed in the window, as shown in Figure 7.1. If the item being viewed is larger than the window, scroll bars appear to enable the user to scroll around the entire window.

Figure 7.1.

Generic window.

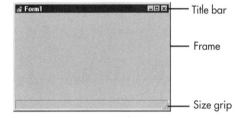

The window frame (if sizable) should include a size grip in the lower-right corner of the window. In addition to the title bar, there are a number of other elements than can be present on the window, including menus, toolbars, status bars, and more. The following sections describe each of the items in a window, focusing on how the items are constructed to conform to the requirements for a clean design.

Title Bar Icons

When you construct a Windows application, your primary window should have a small version of your application icon in the upper-left corner of the window. This icon would represent the product, if that product were a utility or tool of some sort that did not create or view documents of any kind. Figure 7.2 shows a typical Windows application window.

If the primary window is used to view documents of some sort, you want to place a document icon, instead of the application's icon, in the upper-left corner of the window. Place the document icon there even if the user has not saved the document she is creating or viewing. This is done purely for consistency's sake. Remember that you are trying to make the applications be uniform and consistent in their presentation of data and in their form. Figure 7.3 shows a typical Windows document application window.

7

Figure 7.2.
Utility or tool title bar.

Application or document icon

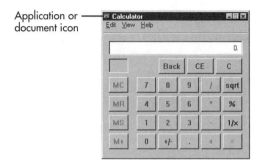

Figure 7.3.
Document title bar icon.

Document icon

MDI applications are a special case. In an MDI application, the application icon is placed in the primary window, and the document icon is placed in all child windows within the parent. Delphi 3 takes care of a lot of the default items as far as the behavior of windows so that you don't have to worry about them. Figure 7.4 shows a typical MDI application window.

Figure 7.4.
An MDI application.

Application icon

Document icon

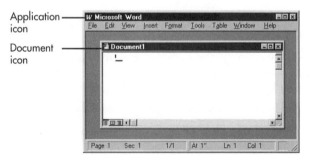

Title Bar Text

The main function of the title bar is to identify the name of the document being viewed in the window. For instance, if the user opens a document called "My Resume" in an MDI application, the title bar should display the document icon representing that document type followed by the name of the document "My Resume." In addition, you can include the name of the application after the document name. If you include the application name, you must include a dash between the document and application name. Figure 7.5 shows a typical text title bar window.

Figure 7.5.

Sample title bar text order.

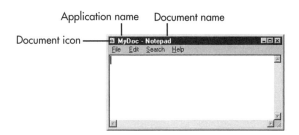

If the application is a utility or tool and does not have a particular document name associated with it, you can use just the application icon followed by the application name, which is how the Windows Calculator is. In the case of an application such as Windows Explorer (where it is browsing a wide variety of things), you can place the application's name followed by some text that specifies what is being viewed currently.

MDI applications again are a special case. In this instance, you display the name of the application in the parent window and the document name in the child window. When the user maximizes the child, the parent window follows the same convention as a utility: The application name first, then a dash, and then the document name.

New Documents

Several issues are related to the titling of windows. If your application enables the user to create new documents, your application should automatically name the windows using the type of file followed by a unique identifier. For example, using document(1) or sheet(1), such as Word and Excel do, provides a quick way to continue after the user has created a document. You never want to ask users for a document name when they create the file. Users should be asked for a filename when the document is saved for the first time.

It is also important that when your application creates the temporary window (and filename), the name should be unique. That is why many applications simply increment the unique number at the end of the file type name (for example, document1, document2, and so on). It is very important that the name not conflict with the name of any other open window. That temporary name (document1) should be the title of the document window until such time as the user is asked for a permanent name for the document. At that point, the user-designated name should be substituted for the temporary one.

7

Title Bar Buttons

The last item to discuss in relation to the title bar is the title bar button. Table 7.1 lists the buttons that are supported by Windows 95.

Table 7.1. Title bar buttons.

Button	Command	Function
✖	Close	Closes the current window
▬	Minimize	Minimizes the current window
◻	Maximize	Maximizes the current window
⧉	Restore	Restores the current window to its original size—the size it was before a minimize or maximize

The Close button closes the current window the same as pressing Alt+F4 does. The Close button always should be the right-most button, separated by a space from the other buttons. The Minimize button always should precede the Maximize button, and the Restore button should replace the Minimize or Maximize button after that button has been used. As the programmer, you can control whether these buttons appear on your forms by changing the `BorderIcon`'s attributes for that form.

Opening and Closing Windows

One of the nicest features in any Windows application is being able to save your settings when you leave your application. This saves the size and position of the application window. The next time you run the program, it comes up in that same place and size. You can make your own entries in the Registry to store the size and position information (making Registry entries is covered in Bonus Day 15, "Deploying Applications"). Another method for sizing is to get the size of the screen and make your application window the size of the entire screen or a portion of the screen size, centered on the screen.

The behavior of a Windows application varies according to its design. For instance, a NotePad-like program would enable multiple instances of the program to run at the same time. When you start the application from the Start menu, another instance is run. For Delphi 3, and applications like it, if the user tries to start another copy, the instance running is simply brought to the foreground. This type of response works well for applications in which only a single instance can be run. You also can bring up a dialog box and give the user the option to bring to the front the running application or run another application.

Window Colors

Using color in your application can add some real sparkle. Using too much color also can make it look as if a paint store exploded. Delphi 3 provides the system colors in the palette so that you can have your application colors match the overall Windows color scheme. If you look for colors in the Object Inspector, you'll find colors such as clWindowActive. These are the current system colors that have been chosen by the user. If you pick these colors to be your application's colors, your application will be changed to match them whenever the user changes the overall Windows color scheme. You also can make your colors *static* (that is, your application's colors do not change when the user changes the Windows color scheme). When you create a new form or add components to a form, Delphi 3 sets the colors of these items to match the Windows 95 color scheme. You have to change the colors manually with the Object Inspector if you wish override Delphi's behavior.

There are several reasons why you should not override the system colors in favor of your own. The user's color choices may have a functional purpose, such as power management (black backgrounds consume less battery power). Visibility may also play a role (the user picked grayscale because he is colorblind). There are many instances in which you may not know best. If you do change the colors in your application, try to stick with the 16 basic colors. Using 256 (or worse yet, 16 million) colors has a tendency to slow down your application, and it may not look right on users' machines that are using 16 colors. The color palette is shown in Figure 7.6.

Figure 7.6.

The Object Inspector color drop-down.

Menus

We have all used menus in Windows applications at one time or another. They are a convenient way to access a program's functionality by recognition (we all know the File | Open routine) rather than having to remember some cryptic command syntax. There are several different types of menus, including pop-up menus, drop-down menus, and cascading menus. Let's take a look at each one of these types of menus and what they have to offer.

The drop-down menu exists mostly in the context of a menu bar. The menu bar is a part of most applications today. The menu bar contains elements called *menu titles*. These titles,

7

when selected, provide access to drop-down menus. The drop-down menus then contain the next level of selection—menu items. Figure 7.7 shows a typical menu bar.

Figure 7.7.

Typical menu bar.

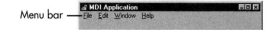

The visual controls, provided with Delphi 3, enable you to construct your own menu bar and associated drop-down menus. The actual menu choice you give your user depends on the functionality of your application. It is possible for you to enable the user to change or customize the menus in your application. If you decide to go this route, make sure that you give the user access to the standard set of choices through a standard mechanism, such as pop-up menus and toolbars. This way, users do not customize the interface to the point where they cannot use it.

TIP

If you select File | New, the Projects tab, and then SDI application, you get a minimal menu structure consisting of File and Help commands. If you create an MDI application, you get a more extensive menu bar including the Edit and Window menu titles.

Let's look at some of the most common menu titles and their functions.

The File Menu

The File menu is the primary way the user accesses the major commands in your application. Usually, you would include a New, Open, Save, and Save As command set if your application opens documents of any kind. A feature for Windows 95 and NT 4.0 is the Send To command that also could be included here. If your application provides a printed output capability, a Print command would go here as well. If your application supports the Exit command, it should be the last item on the File menu. If the application remains active even when the window is closed (such as the Volume control on the taskbar), use the Close command in place of the Exit command.

It is important that menu items be in the same place every time so that the user does not have to learn the basics over again with each new application. File | Exit or File | Print should be natural reactions for the user and should be the same every time.

NOTE

You may have noticed that each menu item has one underlined key or a combination of keys next to it, as shown in Figure 7.8. You'll learn how to establish these accelerator keys in the section titled "Menu Labels, Shortcuts, Access Keys, and Types" later in this chapter.

Figure 7.8.

Typical File drop-down menu.

The Edit Menu

The Edit menu is critical in applications where documents are being edited or viewed. This menu usually contains the Cut, Copy, and Paste items, as shown in Figure 7.9. You can place OLE object items into this menu, as well as several of the more "deluxe" items found in some applications. These items could include Undo (for reversing the last action), Repeat (to repeat the last action), Find and Replace (for searching for and replacing text, respectively), Delete (for removing the currently selected item), and Duplicate (for creating a copy of the currently selected item). The Select All command also comes in handy for selecting an entire document.

Figure 7.9.

Typical Edit drop-down menu.

The View Menu

The View menu provides a way for users to change their view of the data. This change could be something such as zooming in or out (sizing), or viewing additional items on the screen (such as a ruler or toolbar). In this menu, you should support the selection of items, such as a ruler, with a check box to show that it has been selected. Figure 7.10 shows a typical View menu.

Figure 7.10.

Typical View drop-down menu.

The Window Menu

The Window menu is typically present only in an MDI application where it is necessary to control more than one window. This menu usually contains the New Window, Tile, Cascade, Split, and Minimize All functions, as appropriate. The purpose of this menu is to provide a way for the user to manage a number of windows at one time. In this menu, you may also want to provide access to all windows that are currently open. Usually this is done with a list of windows, by name, at the bottom of the Window drop-down menu. This enables the user to access any window by simply choosing it from the menu. Figure 7.11 shows a typical Window menu.

Figure 7.11.

Typical Window drop-down menu

 TIP

Delphi 3 automatically includes the current window list feature as part of the standard MDI application skeleton generated by choosing File | New, the Projects tab, then MDI Application.

The Help Menu

One of the most important of all the menus is the Help menu. This menu provides you with the first line of defense against the user calling you with simple questions that are more efficiently answered online. As a standard part of the Windows Help, you should provide a Help Topics item that provides access to the Help Topics browser, as well as possible individual items such as Topic Search and any Help Wizards (such as in Microsoft Word). If you are going to include any information about the version number or your company, you should include the information in an About dialog box that is accessed through the Help | About menu selection. Remember that the better your help system is designed, the fewer calls you will have to answer. Figure 7.12 shows a typical Help menu.

Pop-Up Menus

Pop-up menus did not really exist in the mainstream of Windows computing, prior to Windows 95. The right (or alternate) mouse button has taken on a whole new meaning in Windows now. The right button offers users a set of functions that can be performed on the object they right-click on. For instance, when you right-click on the background in Windows 95, a pop-up menu appears that gives you all the functions you can perform in relation to the display (the screen).

Figure 7.12.

Typical Help drop-down menu.

The nice part about pop-up menus is that they provide only those choices that are relevant for the object that is currently selected. You always should include a pop-up menu for the user if you provide a menu bar (this is because some of the items on the menu bar are assumed to be relevant to specific objects in your application).

As far as the organization of the pop-up menu goes, use as few items as possible on the menu itself. The selection names should be short, and individual properties should never be listed. Always provide a Properties menu item and let the user navigate through a separate screen instead. It is permissible for a pop-up menu to contain items that are not part of the regular menu bar commands, and vice versa, but make sure that your pop-up menu is not the only way in which the user can access commands in your application. Figure 7.13 shows a typical pop-up menu.

Figure 7.13.

Typical pop-up menu.

The order of the items is critical to providing the common look and feel. The top (first) items should be the primary functions that are performed on that object, such as Open, Explore, Run, Print, and Play. The transfer items, such as Send To, should go next, as well as the "What's This?" command, if supported by your application. Cut, Copy, and Paste should be placed in that order. And finally, the Properties command should be the last item on the pop-up menu.

Pop-up menus are used extensively in the Windows environment. If you right-click on your application's executable file in Windows Explorer, you will notice that several choices are available for you. It is possible for you to add specific menu items to support your application. For instance, if you install WinZip for Windows 95 (an indispensable product), you will see that WinZip places an Add To Zip command in the Windows Explorer. This enables the user to add any file in Explorer to a WinZip file from within the Windows Explorer without having to start WinZip first. This is just one example of how to use pop-up menus to help users be more efficient at their tasks.

7

Cascading Menus

You probably have used an application that has cascading menus in it (Delphi 3 is one of them). Child menus (another name for cascading menus) are used to help minimize the confusion of overburdening the user with too many choices on a single menu. Think for a minute of the File menu in Delphi 3 and all the menu choices under it. Can you imagine how confusing it would be to place all these choices at the highest menu level, instead of separating each into its own child?

If you want a good example of how child menus should be used, look at Delphi 3. The presence of a child menu is indicated by a triangular arrow on a menu item in the parent menu. An example of its use in Delphi 3 is the File | Reopen menu choice. Figure 7.14 shows a typical submenu.

Figure 7.14.

Typical submenu layout.

WARNING

Although child menus are available, use them sparingly. They have a tendency to add complexity by forcing the user to make several directional changes with the mouse. Even Delphi 3 itself makes scarce use of this feature in its menus.

Also try to limit the number of levels. Try not to put a commonly executed task under five levels of submenus. That would make for some very unproductive time for the user.

Menu Labels, Shortcuts, Access Keys, and Types

When creating your menus, you also should consider several concepts that bear some discussion. The first concept is the labels used in a menu. The items on the menu bar and all submenus should be single-word identifiers, if possible. The names should be succinct and clearly understandable. Do not use phrases or more than two words because they add complexity and cause the user to take longer to scan the menu to make his choice.

Two alternate methods (besides using the mouse) to select items from the menu is to use either a shortcut or an access key combination.

A *shortcut* is a key combination, such as Ctrl+F4, that you assign to a menu command to enable users to execute the command more quickly.

Shortcuts enable the user to do things such as a "fast save" of the current document by pressing F2 (as used in Word). You can assign shortcut keys to just about any task, as long as you do not reassign crucial key combinations such as Alt+F4 (close the current window). In the Delphi 3 menu visual control, you can assign shortcut keys by changing the shortcut attribute of each menu item. Delphi displays a list of all available shortcut keys, and you simply pick one. Figure 7.15 shows a typical shortcut menu.

Figure 7.15.
ShortCut *property*
drop-down list.

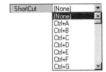

Besides the assignment of shortcut keys, you also can use access key combinations.

 Access keys are used in combination with the Alt key on your keyboard. For instance, in Delphi, you can access the New Items dialog box by pressing Alt+F, N.

 NOTE

When using access keys in multiple layers of menus, the Alt key should be held down only for the first access key. After that selection, just the letters themselves need to be entered.

The keys you can use in combination with the Alt key are underlined. If you see the word File (with the F underlined), you know that the Alt+F combination can be used. When using the menu visual control, you can place an access character (the one that is underlined) in the title by placing an ampersand (&) in front of the letter in the menu item name that you wish to highlight. For example, the word File with the F highlighted would be written &File. Figure 7.16 shows a typical menu item caption.

Figure 7.16.
The menu item
caption property.

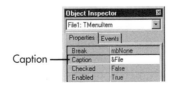

Many things need to be taken into consideration when creating the menu system for your application. This section covered some of the major areas. Usability testing helps bring out the deficiencies in your design. Don't hesitate to take input from those who will use the product, and your product will be a great one!

Controls

In order for your applications to be useful, they must interact with the user. This is done through the use of controls. Controls provide a method for the user to control the actions or properties of other objects. Controls come in many forms (no pun intended) and in many styles.

NEW TERM Controls usually are activated by using the mouse pointer in conjunction with the left mouse button. Most controls have what is referred to as a *hot zone*. This hot zone is an area that is sensitive to left mouse clicks and activates the control when a mouse pointer is clicked in that area. Some controls' hot zones are very apparent, such as the hot zone on a button, which corresponds to the area inside the border of the button. Other controls may have hot zones that are smaller or larger than the control itself. A check box, for instance, has a hot zone that is larger than just the check box itself, because the label for the check box is included.

Labels are important so that the purpose of your controls can be quickly ascertained by the user. Labels, just like menu items, should be concise and to the point. As with menus, it is important to provide access keys for controls so that the user can use the keyboard directly, instead of relying entirely on the mouse.

Command Buttons

Several types of buttons are used in Windows 95. The first is the command button. The command button is used to activate a command associated with that button. The normal behavior is for users to press the command button. When the button is released, if the mouse pointer is on the button, the command associated with the button is executed. If the mouse pointer is off the button, the command is not executed. This enables the user to have a second chance to cancel the command after the button already has been pushed.

This second chance works only if you are using the mouse to visually activate the button. If the button has the current focus and you press the Enter key, that's it. The button has been activated. There is no second-chance mechanism.

NOTE

> The term *press* in relation to buttons on forms can mean two separate things. A button can be "visually" pressed or activated by using the mouse. The button appears to be pushed in when you click that primary button on your mouse. You can also press, or activate, the form's button by making sure the button has the focus, and then pressing the Enter key. They both accomplish the same thing: pressing the button.

Windows 95 uses a special kind of command button called the *unfold* button. It expands a window to a larger view when activated. When you use a command button as an unfold button, you should include the double greater-than signs (>>) in the label to signify that the button will expand the current view. This enables the user to view only primary information by default but then press the unfold button to view additional information.

If your command button requires additional information in order for its associated command to execute correctly, place the ellipses (. . .) after the command button's label. This indicates to the user that more information needs to be given (usually in a dialog box) by the user for the button's command to execute successfully. When command buttons are unavailable, they should be grayed out. This can be accomplished by setting the `Enabled` property for that button to `FALSE`.

Radio Buttons

A radio button is a control that assists the user in selecting options in your application. This is why radio buttons are also referred to as *option* buttons. Radio buttons are shown as small circles and should be presented in groups of two to seven. If you need more buttons than that, consider using another control, such as a list box.

You can present radio buttons in two ways. The first is in exclusive mode (their most common use, as shown in Figure 7.17). In this state, only one button in the group can be selected at any given time. You would present radio buttons this way whenever each option is mutually exclusive.

Figure 7.17.

Radio buttons in exclusive mode.

The second mode in which you can present radio buttons is called mixed-value mode. This means that more than one radio button can be selected at any given time, as shown in Figure 7.18. This is useful in situations such as the selection of file attributes where a file can be read-only, hidden, and archived all at the same time.

Figure 7.18.

Radio buttons in mixed-value mode, with no buttons selected.

Most Windows users assume that radio buttons are used in exclusive mode, which means that one button always is selected. During the design of the application, you (the developer) usually pick the button that is selected by default. You do so by setting the value attribute to TRUE for one of the buttons. The way you make the radio buttons act as an exclusive group is to place them into a RadioGroup, Panel, or Bevel control. These controls ensure that only one radio button is active at any given time.

If you are going to use the radio buttons in mixed-value mode, simply do not place them in a group box control. This enables the radio buttons to act independently of one another. In this instance, you could set the value attribute of all the radio buttons to FALSE and let the user choose them at will.

NOTE

You've just learned about using radio buttons in mixed-value mode. If each radio button really were acting independently and were unrelated to one another, it would be more appropriate to use check boxes instead. I was trying to relay the concept of mixed-value mode, using the radio buttons as an example. Radio buttons should not be used in mixed-value mode.

As with any other Windows control, it is important that you assign access keys to the controls. These keys would enable the user to select a specific radio button from the keyboard directly. Another method for selecting a radio button is to tab around the screen until that control is highlighted and then press the space bar to select it.

NOTE

There is an alternate method of accessing radio buttons without assigning them all individual access keys. If you assign an access key to the GroupBox, or other control of which the radio buttons are a part, when you press the access key for that group control, the focus jumps to the radio buttons in the grouping control. Then you can use the arrow keys on the keyboard to activate the correct radio button.

Check Boxes

Check boxes provide another mechanism for the user to select options in your program. The check box exists in several states. You can use the state attribute to determine whether the check box is checked or not by setting the State property to either cbChecked (the checked state), cbUnChecked (the unchecked state), or cbGrayed (a state where the box is checked but grayed out. This last state is provided for your own use, and your application would have to define what that state means. A check box illustrating all three states is shown in Figure 7.19.

Figure 7.19.

Check boxes in all three states.

When using check boxes, group related check boxes together. This helps the user see the relationship between them. As with other controls, use access keys to enable the user to interact with the check boxes directly from the keyboard. Also, as with other controls, if you check a check box with the mouse, your selection can be undone by moving the mouse off of the control prior to releasing the mouse button. This leaves your selection unchanged. You also can gray out the entire check box control by changing the Enabled attribute to FALSE. This would make the control unavailable to the user regardless of the state.

List Boxes

List boxes are a convenient and succinct way for you to display a number of items to the user. The benefit of a list box is that the items can vary in both number and form. Unlike check boxes and other controls, if a selection is not available, it should not be shown in the list box at all. This differs from the graying out concept of other controls. The contents of the list box can be arranged a number of different ways. Use the method that best fits your user's browsing needs. For example, names probably would be arranged alphabetically, numbers in ascending order, and dates in chronological order. Figure 7.20 shows a typical list box.

7

Figure 7.20.

Sample list box (with items listed alphabetically).

NOTE

It is important that you use the `Listbox` and `Combobox` controls for what they are intended. If you have a 4GB database, do not load all that data into one poor `Listbox` control. That method is slow and unwieldy. Think of how long it would take you to use the vertical slider bar to roll through 4GB of data! Instead, you may want to use an `Edit` control and a search button to narrow the choices down to something reasonable.

A list box does not have a label associated with it. If you create a label for the list box, ensure that it is disabled whenever you disable the list box (by setting the `Enabled` attribute to `FALSE`). The Delphi 3 version of the list box has the `Multiselect` attribute, which enables that list box to be used as a single- or multi-select list box. Single-select means just that—the user can select only one item from the list box. If the `Multiselect` attribute is set to `TRUE`, the user can select multiple items from the list box. If the list of items in the list box is longer than the window height, a vertical scroll bar appears.

View Controls

There are two different types of view controls in Windows 95. The first is a list view control. This control enables users to view a list of items in a similar fashion to the right-hand window in Windows Explorer. Users can view the list in one of the four following ways:

Icon View	The items appear as full-sized icons with the label underneath the icon.
Small Icon	Each item appears as a small icon with the label to the right of the icon.
List	Each item appears as a small icon with the label to the right of the icon, and the icons are displayed in columns and are sorted in the ascending order
Report	The items are displayed in column format. All but the leftmost column must be supplied by the application displaying the list box. The icons are full size and are unsorted.

Tree View Controls

Tree view is another form of the list view control. The major difference is that the tree view is more conducive to showing information of a hierarchical nature. There are some major benefits to this approach. The tree view control enables you to associate icons with each of the items in the "tree." The icon for an item can change even when it is collapsed, as well as when it is expanded.

The tree view control enables you to draw lines drawn between items, which reinforces to the user the hierarchical relationship among the items. A prime example of using the tree control is in the Windows Explorer. The left-hand window in the Explorer is a tree control. Notice how the drive icons represent each drive, folder icons represent each directory within the drive, and so on. This control helps give a clear display method to something that would usually be a little more confusing.

Text Entry and Display

Text can be displayed in two ways using Delphi 3. The first is using a label control for displaying static text. This method is used frequently when displaying information that the user cannot change, such as a customer serial number or social security number.

Microsoft guidelines say that you need to ensure that the label control does not receive focus when tabbing between controls on the screen. Delphi 3 goes one better. The label control has no tab order, so it does not receive focus. In addition, if you set the FocusControl attribute to the control that should have the focus, then when the user presses the access key for that label, the item pointed to by the FocusControl receives focus instead! Here you gain the ability to both label controls and to provide proper focus for those controls.

The edit box is the other method for displaying data. The added benefit of this control is that you can edit the data as well. The Delphi 3 edit control supports the MaxLength attribute, which enables you to limit the length of a user's input. The basic editing techniques of insert, overwrite, and delete are supported.

The memo control is another control that provides similar capabilities. The memo control is really a multi-line edit control. It has a MaxLength property as well. The memo control also has a Lines property under which you can set the value of each line in the control.

Tabbed Page Controls

Think of the filing cabinet in your office (if you have one). The tabbed separators of a tabbed dialog box help to organize your information into "drawers," which enable you to find information more easily. Follow the same guidelines for naming the tabbed pages as you do

7

for menu items. The tabbed pages themselves usually are aligned in a single row. If necessary, you can place several rows of tabbed pages on one dialog box. Each tabbed page contains pieces of data, and to access the data on a tabbed page, users just click on the tab.

 NOTE

> There are several usage and design considerations that go into tabbed dialog boxes. Depending on whether you place your OK and Cancel buttons on the tabbed page itself or on the form holding the tabbed pages makes a statement to the user. If they're on the tabbed page, the inference is that the OK locks in changes on that page only. If the only OK button is on the form, the user should be able to go back and forth and change all tabbed pages, and just use the OK button once at the end to commit those changes. Figure 7.21 shows a typical tabbed page.

Figure 7.21.

Typical tabbed page.

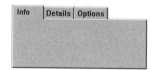

Sliders

Sliders are another way to control the adjustment of data values. You must assign a minimum and maximum value for the slider using the Min and Max properties. This control is ideal for adjusting values such as contrast, volume, and so on. Anything that lends itself to a knob in the real world does very well here. You can control the orientation of the slider (horizontal or vertical), the presence and number of increments, and the size of the slider itself.

 NOTE

> Even though the slider bar requires you to set Min and Max values, you can translate those into other options. For example, Windows 95 uses the slider in the Display Properties dialog box to set the screen size, where each increment is 640×480, 800×600, or 1024×768. You assign each of the three values on the slider to match these screen resolution settings. The result of this mapping of values makes the slider more useful. Figure 7.22 shows a typical slider.

Figure 7.22.
Typical slider.

Tooltips

Tooltips are an important innovation of Windows 95. They provide a quick reference for the user in identifying a control and its function. Delphi 3 provides a "hint" (the Delphi equivalent of a Tooltip) for all relevant controls. You can set the Hint attribute for a control, set the ShowHint attribute to TRUE, and then the hint appears when the user places the mouse pointer over a control and leaves it there. Figure 7.23 shows a typical hint.

Figure 7.23.
Tooltip (hint) in action.

Progress Indicators

When your application performed a lengthy operation in Windows 3.1, you would have used the hourglass icon to tell the user that something was happening. Under Windows 95, a more informative way has been found. The use of a progress indicator shows the user that something is happening and approximately how much of the operation has taken place. Users usually will be more patient when they know something constructive is going on. Figure 7.24 shows a typical progress bar.

Figure 7.24.
Typical progress bar.

Toolbars

Toolbars are a wonderful way to enhance the productivity of the user. They enable fast access to commonly performed operations in your application. There are many different names for toolbars, such as ribbons, palettes, and tool boxes. In Delphi 3, a toolbar usually is implemented using a panel control and a number of speed-button controls. These buttons are placed on the panel and usually appear under the menu bar. If you select File | New, the Projects tab, and then SDI application or MDI application, you get, as part of that default project, a toolbar. Look at the controls carefully and what they represent. The toolbar for a typical SDI application is shown in Figure 7.25.

7

Figure 7.25.

Default toolbar in an SDI application.

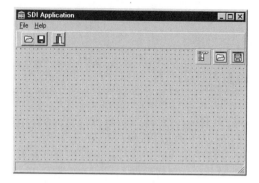

Designing Your Screens

Visual images can have dramatic impact on our minds and emotions. The visual images that software developers present to users can have a number of effects. They can range from inspiration to distraction. This is why it is important to design your applications to inspire the user without distracting them from the task at hand.

When it comes to actually designing your screens, you can leverage a lot of information from companies, such as Microsoft, that have done a great deal of research in this area. This section presents some of the things Microsoft has learned. All this information is part of the Windows 95 design specifications and is on the Microsoft Developer Network (MSDN) CD-ROM. I hope this will give you ideas on how to proceed in your development effort.

Organization

There are really six organizational principles that Microsoft has outlined as being important, and each is described in the following sections:

- ☐ Readability and flow
- ☐ Structure and balance
- ☐ Relationship of elements
- ☐ Focus and emphasis
- ☐ Hierarchy of information
- ☐ Unity and integration

Readability and Flow

The principle of readability and flow asks you to arrange your design to communicate your ideas directly and simply with minimal visual interference. To minimize visual interference and increase readability and flow, ask yourself the following questions when designing a dialog box or window:

- ☐ Is this idea being presented in the easiest manner possible?
- ☐ Can the user easily step through this dialog the way I have designed it?
- ☐ Does everything in this window have a reason for being here?

Structure and Balance

Structure and balance refer to the idea that without a sturdy foundation, the house never will last. The structure of your application is a little esoteric, but it refers to how your overall application is put together. Without a good structure, your application can lack order and meaning. The relationship between screens and the information on those screens play a part in how the application feels to the end user. Balance refers to how your information is balanced on those screens. If too much information is on one screen and not enough on another, the application will feel out of balance. A lack of structure and balance makes it more difficult for the user to clearly understand the interface.

Relationship of Elements

It is important for you to show visually the relationship that exists among elements of your application. If a button expands information in a list box, those two items should be connected visually to each other so that the relationship is obvious to the user. This may involve having both the button and the list box in close proximity on the window, or having them both in the same `bevel` control. If your screen is nothing more than a random grouping of buttons, that is exactly what it will look like.

Focus and Emphasis

The concept of focus refers to identifying the central theme or idea your screen revolves around. The concept of emphasis refers to choosing the central controls or theme and making it stand out so that the user understands which things on the screen are most important. These two concepts reinforce the principles of structure and balance as well. If your application has a solid focus, the structure of the application will seem strong to the user. You do not want your application to be a floor wax *and* a desert topping (sorry, an old joke). It should focus on accomplishing one task, and doing that task well. An example of a well-focused program is WinZip. All that program does is compress and uncompress files. It does not have a disk defragmenter, an Explorer, or a check-book-balancing program built in. It focuses on the task of file compression and does it well. The user interface is concise, focused, and gets the job done.

7

Hierarchy of Information

The concept of a hierarchy applies to screen design as well as to data (as in the `TreeView` control). You must decide what information is the most important and therefore should be on the initial screen, what should be on the second screen, and so on. There are a number of questions you can ask yourself to help decide the structure of your hierarchy:

- ☐ What is the most important information to the user?
- ☐ What tasks should the user do first, second, and so forth?
- ☐ What things should the user see on the first screen, second, and so on?
- ☐ You also need to understand what the priorities of the user are going to be. Will your screen organization help or hurt the user, and which portions do you wish to emphasize?

Unity and Integration

This is sort of the 30,000-foot view. How does your application fit into the overall desktop, and how does it interact with other applications? If your application stands out like a sore thumb, it may be heading for trouble. If you follow some of the guidelines in this chapter, you will find that your application behaves more like a standard application.

Colors and Palettes

As mentioned earlier in this chapter, you can create your application using a rainbow of colors available in Windows. Color provides some mental cues for us, as well as helps draw users' attention to particular areas of the screen. Users also seem to associate color with a particular state.

If you do not practice good color management, color can have a negative effect. Too many (or not the right) colors can distract users or confuse them and make it difficult to work. Here are few other things to remember when choosing colors:

- ☐ Associating color with a particular meaning is not always obvious to the user. In the United States, stop signs are red, but stop signs in other countries could be other colors.
- ☐ Other people may not have the good taste in color you do. Therefore, it's best to use the system colors for your application whenever possible. The user then can change the overall color scheme in Windows, and your application will follow.
- ☐ There actually may be someone out there with a monochrome monitor that wants to use your application.

7

☐ Colors have different meanings in different countries. It would be a shame to create a really cool utility only to have half the world not use it because its color scheme has a negative connotation.

☐ Microsoft estimates that nine percent of the adult male population has a color-confusion problem.

You should use color to add to a display rather than as the primary way to disclose information to the user. Shapes, patterns, and other methods can be used to help distinguish information on your screen. Microsoft even suggests building your screen in black and white, and then adding color later.

Using a limited number of colors also includes using the *right* color combinations. Using bright colors, such as red, on background colors such as green or black, makes it hard for the user to focus. The use of opposite colors is not recommended. A neutral color, such as light gray, is often the best background color (as is evident in most of Microsoft's product line). Remember too that light colors have a tendency to jump out at you, whereas dark colors recede into the background.

Layout

One of the things I found most interesting is a statement in the Windows design guidelines that says one of the goals is to make a predictable environment. As a user, that is what I like—the ability to predict where a menu choice will be (About is always the last item on the Help menu). I think this goal strikes at the very core of your goals. Using your application should be fun, not a chore.

The spacing, font usage, and placement of controls and information on your screen will make or break your application. Font usage in screen design is critical. There are some fonts that are better to use than others. MS Sans Serif eight-point is Microsoft's font choice for all system-related items. There are other factors to take into consideration, too. An italicized font is much harder for the eye to see—the edges are more jagged than a regular font. It is best to use the default system font whenever possible.

It is possible for the user to change the default font, and so you should not make any assumptions that MS San Serif always will be the system font. Your application should try to adjust for new fonts whenever possible. Another factor to take into consideration is that the fonts are not be as readable on the screen as they are in printed form. This is especially true for low-resolution monitors. These are all things to consider when choosing your font.

7

The Unit of Measure

In its specifications, Microsoft uses dialog base units as the unit of measure. This system is used because it is a device-independent measurement system based on the size of the default system font. This compensates for the variations in screen size that different systems can have. There is a GetDialogBaseUnits() function call in the Win32 API that returns a 32-bit value that contains the dialog base units, based on the current system font. The low-order word of the return value contains the horizontal dialog box base unit, and the high-order word contains the vertical dialog box base unit.

> **NOTE**
>
> This presentation of base dialog units is to give you an understanding of where Microsoft is coming from. Delphi 3 uses device units (pixels) for spacing and alignment, not base dialog units. The pixel measurement is easier for programmers to understand and work with.

The horizontal base unit is equal to the average width, in pixels, of the characters ('a' through 'z' and 'A' through 'Z') in the current system font; the vertical base unit is equal to the height, in pixels, of the font. Each horizontal base unit is equal to four horizontal dialog units, and each vertical base unit is equal to eight vertical dialog units. Therefore, to convert dialog units to pixels, your application would use the following formulas:

```
PixelsInX = (DialogUnitsX x BaseUnitsX) / 4

PixelsInY = (DialogUnitsY x BaseUnitsY) / 8
```

And to convert from pixels to dialog units, your application would use the following formulas:

```
DialogUnitsX = (PixelsInX x 4) / BaseUnitsX

DialogUnitsY = (PixelsInY x 8) / BaseUnitsY
```

The multiplication is performed before the division to avoid rounding problems if base units are not divisible by four or eight. The PixelsInX and PixelsInY let you know what the multiplier is for spacing, and so on. There are some general recommendations for the size of different items. For example, edit boxes, labels, spin boxes, and buttons should be 14 dialog base units in height. This gives you just the right amount of space, both above and below the lettering.

Grouping and Spacing Elements

When developing your screens, it is important to provide the proper spacing for the elements on them. It is also important to maintain a constant margin (seven dialog base units) around the entire window. There should be at least four dialog base units between controls. The exception to this rule is when you are trying to group sets of toolbar buttons together. In this case, related buttons should be directly adjacent to one another with no space between them.

You always should group related elements together. The group box control is a good way to accomplish this, although just plain spacing works, too. Group boxes help the user focus on a particular set of elements. It is not recommended to group controls using color (such as a colored shape behind the controls). This method is distracting, and if the user changes the color scheme, it really could get ugly. Figure 7.26 shows a typical grouping.

Figure 7.26.

Grouping controls for focus.

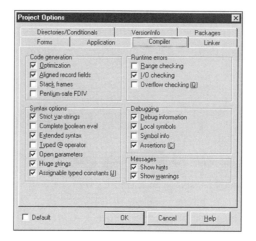

Alignment of Elements

You can use several ways to position data on your screen. People in western countries usually read from left to right, and top to bottom. The most important piece of data is usually in the top-left corner. When the data (or elements) are positioned vertically, the left edges should be aligned. If you attach labels to these controls, the labels should be placed above or to the left of the controls, and should be left aligned as well. This applies to controls such as edit, list box, and combo box. The exceptions to this are the radio box and check box controls. Those controls usually are left aligned, with the label to the right of the control itself.

Using the alignment palette provides an easy way to align controls in Delphi 3. By selecting the controls you wish to align and then choosing the Alignment option from the Alignment Palette, you can quickly move the controls into position. Choosing Edit | Lock Controls in the IDE also keeps the controls from moving once you have them aligned properly.

When you place a command button on a window and the command button is in a group box, it is implied that the button affects only the information within that group. If the command button appears outside any group boxes, the implication is that it affects the entire window. Examples of both types of buttons are shown in Figure 7.27.

Figure 7.27.
Command buttons
(local and global).

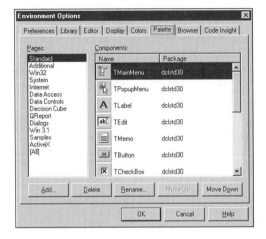

Use of Tabbed Dialog Boxes

Tabbed dialog boxes are an extremely useful aid in keeping your interface clean and simple. When creating tabbed dialogs, you should keep the tabs themselves all the same size (if possible) to give a uniform appearance. Tabs can be arranged on a functional basis, where each tab contains information about a specific topic. A good example of a tabbed dialog box is under Tools | Options in Delphi. Look at how organized the information is on those tabbed dialog boxes. This method in Windows 95 of using tabs helps your interfaces stay neater, and it is easier for the user to use.

Capitalization

When you display text on buttons, labels, tabs, or menus, use headline-style capitalization. This means that you capitalize the first letter of every word, except when the word is a preposition or article that does not appear at the beginning or end of the title. Another exception to the capitalization rule is when the word's conventional usage is not capitalized.

A few examples from Windows and Delphi 3 follow. You can see that capitalization can help add flair to a menu or control.

Save As
Insert Object
Always on Top

Add to Project
Syntax Check
Database Form Expert

Modal Dialog Boxes

A modal dialog box is a window that pops up to provide or request information. Modal dialog boxes can display supplemental information related to information found on a primary window. A modal dialog box is not, however, your application's primary window. It lacks several items found on a primary window. The following list outlines some of these features:

☐ It does not have minimize or maximize buttons.

☐ It can have a close button to dismiss the window (although it's not required).

☐ The title bar text describes what the window does.

☐ The title bar does not have an icon on it.

☐ It does not include a status bar.

☐ It can have a "What's This?" button to give the user help on the components on the window.

When displaying modal dialog boxes, the recommendation is that they not be larger than 263×263 dialog base units. If a secondary window is a property sheet, the three recommended sizes are 218×227, 215×212, and 212×188 dialog base units. These sizes have been determined to give ample viewing area without becoming too big for the screen (especially at lower resolutions).

Window Behavior

Your dialog boxes have to learn how to act in this multi-windowed environment. They appear under two circumstances. The first is that a dialog box is created as a response to a command chosen in a primary window. An example is a Find dialog that comes up in Microsoft Word 97. In this circumstance, when you shut the primary window, you would want all the dialog boxes associated with it to close as well. When the primary window is restored, the dialog boxes return to their positions and "Z order."

New Term   *Z order* is the layered relationship for a set of objects such as windows. The Z order in Windows is the order in which windows are drawn on the screen. The window at the top of the Z order is also the window that will appear on top of all other windows on your screen.

7

The second example of a dialog box is one that is generated from the system, or outside your application. An example of this is the Display Properties window for the Windows 95 display. In this instance, you want that Properties window to stay open when you minimize your application window. These behaviors are part of the Delphi environment. When you minimize your Delphi application, all the child (for MDI) and secondary windows are minimized as well.

Dialog boxes should not appear on the taskbar in Windows 95. Only the primary window should appear there (think of how crowded the taskbar would get if all application windows showed up there). The Delphi applications you generate also provide for this behavior. If you add a dialog box to your project and set the FormStyle attribute to the value sStayOnTop, you can minimize the primary window, the secondary window will minimize with it, and only the primary will show up on the taskbar. Windows that stay on top can be fairly annoying to the user, so use them sparingly.

If you provide for cascading windows in your application (where a secondary window opens another secondary window), keep two things in mind. First, limit the number to three windows (the primary, the secondary, and the sub-secondary). Do not take the levels any further than that because it gets really confusing for the user. Second, make sure when you open the secondary and sub-secondary windows, that you set them off below and to the right of the primary window. This gives the windows a natural cascading effect and lets the user know they are getting deeper into the windows layers.

You learned earlier about unfolding windows. This is where you have a secondary window, you press a button that has a >> next to the label, and the window expands to reveal additional information. This method is very useful for revealing information in stages. If the user is satisfied with the information on the smaller page, that's fine. If more in-depth information is needed, they can expand the window.

You also can open secondary windows in two modes: modeless and modal. If you open the windows in modeless mode, the user still is able to access the other windows in your (and other) applications without dismissing the window first. If you open a secondary window in modal mode, the user must dismiss that window first before gaining access to the windows in your application. This is one of those cases in which you are forcing the user to do something (such as enter a password to continue), and you know how people hate being told what to do. Use the modal dialogs and windows sparingly; they tend to slow productivity.

Summary

Today you explored some of the concepts involved in developing a graphical user interface. You looked at some of the different ways in which you can put users in control (or at least make them feel that way). You also learned some design techniques to help keep your screens uncluttered and easy to read. Although today barely scratched the surface of this topic (the entire topic would be a book of more than a 1,000 pages), I hope you have been able to glean an idea of what designing a good GUI interface takes. It makes me appreciate applications such as Delphi 3 a lot more, now that I see what GUI designers have to contend with. Good luck on your GUI design project!

Q&A

Q I'm getting ready to write an application, and I think it might be a candidate for an MDI application. How would I know?

A That's a good question. As discussed earlier in this chapter, Microsoft is discouraging you from creating MDI applications because most people are not very good at writing them. If you think you should use one, remember that all the children have to be identical. No mixing of document types (documents, spreadsheets, and so on) as children is allowed. You also must give up controlling the windows and let the user do that. You have to give up a lot for MDI.

Q This chapter is good, but I feel like I need to know more. Where can I get additional information?

A There are several sources. The Microsoft Developer Network CD-ROM has a wealth of information about the Win95 logo requirements and GUI design. Another great book is *The Windows Interface Guidelines for Software Design* (from Microsoft Press).

Workshop

The Workshop provides two ways for you to affirm what you've learned in this chapter. The Quiz section poses questions to help you solidify your understanding of the material covered. You can find answers to the quiz questions in Appendix A, "Answers to the Quiz Questions." The Exercises section provides you with experience in using what you have learned. Please try to work through all these before continuing to the next day.

Quiz

1. What is the primary purpose of the right mouse button in Windows 95?
2. Why does Microsoft recommend that you use one of the couple of secondary window sizes, specifically?
3. Why is it important to have the standard menu layout in your application?

Exercises

1. Go through the color palette in Delphi 3 and see if you can find out what all the system colors are used for. If you need help, try to place several types of controls onto a form and notice the default color given to each item.

2. Look at some of the mainstream Windows 95 applications and see how they use pop-up menus to present choices to the user.

3. Examine some of the applications you use every day. How do they measure up to standards you learned about in this chapter?

WEEK 2

8

9

10

11

12

13

14

At A Glance

Putting Delphi To Work

To kick off Week 2, Day 8 walks you through the tools available in the Delphi Visual Component Library (VCL). Day 9 focuses on input/output and printing in Delphi (this is printing without the QuickReport tool). On Day 10, you have some fun and play with graphics. You learn about pens, brushes, drawing, painting, and so on, as well as learn how to save and load graphics. You also touch on DirectX and OpenGL programming, as you explore the fun side of Window 95, by looking at the multimedia and animation support in Delphi 3.

Day 11 focuses on Borland's new database architecture and how it affects you. Day 12 presents the QuickReport and TeeChart components, which enable you to create great output from your Delphi application. Day 13 explains how to create your own VCL and ActiveX components. You finish out the week on Day 14 where you learn how to build Internet applications using Delphi.

After you finish Week 2, you can work through Bonus Day 15. It's an additional chapter that discusses deploying your Delphi applications.

Day **8**

The Visual Component Library

The wonderful thing about Delphi is its rich library of prebuilt components. Up to this point, you have learned some basics with the Delphi IDE as well as programming basics including OOP. You have used some examples from the Visual Component Library (VCL) but really have only scratched the surface. Today, you take a complete tour of the VCL. You learn what is available as you go through every tab on the VCL palette, and take a look at properties and event handlers. You'll put some of these components to use as you build demo programs. Some components such as Internet, Database, Decision Cube, ActiveX, and QReport are mentioned, but they are covered in more detail in other chapters.

By the end of today's lesson, you will have a good idea of what components are available and will have put several of the them to use. So without any further delay, grab your library card, fire up Delphi, and let's get to it!

What Is the VCL?

NEW TERM The *VCL* is made up of prebuilt objects known as components. Simply put, these components are to Delphi what the OCXs and ActiveX controls are to Visual Basic. Unlike OCXs, however, the components in the VCL are written in Delphi's Object Pascal and stored in a single library, not individual files. Any of them that you use become part of your executable. These components save you many hours, if not weeks or months, of coding and testing by providing you with the ability to visually design your application. By selecting components, dropping them on a form, and setting some properties, you actually can create some applications with little or no code.

The VCL is made up of components that provide commonly used features found in most Windows applications. Because of all the components provided in Delphi, you can focus on creating your application rather than reinventing the wheel in creating your GUI, database functions, and program-to-program communication (OLE and DDE). With the power built into Delphi's Object Pascal, you easily can design in record time just about any type of Windows application you can dream up. Your code essentially "glues" the components together. It's like building a pre-fabricated home versus building one from scratch. Building a home from scratch requires many of pieces wood, nails, materials, and so on, as well as a lot of preparation of the wood. By contrast, the pre-fabricated home comes with walls and other major components of the home already cut and assembled. The builder just connects the pieces, and the home takes much less time to build. It still has all the basic components, but the builder doesn't have as much to worry about.

You can create your own visual components in Delphi and add them to the VCL palette for later use. As you go through the various components in the VCL, they are referred to by the name that shows up when you position the mouse pointer over the component (for example, Button). The components' names actually start with a T (for example, TButton) which is the name you see in the Object Inspector as well as the online help. So from this point on, if you see Form, think of TForm; if you see Edit, think of TEdit; likewise, if you see TEdit, you can think of Edit.

What actually happens when you drop a component onto a form? Delphi automatically generates code necessary to use the component and updates the project appropriately. You then only need to set properties, put code in event handlers, and use methods as necessary to get things working.

Component Properties

You have these nice components, but you need a way to tell them how to appear and behave. Delphi components have properties. These properties enable you to change many things about a component's size, shape, visibility, position, and more. To access these properties, use the Object Inspector, as shown in Figure 8.1. The Object Inspector has two tabs: the Properties tab and the Events tab. For now, let's focus on the Properties tab.

Figure 8.1.

The Object Inspector Properties tab.

Many properties are common among components, but not all properties are found in all components. Also, some properties are specific to a component or group of components. It's impossible to cover every property of every component in this book, so it presents only some of the more common properties, as well as the types of properties and how to use them.

First let's look at properties for a component you have used already: the button. In Delphi, open a new project. Select the Standard tab on the Component Palette. Select the button by clicking it, as shown in Figure 8.2, and then click on the form. This adds a new button component to your form. The Object Inspector with the Properties tab selected is shown in Figure 8.3.

Figure 8.2.

The Standard tab Component Palette with the button component selected.

As you can see, there are several properties you can set for the button component. Some properties have number values for their settings, such as the Height property. Some properties have a combo box that enables you to select from a list of pre-defined settings (constants defined in Delphi), such as the Cursor property. Still other properties give you a true/false selection, such as the Default property. Some properties take plain old text as their setting, such as the Caption property. Finally, some properties have pop-up menus and editors that you use to make changes.

Figure 8.3.

The Properties tab for the button component in the Object Inspector.

There is another type of property you need to be aware of: the *nested property*. A nested property always is preceded with a +, as in the +Font property. Basically, a nested property is a property of a property. When you double-click on a property with nested properties, it expands, showing you the nested properties. The + changes to a –. Nested properties can go down several levels. The + and – are used the same way for each level. To collapse a nested property list, double-click the –. The list is collapsed, and the – changes back to a +. Take a look at the following list of properties for the button component. All the nested properties have been expanded.

```
Cancel
Caption
Cursor
Default
DragCursor
DragMode
Enabled
+Font
   Color
   Height
   Name
   Pitch
   Size
   +Style
      fsBold
      fsItalic
      fsUnderline
      fsStrikeOut
Height
HelpContex
Hint
```

8

```
Left
ModalResult
Name
ParentFont
ParentShowHint
PopupMenu
ShowHint
TabOrder
TabStop
Tag
Top
Visible
Width
```

By changing these properties, you can control the appearance, size, behavior, color, font, and more. One of the most commonly used properties for components such as the button is the Caption property. If you are creating an OK button, you change the button's Caption property to OK. Then your button displays OK. Likewise, you might want to have your button's Name property something like MyOKButton to make the code in the unit file more readable.

NOTE

As mentioned earlier, there are far too many properties to cover in this book. As you go through this chapter and the rest of the book, you will be introduced to many of them. When you need information about a particular property, all you need to do is click on it and press F1. Delphi's online help explains each property in detail. A good study assignment for you is to spend a little time each day going through some of the properties for components and reading the online help for each of them. Don't forget that forms have properties, too.

Another thing you should know is that some properties are dependent on the settings of other properties. An example of this is the Hint property. You set Hint to a text message you want displayed when the mouse cursor is over the control for a short period of time. This won't work unless you either have set the ShowHint property on the control to True, or set the parent form or container's (for example, a GroupBox) ShowHint property to True. This is because the control's ParentShowHint property is set to True by default, which passes down the default setting of False to the child controls. Another example is the ParentFont property. If ParentFont is set to True, the component gets its font information from the parent form or container. You can see that there are many, but rest assured that the defaults for most of these properties are fine for most projects. As you work with Delphi, these become second nature.

The names are fairly descriptive, so you should be able to figure out a lot of them just by looking at the names. When all else fails, help is just an F1 key away.

Events

Delphi components have a number of events or event handlers associated with them. As you know, any code you store in these event handlers is executed when a specific event occurs (for example, mouse move, mouse click, and so on). Take a look at the Object Inspector Events tab for the button component, as shown in Figure 8.4.

Figure 8.4.

The Object Inspector Events tab.

To create an event handler, simply double-click the event you want to create, and you are placed inside the handler and are ready to enter your code. If you decide not to use the event handler, Delphi deletes it for you the next time you compile, assuming you have no code stored in it. As in the Properties tab, you can click an event you need help with and press F1 for a description. Also notice that when you click the box to the right of an event in the Object Inspector, you get a combo box. When you click the combo box's down arrow, you get a list of currently defined and available events. This enables several controls and events to share the same event handler, which enables you to save typing and eliminate code duplication in your projects.

Methods

There are several types of methods, but what you are interested in here are the methods associated with the various components and how they affect them. Methods give you a another way to control components. Because components are objects, they can have functions and procedures declared in them. That is what a method is: a public function or procedure declared inside an object that you can call. Take the example of your button component. If you wanted to make it invisible, you could execute a line of code such as Button1.Hide, and the button would become invisible.

8

To find out about the methods available for a particular component or object, click the component or object and press F1. In Delphi's online help, click on methods, and you will be presented with a list of methods available. You then can click on the method for which you need information and view its help. The following list contains methods available for the button component:

```
BeginDrag
BringToFront
CanFocus
ClientToScreen
Create
Destroy
Dragging
EndDrag
Focused
Free
GetTextBuf
GetTextLen
Hide
Refresh
Repaint
ScaleBy
ScreenToClient
ScrollBy
SendToBack
SetBounds
SetFocus
SetTextBuf
Show
Update
```

As with properties, the names are fairly descriptive and usually give you an idea of what they do. Unlike properties, methods are not accessible in the Object Inspector. To find out about methods, you must use the online help. If you click the component for which you need help and press F1, you find the help screen for that component. Click on methods, and you are given the list of methods available. Of course, clicking any of the methods listed gives a description of what it does and how to use it.

This is another area where it would be good for you to make a practice of regularly looking through the help to learn about the available methods and what they do. You don't need to memorize all this, but once you know what is available to you, it will take much less effort to create applications that do what you want. You don't want to reinvent the wheel or to do without because you didn't know a method existed that did just what you want.

Visual and Nonvisual Components

You will find two types of components in Delphi: visual and nonvisual. The visual components are those you use to build your user interface. Both types of components appear at design time, but nonvisual components are not visible at runtime. `Button`, `Edit`, and `Memo` are examples of visual components.

Nonvisual components are used for a variety of different tasks. `Timer`, `OpenDialog`, and `MainMenu` are examples of nonvisual components. You use `Timer` to activate specific code at scheduled intervals, and it is never seen by the user. `OpenDialog` and `MainMenu` are nonvisual components that ultimately produce visible and usable results on the screen, but the components themselves are not visible to the user. Nonvisual components are easy to spot because they can't be resized and look just like the button that you use to select them when you drop them on a form. Visible or not, all the components are very useful and save you much time and effort.

The Library

The library is broken into 13 logically grouped tabs. Included in these, there is a Samples tab as well as an ActiveX tab. These extra tabs have sample controls and components in them for you to experiment with. Please note that this complete list of tabs and components is for the Client/Server Edition of Delphi 3; some components are not available on other versions:

- ☐ Standard
- ☐ Additional
- ☐ Win32
- ☐ System
- ☐ Internet
- ☐ Data Access
- ☐ Data Controls
- ☐ Decision Cube
- ☐ QReport
- ☐ Dialogs
- ☐ Win 3.1
- ☐ Samples
- ☐ ActiveX

8

Features are accessible by selecting the appropriate tab. Although you don't learn the details of and use every component and its properties in this book, you will see all the components and learn about some of their properties as you go. You'll build demo forms for some of the tabs covered. Delphi's online help is a great help to you in determining what a particular component is used for. You can move the cursor over a component and look at the hint. If you need more information about a component, simply click on it and press F1. The Help screens give you information about what a component is for and how to use it. You are never more than just a few clicks and a key press away from the help you need with the library.

Now let's take a look at each of these tabs and build an application using some of these components. This application is not going to do anything useful; it's only purpose is to demonstrate the use of components. You no doubt will get some ideas for using them in other projects as you put this demo application together.

Open a new project and save UNIT1.PAS as STANDARD.PAS. Save the project as VCLDEMO.DPR. Now you are ready to go through the Standard tab and start building the VCLDEMO application.

The Standard Tab

In the Standard tab, you find the most commonly used components. This tab is the default when you start Delphi, and it contains 14 components, as listed in Table 8.1. Let's take a quick look at them, and then you'll build the first form of the demo application using some of them. Note that depending on your screen-resolution settings, Delphi will put arrows at each end of the VCL tabs if there are more components that will fit on one screen You might need to use the arrows to scroll through the available components and tabs, as shown in Figure 8.5.

Figure 8.5.

The VCL palette's Standard tab.

Click this arrow to see more components

Table 8.1. The components available on the Standard tab.

Component	Description
	The MainMenu component enables you to design and create your form's menu bar and drop-down menus. This is a nonvisual component.
	The PopupMenu component enables you to design and create pop-up menus that appear when the user clicks the right mouse button. This is a nonvisual component.
	The Label component enables you to place text in forms and other containers that cannot be changed by the user. This is a visual component.
	The Edit component is used to input single lines of text from the user. The Edit component can also be used to display text. This is a visual component.
	The Memo component enables you to input and/or display multiple lines of text. This is a visual component.
	The Button component enables you to create buttons that the user will use to select options in an application. This is a visual component.
	The Checkbox component is used to enable the user to select or deselect options by clicking on the check box. This is a visual component.
	The RadioButton component enables you to offer a set of options in which only one option in the set can be selected. A set is any number of RadioButtons in a container such as a form, panel, and so on. This is a visual component.
	The ListBox component is the standard Windows list box that enables you to create a list of items that the user can select from. This is a visual component.
	The ComboBox is a component that is like the ListBox component but adds the benefits of an Edit component. The ComboBox component gives the user the option of either selecting from a list or entering the text into the box. This is a visual component.
	The ScrollBar component is the standard Windows scrollbar used to scroll forms or controls. This is a visual component.
	The GroupBox component is a container used to group related controls and containers, such as the RadioButton, CheckBox, and so on. This is a visual component.

8

Component	Description
![]	The RadioGroup component is a combination of a GroupBox and RadioButtons and is designed specifically for creating groups of radio buttons. Multiple radio buttons can be set up, but no other controls are allowed here. This is a visual component.
![]	The Panel component is another container to group controls or containers. Panels also can be used to build status bars, toolbars, and tool palettes. This is a visual component.

Now you're ready to start work on the demo application and put the VCL to work. In your VCLDEMO.DPR project that you created earlier, change the form caption to read The Standard tab. You are going to create a very busy form using at least one of every component on the Standard tab. Look at Figure 8.6 and refer back to it as you add components to the form to make sure that you place the components in the correct location and get the proportions close to the example.

Figure 8.6.

The Standard Tab form for VCLDEMO.

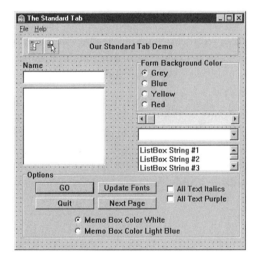

Start by changing the Name property to read Standard tab. Next, add a Panel component to the top of the screen. Stretch it out like a banner. You'll use this to label your form with a title. Set the Caption property for the Panel component to read Our Standard tab Demo. The Panel is very useful for creating labels with a 3D look, but it also works great as a container for other controls. Next, add a label to the screen, and change its caption to Name. The label component has a property called AutoSize, which is set to True by default. AutoSize causes the label to increase or decrease in size as you change the caption, font size, and so on. If the label's background color is the same as the form (which is the default), you may lose track of your label if it shrinks down to no characters and is not selected. If this happens, you can easily find it by going to the Object Inspector and using the combo box to pull down a list of components and selecting it from the list, as shown in Figure 8.7. You then can type the text you want into the Caption property.

Figure 8.7.

Object Inspector's
Name combo box.

Now add an Edit component under the label. Use the Object Inspector to delete all the characters from the Edit component's Text property. Add a MainMenu and PopupMenu component to the form. Remember, these are nonvisual components, so it really doesn't matter where you place them. You probably will find it easy just to move them into a corner out of the way so they are not distracting you as you add other components. Next, add a Memo component.

Take a minute and look at some of the properties available for the Memo component (for example, ScrollBars, WordWrap, WantReturn). Use Delphi's online help to view the descriptions of some of these properties. The Memo component is a pretty powerful component that enables you to design your own text editor. You won't use many of the properties that Memo has available in this example, but you should know they exist. In the Object Inspector, double-click the Lines property, and delete the text, Memo1. Press Enter four times. This adds space to the Memo component's text buffer (you need at least three or four lines available to modify for this demo, and this creates them). If you don't do this, the demo will not work. Now add RadioGroup, ScrollBar, ComboBox, and ListBox to the form. Make sure all the components you have dropped onto the form look like those shown earlier in Figure 8.6.

Double-click the RadioGroup component that you placed on the form, and add the following code to its OnClick event:

```
procedure TStandardTab.RadioGroup1Click(Sender: TObject);
begin
     If RadioGroup1.ItemIndex=0 Then StandardTab.Color:=clSilver;
     If RadioGroup1.ItemIndex=1 Then StandardTab.Color:=clBlue;
     If RadioGroup1.ItemIndex=2 Then StandardTab.Color:=clYellow;
     If RadioGroup1.ItemIndex=3 Then StandardTab.Color:=clRed;
end;
```

Double-click the ScrollBar component, and add the following code to the ScrollBar component's OnChange event:

```
procedure TStandardTab.ScrollBar1Change(Sender: TObject);
begin
    RadioGroup1.ItemIndex := ScrollBar1.Position;
end;
```

Drop a GroupBox onto the form and make sure it has room for some components on it. Add four buttons, two radio buttons, and two check boxes to the GroupBox. Change the Caption property on each of the buttons: Go for Button1, Update Fonts for Button2, Quit for Button3, and Next Page for Button4. These are all the components you'll use on this form. Adjust the component locations and sizes until your form looks as close to Figure 8.6 as possible.

Now you're ready to add some code to these buttons. Here is the code for Button1's OnClick event:

```
procedure TStandardTab.Button1Click(Sender: TObject);
Var
   x : Integer;
begin
{Clear the current contents of the TMemo}
    Memo1.Clear;
    {Copy the text typed in the Name Box (Edit1) to the Memo}
    Memo1.Lines.Add(Edit1.Text);
    {Copy the text from the text box in the Combobox tp the Memo}
    Memo1.Lines.Add(ComboBox1.Text);
    {Copy the selected text from the list box to the memo}
    Memo1.Lines.Add('ListBox String
        #'+IntToStr(ListBox1.ItemIndex+1));
    If RadioButton1.Checked then Memo1.Color:=clWhite;
    If RadioButton2.Checked then Memo1.Color:=ClAqua;
end;
```

Add code for Button2's OnClick event:

```
procedure TStandardTab.Button2Click(Sender: TObject);
begin
    If CheckBox1.State = cbChecked then
       StandardTab.Font.Style:=[fsItalic]
    else StandardTab.Font.Style:=[];
    If CheckBox2.State = cbChecked then
       StandardTab.Font.Color:=clPurple
    else StandardTab.Font.Color:=clBlack;
end;
```

And here's the code for Button3's OnClick event:

```
procedure TStandardTab.Button3Click(Sender: TObject);
begin
    Close;
end;
```

Don't add the code for Button4 just yet. It is used to hide this form and display the next, and you'll add it later—after you create a second form for the Additional tab.

NOTE

Remember that when you double-click a component, it creates the procedure declaration with the begin and end keywords. You simply need to fill in the code from the examples given. Also, remember that you will not see code for all of the controls. Delphi cleans up empty event handlers that get created when you double-click on a component each time it compiles. In fact, it is best to let Delphi clean up unused event handlers because you can cause problems if you delete them yourself.

Finally, add code for the MainMenu and PopupMenu components. Look at the MainMenu component. At first, this component and the way it is used may seem a bit strange, especially if you come from a Visual Basic background. You may be wondering where the Menu Designer is. One way it is activated is via the Items property in the Object Inspector for the MainMenu component, which is shown in Figure 8.8.

Figure 8.8.

Object Inspector for the MainMenu *component.*

If you double-click the property value for the Items property where it says (Menu), you are presented with the Menu Designer, which is shown in Figure 8.9. You can also right-click the MainMenu component on your form to use the speed menu.

As you can see in Figure 8.10, the Object Inspector changes to accommodate the Menu Designer.

Figure 8.9.

The Menu Designer.

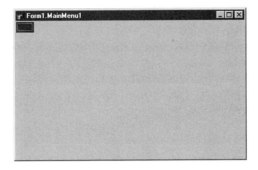

Figure 8.10.

Object Inspector for the Main Menu Designer.

Here you simply change the caption to the menu selection you plan to add. Change this to &File. The & tells Delphi to underline the following character and set up the hot key sequence for the menu selection. In this example, pressing Alt+F brings up the File menu when the program is running. After you have added the File menu option, notice that a box appears to the right of it. This enables you to click on it and add another menu option by changing the Object Inspector Caption property as before. You also can click on existing menu options to add the submenu options. Click on File, and a box appears below it. Click on the box to highlight it, and the Object Inspector is ready to change its caption. Add an Exit option to the File menu. Change the Caption property in the Object Inspector to E&xit, and you should see Exit added below the File menu option.

Notice the blank boxes below and to the right of the menu options in the menu box as you add them. You click on these as you want to add options. If you don't click on them, they will not appear on your menu.

Next, you'll add a Help menu with a Help option, a separator line, and an About option. To add the Help menu and the Help option, type **&Help** into the caption properties as you did with the File and Exit menu options. To create the separator line, simply add a hyphen (-) to the caption property of the submenu—in this case just below the Help option under the Help menu. As soon as you do this, you will see the separator. Next, to add the About option, type *&About* below the separator line, as shown in Figure 8.11.

Figure 8.11.

Menu Designer with menu options.

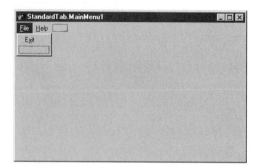

When you are done designing the menu, double-click on the control box for the Menu Designer screen. The Menu Designer closes, and you see your menu options on your form. You then can go through them as you would in a regular menu by clicking on an option, holding the mouse button down, and dragging through the options. To add code to any of the options, just select the menu option as if the program were running, and you are put into the proper event handler code section. For example, you could choose File | Exit on your Exit option, and then add code to close the application when the user selects Exit. Instead, use the existing event handler you already have created from the Object Inspector, and select Exit1 (your File | Exit Menu option) using the combo box. Next, select the Events tab in the Object Inspector, and click the down arrow on the combo box for the OnClick event to show the available options. Select Button3Click. In this case, you have saved only one line of code, but in a large event handler, you could save quite a bit.

This simply closes the application. You don't need to add code to the other options; this was just an example of how to create a menu. Later in your exercises, you get a chance to come back and fill in the code for the Help and About menu options under the Help menu.

NOTE

If you did not leave much room at the top of your form, the menu might cover up some of your components and scroll bars might be present. This isn't desirable for this example, so you need to resize the form so that everything fits. Make the form longer and move the components down a bit to make room for the menu if necessary.

Add the pop-up menu and you'll be done with the form. Click the PopupMenu component that you placed on the form earlier. Right-click the component to bring up the speed menu, and select Menu Designer. This Menu Designer works like the MainMenu component's menu designer with the exception that all the menu options run vertically down a single box. To add code to the menu options in the pop-up menu, you must select the menu option in the Menu Designer. You are then put into the event handler code. Add two options: Go and Update Fonts. When you are finished, exit the Menu Designer. Use existing methods for these just as you did with the File | Exit menu option. From the Object Inspector, select Go and then select Button1Click for the OnClick event. Next, use the Object Inspector to select UpdateFonts1, and select Button2Click for the OnClick event. This saves some more code and gets the pop-up menu working.

If everything went well, you should be done with this part of the VCLDEMO application. Make sure to save your work. Take a look at Listing 8.1, which contains the complete code you should have for this form unit.

TYPE **Listing 8.1. VCLDEMO Standard tab form.**

```
unit Standard;

interface

uses
  Windows, Messages, SysUtils, Classes, Graphics, Controls, Forms,
  Dialogs, Menus, StdCtrls, ExtCtrls,Addition;

type
  TStandardTab = class(TForm)
    MainMenu1: TMainMenu;
    PopupMenu1: TPopupMenu;
    Panel1: TPanel;
    Label1: TLabel;
    Edit1: TEdit;
    RadioGroup1: TRadioGroup;
    GroupBox1: TGroupBox;
    Button3: TButton;
    Button2: TButton;
    CheckBox1: TCheckBox;
    CheckBox2: TCheckBox;
    ScrollBar1: TScrollBar;
    Memo1: TMemo;
    ComboBox1: TComboBox;
    ListBox1: TListBox;
    Button1: TButton;
    Button4: TButton;
    RadioButton1: TRadioButton;
    RadioButton2: TRadioButton;
    File1: TMenuItem;
    Exit1: TMenuItem;
```

continues

Listing 8.1. continued

```
Help1: TMenuItem;
  Help2: TMenuItem;
  N1: TMenuItem;
  About1: TMenuItem;
  Go: TMenuItem;
  UpdateFonts1: TMenuItem;
  procedure RadioGroup1Click(Sender: TObject);
  procedure ScrollBar1Change(Sender: TObject);
  procedure Button3Click(Sender: TObject);
  procedure Button2Click(Sender: TObject);
  procedure Button1Click(Sender: TObject);
  procedure GoClick(Sender: TObject);
  procedure UpdateFonts1Click(Sender: TObject);
  procedure Button4Click(Sender: TObject);
private
  { Private declarations }
public
  { Public declarations }
end;

var
  StandardTab: TStandardTab;

implementation

{$R *.DFM}

procedure TStandardTab.RadioGroup1Click(Sender: TObject);
begin
    If RadioGroup1.ItemIndex=0 Then StandardTab.Color:=clSilver;
    If RadioGroup1.ItemIndex=1 Then StandardTab.Color:=clBlue;
    If RadioGroup1.ItemIndex=2 Then StandardTab.Color:=clYellow;
    If RadioGroup1.ItemIndex=3 Then StandardTab.Color:=clRed;
end;

procedure TStandardTab.ScrollBar1Change(Sender: TObject);
begin
    RadioGroup1.ItemIndex := ScrollBar1.Position;
end;

procedure TStandardTab.Button3Click(Sender: TObject);
begin
    Close;
end;

procedure TStandardTab.Button2Click(Sender: TObject);
begin
    If CheckBox1.State = cbChecked then
        StandardTab.Font.Style:=[fsItalic]
    else StandardTab.Font.Style:=[];
    If CheckBox2.State = cbChecked then
        StandardTab.Font.Color:=clPurple
    else StandardTab.Font.Color:=clBlack;
end;
```

8

```
procedure TStandardTab.Button1Click(Sender: TObject);
Var
    x : Integer;
begin
    {Clear the current contents of the TMemo}
    Memo1.Clear;
    {Copy the text typed in the Name Box (Edit1) to the Memo}
    Memo1.Lines.Add(Edit1.Text);
    {Copy the text from the text box in the Combobox tp the Memo}
    Memo1.Lines.Add(ComboBox1.Text);
    {Copy the selected text from the list box to the memo}
    Memo1.Lines.Add('ListBox String#'+IntToStr(ListBox1.ItemIndex+1));
    If RadioButton1.Checked then Memo1.Color:=clWhite;
    If RadioButton2.Checked then Memo1.Color:=ClAqua;
end;

procedure TStandardTab.GoClick(Sender: TObject);
begin
    Button1Click(StandardTab);
end;

procedure TStandardTab.UpdateFonts1Click(Sender: TObject);
begin
    Button2Click(StandardTab);
end;

procedure TStandardTab.Button4Click(Sender: TObject);
begin
    StandardTab.Hide;
    AdditionalTab.Show;
end;
end.
```

ANALYSIS If you have not done so already, save your project and test it out. When you run the project, the form should come up looking like Figure 8.12. The only menu option that does anything is File | Exit. When you make changes to the Edit, Listbox, or ComboBox components and click the Go button, updates are shown in the Memo component. When you click Go, the background color is also updated to the color selected by the radio buttons at the bottom of the form. You can change the color of the form background by using the scrollbar or selecting the color you wish from the radio buttons in the RadioGroup. Form font colors can be changed to purple and the font to *italic* by checking the check boxes and clicking the Update Fonts button. Finally, you can select Go or Update Fonts from the pop-up menu by right-clicking anywhere on the form.

You have just covered all the components on the Standard tab and tested your application to see how they all work. You should notice that you really didn't write much code or need to change many properties to get it all working. This demonstrates the power available to you in the Delphi VCL.

Figure 8.12.
*The VCLDEMO
Standard tab form.*

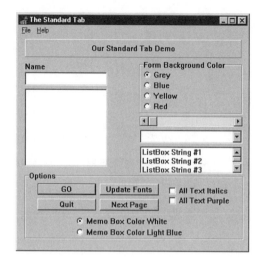

The Additional Tab

The Additional tab contains a group of 13 components, as shown in Figure 8.13. You're likely to use these components often. You'll put some of them to work when you create a second form for the VCLDEMO project. Table 8.2 briefly describes each component.

Figure 8.13.
The Additional tab.

Table 8.2. The components available on the Additional tab.

Component	Description
	The BitBtn component is used to create a button with a bitmap graphic on it (an OK button with a checkmark, for example). This is a visual component.
	The SpeedButton is a specialized button designed to work with the Panel component. The SpeedButton is used to create toolbars and specialized sets of buttons, including buttons that stay pressed. This is a visual component.
	The MaskEdit component is used to format data correctly by requiring proper character input. This is a visual component.
	The StringGrid component is used to display string data in rows and columns. This is a visual component.

8

Component	Description
	The DrawGrid component is used to display information other than text in rows and columns. This is a visual component.
	The Image component is used to display graphics such as icons, bitmaps, and metafiles. This is a visual component.
	The Shape component is used to draw shapes such as squares, circles, and so on. This is a visual component.
	The Bevel component is used to draw a rectangle that can appear inset or raised. This is a visual component.
	The ScrollBox component is used to create a display area that is scrollable. This is a visual component.
	The CheckListBox component combines the features of a ListBox and a CheckBox into one component. This is a visual component.
	The Splitter component is used to create user-sizable panes in applications. This is a visual component.
	The StaticText component is similar to the Label component but provides additional features such as configurable border styles. This is a visual component.
	The Chart component part of the TChart family is used to create charts and graphs. This is a visual component.

Now you're ready to use these components to build the second page of your VCLDEMO application and learn how to tap into their power. First, add a new form to the VCLDEMO project. Change the form's Name property to additionaltab. Change the caption to The Additional tab. Choose File | Save As, and save the new form as ADDITION.PAS. As you add components to the form, refer to Figure 8.14 for approximate size and location.

Next, you need to make this form come up centered on the screen by setting the Position property. By default, this property is set to poDesigned, which means it shows up in the position at which it was designed. Click on poDesigned and you get a combo box. Select poScreenCenter. This setting takes effect when the form is activated.

You also need to add Addition to the original (Standard) form's uses clause. Before you move on, you need to go back to the StandardTab form, and add code that enables you to access your new page when you test the program. Choose View | Forms to bring up the Forms menu, and select StandardTab. Double-click on Button4 (Next Page), and set its Click event code to be as follows:

```
procedure TStandardPage.Button4Click(Sender: TObject);
begin
    StandardPage.Hide;
    AdditionalPage.Show;
end;
```

Next, you'll add components to the form. Refer to Figure 8.14 for the components' approximate size and location.

Figure 8.14.

The Additional Tab form for VCLDEMO.

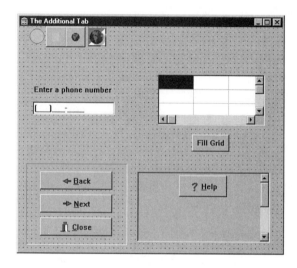

First up is the BitBtn component. Drop three of these in the lower-right corner of the form. For BitBtn1 and BitBtn2, set the Kind properties to bkCustom. Set the caption property for BitBtn1 to Back and for BitBtn2 to Next.

NEW TERM The BitBtn component enables you to set a graphic on the button called a *glyph*. Glyphs are simply small bitmaps that can contain multiple images which can be displayed depending on the state of a BitBtn or SpeedButton. You can use one of the predefined glyphs that come with Delphi, or you can create your own using the Image Editor found in the Tools menu. For our purposes, use the glyphs provided with Delphi. For BitBtn1, double-click on Tbitmap in the Glyph property. This brings up the Picture Editor, as shown in Figure 8.15. This editor does not actually allow you edit the picture, it simply lets you select the filename of the glyph you wish to load and view it before you add it to the button.

Click on the Load button, and you are presented with the a file selection dialog box. Change to the directory C:\Program Files\Borland\Delphib2.0\Images\Buttons (assuming that is where you have Delphi stored), and select ARROW1L.BMP. You should see a red arrow pointing to the left as well as a white arrow. The red arrow is displayed when the button is in the enabled state. The white arrow is displayed in the disabled state, which gives the grayed-out effect.

You can toggle the Enabled property for the button between True and False to see the difference. Make sure that the button's Enabled property is set to True when you are done.

Figure 8.15.
The Picture Editor.

Now repeat the steps you used for BitBtn1, and set the glyph for BitBtn2 to ARROW1R.BMP. Setting up BitBtn3 is going to be easier because of a predefined type that you use in the Kind property. For BitBtn3, click on Kind, and select bkClose. This sets the button's glyph to an open door and the Caption property to Close. For future reference, the Kind property has 10 predefined types and one type called bkCustom, which enables you to create your own type of button. Here are the names of the types:

```
bkAbout
bkAll
bkCancel
bkClose
bkCustom
bkHelp
bkIgnore
bkNo
bkOk
bkRetry
bkYes
```

The names are self-explanatory. These types are commonly used buttons in Windows applications. The bkCustom is, of course, used when you need to create a new button type as you already have done.

Give your buttons a nice grouped appearance by adding a Bevel component. Select the Bevel component on the Additional tab and draw it around the box. This gives you a box with an inset appearance around your buttons. Add some code to the buttons by double-clicking BitBtn1 and adding the following code to its Click event:

```
procedure TAdditionalTab.BitBtn1Click(Sender: TObject);
begin
   Standard.StandardTab.Show;
   AdditionalTab.Hide;
end;
```

You'll come back to BitBtn2 later. For BitBtn3, add this code now:

```
procedure TAdditionalTab.BitBtn3Click(Sender: TObject);
begin
  Standard.StandardTab.Close;
end;
```

To make the Close button work properly, add the following code to the form's Close event:

```
procedure TAdditionalTab.FormClose(Sender: TObject;
  var Action: TCloseAction);
begin
    Application.Terminate;
end;
```

If you do not add the code, the form will close when the Close button is selected, but the application will remain in memory wasting resources.

Next, create a toolbar. For this, you need to use a Panel component from the Standard tab as the container for your buttons. Add a Panel near the upper-left corner of the form, and make it large enough to hold two square buttons. Add two SpeedButtons to the panel from the Additional tab. The SpeedButton enables you to do things you can't do with other buttons. For example, you can create buttons that stay pushed in, you can group buttons together, and you even can create buttons that change the glyph depending on the state of the button. The states available for a SpeedButton are Up, Disabled, Down, and Stay Down. These states cause the proper part of a glyph to be displayed. To take advantage of these states, you can use the Image Editor to create a four-image glyph for use with your button.

NOTE

> Because the Image Editor is not installed automatically when you install Delphi, you must add it separately from the Delphi Tools | Configure Tools menu option (see Delphi's online help or manuals if you need help installing or using it).

The Image Editor, which is shown in Figure 8.16, is a simple draw program designed for creating resources, icons, bitmaps, and so on. If you have ever used any drawing program such as Windows Paint or Draw, you should have little trouble using the Image Editor. If you not ready to use Image Editor at this point, feel free to skip over it and come back to it l

Figure 8.16.

The Image Editor.

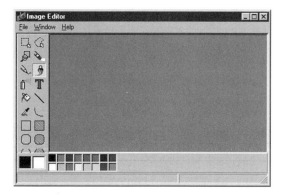

Basically, you want to create a bitmap that is 16×64 with 16 colors. The image will have four equally sized square boxes, each a different color. Going from left to right, you can color them green, gray, purple, or red. I decided on this example because even those of us with no artistic abilities can participate in it...okay, I admit it; I can't draw!

Moving right along, when you are finished, you can choose File | Save as, set the file type to BMP, and save your glyph to the name of your choice (I called it GRNRED.BMP). Using the same procedure you used for setting the BitBtn component's Glyph property, set the SpeedButton1 component's Glyph property to the GRNRED.BMP file, which you just created. Set the Glyph property of SpeedButton2 to the following path (if this is where you installed Delphi 3.0):

```
\PROGRAM FILES\BORLAND\DELPHI 3.0\IMAGES\BUTTONS\GLOBE.BMP
```

For SpeedButton1, make sure the NumGlyphs property is set to 4 (4 is the default). This tells it that there are four glyphs available for each of the states mentioned earlier. Set the GroupIndex property to 1. This tells the button that it belongs to group number 1. Only one button in a group can be in the down position at any given time. Just like the RadioButton, if you press down one button in the group, the other buttons are forced to the up position. Set both the GroupIndex property for SpeedButton2 and its NumGlyphs property to 2. Set the Visual property for SpeedButton2 to False. This completes the design of your toolbar. Now you can add the code.

Double-click SpeedButton1, and make its Click event look like this:

```
procedure TAdditionalTab.SpeedButton1Click(Sender: TObject);
begin
     If SpeedButton1.Down=True then
        Begin
           Image1.Visible:=False;
           Shape1.Brush.Color:=clRed;
        end;
end;
```

The `Click` event code for `SpeedButton2` should look like this:

```
procedure TAdditionalTab.SpeedButton2Click(Sender: TObject);
begin
     If SpeedButton2.Down=True then
        Begin
           Image1.Visible:=True;
           Shape1.Brush.Color:=clLime;
        end;
end;
```

Now add a `Shape` component to the left of the toolbar. Draw it about the same size as the `SpeedButtons` on the toolbar. Set its `Shape` property to `stEllipse`. Double-click the `Pen` property to expose its nested properties, and set the `Color` property to `clGreen`. Double-click the `Brush` property to expose its nested properties, and set its `Color` property to `clLime`. The `Pen` properties are used to set attributes used when drawing the shape (for example, color of the line, and so on). The `Brush` properties are used to set attributes used to fill the shape.

Next, add an `Image` component to the right of the toolbar. Make the `Image` component about the size of the `SpeedButton`, just as you did with the shape. The `Image` component can display graphics such as an icon, bitmap, or metafile. For this example, use an icon. Double-click the `Picture` property, and you are presented with the Picture Editor. Load the icon file `\PROGRAM FILES\DELPHI 3.0\IMAGES\ICONS\EARTH.ICO`. The code you added to the two `SpeedButtons` is used to affect the appearance of the `Shape` and the `Image` components.

On `SpeedButton1`, use another property that is available on all visual components: the `Hint` property. The `Hint` property stores a string of text that will be displayed when the user holds the mouse pointer over the component for a short period of time. Change the `Hint` property to `My SpeedButton Hint`. To enable the `Hint` property, you must set the `ShowHints` property to `True` because it is `False` by default. You'll test this at runtime.

Add a `Label` component to the form with the `Caption` property set to `Enter a Phone Number`. Next, just below the label, add a `MaskEdit` component. Double-click the `EditMask` property to bring up the Input Mask Editor. Click on Phone, and then press OK. This sets the `EditMask` component to accept only numbers that are in the form of an area code and phone number.

Put a `StringGrid` component on the form. Set the `StringGrid1`, `RowCount`, and `ColCount` properties to 3. Set the `FixedCols` and `FixedRows` to 0. Adjust the size of the `StringGrid` so that only the nine cells are visible. Add a button to the form, and set its caption to `Fill Grid`. Double-click the button, and add the following code:

```
procedure TAdditionalTab.Button1Click(Sender: TObject);
var
  x, y: Integer;
begin
  with StringGrid1 do
    for x := 0 to ColCount - 1 do
```

8

```
        for y:= 0 to RowCount - 1 do
          Cells[x,y] := 'Cord. '+ IntToStr(x)+'-'+IntToStr(y);
end;
```

And, finally, the last component covered on this tab is the ScrollBox. Draw the ScrollBox
on the form in the lower-right corner, and size it as shown earlier in Figure 8.14. You will
add a few components to it to demonstrate its ability to scroll components that may not fit
in the area in which they need to be used.

Add a BitBtn to the scroll box, and set its Kind property to bkHelp. Add a Panel to the scroll
box. Notice that if you drag the Panel down below the bottom border of the scroll box, scroll
bars appear. Temporarily stretch the ScrollBox from top to bottom so that it is two to three
times longer than you will need it. Place the button at the top and the panel at the bottom.
Set the Caption property on the panel to Panel in ScrollBox. Now resize the scroll box to fit
on the form (as shown earlier in Figure 8.14). Double-click the Help button in the scroll box,
and add the following code to its Click event:

```
procedure TAdditionalTab.BitBtn4Click(Sender: TObject);
begin
    ShowMessage('Testing Help Button in Scrollbox!');
end;
```

Now double-click on BitBtn2 and add the following code:

```
procedure TAdditionalTab.BitBtn2Click(Sender: TObject);
begin
    ShowMessage('This feature not active');
end;
```

You are done with the Additional tab form and ready to test it. The complete source code
for the Addition unit created as you built your form should look like Listing 8.2.

TYPE   **Listing 8.2. The VCLDEMO Additional tab form.**

```
unit Addition;

interface

uses
  Windows, Messages, SysUtils, Classes, Graphics, Controls, Forms,
  Dialogs, Buttons, StdCtrls, ExtCtrls, Grids, Outline, Mask;

type
  TAdditionalTab = class(TForm)
    BitBtn1: TBitBtn;
    BitBtn2: TBitBtn;
    Panel1: TPanel;
    SpeedButton1: TSpeedButton;
    SpeedButton2: TSpeedButton;
    Bevel1: TBevel;
    Image1: TImage;
```

continues

Listing 8.2. continued

```
  Shape1: TShape;
    ScrollBox1: TScrollBox;
    BitBtn3: TBitBtn;
    BitBtn4: TBitBtn;
    Panel5: TPanel;
    Label1: TLabel;
    MaskEdit1: TMaskEdit;
    StringGrid1: TStringGrid;
    Button1: TButton;
    procedure BitBtn1Click(Sender: TObject);
    procedure BitBtn3Click(Sender: TObject);
    procedure Button1Click(Sender: TObject);
    procedure SpeedButton2Click(Sender: TObject);
    procedure SpeedButton1Click(Sender: TObject);
    procedure FormClose(Sender: TObject; var Action: TCloseAction);
    procedure BitBtn4Click(Sender: TObject);
    procedure BitBtn2Click(Sender: TObject);
  private
    { Private declarations }
  public
    { Public declarations }
  end;

var
  AdditionalTab: TAdditionalTab;

implementation

Uses
     Standard;

{$R *.DFM}

procedure TAdditionalTab.BitBtn1Click(Sender: TObject);
begin
   StandardTab.Show;
   AdditionalTab.Hide;
end;

procedure TAdditionalTab.BitBtn3Click(Sender: TObject);
begin
  StandardTab.Close;
end;

procedure TAdditionalTab.Button1Click(Sender: TObject);
var
  x, y: Integer;
begin
  with StringGrid1 do
    for x := 0 to ColCount - 1 do
      for y:= 0 to RowCount - 1 do
        Cells[x,y] := 'Cord. '+ IntToStr(x)+'-'+IntToStr(y);
end;
```

8

```
procedure TAdditionalTab.SpeedButton2Click(Sender: TObject);
begin
    If SpeedButton2.Down=True then
        Begin
            Image1.Visible:=True;
            Shape1.Brush.Color:=clLime;
        end;
end;

procedure TAdditionalTab.SpeedButton1Click(Sender: TObject);
begin
    If SpeedButton1.Down=True then
        Begin
            Image1.Visible:=False;
            Shape1.Brush.Color:=clRed;
        end;
end;

procedure TAdditionalTab.FormClose(Sender: TObject;
  var Action: TCloseAction);
begin
    Application.Terminate;
end;

procedure TAdditionalTab.BitBtn4Click(Sender: TObject);
begin
    ShowMessage('Testing Help Button in Scrollbox!');
end;

procedure TAdditionalTab.BitBtn2Click(Sender: TObject);
begin
    ShowMessage('This feature not active');
end;

end.
```

ANALYSIS Save the project and test it out. You should be able to go through the two forms and experiment with the components you have placed on each page. Click on the toolbar (SpeedButton) buttons and observe the results. Use the scrollbar to view the Help button and the panel. Click on the Help button in the scroll box to see a message box. When you are satisfied, click Close to exit the program.

You have just gone through a lot of components, done a lot of work, and haven't built anything useful. Remember, the point has been for you to become familiar with the VCL and practice using it. About now you probably are thinking "four more tabs plus the OCX tab and the sample tab to go—I'm tired!" Rest easy because the majority of the work is behind you for this chapter. The Data Access and Data Controls tabs are only briefly mentioned here (they are covered in detail on Day 11, "Delphi's Database Architecture"). The Win32 tab, Dialogs tab, and System tab also are covered only briefly. Several of the components in the System tab are covered in other sections of the book. The OCX and Sample tabs are not covered at all because they are samples only and not officially supported or documented.

So, let's quickly go through the rest of the tabs here and build another small application to test out some of the remaining components.

The Win32 Tab

The Win32 tab, shown in Figure 8.17, contains 16 components that enable you to create applications with the Windows 95/NT 4.*x* look and feel. Several of these components are similar to those that can be found in the Win 3.1 tab. Table 8.3 briefly describes each component.

Figure 8.17.

The Win32 tab.

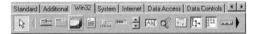

Table 8.3. The components available on the Win32 tab.

Component	Description
	The TabControl is a Windows 95-style tab component that enables you to add tabs to a form for user selection. This is a visual component.
	The PageControl is a Windows 95-style component used to create pages that can be changed using tabs or other controls to conserve desktop space. This is a visual component.
	The ImageList is a new object provided for working with image lists. See the Delphi documentation for more information. This is a nonvisual component.
	The RichEdit component is a Windows 95-style edit box that enables you to use multiple colors, fonts, text search, and more. This is a visual component.
	The TrackBar is a Windows 95-style slider control. This is a visual component.
	The ProgressBar component is a Windows 95-style progress bar. This is a visual component.
	The UpDown component is a Windows 95-style spin button. This is a visual component.
	The HotKey component enables you to add hot-key support to an application. This is a visual component.

Component	Description
	The Animate component is used to play silent AVI movie clips (a sequence of bitmap images) such as the Windows 95-style sequences showing files moving from one folder to another on the screen during a copy or move operation. This is a visual component.
	The DatePicker component provides data selection from a component similar to a ComboBox, but with a drop-down calendar. This is a visual component.
	The TreeView is a Windows 95-style component that views data in a hierarchical format. This is a visual component.
	The ListView is a Windows 95-style component that visually displays lists in columns. This is a visual component.
	The HeaderControl component is a Windows 95-style header component that enables you to create multiple, moveable headers. This is a visual component.
	The StatusBar component is a Windows 95-style status bar enabling you to display status information in multiple panels if necessary. This is a visual component.
	The ToolBar component is used to create toolbars for quick access to common features in an application.
	The CoolBar component is a container that is used to place components in bands that can be resized by the user. This is a visual component.

The System Tab

The System tab contains 8 important components that enable you to take advantage of Windows features, as shown in Figure 8.18. Table 8.4 briefly describes each component. The PaintBox, MediaPlayer are discussed in more detail on Day 10, "Graphics, Multimedia, and Animation." The DDE and OLE components are not covered in any detail here and are beyond the scope of this book. Examples of how to use some of the components from this tab are included the final application you'll create for this chapter.

Figure 8.18.

The System Tab.

Table 8.4. The components available on the System tab.

Component	Description
⏰	The `Timer` component is used to activate procedures, functions, and events at specified time intervals. This is a nonvisual component.
🖌	The `PaintBox` is used to create in the form an area that can be painted. This is a visual component.
🎬	The `MediaPlayer` component is used to create a control panel that looks like that of a VCR. This control is used to play sound, video files, and multimedia devices. This is a visual component.
OLE	The `OLEContainer` component is used to create an OLE client area. This is a visual component.
▣	The `DDEClientConv` component is used by a DDE client to set up a conversation with a DDE Server. This is a nonvisual component.
▣	The `DDEClientItem` component is used to specify client data that will be sent to a DDE server during a conversation. This is a nonvisual component.
▣	The `DDEServerConv` component is used by a DDE server application to set up a conversation with a DDE client. This is a nonvisual component.
▣	The `DDEServerItem` component is used to specify data that will be sent to a DDE client during a conversation. This is a nonvisual component.

The Internet Tab

The Internet tab, shown in Figure 8.19, contains 15 components that greatly reduce the amount of work required to write Internet and TCP/IP network-based applications. Most of these components are covered on Day 14, "Building Internet Applications with Delphi." Table 8.5 briefly describes each component.

Figure 8.19.

The Internet Tab.

Table 8.5. The components available on the Internet tab.

Component	Description
	The FTP component is used to transfer files between computers over the Internet or TCP/IP network using the FTP protocol. This is a nonvisual component.
	The HTML component is used to display HTML pages from HTML code such as in a Web browser. This is a visual component.
	The HTTP component is used to connect to Web servers. This is nonvisual component.
	The NNTP component is used to connect to news servers. This is a nonvisual component.
	The POP component is used to connect to POP3 servers for Internet mail retrieval. This is a nonvisual component.
	The SMTP component is used to send Internet mail. This is a nonvisual component.
	The TCP component is used to communicate with other computers over the Internet or TCP/IP network. This is a nonvisual component.
	The UDP component is used to make UDP connections over a network. This is a nonvisual component.
	The ClientSocket component is used to create a connection to another machine on the network. This is a nonvisual component.
	The ServerSocket component is used to respond to client requests from other machines on the network. This is a nonvisual component.
	The WebDispatcher component is used to convert an ordinary data module to a Web module. This is a nonvisual component.
	The PageProducer is used to convert an HTML template into a string of HTML code that can be viewed by a Web browser or other HTML viewer. This is a nonvisual component.
	The QueryTableProducer is used to produce an HTML table from records of a TQuery object.
	The DataSetTableProducer component is used to produce an HTML table from records of a TDataSet object.

The Data Access Tab

The Data Access tab, shown in Figure 8.20, contains 11 components that enable you to link to and communicate with databases. Some of these components are discussed in more detail on Day 11. For further information, refer to Delphi's online help or printed documentation. Table 8.6 briefly describes each component.

Figure 8.20.

The Data Access tab.

Table 8.6. The components available on the Data Access tab.

Component	Description
	The DataSource component is used to connect the Table or Query components to data-aware components. This is a nonvisual component.
	The Table component is used to link a database table to the application. This is a nonvisual component.
	The Query component is used to create and execute SQL queries to a remote SQL Server database or a local database. This is a nonvisual component.
	The StoredProc component is used to execute procedures that have been stored on a SQL Server. This is a nonvisual component.
	The Database component is used to make connections to remote database servers. This is a nonvisual component.
	The Session component is used to provide global control over an application's database connections. This is a nonvisual component.
	The BatchMove component enables you to perform work on records and tables locally, and then move the updated information back to the server. This is a nonvisual component.
	The UpdateSQL component is used to make updates to a SQL Database. This is a nonvisual component.
	The Provider component is used to provide a connection between a remote database application server and a client dataset in a multi-tiered, desktop client application. This is a nonvisual component.
	The ClientDataSet component is used to provide client access to a multi-tiered database. This is a nonvisual component.
	The RemoteServer component is used connect to a multi-tiered database on a remote server. This is a non-visual component.

The Data Controls Tab

The Data Controls tab, shown in Figure 8.21, contains 15 data-aware components. Most of these components are data-aware versions of commonly used components found in the Standard and Additional tabs. These are covered later in the book. Table 8.7 briefly describes these components. Some of these components are discussed briefly on Day 11. Please refer to Delphi's online help or printed documentation for more information.

Figure 8.21.

The Data Controls tab.

Table 8.7. The components available on the Data Controls tab.

Component	Description
	The DBGrid component is used to create a data-aware grid where data can be displayed in rows and columns. This is a visual component.
	The DBNavigator component is used to create a control that navigates through a database with the ability to edit data. This is a visual component.
	The DBText component is a data-aware version of the Label component. This is a visual component.
	The DBEdit component is a data-aware version of the Edit component. This is a visual component.
	The DBMemo component is a data-aware version of the Memo component. This is a visual component.
	The DBImage component is a data-aware version of the Image component. This is a visual component.
	The DBListBox component is a data-aware version of the ListBox component. This is a visual component.
	The DBComboBox component is a data-aware version of the ComboBox component. This is a visual component.
	The DBCheckBox component is a data-aware version of the CheckBox component. This is a visual component.
	The DBRadioGroup component is a data-aware version of the RadioGroup component. This is a visual component.

continues

Table 8.7. continued

Component	Description
	The DBLookupListBox component is used to create a lookup ListBox that is data-aware. This is a visual component.
	The DBLookupComboBox component is used to create a lookup CombBox that is data-aware. This is a visual component.
	The DBRichEdit component is used to create a RichEdit field that is data aware. This is a visual component.
	The DBCtrlGrid component is used to create a data grid that is data-aware. This is a visual component.
	The DBChart is a data-aware version of the TChart component. This is a visual component.

The Decision Cube Tab

The Decision Cube tab, shown in Figure 8.22, contains six multidimensional charting and graphing components to simplify writing software used for data analysis. These components are available only in the Client/Server Edition of Delphi 3 and so are only briefly described in Table 8.8 in this book. Refer to Delphi's online help or manuals for more information about each of them.

Figure 8.22.
The Decision Cube tab.

Table 8.8. The components available on the Decision Cube tab.

Component	Description
	The DecisionCube is a component a multidimensional data store that can be used to fetch data from a dataset. This is a nonvisual component.
	The DecisionQuery component is a specialized version of the TQuery component designed for use with the DecisionCube. This is a nonvisual component.
	The DecisionSource component is used to define the current pivot state of DecisionGrid or DecisionGraph components. This is a nonvisual component.

8

Component	Description
	The DecisionPivot component is used to open or close DecisionCube dimensions or fields by pressing a button. This is a visual component.
	The DecisionGrid component is used to display data from a DecisionCube component that is bound to a DecisionCube datasource in a grid.
	The DecisionGraph component is used to display data from a DecisionCube component that is bound to a DecisionCube datasource in a graph.

The QReport Tab

The QReport tab contains 17 components for use in report generation, as shown in Figure 8.23. Some of these components are covered in more detail on Day 12, "Reports and Charts." Table 8.9 briefly describes them here.

Figure 8.23.

The QReport tab.

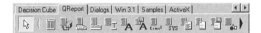

Table 8.9. The components available on the QReport tab.

Component	Description
	The QuickReport component is used to add QuickReport printing capabilities to applications. This is a nonvisual component.
	The QRSubDetail component is used link additional datasets to a report. This is a visual component.
	The QRBand component is used to build reports by placing printable components on it. This is a visual component.
	The QRChildBand component enables you to create child bands that can contain other QuickReport components and bands. This is a visual component.
	The QRGroup component is used to create data groups. This is a nonvisual component.
	The QRLabel component is used to put text on a report. This is a visual component.

continues

Table 8.9. continued

Component	Description
	The QRDBText is a data-aware component for placing text on a report. This is visual component.
	The QRExpr component enables you to build and display expressions based on dataset values as well as system values (such as time or Date). The component's expression property includes an Expression Builder dialog that enables you to graphically build the expression.
	The QRSysData component is used to display system data. This is a visual component.
	The QRMemo component is used to put multi-line text on a report. This is a visual component.
	The QRRichText component is used to put RichText into a report. This is a visual component.
	The QRDBRichText component is used to put text from a database RichText field into a report. This is a visual component.
	The QRShape component is used to draw a shape on a report. This is a visual component.
	The QRImage component is used to print images on a report. This is a visual component.
	The QRDBImage component is used to print images from a database on a report. This is a visual component.
	The QRCompositeReport component is used to build composite reports. This is a nonvisual component.
	The QRPreview component is used to create preview forms for viewing reports onscreen. This is a visual component.
	The QRChart component is used to print charts from data in a report. This is a visual component.

The Dialogs Tab

The Dialogs tab, shown in Figure 8.24, contains ten components used to create the various dialog boxes that are common to Windows applications. Dialogs are used to specify files or select settings. Using the dialog boxes provided in Delphi can save you time and help give a consistent look and feel to your applications. These components are described only briefly in Table 8.10 in this book. Refer to Delphi's online help or manuals for more information about each of them.

Figure 8.24.

The Dialogs tab.

Table 8.10. The components available on the Dialogs tab.

Component	Description
	The OpenDialog component is to create a File Open common dialog box. This is a nonvisual component.
	The SaveDialog component is used to create a File Save common dialog box. This is a nonvisual component.
	The OpenPictureDialog component is used to create an Open Picture dialog box. This is a nonvisual component.
	The SavePictureDialog component is used to create a Save Picture dialog box. This is a nonvisual component.
	The FontDialog component is used to create a Font dialog box. This is a nonvisual component.
	The ColorDialog component is used to create a Color dialog box. This is a nonvisual component.
	The PrintDialog component is used to create a Print dialog box. This is a nonvisual component.
	The PrinterSetupDialog component is used to create a Printer Setup dialog box. This is a nonvisual component.
	The FindDialog component is used to create a Find dialog box. This is a nonvisual component.
	The ReplaceDialog component is used to create a Replace dialog box. This is a nonvisual component.

The Win 3.1 Tab

The Win 3.1 tab stores components that have been replaced by newer components, as shown in Figure 8.25. These 11 components are here for backward compatibility when porting applications between Delphi 1.0 and 2.0 or Delphi 3.0. Components in this tab should not be used with 32-bit applications. Table 8.11 briefly describes these components.

Figure 8.25.

The Win 3.1 Tab.

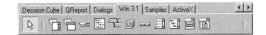

Table 8.11. The components available on the Win 3.1 tab.

Component	Description
	The DBLookupList component is a Windows 3.1 data-aware control used to look up a value in a lookup table using a list box. This is a visual component.
	The DBLookupCombo component is a Windows 3.1 data-aware control used to look up a value in a lookup table using a combo box. This is a visual component.
	The TabSet component is used to create notebook tabs. This is a visual component.
	The Outline component enables you to create a tree-like control used for visually displaying data in a hierarchical format.
	The TabbedNoteBook is used to create multi-page forms with tabs. This is a visual component.
	The NoteBook component is used to create a stack of pages that can be used with the TabSet. This is a visual component.
	The Header component is used to create a control that displays text in resizable sections. This is a visual component.
	The FileListBox component is used to create a list box for displaying the files in the selected directory. This is a visual component.
	The DirectoryListBox component is used to create a list box for displaying directories on the selected drive. This is a visual component.
	The DriveComboBox component is used to create a combo box that is used to display and/or choose a drive. This is a visual component.
	The FilterComboBox component is used to create a combo box that can display and/or select the file filter(s). This is a visual component.

The Samples Tab

The Sample tab contains six sample VCLs, as shown in Figure 8.26. These are provided only as samples, and Delphi provides minimal documentation. You can find the source code for them in the directory \DELPHI\SOURCE\SAMPLES. Table 8.12 briefly describes these samples.

Figure 8.26.

The Samples tab.

8

Table 8.12. The components available on the Samples tab.

Component	Description
	The Gauge sample component is used to create a progress indicator that can appear as a bar, text, or pie-shaped gauge. This is a visual component.
	The ColorGrid sample component is used to create a grid of colors from which the user can make a selection. This is a visual component.
	The SpinButton sample component is used to create spin buttons. This is a visual component.
	The SpinEdit sample component is used to create an edit box combined with the features of a spin control. This is a visual component.
	The DirectoryOutline sample component is used to create a display of the selected drives directory structure. This is a visual component.
	The Calendar sample component is used to display a calendar that can be used to display or retrieve date information in a standard, monthly calendar format. This is a visual component.
	The IBEventAlerter is a database event alert component. This is a nonvisual component.

The ActiveX Tab

The ActiveX tab contains five sample ActiveX controls, as shown in Figure 8.27. These are provided only as samples, and Delphi provides minimal documentation. This area is also where OCXs you add to Delphi are stored. Delphi VCLs are the better way to go (in my opinion) for your Delphi projects, but if you really need to use an OCX control, by all means do so. Remember, however, that if you use an OCX in your Delphi application, you must include it with your application when you distribute it. Table 8.13 briefly describes these samples.

Figure 8.27.

The OCX tab.

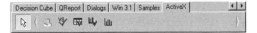

Table 8.13. The components available on the ActiveX tab.

Component	Description
	The ChartFX control is used to add charting capability to a Delphi application. This is a visual control.
	The VCSpeller control is used to add spell-check features to a Delphi application. This is a nonvisual control.
	The V1Book control is used to add a spreadsheet capability to a Delphi application. This is a visual control.
	The VTChart control is used to add a 3D chart to a Delphi application that uses a graphics server. This is a visual control.
	The Graph control is used to add 2D graphs to a Delphi application. This is a visual control.

Finishing Up with the VCL

Now that you have all the tabs under your belt, let's build a small application to demonstrate some of the components you didn't use in the VCLDEMO.DPR project. In the sample application you build in this section, you'll tap into the Win32, Dialog, and System tabs. From the Win32 tab, you'll use the ProgressBar and TrackBar, as well as the TreeView and TabControl. From the Dialog tab, you'll use the OpenDialog component. You'll also use the Timer component from the System tab, along with a few other components you already have used on the Standard tab.

The project for this application is called MOREVCL.DPR and the unit is MORE.PAS. Follow the layout shown in Figure 8.28 as you build the form. On the left side of the form starting at the top and working down, drop the following components on the form: TabControl, Panel (place it on the TabControl), ProgressBar, and TrackBar. Drop a Timer and OpenDialog component on the form (anywhere—remember these are nonvisual). In the upper-right corner, draw a Panel. Working down on the right side, drop a Label, TreeView, Label, Edit, and Button component.

Figure 8.28.

The MOREVCL
Demo Form.

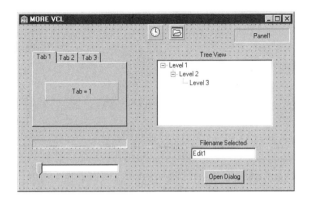

To get this thing working, you need to set up a few properties and add some code. For the TabControl component, double-click on the Tabs property in the Object Inspector and bring up the TStrings edit box. Here, you can type the names of the tabs. Each tab name starts on a new line. Type **Tab 1**, **Tab 2**, and **Tab 3**. For the panel you placed in the TabControl, set its caption to **Tab = 1**. Next set the Max properties for the ProgressBar and the TrackBar to **10**. Add the following code to the TrackBar OnChange event:

```
ProgressBar1.Position:=TrackBar1.Position;
```

Now double-click on the timer, and add the following code to the OnTimer event:

```
Panel1.Caption:=TimeToStr(Time);
```

Change the label just above the TreeView to **TreeView** and the label below the TreeView to **FileName Selected**.

For the TreeView component's properties, double-click to the right of the Items Property where it says TTreeNodes, and this brings up the TreeView Items Editor. Here you can add items and sub-items to build your TreeView. Add an item called Level 1. Next, add a sub-item for Level 1 called Level 2, and add a sub-item of Level 2 called Level 3.

Finally, add the following code to the OpenDialog button:

```
OpenDialog1.FileName := '*.*';
  if OpenDialog1.Execute then
    Edit1.Text := OpenDialog1.FileName;
```

When you are finished, the code should look like Listing 8.4.

TYPE **Listing 8.3. The MOREVCL demo.**

```
unit more;

interface

uses
  Windows, Messages, SysUtils, Classes, Graphics, Controls, Forms,
  Dialogs, ExtCtrls, ComCtrls, StdCtrls, Buttons;


type
  TForm1 = class(TForm)
    Timer1: TTimer;
    Panel1: TPanel;
    OpenDialog1: TOpenDialog;
    TabControl1: TTabControl;
    TrackBar1: TTrackBar;
    ProgressBar1: TProgressBar;
    Panel2: TPanel;
    Button1: TButton;
    TreeView1: TTreeView;
    Label1: TLabel;
    Edit1: TEdit;
    Label2: TLabel;
    procedure Timer1Timer(Sender: TObject);
    procedure TrackBar1Change(Sender: TObject);
    procedure BitBtn1Click(Sender: TObject);
    procedure TabControl1Change(Sender: TObject);
    procedure Button1Click(Sender: TObject);
  private
    { Private declarations }
  public
    { Public declarations }
  end;

var
  Form1: TForm1;

implementation

{$R *.DFM}

procedure TForm1.Timer1Timer(Sender: TObject);
begin
     Panel1.Caption:=TimeToStr(Time);
end;

procedure TForm1.TrackBar1Change(Sender: TObject);
begin
     ProgressBar1.Position:=TrackBar1.Position;
end;

procedure TForm1.BitBtn1Click(Sender: TObject);
begin
     Application.Terminate;
end;
```

```
procedure TForm1.TabControl1Change(Sender: TObject);
begin
     If TabControl1.TabIndex=0 then Panel2.Caption:='Tab = 1';
     If TabControl1.TabIndex=1 then Panel2.Caption:='Tab = 2';
     If TabControl1.TabIndex=2 then Panel2.Caption:='Tab = 3';
end;

procedure TForm1.Button1Click(Sender: TObject);
begin
  OpenDialog1.FileName := '*.*';
  if OpenDialog1.Execute then
    Edit1.Text := OpenDialog1.FileName;
end;

end.
```

ANALYSIS Save the program and run it. If all went well, you should be able to move the `TrackBar` and watch the `ProgressBar` follow along. You should be able to select from the three tabs on the `TabControl` and watch the `Panel` caption change to reflect the tab number selected. You also should be able to open the `TreeView` down three levels by clicking on each item as it is displayed. Finally, you should be able to pull up the `OpenDialog` by pressing on the button and selecting a file. The filename should display in the edit box. If you have any problems, go back and check the code and properties. If you don't, the application is complete.

Although you have covered a lot of components, you haven't come close to covering them all. As discussed earlier in the chapter, there are far too many components, properties, methods, and so on, to cover everything in detail, but you should be fairly comfortable with the VCL at this point and be able to use the online help to quickly find the information you need to be productive. You should now be ready to move on and start building applications that actually do something useful from Delphi's rich selection of components.

Summary

Today you learned what the VCL is and what it is used for. You learned about properties, events, methods, and so on. You learned how to use Delphi's online help to quickly find valuable information for each of these topics. You briefly talked about every component in the VCL, including the sample ActiveXs and sample VCLs. As you went, you built a "do-nothing application" to demonstrate as many of the commonly used components as possible from the Standard tab and Additional tab. You also built yet another do-nothing application using components from the Win32, Dialogs, and System tabs. In short, you had a pretty good work out! Take some time to finish up with the Q&A and the Workshop, pat yourself on the back, and take a rest—you deserve it.

Q&A

Q **What's the difference between the 32-bit Delphi VCL and the 16-bit version?**

A Delphi 1.0 has 75 components, and Delphi 3 has over 130 (counting all the sample VCLs and ActiveX components). Delphi 3 uses 32-bit components and ActiveX controls as opposed to the 16-bit components and VBXs supported in Delphi 1.0.

Q **Can I recompile my 16-bit applications from Delphi 1.0 to 32-bit with Delphi 3.0?**

A Yes. Because Delphi components are written in Delphi, you simply need to recompile your application with the new 32-bit version to convert from 16- to 32-bit. Most applications will recompile with little or no changes. You should note, however, that a 16-bit application using VBXs will require the 32-bit equivalent OCX or ActiveX control.

Workshop

The Workshop provides two ways for you to affirm what you've learned in this chapter. The Quiz section poses questions to help you solidify your understanding of the material covered. You can find answers to the quiz questions in Appendix A, "Answers to the Quiz Questions." The Exercises section provides you with experience in using what you have learned. Please try to work through all these before continuing to the next day.

Quiz

1. What is the difference between a visual and nonvisual component?
2. What is a nested property?
3. What is a method?
4. What are events?
5. What component would you use if you wanted to accept input from a user in a particular format?
6. What component would you use if you wanted to run a procedure or task every five minutes?

8

Exercises

1. Go back and fill in code for the Help and About Menu options in the VCLDEMO application. Hint, you can use the ShowMessage procedure for this.

2. Write a Windows alarm clock application. Your application should be able to display the time, enable you to set an alarm and display a message when the selected time arrives. Hint: Use Timer and Panel as well as any other components that you like to complete the project.

Day 9

Input, Output, and Printing

This chapter focuses on how to get information into and out of your applications. Of course, there are a number of ways that information can pass between your application and the computer. Today you learn about file I/O, including a number of ways to pass, store, and retrieve information in disk files. You also learn about the basics of getting your work down on paper—printing. There's a lot of ground to cover, so let's get started!

File Input and Output

One of the most common and valuable tasks every programmer must do at some point is work with files. A file is nothing more than an organized collection of data that is stored on hard disk, floppy disk, CD-ROM, tape, or other storage media. Obviously, database applications need to create, read, and write files, but files have many uses of their own. Files can be used to store a program's setup information. They can be used to store information temporarily so that a program can use valuable system memory for other tasks and load information back in memory only when needed. Files can even be used to easily pass information between programs; and of course, files commonly are used to save your work such as in a word processor or spreadsheet. Delphi handles files very well, and the programming behind file input and output is not all that difficult to do.

In this section, you examine attributes and file types. You learn how to work with text files, binary typed files, and untyped files. You also learn about some of the file- and directory-related functions that mimic familiar DOS commands such as MkDir. Lastly, you learn about long filenames.

File Attributes

NOTE

> Before starting this section, you should be aware that a basic knowledge of binary numbers and Boolean math would be helpful. As you progress through this section, if you find you are having trouble understanding the topic, you may want to consider obtaining some information about the binary numbering system and Boolean operations. You always can come back and read this section again when you have a better understanding of binary numbers and operations.

 Files have special attributes. An *attribute* is a property that a file exhibits based on its setting. For example, if a file has its read-only attribute set to "on," it can be read but not updated or deleted by most commands or programs. Each file has an attribute byte that is used to store the attribute settings. Each setting is stored in one of the eight bits that make up the byte. Only six bits are used, two of which are for directories and volume labels. That leaves the following attributes to worry about when you're working with files:

File Attribute	Delphi Constant	Description
Read-only files	faReadOnly	Allows files to be read from, but not updated or deleted.
Hidden files	faHidden	Prevents the file from appearing on normal directory listings.
System files	faSysFile	Marks a file for system use and prevents viewing in a directory listing.
Archive files	faArchive	This attribute is turned off if a file has been backed up.
Volume ID	faVolumeID	This attribute is used to create a volume ID.
Directory files	faDirectory	This attribute is used to mark a file as a directory.

The following constant is used for searching, not setting attributes:

File Searching	faAnyFile	This constant is useful in searching for all files regardless of its attribute settings.

These attribute settings are toggled on or off as appropriate by programs using or creating the files. By default, all the attributes are turned off except for the archive bit (bit 5) when a file is created. In Delphi, as with other languages, you can change these attributes before or after you work on files as needed. Delphi provides functions such as FileGetAttr and FileSetAttr to enable you to get and set the attributes as needed. As an example, you might need this if a file you needed to work on was read-only. You might set the read-only attribute to off, work on the file, and then set it back to on, thus protecting it from unwanted or accidental changes.

Another thing worth noting here is that any combination of these attributes can be set on or off for any given file. So how does this all work? Let's break down the attribute byte binary representation and look at the bits. Remember that each byte is made up of eight bits. Each bit can have only one of two values, 0 and 1. When a bit has a value of 1, it is considered "set." When a bit has a value of 0, it is considered "clear" (or not set). As you look at the attribute byte bitmap, think of the attribute bits as switches that can be turned "on" when a 1 is placed in the bit, and turned "off" when a 0 is placed in the bit.

Attribute Byte	Bitmap
Bit 0	Read-only bit
Bit 1	Hidden file bit
Bit 2	System file bit
Bit 3	Volume ID bit
Bit 4	Directory bit
Bit 5	Archive bit
Bit 6	Not used
Bit 7	Not used

A newly created file's attributes would look like this:

Bit 7	Bit 6	Bit 5	Bit 4	Bit 3	Bit 2	Bit 1	Bit 0
0	0	1	0	0	0	0	0

In other words, 00100000 binary or 20 hex. Now suppose you wanted to set the read-only attribute. You could use Delphi's `FileSetAttr` function with the `faReadOnly` constant. The `faReadOnly` constant is set to `00000001` binary or `01` hex. When the filename and `faReadOnly` value is fed to the `FileSetAttr` function, it is OR'd into the attribute byte. This example would clear the archive bit, which may or may not be desirable depending on what you want to do. You learn how to work with multiple bits shortly.

Looking at `$AD` or binary `10101101` (reading from right to left), you know from the attribute byte bitmap you saw earlier that this would indicate a file with the following bits on: read-only, system, volume ID, and archive. Bit 8 is also set but not used. This would not be a valid attribute byte for a file you would be working on. Remember, volume ID and subdirectory are attributes that you will leave alone because they are taken care of when you create a volume label or subdirectory. They are not to be changed by the user or programmer. A more realistic number would be binary `100001` or `$21`. If you check the bitmap against this number, you will find that it shows that the read-only and archive bits are set (file is read-only, and file has not been backed up).

Now take a look at how these bits are actually set. Suppose you wanted to set just the read-only bit of a file called JUNK.TXT. You could place the following line of code in your program:

```
FileSetAttr('JUNK.TXT',faReadOnly);
```

In the `FileSetAttr` statement, the `faReadOnly` constant equates to binary `00000001` or `$01`. This value in `faReadOnly` is copied to the attribute byte. This example sets the read-only bit to `1` and all the other bits in the attribute byte to `0`.

If you want to combine this constant with other constants or numbers, you can OR them together. When you OR two numbers, bit 0 of one number is OR'd with bit 0 of the next number, bit 1 is OR'd with bit 1, and so on. The OR function works just as it sounds. If one of the bits being OR'd is equal to 1, the result is 1. If neither bit is 1, the result is 0. Following is the truth table for the OR function and some examples of OR operations. In this case, you can achieve the same effect by adding the numbers or constants together, but it is useful to understand what happens when you OR numbers together.

OR Truth Table (Possible results for an OR operation)

```
1 OR 1 = 1
1 OR 0 = 1
0 OR 1 = 1
0 OR 0 = 0
```

Examples

```
10110010
OR
10010111
- - - - - - - - - - -
10110111

10110101
OR
10010111
- - - - - - - - - - -
10110111
```

The other operation you should be familiar with is AND. When you AND two bits together, you get only a 1 if both bits were set to 1. This also works just like it sounds: If one bit1=1 AND bit2=1, the result will be 1.

AND Truth Table (Possible results for an AND operation)

```
1 AND 1 = 1
1 AND 0 = 0
0 AND 1 = 0
0 AND 0 = 0
```

Example

```
10110101
AND
10010111
- - - - - - - - - - -
10010101
```

NEW TERM In both of the OR examples, you can see that the top numbers are different, but the bottom number stays the same. This, of course, causes the results to be different. This is called *masking*. Masking is a process that enables you to selectively view or change bits in a byte when it is used in an AND or OR operation with a predefined byte called a mask. By changing the mask (the number on the top), you can selectively turn on or off any bit or combination of bits. You can add constants and numbers or OR them together to create a mask that will be used to set more than one bit (attribute). In other words, if you wanted to set the read-only and archive bits, you could do so with a statement like this, which would create a mask of 00100001:

```
FileSetAttr('JUNK.TXT',faReadOnly+faArchive);
```

Now, that you have two bits on, what if you want to turn one off? You simply call `FileSetAttr` again and pass a mask containing only the bits that you want to stay on; others will be turned off. The following causes the archive bit to be turned off while maintaining the read-only setting.

```
FileSetAttr('JUNK.TXT',faReadOnly);
```

If you use the example, all bits will be set to 0 except for the read-only bit (which may not be desired). This is because the `faReaOnly` constant has only one bit set, and it is copied to the attribute byte. The easiest way to solve this problem is to first get the attributes of a file and store them in a variable. Then you can create a mask that can be OR'd with the original settings so that you change only the bits you select. The following is code to do this:

```
Procedure SetFile2ReadOnly;
Var
     FileAttr : Integer;
Begin
     {Get the contents of the Attribute byte for MYFILE.TXT}
     FileAttr:=FileGetAttr('MYFILE.TXT');
     {OR  the mask (faReadOnly) with the attribute byte value that
     stored in FileAttr and put the results in FileAttr}

     FileAttr:=FileAttr OR faReadOnly;
     {Set the Attribute byte to the new value stored in FileAttr}
     FileSetAttr('MYFILE.TXT',FileAttr);
end;
```

Look at what would happen if you created a new file and ran it through the preceding routine. You create your file called MYFILE.TXT. The attribute byte for the new file looks like this:

```
00100000    (Bit 5, the archive bit is set)
```

Retrieve the attribute byte and store it in a variable called `FileAttr`. Next, OR `FileAttr` with the predefined mask, `faReadOnly`, storing the results in `FileAttr`. This gives you a new mask that combines the old settings with the new ones.

```
00100000
    OR
00000001
    =
00100001
```

Working in binary makes it easier to understand what bits you need to turn on and off and what the results will look like. If you convert the above to hex, you can see what is going on in your code. For example, the numbers above in hex would look like this:

```
$20 OR $01 = $21
```

The original attribute byte contains $20 and is OR'd with `faReadOnly` (which equals $01), and the result is $21.

Now suppose you wanted to see if a bit was set in the attribute byte. For this, use the AND operator. Using the same numbers as above, you would find that none of the bits you are looking for are on. The following example looks for the read-only bit:

```
00100000
   AND
00000001
   =
00000000
```

If you wanted to check the status of all the bits, you would AND the attribute byte with $FF or 11111111, like this:

```
00100000
   AND
11111111
   =
00100000
```

As you can see, all the bits that are on in the attribute byte would be passed on through.

All this binary, hex, and file attribute theory is fine, but what about in practice, you ask? I knew you'd ask that question, so you're going to create a small program that enables you to view and toggle the four file attributes that were discussed (read-only, system, hidden, and archive) for a specified file. This gives you the chance to really see this all in action in a useful Windows utility.

First, create a new project with a single form called FILEATTR.DPR. The unit name should be ATTRSCR.PAS. Using Figure 9.1 as your guide, add the following components to the form:

Quantity	Component Type
1	Bevel
1	GroupBox
3	BitBtn
4	CheckBox
1	Label
1	Edit
1	DirectoryListBox
1	FileListBox
1	DriveComboBox

Starting at the top, the label comes first, and next up is the edit box. Below the edit box and to the left is the DirectoryListBox, and FileListBox is to its right. Below this is the DriveComboBox. On the bottom of the form to the left is the Bevel with the three BitBtns inside. Finally, on the bottom right is the GroupBox with the four CheckBoxs inside.

Figure 9.1.

File Attribute
Manager dialog box.

Now go make the necessary changes to the component properties, add some code, and get this thing running. Change the Label1 Caption property to Filename:. Next, delete all the characters from Edit1.Text property (for example, Edit1).

Assuming you have added the DirectoryListBox, FileListBox, and DriveCombo components, you now can easily tie them together. First, change the FileList property on the DirectoryListBox to FileListBox1. Notice that FileListBox1 was a choice you could select from. This makes connecting these components very easy. Next, go to the DriveComboBox and change the DirList property to DirectoryListBox1. Now go to the FileListBox and change the FileEdit property to Edit1. These changes cause these components to work together as one component, as in a File dialog box.

You need to make a few other changes to make your utility work properly. If you want File Attribute Manager to be able to read hidden and system files and display them, you need to change a few properties in the FileListBox. Notice a property for the FileListBox called FileType. This property has some nested properties that you must change. Make sure the following properties are set to True: ftReadOnly, ftSystem, ftHidden, ftArchive, and ftNormal. The two remaining properties (ftVolumeID and ftDirectory) should be set to False. Change the Caption property for the four check boxes to: Read Only for CheckBox1, Hidden File for CheckBox2, System for CheckBox3, and Archive for CheckBox4.

Change the names of the three BitBtns to BitBtnOk, BitBtnSave, and BitBtnClose. On BitBtnOk, change the Kind property to bkOk. On BitBtnSave, change the Kind property to bkAll. On BitBtnClose, change the Kind property to bkClose. On the bkSave button, change the caption property to &Save.

Now add some code to the buttons. The BitBtnOk code should look like the following code:

```
procedure TForm1.BitBtnOKClick(Sender: TObject);
begin
    {Get file attributes for selected file}
    {Check to see which attributes bits are set and check
     appropriate boxes}
    fname:=Edit1.Text;
    AttrByte:=FileGetAttr(fname);
    If AttrByte AND faReadOnly = faReadOnly Then
       CheckBox1.Checked:=True
    else
       CheckBox1.Checked:=False;
    If AttrByte AND faHidden = faHidden then
       CheckBox2.Checked:=True
    else
       CheckBox2.Checked:=False;
    If AttrByte AND faSysFile = faSysFile then
       CheckBox3.Checked:=True
    else
       CheckBox3.Checked:=False;
    If AttrByte AND faArchive = faArchive then
       CheckBox4.Checked:=True
    else
       CheckBox4.Checked:=False;
end;
```

The BitBtnSave code should look like the following:

```
procedure TForm1.BitBtnSaveClick(Sender: TObject);
begin
    {Clear Attribute byte}
    AttrByte:=0;
    {update file attribute byte from check box settings}
    If CheckBox1.Checked = True then
       AttrByte:=AttrByte OR faReadOnly;
    If CheckBox2.Checked = True then
       AttrByte:=AttrByte OR faHidden;
    If CheckBox3.Checked = True then
       AttrByte:=AttrByte OR faSysFile;
    If CheckBox4.Checked = True then
       AttrByte:=AttrByte OR faArchive;
    {Write settings in checkboxes to file attribute byte}
    FileSetAttr(fname,AttrByte);
end;
```

The BitBtnClose code should look like the following:

```
procedure TForm1.BitBtnCloseClick(Sender: TObject);
begin
    Application.Terminate;
end;
```

You need to add the following to the Implementation section:

```
Var
   fname:string;
   AttrByte:integer;
```

The code for the OnDblClick event handler for FileListBox1 should be as follows:

```
procedure TForm1.FileListBox1DblClick(Sender: TObject);
begin
     Form1.BitBtnOkClick(self);
end;
```

If you have typed everything correctly into the correct sections up to this point, your finished unit should be the same as Listing 9.1.

TYPE   Listing 9.1. File Attribute Manager.

```
unit Attrscr;

interface

uses
 Windows, Messages, SysUtils, Classes, Graphics, Controls, Forms,
 Dialogs, Menus, StdCtrls, Buttons, FileCtrl, ExtCtrls;

type
  TForm1 = class(TForm)
    Label1: TLabel;
    Edit1: TEdit;
    GroupBox1: TGroupBox;
    CheckBox1: TCheckBox;
    CheckBox2: TCheckBox;
    CheckBox3: TCheckBox;
    CheckBox4: TCheckBox;
    BitBtnOK: TBitBtn;
    BitBtnClose: TBitBtn;
    FileListBox1: TFileListBox;
    DirectoryListBox1: TDirectoryListBox;
    DriveComboBox1: TDriveComboBox;
    BitBtnSave: TBitBtn;
    Bevel1: TBevel;
    procedure BitBtnCloseClick(Sender: TObject);
    procedure BitBtnOKClick(Sender: TObject);
    procedure BitBtnSaveClick(Sender: TObject);
    procedure FileListBox1DblClick(Sender: TObject);
  private
    { Private declarations }
  public
    { Public declarations }
  end;
```

```
var
  Form1: TForm1;

implementation
Var
   fname:string;
   AttrByte:integer;
{$R *.DFM}

procedure TForm1.BitBtnCloseClick(Sender: TObject);
begin
     Application.Terminate;
end;

procedure TForm1.BitBtnOKClick(Sender: TObject);
begin
     {Get file attributes for selected file}
     {Check to see which attributes bits are set and check
      appropriate boxes}
     fname:=Edit1.Text;
     AttrByte:=FileGetAttr(fname);
     If AttrByte AND faReadOnly = faReadOnly Then
        CheckBox1.Checked:=True
     else
        CheckBox1.Checked:=False;
     If AttrByte AND faHidden = faHidden then
        CheckBox2.Checked:=True
     else
        CheckBox2.Checked:=False;
     If AttrByte AND faSysFile = faSysFile then
        CheckBox3.Checked:=True
     else
        CheckBox3.Checked:=False;
     If AttrByte AND faArchive = faArchive then
        CheckBox4.Checked:=True
     else
        CheckBox4.Checked:=False;
end;

procedure TForm1.BitBtnSaveClick(Sender: TObject);
begin
     {Clear Attribute byte}
     AttrByte:=0;
     {update file attribute byte from check box settings}
     If CheckBox1.Checked = True then
       AttrByte:=AttrByte OR faReadOnly;
     If CheckBox2.Checked = True then
       AttrByte:=AttrByte OR faHidden;
     If CheckBox3.Checked = True then
       AttrByte:=AttrByte OR faSysFile;
     If CheckBox4.Checked = True then
       AttrByte:=AttrByte OR faArchive;
     {Write settings in checkboxes to file attribute byte}
     FileSetAttr(fname,AttrByte);
end;
```

continues

Listing 9.1. continued

```
procedure TForm1.FileListBox1DblClick(Sender: TObject);
begin
 BitBtnOkClick(self);
end;

end.
```

ANALYSIS   The File Attribute Manager code has two primary sections of code that you need to be concerned about. These sections are contained in buttons: the OK button (BitBtnOKClick) and the Save button (BitBtnSaveClick). The code for the OK button is used to read the file attributes of the file selected in the list box and to show the results by updating the check boxes on the File Attribute Manager form. The code in the Save button updates the selected file's attributes to match that of the check box settings.

To test the program, create a temporary file and run the File Attribute Manager. The Archive check box should be checked, and all the other boxes should be unchecked. Check the Hidden File check box and click Save. Do a directory listing, and look for the filename. The filename should not appear in the directory listing (unless you are using a program that displays hidden files). You then can uncheck the Hidden File check box. Click Save, and the file again appears in a directory listing. You should have a good understanding of file attributes now, so let's move on to file types.

File Types

There are two basic types of files: *text* and *binary*. There are many different ways you can store or format the data in these two file types, but the files always fit into one of these two categories. So why the different types? Like anything, each file type has its advantages and disadvantages. What works well for one situation may not work well for another. This section gives you a look at the file types and some examples of how they might be used. Keep in mind that these are examples. You are free to determine how to format and work with the data stored in a file to suit your needs.

Text Files

NEW TERM   Most of us are familiar with text files. *Text* files are simple files containing plain ASCII characters. Data in a text file is typically stored and retrieved sequentially one line at a time, and each line ends with carriage return ($D) and line feed ($A) characters. Because data is handled sequentially, doing searches on large files or making a lot of changes to a text file can be quite tedious and inefficient. However, there are many situations, such as exporting data to a standard format, in which using text files is the best choice. As a general rule, if you plan to work with data sequentially and don't need to jump to different locations in a file, a text file is probably a good choice.

Let's look at some of the functions and procedures you need to know about for working with text files, and then build a program that stores and reads data in a text file.

The first item you need to look at is a variable type called `TextFile`. With `TextFile`, you declare a variable that will be used to identify the file type you wish to work with. Your declaration might look like the following:

```
Var
    MyFile : TextFile;
```

Now that you have a variable associated with the type, you need a way to pass this information to Delphi, as well as the name of the file you wish to work with. You do so with a procedure called `AssignFile`. If you are familiar with Pascal, you remember the `Assign` procedure. Delphi is backward compatible with the `Assign` procedure, but you should use `AssignFile` in Delphi because it avoids scope conflicts. Use `AssignFile` like this:

```
AssignFile(MyFile,filename)
```

In this example, `MyFile` is the variable you defined as a text file, and *filename* is a string containing the name of the file you wish to work with. Once you have used `AssignFile`, you can refer to the file as `MyFile`.

There are few other procedures you need to know about for writing to text files. Read their descriptions in the following list, and then look at the syntax and descriptions in the online help for each of these procedures. Make sure to study the code for the Text File Demo application coming up shortly as well as the comments preceding each procedure in the code.

For writing text files, you will need the following procedures:

Procedure	Description
ReWrite	Creates and opens a new file. Any existing files with same name will be overwritten.
Writeln	Writes a line of text to the open file with a CR/LF combination at the end.
CloseFile	Finishes updating the current file and closes it.

For reading text files, you will need the following procedures:

Procedure	Description
Reset	Opens an existing file. Text files are opened as read only.
Readln	Reads the current line of text from an open text file. Each line ends with CR/LF combination.

Now that you have some definitions under your belt, you're ready to build a program that reads and writes a simple text file and see how these procedures work. Open a new project in Delphi, and use Figure 9.2 as a guide to build the following Text File Demo application.

Figure 9.2.

Text File Demo application.

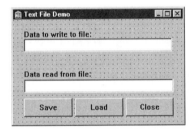

From top to bottom, place Label1, Edit1, Label2, Edit2. Working from left to right, place three buttons along the bottom. Set the captions of each component to match Figure 9.2. All the code that you need to add to make this application work is in the three buttons. Add the following code to the appropriate buttons.

Add this code to the Save button (Button1):

```
procedure TForm1.Button1Click(Sender: TObject);
Var
    OutFile : TextFile;
    fname,OutString : string;
begin
    {Assign a filename to the variable}
    fname:='JUNKFILE.TXT';
    {Identify the filename and type as OutFile}
    AssignFile(OutFile,fname);
    {create and open a new file identified as OutFile}
    Rewrite(OutFile);
    {Get text from the write edit box}
    OutString:=Edit1.Text;
    {Write out the text in OutString to file}
    Writeln(OutFile,OutString);
    {Upadate and close the file}
    CloseFile(OutFile);
end;
```

Add this code to the Load button (button2):

```
procedure TForm1.Button2Click(Sender: TObject);
Var
   InFile : TextFile;
   fname,InString : string;
begin
   {Assign text file name to variable}
   fname:='JUNKFILE.TXT';
   {Identify the text file as InFile}
   AssignFile(InFile,fname);
   {Open the file identified with InFile}
   Reset(Infile);
   {Read in a line of text}
   Readln(InFile,InString);
   {Store the line read in to the Read Text box}
   Edit2.Text:=InString;
   {Close the file}
   CloseFile(InFile);
end;
```

Add this code to the Close button (Button3):

```
procedure TForm1.Button3Click(Sender: TObject);
begin
    Application.Terminate;
end;
```

The full listing should look like the one shown in Listing 9.2.

TYPE Listing 9.2. The Text File Demo application.

```
unit Textform;

interface

uses
 Windows, Messages, SysUtils, Classes, Graphics, Controls, Forms,
 Dialogs, StdCtrls;

type
  TForm1 = class(TForm)
    Edit1: TEdit;
    Edit2: TEdit;
    Label1: TLabel;
    Label2: TLabel;
    Button1: TButton;
    Button2: TButton;
    Button3: TButton;
    procedure Button3Click(Sender: TObject);
    procedure Button1Click(Sender: TObject);
    procedure Button2Click(Sender: TObject);
```

continues

Listing 9.2. continued

```
private
  { Private declarations }
public
  { Public declarations }
end;

var
  Form1: TForm1;

implementation

{$R *.DFM}

procedure TForm1.Button3Click(Sender: TObject);
begin
    Application.Terminate;
end;

procedure TForm1.Button1Click(Sender: TObject);
Var
    OutFile : TextFile;
    fname,OutString : string;
begin
    {Assign a filename to the variable}
    fname:='JUNKFILE.TXT';
    {Identify the filename and type as OutFile}
    AssignFile(OutFile,fname);
    {create and open a new file identified as OutFile}
    Rewrite(OutFile);
    {Get text from the write edit box}
    OutString:=Edit1.Text;
    {Write out the text in OutString to file}
    Writeln(OutFile,OutString);
    {Upadate and close the file}
    CloseFile(OutFile);
end;

procedure TForm1.Button2Click(Sender: TObject);
Var
    InFile : TextFile;
    fname,InString : string;
begin
    {Assign text file name to variable}
    fname:='JUNKFILE.TXT';
    {Identify the text file as InFile}
    AssignFile(InFile,fname);
    {Open the file identified with InFile}
    Reset(Infile);
    {Read in a line of text}
    Readln(InFile,InString);
    {Store the line read in to the Read Text box}
```

9

```
    Edit2.Text:=InString;
    {Close the file}
    CloseFile(InFile);
  end;

end.
```

ANALYSIS This simple little application enables you to type text into the top edit box, press the Save button, and have the text written to a file called JUNKFILE.TXT. You can read the same file and have the text read from the file displayed in the bottom edit box. Take a minute or two to experiment with this application. You might even use Notepad or another editor to edit JUNKFILE.TXT by hand just to verify that the program is working properly and the way you would expect.

You have seen how to read and write a single line of text, and it should be fairly obvious that you could set up a loop to read or write several lines of text. There is one catch here; you can write to a file until you run out of disk space, but how do you know when to stop reading text in? In other words, how do you know when you are at the end of the file? Glad you asked! Delphi, like other languages, has a function to tell you when you have gone past the end of the file: Eof. To use Eof, you simply give it the file variable used with AssignFile, and it returns a Boolean value that can be used in a determinate loop, such as a while loop.

The following illustrates the use of Eof:

```
while not Eof(InFile) do
    Begin
        Readln(InFile,MyString);
    end;
```

This loop continues until a True is returned by Eof. With this in mind, write a quick-and-dirty text editor called WinEdit and see how it works. In this example, use the Memo, OpenDialog, SaveDialog, and MainMenu components. Drop one of each of these components onto a new form (use Figure 9.3 as a basis for building the editor). Click the OpenDialog component and double-click the Filter property in the Object Inspector to bring up the Filter Editor. Add the following two filters to the Filter Editor:

Filter Name	Filter
Text Files	*.txt
All Files	*.*

Figure 9.3.

The WinEdit text-editor application.

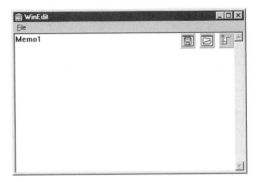

Do the same thing for the SaveDialog component. Using the MainMenu component, add a File menu with Open, Save, a separator line, and Exit options under it. Change the Align property for the Memo component to alClient. This causes the Memo component to automatically size to fill the entire form client area. Set the Memo's ScrollBar property to ssVertical. Now just add a bit of code to these File Menu options, and you have a simple text editor.

To the File | Open menu option, add the following code:

```
procedure TForm1.Open1Click(Sender: TObject);
Var
    InFile : TextFile;
    fname,InString : string;
begin
    If OpenDialog1.Execute then
    Begin
        fname:=OpenDialog1.FileName;
        AssignFile(InFile,fname);
        Reset(Infile);
        While not Eof(InFile) do
            Begin
                Readln(InFile,InString);
                Memo1.Lines.Add(InString);
            end;
        CloseFile(InFile);
        {Set filename in caption}
        Form1.Caption:=Form1.Caption + '['+fname+']';
    end;
end;
```

The preceding code uses a loop to load one line of text at a time into the Memo box until it reaches the end of the file. This is not the best way to load text into the Memo component, but the idea here is to show how Eof works. You could have used the following line to load your file and saved about 10 lines of code:

```
Memo1.Lines.LoadfromFile(OpenDialog1.FileName);
```

The following code illustrates how you might use this method:

```
begin
  if OpenDialog1.Execute then
  begin
    Memo1.Lines.LoadfromFile(OpenDialog1.FileName);
  end;
```

To the File | Save menu option, add the following code:

```
procedure TForm1.Save1Click(Sender: TObject);
Var
   OutFile : TextFile;
   fname : string;
begin
   If SaveDialog1.Execute then
     begin
        fname:=SaveDialog1.FileName;
        AssignFile(OutFile,fname);
        Rewrite(OutFile);
        {Write the contents of memo out in one block}
        Writeln(OutFile,Memo1.Text);
     end;
   CloseFile(OutFile);
   {Set filename in caption}
   Form1.Caption:=Form1.Caption + '['+fname+']';
```

The File | Save code writes out the text in the Memo box as one block of text so that you don't need a loop. There are other circumstances that you may run into where you will need a loop to write data one line at a time out to a file. The process is similar to reading in with a loop except that you either need to know the number of lines to be written or have some other method of determining when the loop should end.

Finally, to the File | Exit menu option, add this code:

```
procedure TForm1.Exit1Click(Sender: TObject);
begin
    Application.Terminate;
end;
```

Listing 9.3 shows the complete code for the editor.

TYPE **Listing 9.3. The WinEdit text-editor application.**

```
unit Edit;

interface

uses
 Windows, Messages, SysUtils, Classes, Graphics, Controls, Forms,
 Dialogs, StdCtrls, Menus;
```

continues

Listing 9.3. continued

```
type
  TForm1 = class(TForm)
    MainMenu1: TMainMenu;
    File1: TMenuItem;
    Open1: TMenuItem;
    Save1: TMenuItem;
    N1: TMenuItem;
    Exit1: TMenuItem;
    Memo1: TMemo;
    OpenDialog1: TOpenDialog;
    SaveDialog1: TSaveDialog;
    procedure Open1Click(Sender: TObject);
    procedure FormCreate(Sender: TObject);
    procedure Exit1Click(Sender: TObject);
    procedure Save1Click(Sender: TObject);
  private
    { Private declarations }
  public
    { Public declarations }
  end;

var
  Form1: TForm1;

implementation

{$R *.DFM}

procedure TForm1.Open1Click(Sender: TObject);
Var
    InFile : TextFile;
    fname,InString : string;
begin
    If OpenDialog1.Execute then
    Begin
       fname:=OpenDialog1.FileName;
       AssignFile(InFile,fname);
       Reset(Infile);
       While not Eof(InFile) do
          Begin
             Readln(InFile,InString);
             Memo1.Lines.Add(InString);
          end;
       CloseFile(InFile);
       {Set filename in caption}
       Form1.Caption:=Form1.Caption + '['+fname+']';
    end;
end;

procedure TForm1.FormCreate(Sender: TObject);
begin
     {Clear text from memo box}
     Memo1.Text:='';
end;
```

```
procedure TForm1.Exit1Click(Sender: TObject);
begin
    Application.Terminate;
end;

procedure TForm1.Save1Click(Sender: TObject);
Var
   OutFile : TextFile;
   fname : string;
begin
   If SaveDialog1.Execute then
     begin
        fname:=SaveDialog1.FileName;
        AssignFile(OutFile,fname);
        Rewrite(OutFile);
        {Write the contents of memo out in one block}
        Writeln(OutFile,Memo1.Text);
     end;
   CloseFile(OutFile);
   {Set filename in caption}
   Form1.Caption:=Form1.Caption + '['+fname+']';
end;

end.
```

ANALYSIS The finished program will look like your basic Windows text editor, such as Notepad, with fewer options and features of course. If you have not done so already, choose File | Project Save As, and save the unit as EDIT.PAS and the project file as WINEDIT.DPR. Run the program and try loading a text file to test it. Make some changes to the file and save it back to a new filename. Use Notepad or another editor to create your test text files and verify that the files were created or updated by your editor.

As mentioned earlier, there are many ways you can format and work with text files. Use your imagination, and remember that there is no single right answer. You must determine what is best for the task at hand.

Binary Files

NEW TERM The other file type is *binary*. All non-text file types fit this category. A binary file is simply a file containing the binary information written to it by the program. In the case of ASCII characters, the ASCII code is the binary information written to the file. Unlike text files, however, any file opened as binary—including text files, program files, bitmaps, and so on—can be read by your program. In this mode, you are responsible for determining how to handle data when it comes in.

Binary files come in two flavors: typed and untyped. They're described in detail in the following sections.

Typed Files

NEW TERM This first flavor of a binary file is the *typed file*. These are files for which you have decided on the format or structure of the file and the type of data to be stored in it, such as integers, reals, strings and their lengths, and so on. A good example of this is a simple phone/address book program.

Create a simple program to demonstrate this by first creating a new project, saving the unit as ADDR.PAS, and saving the project as ADDRESS.DPR. Then, create your record structure. In the implementation section, put the following code just below the {$R *.DFM}:

```
type
  Address = record
      Lastname: String[20];
      Firstname: String[20];
      Phone: String[15];
      StreetAddress : String[50];
      City : String[40];
      State : String[2];
      ZipCode : String[10];
  end;
```

Here you created your own type called Address. This example uses only strings, but you could use any other variable types (for example, integer, real, byte, and so on) in your record type. Use this new type to create some variables for your program. Next, immediately following the preceding code, add this code:

```
Var
   AddressFile : File of Address;
   AddressData : Address;
```

AddressFile is a file variable of type Address. File variables are used with many of the file I/O procedures and functions. AddressData is a variable of type Address. Because your new type, Address, is a record, AddressData becomes a buffer with the structure of the Address type. This enables you to easily read or write the data in the buffer with one line of code while maintaining some order. Each record saved to disk will be the same size regardless of the data entered into it. This is also known as a *fixed-length record* and is the idea behind typed files.

Before you get too much farther into your program, take a look at the functions and procedures you will be using to work with typed files. For more detail on these, refer to Delphi's online help and manuals. The purpose here is to show you the functions and procedures available for the task at hand.

AssignFile

Syntax   procedure AssignFile(var F, String);

Purpose   Used to assign a filename to a file variable for use by other file I/O functions.

Reset

Syntax   `procedure Reset(var F [: File; RecSize: Word ] );`

Purpose   Used to open an existing file that has been assigned to a file variable with `AssignFile`.

Rewrite

Syntax   `procedure Rewrite(var F: File [; Recsize: Word ] );`

Purpose   Used to create and open a file that has been assigned to a file variable with `AssignFile`.

Seek

Syntax   `procedure Seek(var F; N: Longint);`

Purpose   Used to move the file pointer to the specified record or location within the open file.

Read

Syntax   `procedure Read(F , V1 [, V2,...,Vn ] );`

Purpose   Used to read records in from a file.

Write

Syntax   `procedure Write(F, V1 [V2,...Vn]);`

Purpose   Used to write records to a file.

Eof

Syntax   `function Eof(var F): Boolean;`

Purpose   Used to determine if the program is at the end of the file. Used in conjunction with `Read`.

CloseFile

Syntax   `procedure CloseFile(var F);`

Purpose   Used to update the file with any final changes and then close it.

Sample Project

On with the program! Earlier you created the project, added a type called Address, and added some variables. Immediately following the line containing AddressData : Address;, add the following variables:

```
Fname : String;
RecSize,CurRec : Longint;
```

Now add seven edit boxes, seven labels, four buttons, and one BitBtn. Using Figure 9.4 as a guide, lay out the edit boxes and the labels starting with Edit1 and Label1. Work from top to bottom, left to right to add the rest of the items. Change the caption and name properties for the buttons as well as the BitBtn.

You may want to note that Read() and Write() are two of the very few procedures that accept a varying number of parameters. This is something you should keep in mind as you study and use them to prevent confusion.

Figure 9.4.

Typed file demo–Address/Phone Book design.

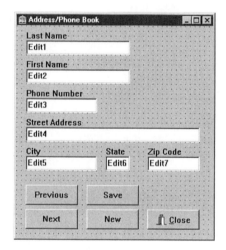

Examine the code in Listing 9.4, and then use it to add the code to the appropriate controls.

TYPE | **Listing 9.4. The Address/Phone Book application.**

```
unit Addr;

interface

uses
  Windows, Messages, SysUtils, Classes, Graphics, Controls, Forms,
  Dialogs, StdCtrls, Buttons;
```

```
type
  TForm1 = class(TForm)
    Edit1: TEdit;
    Edit2: TEdit;
    Edit3: TEdit;
    Edit4: TEdit;
    Edit5: TEdit;
    Edit6: TEdit;
    Edit7: TEdit;
    Label1: TLabel;
    Label2: TLabel;
    Label3: TLabel;
    Label4: TLabel;
    Label5: TLabel;
    Label6: TLabel;
    Label7: TLabel;
    Previous: TButton;
    Next: TButton;
    Save: TButton;
    New: TButton;
    Close: TBitBtn;
    procedure FormCreate(Sender: TObject);
    procedure NewClick(Sender: TObject);
    procedure PreviousClick(Sender: TObject);
    procedure NextClick(Sender: TObject);
    procedure SaveClick(Sender: TObject);
    procedure CloseClick(Sender: TObject);
  private
    { Private declarations }
    procedure LoadRecord;
    procedure SaveRecord;
    procedure ShowRecord;
    procedure ClearData;
  public
    { Public declarations }

  end;

var
  Form1: TForm1;

implementation
{$R *.DFM}

type
  Address = record
      Lastname: String[20];
      Firstname: String[20];
      Phone: String[15];
      StreetAddress : String[50];
      City : String[40];
      State : String[2];
      ZipCode : String[10];
  end;
```

Listing 9.4. continued

```
Var
    AddressFile : File of Address;
    AddressData : Address;
    Fname : String;
    RecSize,CurRec : Longint;

procedure TForm1.LoadRecord;
begin
  {Load record}
  Read(AddressFile,AddressData);
  {Display record on screen}
  ShowRecord;
end;

procedure TForm1.SaveRecord;
begin
  {Copy record from screen to record}
  AddressData.Lastname:=Edit1.Text;
  AddressData.Firstname:=Edit2.Text;
  AddressData.Phone:=Edit3.Text;
  AddressData.StreetAddress:=Edit4.Text;
  AddressData.City:=Edit5.Text;
  AddressData.State:=Edit6.Text;
  AddressData.ZipCode:=Edit7.Text;
  {Write record to disk}
  Write(AddressFile,AddressData);
end;

procedure TForm1.ClearData;
begin
      {Clear the edit boxes}
      Edit1.Text:='';
      Edit2.Text:='';
      Edit3.Text:='';
      Edit4.Text:='';
      Edit5.Text:='';
      Edit6.Text:='';
      Edit7.Text:='';
end;

procedure TForm1.FormCreate(Sender: TObject);
begin
    {Clear the edit boxes}
    ClearData;
    {Clear Current Record Counter}
    CurRec:=0;
    {Set Filename}
    Fname:='ADDRESS.DAT';
    {Set File Variable}
    AssignFile(AddressFile,Fname);
    {Get Record Size}
    RecSize:=SizeOf(AddressData);
    {If file exists, load it}
    If FileExists(Fname) then
```

```
       Begin
           Reset(AddressFile);
           If not Eof(AddressFile) then
               begin
                   Read(AddressFile,AddressData);
                   ShowRecord;
               end;
       end

       {Else create it}
       else
           Begin
               ClearData;
               Rewrite(AddressFile);
           end;
end;

procedure TForm1.NewClick(Sender: TObject);
begin
     repeat
         CurRec:=CurRec+1;
         Seek(AddressFile,CurRec);
     until Eof(AddressFile);
     {Clear edit boxes}
     ClearData;
     {Create a new record}
     SaveRecord;
     {Roll back to current record}
     Seek(AddressFile,CurRec);
end;

procedure TForm1.PreviousClick(Sender: TObject);
begin
       If CurRec-1 < 0 then
       begin
       {If past begining of file, put to first record
        and display message}
           CurRec:=0;
           Seek(AddressFile,CurRec);
           ShowMessage('This is the begining of the file');
       end
       {Otherwise, move back one record and display}
       else
       Begin
           CurRec:=CurRec-1;
           Seek(AddressFile,CurRec);
           Read(AddressFile,AddressData);
           Seek(AddressFile,CurRec);
           ShowRecord;
       end;
end;

procedure TForm1.NextClick(Sender: TObject);
```

continues

Listing 9.4. continued

```
begin
    {Advance to next record}
    CurRec:=CurRec+1;
    Seek(AddressFile,CurRec);
    {If not past end of file, read record and display}
    If not Eof(AddressFile) Then
        begin
          Read(AddressFile,AddressData);
          Seek(AddressFile,CurRec);
          ShowRecord;
        end
    {If past end of file, roll back to last record and
     display message}
    else
        begin
          CurRec:=CurRec-1;
          Seek(AddressFile,CurRec);
          ShowMessage('This is the end of the file');
        end;
end;

procedure TForm1.ShowRecord;
begin
  {Copy record data to edit boxes}
  Form1.Edit1.Text:=AddressData.Lastname;
  Form1.Edit2.Text:=AddressData.Firstname;
  Form1.Edit3.Text:=AddressData.Phone;
  Form1.Edit4.Text:=AddressData.StreetAddress;
  Form1.Edit5.Text:=AddressData.City;
  Form1.Edit6.Text:=AddressData.State;
  Form1.Edit7.Text:=AddressData.ZipCode;
end;

procedure TForm1.SaveClick(Sender: TObject);
begin
    {Save Record}
    SaveRecord;
    {Display record in edit boxes}
    ShowRecord;
end;

procedure TForm1.CloseClick(Sender: TObject);
begin
    {Save current record}
    SaveRecord;
    {Close File}
    CloseFile(AddressFile);
    {Exit application}
    Application.Terminate;
end;

end.
```

ANALYSIS You have just written your own Address/Phone Book database application without using a database engine. This program creates a data file called ADDRESS.DAT, takes input from the user, and stores it in the file in the form of records. The code in the New button clears the input fields and enables the user to enter a new record. The Save button writes the data out to the ADDRESS.DAT file. The Previous and Next buttons enable users to move back and forth in the database from one record to another. And of course, the Close button exits the application. As an extra feature, you may wish to set the MaxLength property of each edit control to that of the string size where the data is to be stored. This will limit the length of data entered into that field by the user and prevent strings longer than permitted from being entered and truncated by the program.

You now should be ready to test the Address/Phone Book application. Follow these steps:

1. Run the application, and you should see the screen in Figure 9.5. When the program runs for the first time, it detects whether the data file is present. In this case, it should find no file and create it (ADDRESS.DAT).

Figure 9.5.

*Typed file demo–
Address/Phone Book
application.*

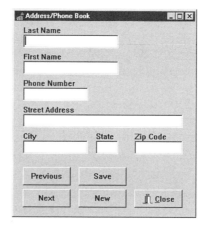

2. To enter the first record, type your name, address, and phone number into the edit boxes and select Save.

3. To enter the next record, press the New button. The boxes clear and are ready for you to enter the next record.

4. Enter a few more records by typing some data and pressing Save when you are done with each record.

5. Now test the application by moving through the records using the Previous and Next buttons. You should notice that when you get to the beginning or end of the file, a message box appears and indicates that you are at the end of the record. It is

obviously important to prevent or trap errors as well as attempts to move past the beginning or end of the file. The code you added to do this adds a nice touch to the application by notifying users that they are at the beginning or end.

6. Exit the program and then run it again. This time, it finds the data file (ADDRESS.DAT) and loads it displaying the first record. As before, you should be able to move through, edit, save, and add new records.

Now that you have created a working application, take a few minutes to go back and study the code. Read the comments in the listing to understand what is going on. In the FormCreate event, notice the code that checks for the existence of a data file. If one is found, it is opened using Reset. The first record is loaded and displayed on the screen; otherwise, it is created using Rewrite, and you are presented with a blank screen ready to input data. Study the code and comments in each of the buttons as well as these procedures: LoadRecord, SaveRecord, ShowRecord, ClearData. Once you are comfortable with typed files, continue on.

Untyped Files

Untyped files give you more flexibility in how you work with files. You essentially can jump to any location, change one byte or an entire block, save the data, and close the file. When you write your code, you have no rigid structure to worry about, and your code can work with any type of file you want, and in any fashion you choose. There is a catch, however. You must write your code to determine exactly where in the file you want to work. You do this by using file pointers, having some knowledge of the file, and building some intelligence into the program. Record sizes can vary, and it is entirely up to you to determine where and how big any record or piece of data is.

Caution is advised when working with untyped files, but they can be very useful. What if you had a file that was quite large, and you wanted to replace all the spaces with commas? You could write a simple Delphi program that would read the file into a buffer one block at a time, scan the buffer for spaces, change them to commas as it goes, and then save the changes back to disk. Again, it wouldn't matter if it was a text or binary file, nor does it matter how the data was stored. The point here is that you really have no restrictions as to how you access or work with data in untyped files. You're the boss!

Before you go any further, let's look at a few more procedures and a functions that you'll be using to build a sample application.

BlockRead

Syntax   `BlockRead(var F: File; var Buf; Count: Word`
                   `➥[; var Result: Word]);`

Purpose   Reads a block of data from disk into a buffer.

BlockWrite

Syntax   BlockWrite(var f: File; var Buf; Count: Word
                          ➡[; var Result: Word]);

Purpose   Writes a block of data from memory to disk.

FilePos

Syntax   FilePos(var F): Longint;

Purpose   Retrieves the current file pointer position.

Sample Project

These functions are discussed more as you go through the lesson, but now let's create a program to read a file and convert all spaces to commas.

Follow these steps to create the form for this application:

1. Create a new Delphi project, and save the unit as SP2CMA.PAS.
2. Save the project as SP2COMMA.DPR.
3. Using Figure 9.6 as a design guide, add three buttons, one edit box, and one label to the form.

Figure 9.6.

Space-to-comma
conversion program.

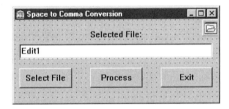

4. Change the form's caption to read Space to Comma Conversion.
5. Add an OpenDialog component to the form.
6. Double-click the Filter property, and use the Filter editor to set the Filter name to **All Files** and the Filter to ***.***.
7. Set the edit box and Label Visible property to False.

The meat of the program is in the OnClick event for the Process button. This is where code that loads data from disk, converts the spaces to commas, and saves the data back to disk. Let's take a look at some of the code.

In the following code, you set up some variables needed for this operation:

```
Var
   InFile : File;
   FBuffer : array [0..1023] of Byte;
   FPointer : Longint;
   BytesRead : Integer;
   x : Integer;
```

InFile is a variable of type File that you already have been exposed to. Fbuffer is an array of type Byte, which is a 1KB buffer that you can use to store the data read from the file. FPointer is used to store the file pointer (position in the file) so that you can return to this position after a read or write operation.

Next, you need to identify and prepare the file for use, as shown in the following code. You have seen AssignFile before, but notice that you have added another parameter to the Reset function. This is the record size for which the default is 128 bytes. Set it to 1 for this example.

```
begin
{Set the filename to a file variable}
AssignFile(InFile,Fname);
{Set record size to 1 byte}
Reset(InFile,1);
```

Once the file is opened, you need to load it 1KB at a time. Notice the while loop, which runs until you reach the end of the file. Also notice that on each pass through the loop, you get the file pointer position. Read a block using the BlockRead procedure to pull a 1KB block of data into the buffer. You then scan the data in the buffer one byte at a time, changing all spaces to commas. After the buffer is processed, use the Seek procedure to place the file pointer back to the beginning of the record. This is necessary because the file pointer is moved to the start of the next block of data after a read or write operation. Then use the BlockWrite to save the buffer back to disk. If there is more data to process, go through the loop again; otherwise, the file is updated and closed with CloseFile. When you are all done, you display a message saying Processing Complete!. See the following code:

```
While Not Eof(InFile) Do
      Begin
            {Get File Position}
            FPointer:=FilePos(InFile);
            {Read a 1K Byte Block into the buffer}
            BlockRead(InFile,FBuffer,SizeOf(FBuffer),BytesRead);
            {Convert spaces to commas}
            For x:= 0 to BytesRead-1 do
            Begin
                  If FBuffer[x]=32 then FBuffer[x]:=44;
            end;
            {Move Filepointer back to start of block}
            Seek(InFile,FPointer);
            {Write 1K Byte Buffer back to disk}
            BlockWrite(InFile,FBuffer,BytesRead);
      end;
```

```
        {Flush buffers to disk and close the file}
        CloseFile(InFile);
        ShowMessage('Processing Complete!');
end;
```

This code will be quite fast for a couple of reasons. First, the BlockRead and BlockWrite procedures load an entire block of data in one operation. Then, processing takes place in memory (the buffer), which is much faster than reading and writing a byte at a time. The buffer size could be set to a higher number if you wanted even more performance (especially with larger files).

Listing 9.5 is the entire listing; take a look at it and make sure to fill in the rest of the code in the correct buttons. When you are done, test it out.

TYPE **Listing 9.5. Space-to-Comma Conversion application.**

```
unit Sp2cma;

interface

uses
  Windows, Messages, SysUtils, Classes, Graphics, Controls, Forms,
  Dialogs, Menus, StdCtrls;

type
  TForm1 = class(TForm)
    Button1: TButton;
    Button2: TButton;
    Button3: TButton;
    OpenDialog1: TOpenDialog;
    Edit1: TEdit;
    Label1: TLabel;
    procedure Button2Click(Sender: TObject);
    procedure Button1Click(Sender: TObject);
    procedure Button3Click(Sender: TObject);
  private
    { Private declarations }
  public
    { Public declarations }
  end;

var
  Form1: TForm1;

implementation
Var
   Fname : String;
{$R *.DFM}
procedure TForm1.Button2Click(Sender: TObject);
```

continues

Listing 9.5. continued

```
Var
    InFile : File;
    FBuffer : array [0..1023] of Byte;
    FPointer : Longint;
    BytesRead : Integer;
    x : Integer;
begin
{Set the filename to a file variable}
AssignFile(InFile,Fname);
{Set record size to 1 byte}
Reset(InFile,1);
While Not Eof(InFile) Do
      Begin
            {Get File Position}
            FPointer:=FilePos(InFile);
            {Read a 1K Byte Block into the buffer}
            BlockRead(InFile,FBuffer,SizeOf(FBuffer),BytesRead);
            {Convert spaces to commas}
            For x:= 0 to BytesRead-1 do
            Begin
                 If FBuffer[x]=32 then FBuffer[x]:=44;
            end;
            {Move Filepointer back to start of block}
            Seek(InFile,FPointer);
            {Write 1K Byte Buffer back to disk}
            BlockWrite(InFile,FBuffer,BytesRead);
      end;
      {Flush buffers to disk and close the file}
      CloseFile(InFile);
      ShowMessage('Processing Complete!');
end;
procedure TForm1.Button1Click(Sender: TObject);
begin
  {Display Open File Dialogbox}
  OpenDialog1.FileName := '*.*';
  if OpenDialog1.Execute then
    {Get the selected filename}
    Fname := OpenDialog1.FileName;
    {Display selected filename}
    Edit1.Text:=Fname;
    {Show the Edit box and label now that we have the filename}
    Edit1.Visible:=True;
    Label1.Visible:=True;
end;

procedure TForm1.Button3Click(Sender: TObject);
begin
    {Exit the application}
    Application.Terminate;
end;

end.
```

ANALYSIS This program reads a text file (selected by the user) into FBuffer in blocks of up to 1,024 bytes. The contents of the buffer are then scanned, and the spaces are converted to commas (when the user presses the Process button). The file pointer is repositioned to the beginning of the block (because it was advanced after the BlockRead statement), and the changed data is written back out to the file. When the processing is done, the program displays the message Processing Complete!. At this point, the user can choose to process another file or select Exit to terminate the program.

Save the code, and then compile and run it. If all looks well, go to Notepad and create a simple text file with a sentence or two to use for testing. Switch back to the application, and press the Select File button. Using the dialog box, select the text file you created. Next, click the Process button. A message box should appear very quickly indicating that the program is finished. Exit the program, go back to Notepad, and load the file back in. If you had no errors in the code, you should see commas where before there were spaces. You might want to test this on other files as well. To verify operation on binary files, use a large document file written in a word processor, such as MS Write or Word 6, that saves files in a binary format.

This covers the basics for untyped files but only scratches the surface of what can actually be done with them. Use your imagination.

File Management, Directory Management, and Other File-Support Functions

There are a number of other file I/O and management functions and procedures that you should know about, but it's beyond the scope of this book to cover them all. It's up to you to familiarize yourself with the functions and procedures listed in Delphi's online help under the following three help categories:

> File Management Routines
> I/O Routines
> Text File Routines

At this point, you have used several of the functions and procedures you will find in these areas. Many of the functions do the same types of operations in a different way. For example, the following routine creates a File variable and assigns a filename to it:

```
Var
    MyFileVar : File
Begin
    {Create a file Variable and open a new file}
    AssignFile(MyFileVar,filename);
    ReWrite(MyFile);
End;
```

The File variable is used by the Rewrite procedure to create and open the file. You could also do the same thing with the FileCreate function, as shown in the following code:

```
Var
    Handle : Integer;
Begin
    Handle :=FileCreate('Filename');
End;
```

NEW TERM   The FileCreate function returns a file handle if the operation is successful. A *file handle* is nothing more than an integer value that will be used to identify the file until it is closed. If more than one file is opened, each file will have its own unique handle assigned. This file handle is used by an entire set of functions and procedures to read, write, move file position, and so on, similar to what you already have used earlier based on file variables.

There are some advantages to using the procedures based on file handles versus those that use file variables. For example, the FileOpen function enables you to OR a set of constants together to set the mode in which the file is opened. The following list shows constants from which you can choose two or more to OR together setting the mode at which the file will be opened:

fmOpenRead

fmOpenWrite

fmOpenReadWrite

fmShareCompat

fmShareExclusive

fmShareDenyWrite

fmShareDenyRead

fmShareDenyNone

The names are fairly descriptive, but see Delphi's online help if you need more information. You can find them under help for the SysUtils unit under the "Constants in the File Open Mode Constants" section.

If you wanted to open a file with exclusive access and deny access to all other programs or users, you would use the fmShareExclusive, as in the following example:

```
MyHandle:=FileOpen(fname,fmShareExclusive);
```

Remember, you can OR these constants together to get the desired access to the file. This can be important if you are sharing files with other programs on the same system or other users on a network.

The following are some other functions and routines of which you should be aware. Take a minute to look them over and see online help for more detail.

Erase	Deletes a file.
FileSize	Returns the size of a specified file.
GetDir	Returns the current directory for the specified drive.
MkDir	Creates a subdirectory.
Rename	Renames a file.
RmDir	Removes subdirectory.

There are many other functions and procedures available to you that have not been covered in this section. If you have reviewed online help for the three categories dealing with files suggested earlier, you should have a good idea what can be done with files in addition to what has been covered here.

Long Filenames

They are finally here...long filenames at last! No longer are you limited to the eight-character name with a three-character extension (8.3). Windows 95 and Windows NT allow long filenames. In Windows 95, these filenames can be up to 255 characters long, including a NULL, and they enable you to be much more descriptive when naming your files. The maximum path length is 260 characters, including NULL.

For backward compatibility, a short filename is created based on the first six characters of the filename. If multiple long filenames have the same first six characters and the same extension, the operating system uses an algorithm to add numbers in the filename to create a short filename compatible with older versions of DOS and Windows. Here are a couple examples:

Long Filename	Short Filename
LongFileName1.TXT	LONGFI~1.TXT
LongFileName2.TXT	LONGFI~2.TXT

Delphi 95 supports long filenames with changes to file-related components, functions, and procedures. You need not do anything because Delphi and the OS (Windows 95, NT) handle the details for you. You simply pass the long filename to your functions, procedures, and programs, and you are done. Finally, you are not required to use the long filenames, so feel free to use the 8.3 filename, if you wish.

Printing

Although we increasingly live in an electronic world in which we send faxes and e-mail and use computers for slide presentations, there always comes a time when you must print text or graphics from a program, such as the one that generates form letters and customized flyers.

This section teaches you how to print without the use of add-in tools such as QuickReport. QuickReport is covered on Day 12, "Reports and Charts." Here you learn two ways to print directly from Delphi programs, which can save on overhead if you do not need the features of a report writer or another printing add-on. You learn about the basic printing methods in which you send one line or string of text at a time to the printer.

This section also examines the printer objects available in Delphi. Using the printer object, you can print text. You learn how to use the printer dialog boxes and how to print graphics, along with all the basic information you need to know to add full print capabilities to your applications without the need for add-ons, report generators, and so on.

Basic Printing with Pascal

If you are familiar with printing in Pascal or other languages, this is nothing new. Basic printing simply involves creating a file variable, which you just learned about, and assigning it to the printer. Then you use a WriteLn statement to send the text to the printer. This type of printing is primitive compared to all the features built into Windows, but you occasionally might want to print this way. Suppose, for example, that a computer is hooked up to a line printer for the purpose of saving readings as they are gathered in a factory. If the computer has a hardware failure, all the readings gathered up to that point are on the printout. Likewise, you might want to print a simple list that does not require graphics, fonts, or other formatting available in Windows.

The following code uses a writeLn statement to print:

```
var
  P : TextFile;
begin
    AssignPrn(P);
    rewrite(P);
    writeln(P,'This is a test of printing');
    CloseFile(P);
end;
```

As you can see, a variable called P of type TextFile is declared. A variation of Assign is used here: AssignPrn. It assigns the variable to the printer port, treating the port like a file. Next, the printer port must be opened, so rewrite is used. Text is sent to the printer with the writeln procedure, and the printer port is closed with CloseFile. It is important to close the printer port to complete the operation. Any text left in memory is sent to the printer, and the port is closed—just like a file.

To see how this works, create a program for selecting a text file and sending it to the printer. Look at Figure 9.7 as you design the screen. Add two buttons, an OpenDialog component, and a label to the form. Use the OpenDialog filter property to add a .TXT filter. Then fill in the code for the controls using Listing 9.6. Save the project as FILE2PRN.DPR and the unit to FILEPRN.PAS.

Figure 9.7.

Text file transfer—
FILE2PRN.DPR.

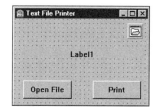

NOTE

You need to add Printers to the uses statement to have access to the printer functions.

TYPE **Listing 9.6. Text file printer.**

```
unit Fileprn;

interface

uses
  Windows, Messages, SysUtils, Classes, Graphics, Controls, Forms,
  Dialogs, StdCtrls,Printers;

type
  TForm1 = class(TForm)
    Button1: TButton;
    OpenDialog1: TOpenDialog;
    Button2: TButton;
    Label1: TLabel;
    procedure Button1Click(Sender: TObject);
    procedure Button2Click(Sender: TObject);
  private
    { Private declarations }
  public
    { Public declarations }
  end;
```

continues

Listing 9.6. continued

```
var
  Form1: TForm1;

implementation

{$R *.DFM}
Var
   Fname : String;

procedure TForm1.Button1Click(Sender: TObject);
begin
  if OpenDialog1.Execute then
  begin
    Fname:=OpenDialog1.FileName;
    Label1.Caption:='Ready to print ' + Fname;
  end;
end;

procedure TForm1.Button2Click(Sender: TObject);
Var
   P,F : TextFile;
   TempStr : String;
begin
   AssignFile(F,Fname);
   Reset(F);
   AssignPrn(P);
   Rewrite(P);
   Label1.Caption:='Now Printing '+ Fname;
   While Not Eof(F) Do
   begin
        Readln(F,TempStr);
        Writeln(P,TempStr);
   end;
   CloseFile(F);
   CloseFile(P);
   Label1.Caption:='Printing Complete!';
end;

end.
```

ANALYSIS   This program enables you to use the FileOpen dialog box to choose a file for printing.
It reads the file one line at a time and sends each line to the printer. Give it a try by
printing some text files.

Printing with Delphi's TPrinter **Object**

Rather than going through all the printer object properties, methods, and so on, (which is
beyond the scope of this book), this section has you develop a few programs that show you
how to add printer capabilities to your applications and demonstrate the printer object's use.

In Delphi, you use the `TPrinter` object to access the Windows printer interface. Delphi's `Printers` unit contains the `Printer` variable, which is declared as an instance of the `TPrinter` object:

```
Printer : TPrinter;
```

To use the `TPrinter` object, you must add the `Printers` unit to the `uses` clause of your code, as shown in the following example. Unlike some of the other commonly used units, the `Printers` unit is not added by default to your Delphi project.

```
uses
  Windows, Messages, SysUtils, Classes, Graphics, Controls, Forms,
  Dialogs, StdCtrls,Printers;
```

Once you do this, you can use `Printer` to reference properties in the `TPrinter` object.

Using the `TPrinter` Object

Before you can use the `TPrinter` object, you need to understand the following properties and methods:

Property/Method	Description
Canvas	Declared as an instance of the `TCanvas` object. The `Canvas` is where the page or document is built in memory before it is printed. The `Canvas` has properties, including `Pen` and `Brush`, that enable you to draw and put text on it.
TextOut	A method of the `TCanvas` object. It enables text to be sent to the `Canvas`.
BeginDoc	Used to start a print job.
EndDoc	Used to end a print job. Actual printing does not occur until a call to `EndDoc` is made.
PageHeight	Returns the page height in pixels.
NewPage	Forces a new page on the printer and resets the `Pen` property value of the `Canvas` back to (`0`, `0`).
PageNumber	Returns the number of the page currently being printed.

Suppose, for example, that you want to print text using the printer object. You might have code that looks like this:

```
Printer.BeginDoc;
Printer.Canvas.TextOut(10,10,'I am printing through the printer
➡ object');
Printer.EndDoc;
```

This code causes the text I am printing through the printer object to be printed starting at the tenth pixel to the right and the tenth pixel down on the canvas. BeginDoc starts the print job. The text is sent to the canvas with the Canvas TextOut property. EndDoc causes the text to be printed and ends the print job.

These properties and methods only scratch the surface of what is available, but they are enough to enable you to create the text-file printing program that you wrote earlier with the printer object.

Load the FILE2PRN.DPR project, and resave it as FILE2POB.DPR. Resave the unit as FILEPOBJ.PAS. Edit the code in the Print button—in this case, Button2. The program reads the file one line at a time as before, but it now calculates the position on the canvas to which the text should be sent and puts it on the canvas to be printed.

Listing 9.7 shows the revised text-file printing program. The comments in the listing will help you understand the code. Working with FILEOBJ.PAS, modify the code in the Print button (Button2) so that it looks like the code in Listing 9.7. You can change the Caption property if you want to read the text-file printer using the TPrinter object.

TYPE   **Listing 9.7. Text-file printer using the TPrinter object.**

```
unit Filepobj;

interface

uses
  Windows, Messages, SysUtils, Classes, Graphics, Controls, Forms,
  Dialogs, StdCtrls,Printers;

type
  TForm1 = class(TForm)
    Button1: TButton;
    OpenDialog1: TOpenDialog;
    Button2: TButton;
    Label1: TLabel;
    procedure Button1Click(Sender: TObject);
    procedure Button2Click(Sender: TObject);
  private
    { Private declarations }
  public
    { Public declarations }
  end;

var
  Form1: TForm1;

implementation
```

```
{$R *.DFM}
Var
   Fname : String;

procedure TForm1.Button1Click(Sender: TObject);
begin
  if OpenDialog1.Execute then
  begin
    Fname:=OpenDialog1.FileName;
    Label1.Caption:='Ready to print ' + Fname;
  end;
end;

procedure TForm1.Button2Click(Sender: TObject);
Var
   F : TextFile;
   TempStr,PageNum : String;
   Ctr,x,PHeight,LineSpace: Integer;
begin
   Ctr:=1;
   {Open the text file to be printed}
   AssignFile(F,Fname);
   Reset(F);
   {Start printing}
   Printer.BeginDoc;
   {Get the Page Height}
   PHeight:=Printer.PageHeight;
   {Calculate distance to space lines based on a 60 line page}
   LineSpace:=PHeight DIV 60;
   {Get the current page being printed}
   PageNum:=IntToStr(Printer.PageNumber);
   {Update label with current page number}
   Label1.Caption:='Now Printing '+ Fname + ' Page ' + PageNum;
   While Not Eof(F) Do
   begin
        {Read a line of text from the text file into TempStr}
        Readln(F,TempStr);
        {Send the contents of TempStr to the printer}
        Printer.Canvas.TextOut(0,x,TempStr);
        {Increment x the appropriate number of pixels
         to print the next line }
        x:=x+LineSpace;
        {Count the number of lines printed}
        Ctr:=Ctr+1;
        {If 60 lines have been printed, start a new page, get
         page number and reset our counters}

        If Ctr > 59 then
        begin
            Printer.NewPage;
            x:=0;
            Ctr:=0;
            PageNum:=IntToStr(Printer.PageNumber);
            Label1.Caption:='Now Printing '+ Fname + ' Page ' + PageNum;
        end;
```

continues

Listing 9.7. continued

```
    end;
    {Close the text file and cause the job to print}
    CloseFile(F);
    Printer.EndDoc;
    Label1.Caption:='Printing Complete!' + ' Pages printed = '+ PageNum;
  end;

end.
```

 This program behaves much as it did before, except that it is now printing through the printer object. There are also a few changes to the status messages. Make sure that you save your work before you test the new version of the text file printer.

This method of printing enables you to add graphics to a document easily. You also can add code to change the page orientation, font sizes, styles, and much more. You get this extra capability without having to write much code. You simply tell the `Printer` object what to print and how it should be printed.

Using the `TPrinterDialog` and `TPrinterSetupDialog` Components

You have seen commercial applications in which dialog boxes are seen as commercial applications in which dialog boxes are used to choose the print options, such as the number of copies, collating, and the page orientation. In Windows with Delphi, it does not take much to do those things. Just put the `TPrinterDialog` component on the page and add a few lines of code. Your application now has printer dialog boxes for the user. The code that activates this looks like this:

```
if PrintDialog1.Execute then
  Begin
      {your print code}
  end;
```

When this code is executed, the standard Windows Print dialog box appears giving the user choices for the pending print job. After the user makes choices, the print job is completed using the specified settings—except for the number of copies, which requires a loop. For the most part, it is as simple as that.

To see how this works, modify the text-file printing program to enable Print Dialog support. Make a copy of the previous version by saving it to new filenames. First, load `FILE2POB.DPR`. Select Save Project As, and name it `PRINTDLG.DPR`. Select Save File As, and name it `PRNDLG.PAS`.

Once you make a few simple changes, you can test the Print dialog box features. From the Dialogs tab, select the PrintDialog component, and drop it on the form. Modify the code in the Print button to look like the code in Listing 9.8.

TYPE **Listing 9.8. Adding Print dialog support.**

```
procedure PrintFile;
Var
   F : TextFile;
   TempStr,PageNum : String;
   Ctr,x,PHeight,LineSpace: Integer;
begin
   Ctr:=1;
   {Open the text file to be printed}
   AssignFile(F,Fname);
   Reset(F);
   if PrintDialog1.Execute then
   Begin
     {Start printing}
     Printer.BeginDoc;
     {Get the Page Height}
     PHeight:=Printer.PageHeight;
     {Calculate distance to space lines based on a 60 line page}
     LineSpace:=PHeight DIV 60;
     {Get the current page being printed}
     PageNum:=IntToStr(Printer.PageNumber);
     {Update label with current page number}
     Label1.Caption:='Now Printing '+ Fname + ' Page ' + PageNum;
     While Not Eof(F) Do
     begin
        {Read a line of text from the text file into TempStr}
        Readln(F,TempStr);
        {Send the contents of TempStr to the printer}
        Printer.Canvas.TextOut(0,x,TempStr);
        {Increment x the appropriate number of pixels to print
         the next line }
        x:=x+LineSpace;
        {Count the number of lines printed}
        Ctr:=Ctr+1;
        {If 60 lines have been printed, start a new page,
         get page number and reset our counters}

        If Ctr > 59 then
        begin
            Printer.NewPage;
            x:=0;
            Ctr:=0;
            PageNum:=IntToStr(Printer.PageNumber);
            Label1.Caption:='Now Printing '+ Fname + ' Page ' + PageNum;
        end;
```

continues

Listing 9.8. continued

```
      end;
      {Close the text file and cause the job to print}
      CloseFile(F);
      Printer.EndDoc;
      Label1.Caption:='Printing Complete!' + ' Pages printed = '+ PageNum;
    end;
end;
```

ANALYSIS The only difference from the program in Listing 9.7 is the if PrintDialog and begin...end statements:

```
if PrintDialog1.Execute then
begin
        {print code...}
end;
```

When you run the program and select Print, the Print dialog box appears, as shown in Figure 9.8. It waits for the user to make choices before printing the job. You can get to the Properties dialog box, shown in Figure 9.9, by pressing the Properties button.

Figure 9.8.

The Print dialog box.

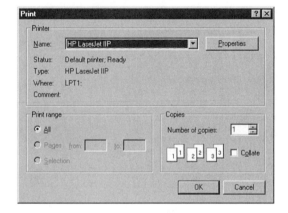

Figure 9.9.

The Properties dialog box.

Fonts and Font Sizes

Changing fonts and font sizes is easy, too. Suppose, for example, that you want to change the font size to 18 and the font to Times New Roman (keep in mind that when you set the font, it must be installed on the users' systems). The Font property of the canvas enables you to do just that. By adding the following lines of code to the print routine in your program, you can easily change the font to fit your needs:

```
{Set Font Size}
Printer.Canvas.Font.Size:=18;
{Set Font Type to Times Roman}
Printer.Canvas.Font.Name:='Times New Roman';
```

One problem remains, though. The original program was based on the default 10-point System font and assumed that there were 60 lines per page. When you change fonts and font sizes, the old code will not work so well.

To eliminate this problem, add code that uses the font size to calculate how many lines can fit on a page. The following code, for example, adds 10 lines to the font size and calculates the LinesPerPage variable so that there is space between the lines when the LineSpace variable is calculated:

```
{Calculate the lines per page based on the font size}
LinesPerPage:=PHeight Div FontSize+10;
{Calculate distance to space lines based on the lines per page}
LineSpace:=PHeight DIV LinesPerPage;
```

The new variables that are added to accommodate these changes are FontSize and LinesPerPage. Add these changes to the Print button code. Make sure that the code looks like the code in Listing 9.9. Then save your code and try it out.

Type   **Listing 9.9. Print button code.**

```
procedure TForm1.Button2Click(Sender: TObject);
Var
    F : TextFile;
    TempStr,PageNum : String;
    Ctr,x,PHeight,LineSpace,LinesPerPage,FontSize: Integer;
begin
    Ctr:=1;
    {Open the text file to be printed}
    AssignFile(F,Fname);
    Reset(F);
    if PrintDialog1.Execute then
    Begin
      {Start printing}
      Printer.BeginDoc;
      {Get the Page Height}
      PHeight:=Printer.PageHeight;
      {Set the Font to 18}
      Printer.Canvas.Font.Size:=18;
      {Set Font Type to Times Roman}
      Printer.Canvas.Font.Name:='Times New Roman';
      {Calculate the number of lines per page based on the font
       adding 10 to leave some room between lines}
      LinesPerPage:=PHeight Div FontSize+10;
      {Calculate distance to space lines based on the lines per page}
      LineSpace:=PHeight DIV LinesPerPage;
      {Get the current page being printed}
      PageNum:=IntToStr(Printer.PageNumber);
      {Update label with current page number}
      Label1.Caption:='Now Printing '+ Fname + ' Page ' + PageNum;
      While Not Eof(F) Do
      begin
          {Read a line of text from the text file into TempStr}
          Readln(F,TempStr);
          {Send the contents of TempStr to the printer}
          Printer.Canvas.TextOut(0,x,TempStr);
          {Increment x the appropriate number of pixels
           to print the next line }
```

```
      x:=x+LineSpace;
      {Count the number of lines printed}
      Ctr:=Ctr+1;
      {If LinesPerPage have been printed, start a new page, get
       page number and reset our counters}

      If Ctr > LinesPerPage-1 then
      begin
          Printer.NewPage;
          x:=0;
          Ctr:=0;
          PageNum:=IntToStr(Printer.PageNumber);
          Label1.Caption:='Now Printing '+ Fname + ' Page ' + PageNum;
      end;
    end;
  {Close the text file and cause the job to print}
  CloseFile(F);
  Printer.EndDoc;
  Label1.Caption:='Printing Complete!' + ' Pages printed = '+ PageNum;
  end;
end;
```

ANALYSIS   This program prints text files in 18-point Times New Roman, calculates the number of lines of text that can be printed on a page, and starts a new page at the appropriate place. Using this technique, you can enable the user to choose the font by means of a Font dialog box. You get the font information from the user instead of hard coding it in the program as you do here.

Now you need to finish up this program by adding the Font dialog box to enable the user to select the font, the font size, the font style, and so on. You need to add a new button called Font. You also need to add code to enable the program to print the number of copies selected by the user.

To change the font settings, you use the Font property and its properties to get information from the Font dialog box and to apply it to the canvas. The following line sets the font size from the Font dialog box settings:

```
Printer.Canvas.Font.Size:=FontDialog1.Font.Size;
```

This line sets the font to Times New Roman:

```
Printer.Canvas.Font.Name:='Times New Roman';
```

This line sets the type from the Font dialog box:

```
Printer.Canvas.Font.Type:=FontDialog1.Font.Type;
```

For the number of copies, you must create a loop that encompasses the print code and executes it the number of times specified by the user. To get the number of copies specified by the user, use the following code. The number of copies is stored in the variable NumCopies for later use.

```
NumCopies:=PrintDialog1.Copies
```

To make these changes, modify the code in the Print button so that it looks like the code in Listing 9.10. Add a second label to the form just below Label1. Pay close attention to the code because some lines have been moved to make the loops work properly.

TYPE   Listing 9.10. Print button that includes code for handling the font and number of copies.

```
procedure TForm1.Button2Click(Sender: TObject);
Var
    F : TextFile;
    TempStr,PageNum : String;
    Ctr,x,PHeight,LineSpace,LinesPerPage,FontSize,CopyNum,
    NumCopies: Integer;
begin
    if PrintDialog1.Execute then
    Begin
      Ctr:=1;
      {Open the text file to be printed}
      AssignFile(F,Fname);
      {Get the number of copies to print from the Print Dialog}
      NumCopies:=PrintDialog1.Copies;
      {Loop through and print for each copy to be printed}
      for CopyNum:=1 to NumCopies do
      begin
        {Open file at begining}
        Reset(F);
        {Clear the counters for next pass}
        x:=0;Ctr:=0;
        {Start printing}
        Printer.BeginDoc;
        {Get the Page Height}
        PHeight:=Printer.PageHeight;
        {Set the Font size from the Font Dialog}
        Printer.Canvas.Font.Size:=FontDialog1.Font.Size;
        {Set the font name from the Font Dialog}
        Printer.Canvas.Font.Name:=FontDialog1.Font.Name;
        {Set the font style from the Font Dialog}
        Printer.Canvas.Font.Style:=FontDialog1.Font.Style;
        {Calculate the number of lines per page based on the font
        adding 10 to leave some room between lines}
        LinesPerPage:=PHeight Div FontSize+10;
        {Calculate distance to space lines based on the lines per page}
        LineSpace:=PHeight DIV LinesPerPage;
        {Get the current page being printed}
```

```
    PageNum:=IntToStr(Printer.PageNumber);
    {Update label with current page number}
    Label1.Caption:='Now Printing '+ Fname + ' Page ' + PageNum;
    While Not Eof(F) Do
      begin
        {Read a line of text from the text file into TempStr}
        Readln(F,TempStr);
        {Send the contents of TempStr to the printer}
        Printer.Canvas.TextOut(0,x,TempStr);
        {Increment x the appropriate number of pixels to
         print the next line }
        x:=x+LineSpace;
        {Count the number of lines printed}
        Ctr:=Ctr+1;
        {If LinesPerPage have been printed, start a new page, get
         page number and reset our counters}

        If Ctr > LinesPerPage-1 then
        begin
            Printer.NewPage;
            x:=0;
            Ctr:=0;
            PageNum:=IntToStr(Printer.PageNumber);
            Label1.Caption:='Now Printing '+ Fname + ' Page ' + PageNum;
        end;
      end;
    {Close the text file and cause the job to print}
    CloseFile(F);
    Printer.EndDoc;
    Label1.Caption:='Printing Complete!' + ' Pages printed = '+ PageNum;
    Label2.Caption:='Number of Copies = ' + IntToStr(NumCopies);
  end;
 end;
end;
```

 These changes read the settings from the Font dialog box, shown in Figure 9.10, and use them for the print job. The print job is printed the number of times specified by the user in the Print dialog box.

Figure 9.10.

The Font dialog box.

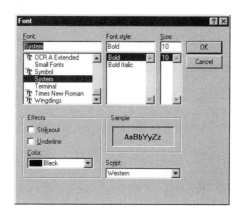

You can look over the properties that are available to you by using the online help. When you have made the changes to the program, it should look like the code in Listing 9.11.

TYPE   **Listing 9.11. Using the Print & Font Dialogs application.**

```
unit Prndlg;

interface

uses
  Windows, Messages, SysUtils, Classes, Graphics, Controls, Forms,
  Dialogs, StdCtrls,Printers;

type
  TForm1 = class(TForm)
    Button1: TButton;
    OpenDialog1: TOpenDialog;
    Button2: TButton;
    Label1: TLabel;
    PrintDialog1: TPrintDialog;
    FontDialog1: TFontDialog;
    Button3: TButton;
    Label2: TLabel;
    procedure Button1Click(Sender: TObject);
    procedure Button2Click(Sender: TObject);
    procedure Button3Click(Sender: TObject);
  private
    { Private declarations }
  public
    { Public declarations }
  end;

var
  Form1: TForm1;

implementation

{$R *.DFM}
Var
   Fname : String;

procedure TForm1.Button1Click(Sender: TObject);
begin
  if OpenDialog1.Execute then
  begin
    Fname:=OpenDialog1.FileName;
    Label1.Caption:='Ready to print ' + Fname;
  end;
end;

procedure TForm1.Button2Click(Sender: TObject);
Var
   F : TextFile;
   TempStr,PageNum : String;
```

```
      Ctr,x,PHeight,LineSpace,LinesPerPage,FontSize,CopyNum,
        NumCopies: Integer;
begin
    if PrintDialog1.Execute then
    Begin
      Ctr:=1;
      {Open the text file to be printed}
      AssignFile(F,Fname);
      {Get the number of copies to print from the Print Dialog}
      NumCopies:=PrintDialog1.Copies;
      {Loop through and print for each copy to be printed}
      for CopyNum:=1 to NumCopies do
      begin
        {Open file at begining}
        Reset(F);
        {Clear the counters for next pass}
        x:=0;Ctr:=0;
        {Start printing}
        Printer.BeginDoc;
        {Get the Page Height}
        PHeight:=Printer.PageHeight;
        {Set the Font size from the Font Dialog}
        Printer.Canvas.Font.Size:=FontDialog1.Font.Size;
        {Set the font name from the Font Dialog}
        Printer.Canvas.Font.Name:=FontDialog1.Font.Name;
        {Set the font style from the Font Dialog}
        Printer.Canvas.Font.Style:=FontDialog1.Font.Style;
        {Calculate the number of lines per page based on the font
        adding 10 to leave some room between lines}
        LinesPerPage:=PHeight Div FontSize+10;
        {Calculate distance to space lines based on the lines per page}
        LineSpace:=PHeight DIV LinesPerPage;
        {Get the current page being printed}
        PageNum:=IntToStr(Printer.PageNumber);
        {Update label with current page number}
        Label1.Caption:='Now Printing '+ Fname + ' Page ' + PageNum;
        While Not Eof(F) Do
          begin
            {Read a line of text from the text file into TempStr}
            Readln(F,TempStr);
            {Send the contents of TempStr to the printer}
            Printer.Canvas.TextOut(0,x,TempStr);
            {Increment x the appropriate number of pixels to print
             the next line }
            x:=x+LineSpace;
            {Count the number of lines printed}
            Ctr:=Ctr+1;
            {If LinesPerPage have been printed, start a new page,
             get page number and reset our counters}

            If Ctr > LinesPerPage-1 then
            begin
                Printer.NewPage;
                x:=0;
```

continues

Listing 9.11. continued

```
                Ctr:=0;
                PageNum:=IntToStr(Printer.PageNumber);
                Label1.Caption:='Now Printing '+ Fname + ' Page ' + PageNum;
            end;
          end;
        {Close the text file and cause the job to print}
        CloseFile(F);
        Printer.EndDoc;
        Label1.Caption:='Printing Complete!' + ' Pages printed = '+ PageNum;
        Label2.Caption:='Number of Copies = ' + IntToStr(NumCopies);
      end;
    end;
end;
procedure TForm1.Button3Click(Sender: TObject);
begin
    FontDialog1.Execute;
end;

end.
```

ANALYSIS This code enables users to select a file to be printed via a Windows OpenDialog box. The Font button enables users to select the font to be used when printed via the standard Windows Font dialog box. Next, the Print button displays the standard Windows Print dialog box, which provides users with access to all the features usually found there. As you can see, the majority of the code is found in the Print button's OnClick event.

The finished program's form should look like the one shown in Figure 9.11.

Figure 9.11.

Using the Print & Font Dialogs application.

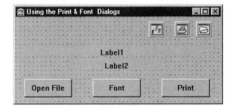

Sending Graphics to the Printer

You have printed text using the old-fashioned method, and you have sent text through the TPrinter object. What about graphics? You might want to create logos, charts, and other non-text information. This section shows you how to create just about any printed graphic. You are limited only by the type of the printer and driver that you are using. Some printer drivers do not support printing images.

Sending graphics to the printer is about the same as sending it to the screen. You use the TPrinter object's Canvas and its properties and methods to draw or place graphics on the canvas. In fact, you can design graphics by first sending them to the screen. When you are happy with what they will look like, you can modify the code to send them to the printer.

Consider the following code, for example. It draws a circle on the surface of Form1 in the upper-left corner.

```
begin
     {Set the width of the pen to be 5 pixels wide}
     Form1.Canvas.Pen.Width:=5;
     {Draw an ellipse with the upper left corner at 0,0
      and the lower right corner at 200,200}
     Form1.Canvas.Ellipse(0, 0, 200, 200);
end;
```

The following code draws the same circle in the same location on the printer canvas and sends it to the printer:

```
begin
     {Start the print job}
     Printer.BeginDoc;
     {Set the width of the pen to be 5 pixels wide}
     Printer.Canvas.Pen.Width:=5;
     {Draw an ellipse with the upper left corner at 0,0
      and the lower right corner at 200,200}
     Printer.Canvas.Ellipse(0, 0, 200, 200);
     {complete and print the print job}
     Printer.EndDoc;
end;
```

By adding the BeginDoc and EndDoc lines and by changing Form1 to Printer to point to the printer canvas instead of the form canvas, you can send the same graphics to the printer. You can create a small program with a Screen button and a Printer button to test this code. You can send almost any graphic to the printer as easily as you can to the screen.

Now create a program that enables the user to use a File Open dialog box to select a graphics file—such as a bitmap (.bmp) or Windows metafile (.wmf)—to display it on the screen, and to send it to the printer. Delphi makes this task easy. You use an image component to store the graphic on the screen and the CopyRect method to move the image to the printer canvas, which sends the image to the printer. In this program, you enable the user to select a divisor for changing the size of the finished printout. You also add code to print the graphic in the center of the page.

First, create the form shown in Figure 9.12 with the following components:

Quantity	Component
2	Buttons
1	image component
1	OpenDialog component
1	Panel
2	Labels
1	SpinEdit component from the Samples tab

Figure 9.12.

The Image Printer form.

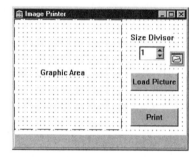

Create a new project. Call it PRINTPIC.DPR, and call the unit PICPRINT.PAS. Lay out the form as shown in Figure 9.12. Change the caption of the form to Image Printer. Change the button captions to Load Picture and Print. Add filters to the OpenDialog component for graphics files (.bmp and .wmf) and all files. For the SpinEdit component, set MinValue to 1 and MaxValue to 10. Change the Label1 caption to Size Divisor and Label2 caption to Graphic Area. Change the Image1.Stretch property to True so that the image is resized to fit in the image box, if possible, when it is loaded. Likewise, make sure that the AutoSize property is set to False.

 NOTE
When you place the image box on the form, make it a reasonably sized square on the form, and position it so that its Top and Left properties are both set to 0. If you have trouble, set them to 0 in the Object Inspector; the box will snap into position. The positioning is important.

To load the image, execute the LoadFromFile method for the image box that you placed on the form. In this case, feed the filename from OpenDialog as a parameter to the LoadFromFile method as shown in the following code sample. When this code is excuted, the image is loaded and displayed.

```
If OpenDialog1.Execute then
        Image1.Picture.LoadFromFile(OpenDialog1.FileName);
```

To print the image, you need to know where the center of the canvas is so that you can place the image in the center. The following code gets the center X,Y-coordinates by getting the printer page height and width and then by dividing the height and width by 2. It then stores the values in the CenterX and CenterY variables.

```
{Find Center on the Canvas}
    PHeight:=Printer.PageHeight;
    PWidth:=Printer.PageWidth;
    CenterX:=PWidth Div 2;
    CenterY:=PHeight Div 2;
```

You calculate the placement coordinates based on the user input divisor. First, get the user input value from the SpinEdit control's Value property. To place the image, you need to know the X,Y-coordinates of the Top,Left and Bottom,Right positions. The variables are as follows:

Variable	Position
X1	Left
Y1	Top
X2	Right
Y2	Bottom

The following code calculates the center position based on the divisor selected by the user:

```
{Calculate center position with the user set size divisor}
    SDiv:=SpinEdit1.Value;
    X1:=CenterX-(PWidth Div (SDiv*2));
    Y1:=CenterY-(PHeight Div (SDiv*2));
    X2:=CenterX+(PWidth Div (SDiv*2));
    Y2:=CenterY+(PHeight Div (SDiv*2));
```

The user-input divisor is multiplied by 2. This product is then divided into the page width or height. This quotient is subtracted from or added to the CenterX and CenterY values to determine the center position. If the user selects the default divisor—1—the image is printed centered on the page, and it takes up the full page. If the printer page measures 2000 by 2000 pixels, the center position is 1000,1000, as in the following example:

```
X1 = 1000 - (2000 Div (1*2))
or X1 = 1000 - 1000
or X1 = 0
```

This sets the X1 (left) position to 0, which is the far left position on the page.

```
X2 = 1000 + (2000 Div (1*2))
or X2 = 1000 + 1000
or X2 = 2000
```

This sets the X2 (right) position to 2000, which is the far right position.

This gives the settings for an image that takes up the full page. By changing the divisor, the user can reduce the size of the printed image. You use the Div operator for division because you are working with integers and want to avoid remainder values. With this formula, the image always is printed in the center of the page regardless of the user-input divisor.

To put the graphic on the printer canvas, you need to use the CopyRect method, which copies a rectangular area from one canvas to another, as shown here:

```
procedure CopyRect(Dest: TRect; Canvas: TCanvas; Source: TRect);
```

The destination and source rectangles are passed as variables of type Trect. In this case, the source canvas is the canvas of Form1.

You position the image box at 0,0 because the CopyRect statement takes the image from the form canvas—not directly from the image box. If you set the image box to 0,0 in the form client area, you do not have to worry about offsets in the calculations. If you move the image box to another location with no offset values calculated in, you might lose part or all of the of the image because it would be out of the rectangular area that you are copying.

Because CopyRect takes two variables of type TRect, you must declare two variables of this type and put the data in them. To declare the variables, use this code:

```
Var
      PrnRect, ImgRect : TRect;
```

TRect is defined as a record in the Windows unit as follows:

```
TRect = record
  case Integer of
    0: (Left, Top, Right, Bottom: Integer);
    1: (TopLeft, BottomRight: TPoint);
end;
```

You feed it four values. Next, you use the Rect function to store data in the new variables. The Rect function takes the X1,Y1,X2,Y2—or Top,Left,Right,Bottom—coordinates as parameters and returns the data as a record of type TRect to the variables, as shown in this example:

```
{Store the desired Printer Canvas Rect Size in PrnRect}
PrnRect:=Rect(X1,Y1,X2,Y2);
{Get the Image Box Canvas Rect Size in ImgRect}
ImgRect:=Rect(0,0,Image1.Width,Image1.Height);
```

Once you assign the values to PrnRect and ImgRect, use the variables in the CopyRect method statement to copy the image to the printer canvas:

```
{Copy the image from image box to printer canvas}
Printer.Canvas.CopyRect(PrnRect,Form1.Canvas,ImgRect );
```

With a few exceptions—such as hiding the label that marks the graphics area when the graphic is displayed, and updating the panel with the program status—you now know how to make a working image printer.

Listing 9.12 shows the completed code for the image printer program. Take some time to study the comments. Input the code in the proper places, and then test the program.

TYPE   **Listing 9.12. Picprint, the image printer program.**

```
unit Picprint;

interface

uses
  Windows, Messages, SysUtils, Classes, Graphics, Controls, Forms,
  Dialogs,Printers,StdCtrls, ExtCtrls, Spin;

type
  TForm1 = class(TForm)
    Button1: TButton;
    Button2: TButton;
    OpenDialog1: TOpenDialog;
    Image1: TImage;
    SpinEdit1: TSpinEdit;
    Panel1: TPanel;
    Label1: TLabel;
    Label2: TLabel;
    procedure Button1Click(Sender: TObject);
    procedure Button2Click(Sender: TObject);
  private
    { Private declarations }
  public
    { Public declarations }
  end;

var
  Form1: TForm1;

implementation

{$R *.DFM}

Var
   PHeight,PWidth : Integer;
```

continues

Listing 9.12. continued

```
procedure TForm1.Button1Click(Sender: TObject);
Var
     PrnRect,ImgRect:TRect;
     CenterX,CenterY,X1,Y1,X2,Y2,SDiv : Integer;
begin
     Panel1.Caption:='Printing...';
     Printer.BeginDoc;
     {Find Center on the Canvas}
     PHeight:=Printer.PageHeight;
     PWidth:=Printer.PageWidth;
     CenterX:=PWidth Div 2;
     CenterY:=PHeight Div 2;
     {Calculate center position with the user set size divisor}
     SDiv:=SpinEdit1.Value;
     X1:=CenterX-(PWidth Div (SDiv*2));
     Y1:=CenterY-(PHeight Div (SDiv*2));
     X2:=CenterX+(PWidth Div (SDiv*2));
     Y2:=CenterY+(PHeight Div (SDiv*2));
     {Store the desired Printer Canvas Rect Size in PrnRect}
     PrnRect:=Rect(X1,Y1,X2,Y2);
     {Get the Image Box Canvas Rect Size in ImgRect}
     ImgRect:=Rect(0,0,Image1.Width,Image1.Height);
     {Copy the image from image box to printer canvas}
     Printer.Canvas.CopyRect(PrnRect,Form1.Canvas,ImgRect );
     Printer.EndDoc;
     Panel1.Caption:='Printing Complete!';
end;
procedure TForm1.Button2Click(Sender: TObject);
begin
     {Load a graphic to image box on Form}
     If OpenDialog1.Execute then
     begin
          Label2.Visible:=False;
          Image1.Picture.LoadFromFile(OpenDialog1.FileName);
     end;
end;

end.
```

ANALYSIS This program enables the user to select an image file by clicking the Load Picture button. The picture is displayed in the form in the Image component. Next, the user can print the picture by clicking the Print button. When the Print button is clicked, the code copies the image from the form canvas and sends it to the printer.

At this point, you should be able to run the program, select a graphics image (bitmap or metafile), and display it on the screen. You can select a number from 1 to 10 for the size divisor and print the image. Your image is sized and centered on the page if everything has been set up correctly. Once you successfully load and print a few graphics files, pat yourself on the back for a job well done.

Summary

Today you learned about file attributes as well has how to read and change them. You learned how to work with text files by writing a simple text editor. Next, you created a simple database program to store address/phone number information using typed files. You then learned about untyped files and how to open any type of file by creating a program that would open a file and replace all its spaces with commas. You learned about some of the other file management and I/O routines available, as well as about long filenames and how they are supported by Delphi 3.

Quite a bit of material about working with files was covered here. With the database controls and other features of Delphi, you may not always need this type of file access. However, the information you learned here may enable you to write that next conversion program, import utility, or custom file editor. At some point in time, file I/O capabilities will prove to be a real asset.

You also learned about basic printing techniques, in which you treat the printer port as a file and use writeln statements to send text to the printer. To demonstrate this, you created a program that reads a text file and sends each line to the printer.

You also learned how to accomplish the same task by using the TPrinter object, which gives you the flexibility to change fonts, font sizes, and so on. You saw how to use the printer dialog boxes to enable users to make printing selections. You learned how to draw on the printer canvas as though you were drawing on the screen and to send it to the printer.

Finally, you learned how to load a graphics image onto the screen and to send it to the printer. Although you learned only the basics of printing text and graphics, you can apply what you learned here to future projects in Delphi.

At this point you should have a decent grasp on file input and output as well as printing. You should be able to create very useful and powerful applications using these essential skills.

Q&A

Q Do I need to do anything special to handle long filenames?

A No, Delphi 3 functions and components have built-in support for long filenames. They recognize short or long filenames with no effort on your part.

Q How can I allow my programs to tell what a file's type is?

A You really can't. Although there are standards for using file extensions to denote a file type, this standard often is not adhered to. You will have to make the determination as to what you are expecting a file to be formatted as and look like, and then do your best to check it and handle errors that might occur. Beyond that, you just have to rely on the user choosing the right file.

Q **I tried to print an icon using the Image Printer. Although it loaded, it will not properly size or center on the screen or paper. Why?**

A An icon, unlike a bitmap or metafile, is not a resizable graphic in the image box. The icon simply displays in the upper-left corner of the image box and prints the same way on the page. When you copied the rectangular image from the image box to the printer canvas, you took the size of the image box. The icon used only a portion of this space. The program is working properly; you just cannot see the image box that contains the icon. The image changes in size and moves towards the center when larger numbers are specified in the divisor.

Q **How can I tell if my print job is printing?**

A Use the `Printing` property of the `TPrinter` object. If `Printing` is set to `True`, the print job has been called with `BeginDoc`, but `EndDoc` has not yet been called. The code might look like this:

```
If Printer.Printing then
    {your code here}
```

Q **How can I abort a print job?**

A By using the `Abort` method of the `TPrinter` object, you can add code to a button or your code to abort a print job. The following line of code causes the print job to abort:

```
Printer.Abort;
```

Workshop

The Workshop provides two ways for you to affirm what you've learned in this chapter. The Quiz section poses questions to help you solidify your understanding of the material covered. You can find answers to the quiz questions in Appendix A, "Answers to the Quiz Questions." The Exercises section provides you with experience in using what you have learned. Please try to work through all these before continuing to the next day.

Quiz

1. What is the difference between typed files and untyped files?
2. What procedure is used to move the file pointer without reading or writing data?
3. What types of files can you work with using untyped files?

4. Do you need to use the Printer object to send text to the printer?

5. To use the printer functions, what must you add in the interface section of the program?

6. Name the two important methods used to print with the Printer object. (Hint: The print job cannot start or complete without them.)

7. Drawing on the printer canvas is much like drawing on a form canvas. True or false?

8. What code is used to activate the Properties dialog box?

9. What method is used to copy an image from the form canvas to the printer canvas?

10. How do you print a small circle or ellipse using the TPrinter object?

Exercises

1. Add the capability in the typed files Address/Phone Book program to move to the first record or the last record.

2. Modify the Image Printer program to enable the user to select among the center, upper-left, and lower-right positions for printing the image.

Day **10**

Graphics, Multimedia, and Animation

Delphi offers many features that enable you to easily create graphics applications. This chapter guides you through the most basic aspects of creating graphics applications in Delphi and finishes with using Delphi to create multimedia and high-performance graphics techniques.

The Graphical Elements

As a developer, you should understand how to display images in applications or how to manipulate points, shapes, lines, and colors. Windows 95 and Windows NT offer some advanced features to enable high-performance graphics applications to use system resources effectively. Delphi offers a rich set of graphical components and methods that hide many of the operating system implementation details from you This is extremely useful if you are new to graphics because you can concentrate on how graphics work rather than learn how to manipulate complex operating system calls.

Coordinates

NEW TERM You probably have a good idea of what a coordinate is. All of the visual components have a Top and Left property. The values stored in these properties determine where a component is placed on a form. Another way to say this is that the component is placed at coordinate X,Y where X is referring to the Left property and Y is referring to the Top property. The values for X and Y (or Left and Top) are stored in pixels. A *pixel* is the smallest region on a drawing surface that can be manipulated.

The Canvas

The Canvas property is the drawing area on forms and many other graphical components. The Canvas property enables Delphi code to manipulate the drawing area at runtime. One main feature of the Canvas property is that it consists of properties and methods that make using graphics in Delphi relatively simple. All of the overhead and bookkeeping that is done is hidden in the implementation of the Canvas object.

The next section explains the basic functions you need to perform graphical operations in Delphi by using the Canvas object.

Pixels

Conceptually, all graphical operations boil down to setting the color of pixels on the drawing surface. In Delphi, you can manipulate pixels individually. In the ancient days of computers, a pixel was considered to be on or off, which meant that it was either black or white (or green or amber). Luckily, in today's world of computers, pixels can take on a wide range of colors. The color of a pixel can be set either as a predefined color such as clBlue or as an arbitrary mix of the colors Red, Green, and Blue.

To access the pixels on a form, use the Canvas property of the form and the Pixels property of the canvas. The Pixels property is a two-dimensional array that corresponds to the colors in the canvas. Canvas.Pixels[10,20] corresponds to the color of the pixel that is 10 pixels to the right and 20 pixels down. Treat the pixel array as any other property; to change the color of a pixel, assign a new value. To determine what color a pixel is, read the value.

Using Pixels

In the following example, you use the Pixels property to draw a sine wave in the main form. The only component on the form is a button that draws the sine wave when it is clicked. You use the form's Width and Height parameters to scale the sine wave to fit into 70 percent of the form's height and all of the form's width. The code that produces the sine wave is shown in Listing 10.1. Figure 10.1 shows the sine program in action.

TYPE **Listing 10.1. Using pixels to form a sine wave.**

```
unit unitSine;

interface

uses
  Windows, Messages, SysUtils, Classes, Graphics, Controls,
  Forms, Dialogs,
  StdCtrls;

type
  TForm1 = class(TForm)
    DrawSine: TButton;
    procedure DrawSineClick(Sender: TObject);
  private
    { Private declarations }
  public
    { Public declarations }
  end;

var
  Form1: TForm1;

implementation

{$R *.DFM}

procedure TForm1.DrawSineClick(Sender: TObject);
.
var
  X  : real;
  Y  : real;
  PX :longint;
  PY :longint;
  HalfHeight : longint;
begin
{ Determine Halfway down the form}
HalfHeight := Form1.Height div 2;
for PX:=0 to Form1.Width do
  BEGIN
    {Scale X in terms of 2 PI to do 1 full sine wave}
    X  := PX * (2*PI/Form1.Width);
    Y  := sin(X);
    PY := trunc(0.7 * Y * HalfHeight) + HalfHeight;
    {Set pixel to black (0 intensity of RGB)}
    Canvas.Pixels[PX,PY] := 0;
  END;
end;
end. .
```

ANALYSIS   This application first determines the height of the form in order to scale the sine wave correctly. The PX counter then loops from 0 to the width of the form where a corresponding Y value is calculated at each point on the sine wave. The Y coordinate is scaled so that the wave fits nicely on the form, and the point is drawn by setting the Canvas.Pixels property.

Figure 10.1.

Sine wave program using the Pixels *property.*

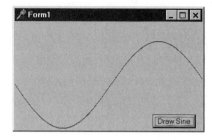

The Pen

Every canvas has an imaginary pen that it uses to draw lines and shapes. Think of the pen on the canvas as a real pen on a piece of paper. Of the two ways to move the pen, one method is to touch the paper and leave a mark. The second method is to lift the pen above the paper so that moving it does not leave a mark. In addition to its different actions, the pen also has attributes associated with it. For example, it has a distinct color and width. To move the pen without actually drawing, you use the MoveTo method. The following line of code moves the pen to the coordinates 23,56:

```
Form1.Canvas.MoveTo(23,56);
```

Drawing Lines

To draw a straight line from the pen's current position to another position, you use the LineTo method. LineTo simply needs the coordinates of the pen's destination, and it draws a straight line from the current position to the new position. The simple procedure in Listing 10.2 uses the LineTo property to draw a neat pattern. This program is shown in action in Figure 10.2.

TYPE | **Listing 10.2. An interesting line pattern.**

```
procedure TForm1.DrawSineClick(Sender: TObject);

var
   X  : real;
   Y  : real;
   PX :longint;
   PY :longint;
   Offset : longint;
   HalfHeight : longint;
begin
```

```
{ Determine the coordinate Halfway down the form}
HalfHeight := Form1.Height div 2;
For OffSet := -10 to 10 do
BEGIN
     PX := 0;
     While PX < Form1.Width  do
       BEGIN
          {Scale X interms of 2 PI to do 1 full sine wave}
          X := PX * (2*PI/Form1.Width);
          Y := sin(X);
          PY := trunc(0.7 * Y * HalfHeight)
           + HalfHeight + (Offset *10);
          IF (PX = 0) Then
            canvas.MoveTo(PX,PY);
          canvas.LineTO(PX,PY);
          PY := trunc(0.7 * Y * HalfHeight) +
             HalfHeight + ((Offset-1) *10);
          canvas.LineTO(PX,PY);
          PX := PX +15;
       END;
END;
end;
end. .
```

Figure 10.2.

Neat pattern drawn using LineTo *and* MoveTo.

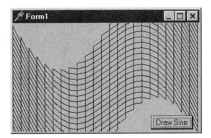

ANALYSIS This program is similar to the previous sine wave program except that now you are providing gaps between the points and connecting them with lines. On the first iteration (when PX = 0), you use the MoveTo method to go to the first point. After moving to the first point, you just need to use LineTo to move to all subsequent points.

Drawing Polygons

In addition to methods for drawing straight lines, the canvas also has methods for drawing shapes. You draw some shapes, such as a rectangle, with their own methods, but you draw others using a series of points. These other shapes are known as *polygons*. Delphi has separate methods to draw filled-in shapes. For now, I discuss only outlined polygons until I cover how to fill graphical objects (discussed in "The Brush and Filled Objects" later in this chapter). Some polygons that you'll recognize include triangles, octagons (like a stop sign), or trapezoids. Figure 10.3 shows some common polygons.

Figure 10.3.

Some common polygons.

Square   Triangle   Octagon

To draw a polygon, you pass the PolyLine function a series of points that the function then connects with lines (just like connect-the-dots). You simply pass the PolyLine function an array of points, which is a new concept. Until now, you did everything with coordinates; you passed the LineTo function an X and Y value.

NEW TERM — Delphi also has a type TPoint, which encapsulates the X and Y value into a single record called a *point*. The easiest way to create a point is using the Point function. Point simply takes an X and Y value and returns a TPoint record. Note that the first and last points are not automatically connected, so the last point must be the same as the first point to form a complete polygon. For example, the following call to PolyLine draws a triangle:

```
Form1.Canvas.PolyLine([Point(10,10),Point(100,100),
                       Point(50,75),Point(10,10)]);
```

You can expand on this to create a procedure that draws a symmetric polygon with an arbitrary number of sides, which the user enters. If the user enters 8, the procedure draws an octagon; 6 draws a six-sided polygon. To do this, use some basic geometric principles to put the vertices on a circle. Listing 10.3 shows what your source code should look like.

TYPE **Listing 10.3. An arbitrary-sided polygon.**

```
procedure TForm1.DrawPolyClick(Sender: TObject);

var
  Sides : integer;
  Count : integer;
  PolyArray : Array[0..15] of TPoint;

begin
    Sides := strtoint(NumSides.Text);
    If Sides > 15 then Sides := 15; /* Array only Holds 15 points*/
    For Count := 0 to Sides do
    BEGIN
      {Using Points From A circle, choose Vericies for points}
      PolyArray[Count] :=
        Point(TRUNC(SIN((2*PI)*COUNT/Sides)* 30)+(Form1.Width div 2),
              TRUNC(COS((2*PI)*COUNT/Sides)* 30)+(Form1.Height div 2));
    END;
    {Hook Last point back to the first point and set all }
    {remaining points equal to the first point           }
    For Count := Sides+1 to 15 do
```

10

```
    PolyArray[Count] := PolyArray[0];
    {Draw the Polygon}
    Form1.Canvas.PolyLine(PolyArray);

end;
```

ANALYSIS   This procedure calculates evenly spaced points on a circle depending on how many sides are selected. The points are connected by using the PolyLine method on the canvas. To close the polygon, set the unused points equal to the starting point. Figure 10.4 shows the polygon application executing.

Figure 10.4.

Arbitrary-sided polygon program.

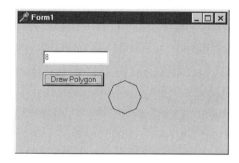

Modifying the Pen Attributes

All the shapes you've drawn to this point used the default pen. It is possible to change the color, width, and style of the pen. In Delphi, you access the pen through the canvas, which has a Pen property. The main properties used with the pen are Color, Width, Style, and Mode.

Color

You can set the pen's color using the same methods you used to set the form's color. For example, to set the color of the pen to blue, you could execute the following:

```
Form1.Canvas.Pen.Color := clBlue;
```

You also could use this line:

```
Form1.Canvas.Pen.Color := RGB(0,0,255);
```

To show all the possible intensities of gray that your computer can show, you could use the following procedure:

```
procedure TForm1.DrawGreyClick(Sender: TObject);

var
  Count : Integer;
begin
```

```
  For Count := 0 to 255 do
  BEGIN
   Form1.Canvas.Pen.Color := RGB(Count,Count,Count);
   Form1.Canvas.MoveTo(Count,0);
   Form1.Canvas.LineTo(Count,100);
  end;
end;
```

Width and Style

The Width property sets the width of the pen in pixels. The Style property enables the pen to draw various styles such as dashed or dotted lines. Valid values for the Style property are psSolid, psDash, psDot, psDashDot, psDashDotDot, psClear, and psInsideFrame. If you wanted your pen to be red, three pixels wide, and dotted, you would execute the following lines of code:

```
Form1.Canvas.Pen.Color := clRed;
Form1.Canvas.Pen.Width := 3;
Form1.Canvas.Pen.Style := psDot;
```

Mode

Another pen property is Mode, which enables the pen to interact with its environment. For example, indicating a mode of pmNot causes the pen to draw the inverse color of the background (and, therefore, the inverse of each bit). The pen uses the mode pmCopy by default, which causes the pen to use the current color. You can determine the color of the pen by checking the color property.

One example of using the Mode property is performing simple animation. You create animation by slightly redrawing a picture and showing the changes in a sequence. It appears to the human brain that the object is moving or changing. For simple animation, you can use the pmXor or pmNotXor mode to draw an object and then remove it without changing the background. Remember that each pixel stores a color as a sequence of bits. Changing a pixel by XORing the current pixel with a color changes the color. The XOR operation takes two bitwise operands and returns True if one of the operands is true but not both. Doing this again sets the pixel back. The following steps illustrate this process:

> The background pixel has a value of 0110011 which you XOR with the value 1111000 resulting in the new pixel having a value of 1001011.

When you want to erase the pixel and set the background back, you simply perform the same steps again:

> Take the pixel that currently has a value of 1001011 and XOR it with the value 1111000 resulting in a pixel which has a value of 0110011 (wow! your original color).

The advantage of using this process is that you do not need to store the background information; it is done automatically. The disadvantage is that you can't get exactly the picture you want because you are embedding information into your pixel's color. In the procedure in Listing 10.4, you use this technique to animate a triangle flying across a form. Note that there is also a red box on the form. The blue triangle will fly through the box but not disturb the box.

TYPE | **Listing 10.4. Simple animation using the Mode property.**

```
procedure TForm1.SimpleAnimateClick(Sender: TObject);
var
    Count : Integer;
    Pause : real ;
begin
{ Draw a Box }
Form1.Canvas.Pen.mode := pmCopy;
Form1.Canvas.Pen.Color := clRed;
Form1.Canvas.PolyLine([point(50,10),
                       point(100,10),
                       point(100,200),
                       point(50,200),
                       point(50,10)]);
{Set the Pen}
Form1.Canvas.Pen.Color := clBlue;
Form1.Canvas.Pen.mode := pmNotXor;
For Count := 0 to (Form1.Width div 5) do
BEGIN
 {Draw the Triangle}
 Form1.Canvas.PolyLine([point(Count*5,100),
                        point(Count*5+10,100),
                        point(Count*5+5,110),
                        point(Count*5,100)]);
 Pause := Time;
 while (Time-Pause) < 1e-12 do; {nothing}
 {Erase The Triangle}
 Form1.Canvas.PolyLine([point(Count*5,100),
                        point(Count*5+10,100),
                        point(Count*5+5,110),
                        point(Count*5,100)]);
end;  {end While}
end;
```

ANALYSIS The program first draws a red box by setting the pen mode to pmCopy and the color to clRed. Next, the program moves a triangle across the screen by using the pmNotXor pen mode. The mode pmNotXor is similar to XOR in that it preserves the background image, but it displays the true color on the foreground. It is necessary to draw the triangle twice in each position. The first time, the triangle is drawn, the second time the triangle is removed.

10

The Brush and Filled Objects

Rather than using only outlines of shapes, you can fill some of the graphics objects that Delphi provides. The Brush property determines how an object is filled. The three main properties that affect the brush are Color, Style, and Bitmap. There are two ways to use the brush—either with the Color and Style properties or with the Bitmap property.

When you use the Color and Style properties, the overall color of the fill comes from the value of the Color property. The Style property defines the style of the fill. In the same way that you use the PolyLine method for outlined (unfilled) objects, you use the Polygon method to draw filled polygons.

The sample program in Listing 10.5 shows all the available styles in eight different triangles. The triangles are displayed in Figure 10.5.

TYPE **Listing 10.5. Drawing triangles filled with different patterns.**

```
procedure Triangle(Iteration : Integer);
begin
Form1.Canvas.Brush.Color := clBlue;
Form1.Canvas.Polygon([Point(TRUNC((Iteration/9)*Form1.Width),50),
                      Point(TRUNC((Iteration/8)*Form1.Width),100),
                      Point(TRUNC(((Iteration-1)/8)*Form1.Width),100),
                      Point(TRUNC((Iteration/9)*Form1.Width),50)]);
end;

procedure TForm1.ShowTrianglesClick(Sender: TObject);
begin
  Form1.Canvas.Brush.Style := bsSolid;
  Triangle(1);
  Form1.Canvas.Brush.Style := bsClear;
  Triangle(2);
  Form1.Canvas.Brush.Style := bsHorizontal;
  Triangle(3);
  Form1.Canvas.Brush.Style := bsVertical;
  Triangle(4);
  Form1.Canvas.Brush.Style := bsFDiagonal;
  Triangle(5);
  Form1.Canvas.Brush.Style := bsBDiagonal;
  Triangle(6);
  Form1.Canvas.Brush.Style := bsCross;
  Triangle(7);
  Form1.Canvas.Brush.Style := bsDiagCross;
  Triangle(8);
end;
```

Figure 10.5.

Triangles filled with different styles.

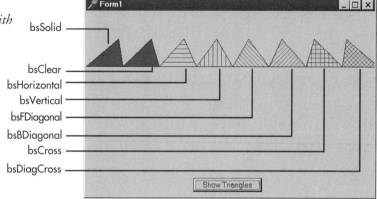

 You create a generic procedure to create triangles in one of eight regions of the screen. The ShowTrainglesClick procedure sets the brush to various settings and calls the triangle procedure passing the position that the triangle should be drawn in.

In addition to using the predefined styles and colors for a brush, you also can use a bitmap to define the pattern that a brush uses to fill objects.

NEW TERM A *brush bitmap* is an 8-pixel × 8-pixel bitmap that defines the pattern with which all objects are filled. To use a bitmap for a brush, you must first create a bitmap, assign it, and then free it when you're done. Creating and manipulating bitmaps are discussed later in this chapter.

Drawing Filled Rectangles

Just as a TPoint type specifies a set of coordinates in Delphi, a TRect data type specifies a rectangular part of a form or graphical area. You specify a rectangular region by giving coordinates for the top-left and bottom-right corners. You use the function Rect to create a TRect type from coordinates. Many of the functions that deal with rectangular regions use TRect types as parameters. For example, you use the FillRect method to draw a filled rectangle. The following code line is an example of the FillRect method. Note that you need to use the Rect function to specify the coordinates.

```
Form1.Canvas.FillRect(Rect(20,20,100,100));
```

In addition to the FillRect procedure, the Rectangle procedure draws a rectangle using the attributes from the current brush for the fill and the attributes from the current pen for the outline. Although it is inconsistent in the way that parameters are passed, the Rectangle procedure takes all four points as parameters as opposed to a TRect type. The following code line is an example of the Rectangle procedure:

```
Form1.Canvas.Rectangle(20,20,100,100);
```

Drawing Circles, Curves, and Ellipses

Everything that you have drawn so far has used either single points or a combination of straight lines. The world would be a pretty dull place without curves. Delphi offers a number of methods for drawing circles, ellipses, arcs, and slices. A circle is simply an ellipse that has a constant radius.

To draw an ellipse in Delphi, you supply the rectangular region of the drawing surface (or canvas) within which the ellipse is contained. To draw a perfect circle, you execute the following:

```
Form1.Canvas.Ellipse(100,100,200,200);
```

To draw an ellipse that has a width greater than its height, you execute the following:

```
Form1.Canvas.Ellipse(100,100,300,200);
```

Drawing part of an ellipse is slightly more complex. The method takes eight parameters. The first four parameters are exactly like the parameters for drawing a complete ellipse. The final two parameters are points that indicate the percentage of the ellipse that should show. These points represent the end points of two lines originating from the origin to define how much of the pie to draw. For example, the following line draws the quarter of a circle shown in Figure 10.6:

```
Form1.Canvas.Pie(100,100,200,200,100,100,100,200);
```

Figure 10.6.

Quarter circle using the pie method.

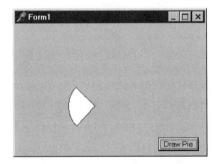

An arc is exactly like a pie slice except that it is not filled. The following code shows only an arc for the same part of a circle drawn by the preceding pie method:

```
Form1.Canvas.Arc(100,100,200,200,100,100,100,200);
```

OnPaint—When a Window Needs To Be Redrawn

In the days of old, a graphics program used the entire screen and assumed that any change on the screen was caused by the program's own action. In a Windows 95 or Windows NT environment, many applications can run simultaneously on a display. What happens when a window is covered by another window or resized? One option that the operating system has is to keep a copy of what the screen looked like in memory and perform in memory any changes to the screen that are out of view. This method requires a lot of overhead, especially if there are many applications running. Instead, the operating system notifies the application that something has changed and that it is the application's job to fix it. Whenever an update is needed, an OnPaint event occurs.

 Delphi redraws only the part of a canvas that has been corrupted, which is known as *invalidation*. When part of a form is invalid, Delphi calls the procedure specified in the OnPaint event handler to redraw the invalidated part of the form.

The example in Listing 10.6 places code that draws a quarter circle on the form in the OnPaint event handler. It also rigs up an edit box to display the number of times that the form has been repainted.

TYPE **Listing 10.6. Demonstration of the OnPaint event handler.**

```
unit unitOnPaint;

interface

uses
  Windows, Messages, SysUtils, Classes, Graphics, Controls,
  Forms, Dialogs,
  StdCtrls;

type
  TForm1 = class(TForm)
    NumRepaints: TEdit;
    procedure FormPaint(Sender: TObject);
    procedure FormCreate(Sender: TObject);
  private
    { Private declarations }
    NumPaints : integer;
  public
    { Public declarations }
  end;
```

continues

Listing 10.6. continued

```
var
  Form1: TForm1;

implementation

{$R *.DFM}

procedure TForm1.FormPaint(Sender: TObject);
begin
    NumPaints := NumPaints + 1;
    Form1.Canvas.Pie(100,100,200,200,100,100,100,200);
    NumRepaints.Text := IntToStr(NumPaints);
end;

procedure TForm1.FormCreate(Sender: TObject);
begin
    NumPaints := 0;
end;
end.
```

ANALYSIS   When you execute this program, you see the updated iteration increment every time the OnPaint handler is called. This is due to the NumPaints variable being incremented and displayed every time the OnPaint event handler is called.

The TPaintBox **Component**

All drawing that you have performed to this point has been on the canvas of a form. It often is useful to confine a graphic to a rectangular region of a form. Delphi offers a component for doing this, the TPaintBox component. Try the following exercise:

1. Drop a TPaintBox component on a form.

2. Drop a TButton on a form.

3. Add the following code for the OnClick event of the button:
   ```
   PaintBox1.canvas.Ellipse(0,0,2*PaintBox1.Width,
                            2*PaintBox1.Height);
   ```

4. Compile and run the application.

What happened? You asked for an ellipse, but Delphi drew only an arc. This happened because the ellipse is bigger than the TPaintBox component, which is the only area that Delphi can draw in. The rest of the ellipse was *clipped*. Imagine the extra complexity you would need to add to an application to ensure that nothing is drawn outside of a region. The TPaintBox handles this for you. The coordinates in a TPaintBox are relative to the TPaintBox, not the form. This also means that as long as an OnPaint handler is responsible for drawing the

10

TPaintBox, you can move the image on the form by changing the Top and Left properties of the TPaintBox. The TPaintBox uses the Align property to keep the image at the top, left, bottom, or right of the form. It also forces the TPaintBox to fill the client area of the form.

The Shape Component: Losing Some Complexity

What if you want to manipulate simple shapes but don't want to deal with events to handle repainting; are there any controls that can make this easier? Of course! The TShape component encapsulates many of the drawing methods in its properties and methods. The TShape component has properties to represent its brush, pen, and shape. The shapes that the component can become include a circle, ellipse, rectangle, rounded rectangle, square, or rounded square. The real advantage to using TShape is that all the code to draw and repaint the object is hidden.

Shapes Are Okay, but How Do I Put Up a Picture?

Using the graphical methods and components works well for many types of applications, but sometimes you may want to add a predrawn graphic image or picture to an application. This would be cumbersome if the only method available was using the graphical components. For example, suppose the Bonzo Soda Pop Company wants to have its founder's picture on every application the company uses. Doing this with the graphical methods would be an eternal nightmare. Instead, you simply take a photo of Frank Bonzo and scan it into the computer using a digital scanner. The scanning program stores the picture in a special format that Delphi can understand and simply displays the picture. Another time that it does not make sense to use the graphical methods is if an artist designs an image in a drawing program and wants to incorporate it into a Delphi application.

Delphi provides native support for working with four types of images: bitmaps, icons, enhanced metafiles, and metafiles. All four types of files store images; the difference is how the images are stored internally to the file and what sorts of tools can manipulate and access the images. When you calculate the memory requirements to store an image on the screen, you have to multiply the color depth (in bits) by the resolution. You can think of a bitmap as a snapshot of a piece of the screen and all of its associated information. This is true in the sense that a bitmap knows only the colors of every pixel in the image and not what the image represents. For example, if you take a bitmap of a red square on a blue background, the only information in the bitmap is that all the pixels are blue except for the pixels in the square with vertices (10,10) in the upper-left corner and (100,100) in the lower-right corner, which are red.

10

Windows 3.1, Windows NT, and Windows 95 have standard file formats for what a bitmap file should look like. Bitmaps on Windows, Windows NT, and Windows 95 are device-independent bitmaps, which means that the information is stored in such a way that any computer can display the picture in the resolution and number of colors that it is configured for. This does not mean that the image looks the same on every computer! It obviously looks better on a screen with 1024×768 resolution and 24-bit color than on a standard VGA screen. The important thing is that users of both computers can view the image. It would definitely be a drag if every Windows 95 programmer had to understand what each byte in the .bmp file represented.

Luckily, the details of the bitmap file format are encapsulated in the operating system and Delphi. The easiest way to display a bitmap in Delphi is to use the TImage component. The TImage component can display different types of graphical images. The TImage component can load a bitmap from a file and then contain the bitmap in the application. This enables you to ship the application without including the bitmap as a separate file with the software.

Icons are simply very small bitmaps. Icons are placed in a separate category because they generally are used to display a shortcut to an application or a minimized view of some information. Internally, icons are stored in a fashion similar to that of bitmaps. Metafiles and enhanced metafiles, on the other hand, are stored completely differently. A metafile stores information about how a picture was created rather than the series of bits that form the picture. Metafiles store the drawing command sequence in order to re-create the image.

To display an image using the TImage component, place a TImage on a form and double-click the Picture property. This brings up a dialog box that enables you to view, load, and save a bitmap into the image. Click on Load and choose any valid .ico, .bmp, .emf, or .wmf file. The bitmap or metafile that you choose is displayed in the TImage component.

Stretching and Sizing Images

By default, an image is displayed at its native resolution, and you see only the part of the image that is displayed within the TImage component. Two key properties affect the way that an image appears in a TImage component. The Autosize property causes the size of the component to match the dimensions of the image. Setting the Stretch property to True forces the image to fit into the dimensions of the TImage component. If you set the Stretch and Autosize properties to False, the image is centered in the component by default. To force the image to be displayed with the top-left corner in the component, set the Center property to False.

Loading an Image from a File at Runtime

You have examined how to use the TImage component to display a bitmap, metafile, or icon by setting the image at design time. You also can load a bitmap from a file at runtime with the LoadFromFile method. The following line loads the Windows 95 setup bitmap into your image component:

```
Image1.Picture.LoadFromFile('C:\WIN95\SETUP.BMP');
```

Note that the method operates on the Picture property of the image component and not the component itself. The image uses most of its properties to describe how the image interacts with the application. The Picture property holds information about the image itself, so you need to load the image into the Picture property.

Getting Fancy: Creating Your Own Bitmap

Earlier in this chapter, I describe how to draw on a form's canvas and a paintbox's canvas. Can you also draw on a bitmap's canvas? The answer is yes. In Delphi, a TBitmap object has a canvas that you can manipulate like a canvas in a TPaintbox or on a TForm. When drawing on a bitmap, you don't have to worry about OnPaint events to redraw the scene when it is invalidated. You can simply reload the image from memory. A disadvantage of using a bitmap is that it requires more system resources because the image is stored in memory. In Delphi, a bitmap by itself has limitations because it is difficult to display. This is because the bitmap by itself is not a component and cannot "fix" itself if something writes over a piece of it. However, when you use a bitmap in conjunction with an image component to display the bitmap, the image component automatically responds to its own OnPaint event by redrawing the bitmap whenever it is necessary to do so.

Creating a Bitmap from Scratch

To create a new bitmap, you need to declare a variable of type TBitmap and then use the Create method as a constructor to allocate space for the bitmap, as shown in this example:

```
Var
   MyBitmap : TBitmap;

BEGIN
   MyBitmap := TBitmap.Create;
```

At this point, the bitmap is created but empty. The next step is to define the dimensions for the bitmap. Use the Height and Width properties, as follows:

```
MyBitmap.Height := 100;
MyBitmap.Width  := 200;
```

Before you draw the bitmap, add some graphics to it—in this case, a diagonal line, using this code:

```
MyBitmap.Canvas.MoveTo(200,100);
MyBitmap.Canvas.LineTo(0,0);
```

To display a bitmap, you can use the Draw method. The Draw method copies a bitmap onto a canvas. All other manipulation of the bitmap is done in memory. To draw the bitmap on Form1 at coordinates 100,100, use the following line:

```
Form1.Canvas.Draw(100,100,MyBitmap);
```

When you are through with the bitmap, you should free its system resources using the Free method, like this:

```
MyBitmap.Free;
```

The other way that you could display the bitmap is to set an image component's picture to the bitmap that you created, as in the following line of code:

```
Image1.Picture.Graphic := MyBitmap;
```

One advantage of using the Image component is that you don't have to worry about the image becoming invalidated because the component takes care of redrawing the image if it becomes invalid.

Saving a Bitmap to a File

In addition to loading and manipulating bitmaps, you also can save a bitmap back to a file. To save the bitmap, use the SaveToFile method as follows:

```
MyBitmap.SaveToFile('C:\CoolStuff\MyBitmap.BMP');
```

Putting Bitmaps To Work with a Sample Program

In this example, you use Delphi's graphics functions to create a program to manipulate bitmaps. A user loads a bitmap into the program, clicks the Mixup Bitmap button, and creates a new bitmap, which is built from random pieces of the original. Figure 10.7 shows the mixup program in action.

Listings 10.7 shows the complete mixup unit.

Figure 10.7.

Mixup sample program.

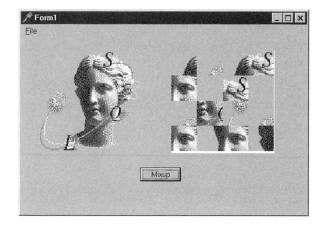

10

TYPE **Listing 10.7. Mixup Bitmap program.**

```
unit unitMixup;

interface

uses
  Windows, Messages, SysUtils, Classes, Graphics, Controls,
  Forms, Dialogs,
  StdCtrls, Menus, ExtCtrls;

type
  TForm1 = class(TForm)
    Orig: TImage;
    NewImage: TImage;
    OpenDialog1: TOpenDialog;
    SaveDialog1: TSaveDialog;
    MainMenu1: TMainMenu;
    File1: TMenuItem;
    Save1: TMenuItem;
    Open1: TMenuItem;
    Exit1: TMenuItem;
    Mixup: TButton;
    procedure Exit1Click(Sender: TObject);
    procedure Open1Click(Sender: TObject);
    procedure MixupClick(Sender: TObject);
    procedure Save1Click(Sender: TObject);
  private
    { Private declarations }
    NewBitmap : TBitmap;   {Bitmap to create}
  public
    { Public declarations }
  end;
```

continues

Listing 10.7. continued

```
var
  Form1: TForm1;

implementation

{$R *.DFM}

procedure TForm1.Exit1Click(Sender: TObject);
begin
   Application.Terminate;
end;

procedure TForm1.Open1Click(Sender: TObject);
begin
  if OpenDialog1.Execute then
    Begin
       Orig.Picture.LoadFromFile(OpenDialog1.FileName);
    End;
end;

procedure TForm1.MixupClick(Sender: TObject);
{ Divide the origional bitmap into 16 pieces.  Create}
{ a new bitmap by randomally selecting one of the 16}
{ pieces for each piece of the new bitmap            }

Var
  NewBitmap      : TBitmap;   {Bitmap to create}
  X,Y,NewX,NewY : integer;   {Used to index the pieces}
  ChunkX,ChunkY : integer;   {X and Y dimension for each piece}

begin

   {Allocate resources for a new bitmap}
   NewBitmap := TBitmap.Create;

   {set the dimensions equal to the original}
   NewBitmap.Height := Orig.Picture.Bitmap.Height;
   NewBitmap.Width := Orig.Picture.Bitmap.Width;
   NewImage.Stretch := true;

   {Calculate the dimensions of each section}
   ChunkX := NewBitmap.Width div 4;
   ChunkY := NewBitmap.Height div 4;

   {Build the new bitmap}
   For X := 0 to 3 do
    For Y := 0 to 3 do
      BEGIN
        NewX := random(3);
        NewY := random(3);
        NewBitmap.canvas.CopyRect(
```

```
            Rect(X*ChunkX,Y*ChunkY,(X+1)*ChunkX,(Y+1)*ChunkY),
            Orig.Picture.Bitmap.Canvas,
            Rect(NewX*ChunkX,NewY*ChunkY,
                 (NewX+1)*ChunkX,(NewY+1)*ChunkY));
    END; {For Y}

  {Display the new bitmap by setting the picture of the new image}
  NewImage.Picture.Graphic := NewBitmap;
  NewBitmap.Free;
end;

procedure TForm1.Save1Click(Sender: TObject);
{Use the save common dialog to save the bitmap}
begin
  if SaveDialog1.Execute then
    Begin
      NewImage.Picture.SaveToFile(SaveDialog1.FileName);
    End; {if}
end; {Procedure}

end.
```

ANALYSIS   Take a look at how this program works. First, you use the following components:

- ☐ Two image components to display the original image and the mixed-up image
- ☐ An OpenDialog component to access the common open dialog box
- ☐ A SaveDialog component to access the common save dialog box
- ☐ A menu and standard button to trigger events

Figure 10.8 shows the component layout.

When a user selects File | Open from the menu, the program displays the common open dialog box. When the user clicks OK, the program loads the bitmap file that the user selected into the Orig image component with the following code:

```
Orig.Picture.LoadFromFile(OpenDialog1.FileName);
```

Next, the user clicks the Mixup Bitmap button. This invokes the MixupBitmapClick procedure to scramble the bitmap. The steps to build a new bitmap and pull in random pieces from the original are as follows:

1. Free any current bitmap and then build a new bitmap by executing the Create method on a bitmap object, like this:

   ```
   NewBitmap := TBitmap.Create;
   ```

Figure 10.8.

Mixup component layout.

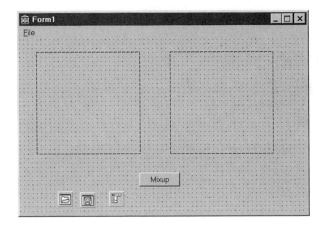

2. Set the dimensions of the bitmap equal to those of the original picture, as in the following code. Note that you use the `Picture.Bitmap` instead of the `Picture.Graphic` to obtain the bitmap dimensions.

```
NewBitmap.Height := Orig.Picture.Bitmap.Height;
NewBitmap.Width := Orig.Picture.Bitmap.Width;
```

3. When the original bitmap is divided into 16 pieces and the new bitmap reassembled, you need to know how big each chunk is. Calculate an integer value of four pieces in each direction, as shown in the following two lines of code. Assume that the possible loss of three bits per section is acceptable (for example, if the bitmap had a width of 43 pixels, `ChunkX` would be only 10 pixels).

```
ChunkX := NewBitmap.Width div 4;
ChunkY := NewBitmap.Height div 4;
```

4. Loop through each sector and select a random piece to put into the new bitmap. This is accomplished by setting up a nested loop to choose each piece of the bitmap to create, as illustrated in the following code. You select a random piece from the original bitmap by using the `random` function to select random X and Y coordinates. You can draw on a bitmap by using any canvas function. One of these functions is `CopyRect`, which copies a rectangular region of one canvas to a rectangular region of another canvas.

```
For X := 0 to 3 do
   For Y := 0 to 3 do
     BEGIN
       NewX := random(3);
       NewY := random(3);
       NewBitmap.canvas.CopyRect(
          Rect(X*ChunkX,Y*ChunkY,(X+1)*ChunkX,(Y+1)*ChunkY),
```

10

```
        Orig.Picture.Bitmap.Canvas,
        Rect(NewX*ChunkX,NewY*ChunkY,
            (NewX+1)*ChunkX,(NewY+1)*ChunkY));
    END; {For Y}
```

5. When the program creates the new bitmap, it displays it by setting the `Picture.Graphic` property of the new image equal to the bitmap with this line of code:

```
NewImage.Picture.Graphic := NewBitmap;
```

To save the image, the program uses the common save dialog box when the user selects File | Save from the menu. If the user gives a valid file, the program uses the `SaveToFile` method on the `NewImage` component, as indicated in this code:

```
NewImage.Picture.SaveToFile(SaveDialog1.FileName);
```

Multimedia and Animation Techniques

10

Today's computers can express information in ways other than still images on a screen. You can view full-motion video and listen to sounds. Users find it intriguing to hear a narration or view a video. Delphi offers components and API calls that make multimedia programming easy.

A Quick Start—Using Sound in Your Applications

There are many ways to play sound in an application. In this section, you learn a very simple way that prepares you for using multimedia from within Delphi, using the `PlaySound()` API call. The `PlaySound()` API call can play sounds from different sources and with different options. For example, you can use the `PlaySound()` API call to play a `.WAV` file or to play one of the default system sounds. There are also many options for how the sounds interact with your application. For example, you can play a sound and pause the program's execution until the sound is completed, or you can play a sound and continue to execute other Delphi commands while the sound is played.

Let's begin with a simple example. Create a new application and add a single button on the main form. In the main form's unit, two steps are necessary to play a sound. First, add the `mmsystem` unit to a uses clause in the `implementation` part of the unit. Next, add the `PlaySound` API call to the `OnClick` event handler on the `TButton` visual component. For this first example, you simply play one of the `.WAV` files that comes with Windows 95. You also specify that the sound should be played synchronously, which means that the application pauses until the sound has executed. The code for this unit is shown in Listing 10.8.

TYPE **Listing 10.8. Using sound in a Delphi application with the PlaySound() API call.**

```
unit mult1;

interface

uses
  Windows, Messages, SysUtils, Classes, Graphics, Controls,
  Forms, Dialogs,
  StdCtrls;

type
  TForm1 = class(TForm)
    Button1: TButton;
    procedure Button1Click(Sender: TObject);
  private
    { Private declarations }
  public
    { Public declarations }
  end;

var
  Form1: TForm1;

implementation
{Note that we need to include mmsystem for this to work}
uses mmsystem;

{$R *.DFM}

procedure TForm1.Button1Click(Sender: TObject);
begin
    {Replace C:\WIN95 with Wherever your Windows 95 Directory is}
    PlaySound('C:\WIN95\MEDIA\The Microsoft Sound', 0, SND_SYNC);
end;
```

ANALYSIS In this example, you simply play the wave file that is in the C:\WIN95\MEDIA subdirectory called The Microsoft Sound. The sound is played synchronously, which means the program pauses until the sound completes.

The three parameters that the PlaySound API call takes are as follows:

Parameter 1   A variant parameter that can be either the name of a file, a memory address, or a system event.

Parameter 2   A parameter used in special circumstances where the sound is stored in a resource file. The chapter does not cover this case, so assume parameter 2 to be 0.

Parameter 3   Specifies all the options, including how to play the sound, and what type of parameter the first parameter should be treated as. Remember that the Win32 API is not object oriented, so there cannot be multiple forms of a call that automatically detect the type of data presented in the first parameter.

The constants used for parameter 3 are defined in the mmsystem unit. The bitwise OR operator can be used to combine multiple options. For example, the following call plays The Microsoft Sound asynchronously (allows execution to continue while the sound plays) and plays the sound over and over until another call to PlaySound is made:

```
PlaySound('C:\WIN95\MEDIA\The Microsoft
➥Sound', 0, SND_ASYNC or SND_LOOP);
```

System events are pre-defined sounds that occur when a program or the operating system is trying to make a statement clear to the user. For example, to play the effect used when the system starts, you can use this code:

```
PlaySound('SystemStart', 0, SND_ASYNC OR SND_NODEFAULT);
```

If you want to play a sound frequently and don't want to access the disk, you can play a sound that is stored in a memory location. This is not often necessary because the operating system is usually good at caching disk information. One advantage of playing a file from memory is that your end users don't have access to the file (if you didn't want someone to steal the cool sound your application uses).

Different Types of Media Files

The PlaySound API used a special kind of file called a wave file. You already know that a wave file can store a sound, but how exactly does it do it? A wave file stores a digital representation of the pitch and volume over the length of the sound clip. Because the wave file does not have any knowledge of what the sound is, it needs to store a great deal of information to store a sound clip.

NEW TERM   Another common type of multimedia file that is used is called a *musical instrument digital interface (MIDI)* file. A MIDI file usually is used to store a musical selection. A MIDI file stores the sound by saving data about which instruments are playing what notes for how long. If you are familiar with music, this would be the digital equivalent of the conductor's score. One of the key advantages of MIDI files is that they are much smaller than wave files. One analogy that can be used is that a wave file is to a MIDI file as a bitmap is to a metafile. In each case, one file format understands the data that it represents, and the other simply contains the raw data that is sent to an output device.

Wave and MIDI files can store only sound or audio. What about video, or animation? There are multiple file formats that can store video; two examples of these are AVI and MPEG files. Most of the video files also support a track for sound so that the audio and video is played in sync with the picture. Now that you know about all of these file formats, how can you use them in Delphi? The answer is the Media Player visual component, which is described in the next section.

The Media Player Visual Component

The *media control interface (MCI)* is a high-level command interface for controlling media files built into the Windows 95 and Windows NT operating system. Delphi provides a visual component that encapsulates the command interface into a visual component resembling a VCR or tape recorder as shown in Figure 10.9.

Figure 10.9.
The media player visual component.

The media player component can be used in two ways. The component contains a user interface that can be enabled, and the end user can manipulate media functions through a set of buttons such as Play, Stop, Record, and Rewind. The second way is to hide the component and manipulate media files by executing the component's methods from within a block of code.

Let's start by creating a simple, yet powerful application that enables the user to load a wave, MIDI, or AVI file and then to play and manipulate the file through the Media Player component interface. The application is quite simple. It requires three components: a TMainMenu component, a TOpenDialog component, and a TMediaPlayer component. Add the capability of choosing File | Open to the menu component. The other two components need to be placed on the form as shown in Figure 10.10.

Figure 10.10.
Component layout for simple media player.

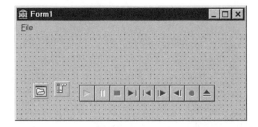

Add the following code behind the File | Open event on the menu:

```
procedure TForm1.Open1Click(Sender: TObject);
begin
 if OpenDialog1.Execute then
 begin
  {Set the file name}
   MediaPlayer1.FileName := OpenDialog1.FileName;
   {Open the file using the open method}
   MediaPlayer1.Open;
 end;
end;
```

You now have a functioning application that can play audio and video files through an easy-to-use interface. Figure 10.11 shows this application playing a standard AVI file.

Figure 10.11.

*The simple media
player playing an AVI
file.*

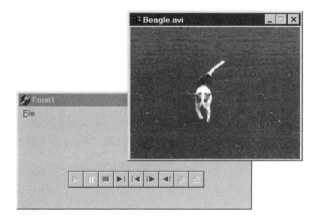

10

It's possible to change how the media player interacts with media files by setting the properties of the component. For example, when the player plays an AVI file, it plays the video in its own window. This behavior can be modified by setting the Display property on the media player. The Display property tells the component where to play a video file. The value can be any form or component derived from a TWinControl. There is also a DisplayRect property that you can use to specify the region of the new window in which to play the video file.

The DisplayRect property is slightly confusing. The confusion comes from the way it accepts its parameters. The DisplayRect property is set to a TRECT type, which you might think is the region to display the image in, but it isn't. The top-left parameter does indicate where to position the image, but the bottom-right parameter is used to specify the width and height. Therefore, the following code indicates that you wish to play the video on Form1 between coordinates 10,10 and 210,210 (not 10,10 to 200,200):

```
MediaPlayer1.Display := Form1;
MediaPlayer1.DisplayRect := RECT(10,10,200,200);
```

Using these two properties, create your next sample application shown in Listing 10.9, which enables the user to load a video file and play it just as before. However, now the image will be shown on part of the main form instead of in its own window. Furthermore, you add a special button that lets the user capture a particular frame. The captured frame is held even if the video continues. Figure 10.12 shows an AVI file playing in the left frame while a frame has been captured in the right frame.

Figure 10.12.

The frame capture application.

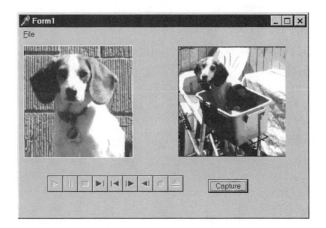

TYPE   **Listing 10.9. The Video Frame Capture application.**

```
unit unitCapture;

interface

uses
  Windows, Messages, SysUtils, Classes, Graphics, Controls,
  Forms, Dialogs,
  ExtCtrls, StdCtrls, Menus, MPlayer;

type
  TForm1 = class(TForm)
    MediaPlayer1: TMediaPlayer;
    MainMenu1: TMainMenu;
    File1: TMenuItem;
    Open1: TMenuItem;
    Capture: TButton;
    PaintBox1: TPaintBox;
    Exit1: TMenuItem;
    OpenDialog1: TOpenDialog;
    procedure Open1Click(Sender: TObject);
    procedure CaptureClick(Sender: TObject);
    procedure FormPaint(Sender: TObject);
    procedure Exit1Click(Sender: TObject);
    procedure FormCreate(Sender: TObject);
```

10

```
    procedure FormClose(Sender: TObject; var Action: TCloseAction);
    procedure PaintBox1Paint(Sender: TObject);
  private
    { Private declarations }
    ImgBitmap : TBitmap;
  public
    { Public declarations }
  end;

var
  Form1: TForm1;

implementation

{$R *.DFM}

procedure TForm1.Open1Click(Sender: TObject);
{open the file and set the display to form1}
{also set the region to display from (10,10,210,210)}
begin
 {Use the OpenDialog component to find a video file}
 if OpenDialog1.Execute then
 begin
   MediaPlayer1.FileName := OpenDialog1.FileName;
   MediaPlayer1.Open;
   MediaPlayer1.Display := Form1;
   MediaPlayer1.DisplayRect := RECT(10,10,200,200);
 end; {if}
end; {procedure}

procedure TForm1.CaptureClick(Sender: TObject);
{when the capture button is pressed, use the CopyRect method}
{to copy the image                                          }
{to a bitmap in memory}
begin
    ImgBitmap.Canvas.CopyRect(Rect(0,0,200,200),
                          Form1.Canvas,Rect(10,10,210,210));
    PaintBox1.Invalidate;
end; {procedure}

procedure TForm1.FormPaint(Sender: TObject);
{When the form is invalidated redraw the background rectangle}
begin
  Canvas.FrameRect(Rect(8,8,212,212));
end; {procedure}

procedure TForm1.Exit1Click(Sender: TObject);
begin
    Application.terminate;
end;

procedure TForm1.FormCreate(Sender: TObject);
{when the form is created we allocate resource for the bitmap and}
{set the initial size.  The bitmap is also cleared             }
begin
```

continues

Listing 10.9. continued

```
  ImgBitmap := Tbitmap.create;
  ImgBitmap.Height := 200;
  ImgBitmap.Width  := 200;
  ImgBitmap.Canvas.Rectangle(0,0,200,200);
end; {procedure}

procedure TForm1.FormClose(Sender: TObject; var Action: TCloseAction);
{When we leave, clean up by freeing the bitmap}
begin
  ImgBitmap.Free;
end; {procedure}

procedure TForm1.PaintBox1Paint(Sender: TObject);
{when the paintbox which displays the captured image}
{is invalidated, copy the                          }
{bitmap from memory into the paintbox.  }
{This prevents us from losing the image }
begin
  PaintBox1.Canvas.CopyRect(Rect(0,0,200,200),
                            ImgBitmap.Canvas,Rect(0,0,200,200));
end; {procedure}

end.
```

ANALYSIS   To load the media, you set up an Open option on the main menu. The event handler, which is called when the user opens a new file, loads the file, determines where the video file will be played, and enables the media player component. To determine which file to open, use the OpenDialog component. When the execute method is executed on the OpenDialog component, it displays the standard open dialog and returns a Boolean value that indicates if the user has chosen OK or Cancel. If the user chooses a valid file, set the FileName property on the media player equal to the FileName property of the OpenDialog component, as shown here:

```
MediaPlayer1.FileName := OpenDialog1.FileName;
```

Next, open the file and enable the media player by calling the Open method, as shown here:

```
MediaPlayer1.Open;
```

The final step in preparing the video clip to run is to specify that you want the image to run on Form1, and that the picture should be confined to a well-defined rectangle. This is necessary so you know where to capture the image. Use the following code to do this:

```
MediaPlayer1.Display := Form1;
MediaPlayer1.DisplayRect := RECT(10,10,200,200);
```

The sample uses the interface provided with the media player to enable the user to control the media that is loaded. Therefore, the user can perform functions such as play, stop, rewind, fast forward, and pause. The application uses this interface to control the player, but it adds a new button (Capture) that takes the current frame and copies it into a bitmap in memory.

Why use a bitmap? You could simply copy the image to another part of the main form, or a paintbox; however, if another window was dragged over the captured frame and then moved away, it would be erased. By copying the image to a bitmap, you have stored the image into a part of memory that you control.

Using a bitmap does add some complexity to the program. Where do you store the bitmap? Only procedures and functions that are used in the form need to access the bitmap. Therefore, you can add the bitmap in the Private portion of the TForm class declaration. Although the bitmap is referenced in the form, you still need to call the Create method and specify the dimensions of the bitmap when the form is loaded. This code can be placed in the OnCreate event handler of the form. Similarly, you need to clean up by deleting the bitmap when the form is closed. Note that storing the image in a bitmap does not display the image anywhere on the form. This is accomplished by placing a PaintBox component on the form and using its OnPaint event to copy the bitmap into the PaintBox whenever an OnPaint event is called. The OnPaint event handler is as follows:

```
procedure TForm1.PaintBox1Paint(Sender: TObject);
begin
   PaintBox1.Canvas.CopyRect(Rect(0,0,200,200),
                      ImgBitmap.Canvas,Rect(0,0,200,200));
end;
```

Therefore, whenever the operating system determines that the image needs to be redrawn, it calls the PaintBox1Paint procedure to reconcile the windows.

Using the Methods To Control the Media Player

Sometimes, you will want to use multimedia capabilities in an application however, and not want to display the media player component. You can do this by setting the Visible property to false on the media player component, and then you can perform all the functionality through the media player's methods. There are methods corresponding to all the buttons on the media player component's interface, as well as methods to provide additional functionality not included in the user interface. An example of a method not in the user interface is the Open method, which is used to open a file.

It is common to hide the media player component when you want to show a video clip during an application; however, you don't want to confuse the user or add clutter to the interface. For example, consider a cookbook application. You may have a feature that enables a user to click on an icon and show a video clip of a chef preparing a recipe. In this case, there is no need for the entire interface to be displayed because the user simply wants to see how the meal is prepared.

Responding to Media Player Events

Although the media player component has many properties and methods, there are relatively few events. The events that are included provide hooks into the user interface provided as well as notification when a media task is complete. One of these abilities is to execute custom code when a user clicks one of the buttons, and to tell the media player whether it should execute the requested task.

How Video Files Are Stored

NEW TERM Previous examples have explained using AVI files in your applications to create video effects. What exactly is a video file and how does it work? The human brain interprets a quick series of images with minor changes as motion. Each one of these pictures is called a *frame*. If you tour Walt Disney World, you actually can watch people draw each frame of a cartoon. Thus, each frame is slightly different from the next. For smooth video, or animation, the brain prefers about 30 frames per second. More than this is not very noticeable, and fewer frames per second gives the appearance of flicker.

NEW TERM Consider that a full-screen bitmap is a few hundred kilobytes. If you needed to store each frame of a video as a bitmap, that would be a lot of storage. For example, using this simple scheme, you could store only about 72 seconds-worth of video on a CD-ROM. If this was the case, there wouldn't be any multimedia applications until storage capacity improved. Luckily, there is a solution: *video compression.*

Instead of going though complex math in describing how video is compressed for a particular file format (such as AVI or MPEG), here is an overview of one of the techniques used. Have you ever watched a Rocky and Bullwinkle cartoon? The images freeze, and the character's mouth continues to move. The animators learned that it is much easier to change part of a scene rather than the entire scene. Video compression uses a similar approach. When a frame is captured, a decision is made by the capture hardware or software. "Can I store this frame using less space by saving what is different from the previous frame, or should I save the whole thing?" Most of the time, it is easier to save the parts of the scene that have changed. However, under certain circumstances, such as switching to a different camera, the overhead of describing the change would take up more space than it would to re-save the entire frame. Multimedia storage has come a long way. It's now possible to store an entire full-length movie on a standard CD-ROM.

Animation Techniques in Delphi

When you're using animation or moving graphics, it's important that the motion appears smooth to the user. Unfortunately, creating a frame by simply drawing a picture, erasing it, and drawing the next frame creates animation with a lot of flicker and isn't pleasant to view.

Double Buffers Using Standard Windows Services

NEW TERM A *double buffer* is a set of drawing surfaces. One surface is displayed, and the other is used as a drawing surface. When the drawing is complete on the drawing buffer, the buffers either switch places so that the one that was hidden is now displayed, or the hidden buffer is quickly copied onto the display buffer.

A simple technique to set up a double buffer in Delphi is to create a bitmap in memory and use it as the temporary buffer. Draw the image on the bitmap, and when each frame is drawn, use a `copyrect` method to copy the bitmap image onto the display buffer.

The Three-Dimensional, Spinning Cube

Now that you understand the concepts in creating animation in Delphi, you're ready to build an interactive example. This example shows that you can perform some pretty cool animation in Delphi without learning how to use the accelerated graphics techniques available in OpenGL or DirectX. This sample application displays a six-sided cube in a form. The user can set the speed at which the cube spins on the X, Y, and Z axis. Figure 10.13 shows the spinning cube application in action.

Figure 10.13.
The spinning cube.

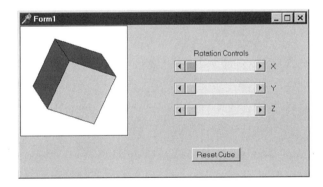

The example in Listing 10.10 illustrates the principles mentioned, plus gives a brief introduction into three-dimensional graphics. The first step in creating the cube is to know how to draw each frame. The cube consists of six faces and eight points. You define the position of each point in three-dimensional space by storing an X, Y, and Z coordinate in a record called TDPoint (for three-dimensional point). You keep track of all these points by using an array of records. The array is defined as follows:

```
Pnts : array[1..8] of TDPoint;    {Origional image}
```

TYPE **Listing 10.10. The rotating cube.**

```
unit unitSpinCube;
{*****************************************************}
{* The 3D Rotating Cube - A Comprehensive example  *}
{* of using animation in Delphi. This application  *}
{* displays a rotating 3 dimensional cube. The user*}
{* can adjust how quickly the cube rotates on each  *}
{* axis.                                            *}
{*****************************************************}

interface

uses
  Windows, Messages, SysUtils, Classes, Graphics, Controls,
  Forms, Dialogs,
  ExtCtrls, StdCtrls;

type
  TForm1 = class(TForm)
    ZRot: TScrollBar;
    YRot: TScrollBar;
    XRot: TScrollBar;
    ResetCube: TButton;
    Timer1: TTimer;
    Label1: TLabel;   {Labels used to make scroll bars}
    Label2: TLabel;
    Label3: TLabel;
    Label4: TLabel;
    procedure FormCreate(Sender: TObject);
    procedure FormClose(Sender: TObject; var Action: TCloseAction);
    procedure Timer1Timer(Sender: TObject);
    procedure ResetCubeClick(Sender: TObject);
  private
    { Private declarations }
  public
    { Public declarations }
  end;

var
  Form1: TForm1;

implementation

{$R *.DFM}
Type
  {Used to create a rotation matrix}
  Matrix = array[0..3,0..3] of Extended;
  {Structure to store a 3D point   }
  TDPoint = record
    X : Extended;
    Y : Extended;
    Z : Extended;
  end;
```

10

```
var
  DoubleBuffer : TBitmap;  {We will draw here then copyrect}
  BlankBuffer  : TBitmap;  {Bitmap to store our background }
  PntsOut :array[1..8] of TDPoint; {Rotated Points}
  TPPnts : array[1..8] of TPoint;  {2D representation of pts}
  Pnts : array[1..8] of TDPoint;   {Original image}
  XAng,YAng,ZAng : Extended;

{*******************************************************}
{Create an array(or matrix) which sets up rotation based }
{on angels passed in terms or radians. Consult a geometry}
{book to understand the math behind rotation.            }
{*******************************************************}
procedure matrixRotate(var m:Matrix;
                          x,y,z : Extended);
var
    sinX, cosX,
    sinY, cosY,
    sinZ, cosZ:Extended; {Store here so we only need to calc once}
    C1,C2 : integer; {for the loops}

begin
    sinX := sin(x); {let's do our geometry...}
    cosX := cos(x);
    sinY := sin(y);
    cosY := cos(y);
    sinZ := sin(z);
    cosZ := cos(z);
    for C1 := 0 to 3 do   {set the matrix to the identity}
     for C2 :=0 to 3 do
       if C1 = C2 then
         M[C1,C2] := 0
       else
         M[C1,C2] := 1;
    {Take my word for it this works!...}
    M[0,0] :=  (cosZ * cosY);
    M[0,1] :=  (cosZ * -sinY * -sinX + sinZ * cosX);
    M[0,2] :=  (cosZ * -sinY * cosX + sinZ * sinX);
    M[1,0] :=  (-sinZ * cosY);
    M[1,1] :=  (-sinZ * -sinY * -sinX + cosZ * cosX);
    M[1,2] :=  (-sinZ * -sinY * cosX + cosZ * sinX);
    M[2,0] :=  (sinY);
    M[2,1] :=  (cosY * -sinX);
    M[2,2] :=  (cosY * cosX);
end;

{Apply the rotation matrix to a 3D point and return a new 3D point}
procedure ApplyMatToPoint(PointIn : TDPoint;
                          var pointOut:TDPoint;mat : Matrix);
var
    x, y, z : Extended;

begin
    x :=(PointIn.x * mat[0,0]) + (PointIn.y * mat[0,1]) +
```

continues

Listing 10.10. continued

```
            (PointIn.z * mat[0,2]) + mat[0,3];
    y := (PointIn.x * mat[1,0]) + (PointIn.y * mat[1,1]) +
            (PointIn.z * mat[1,2]) + mat[1,3];
    z := (PointIn.x * mat[2,0]) + (PointIn.y * mat[2,1]) +
            (PointIn.z * mat[2,2]) + mat[2,3];
    PointOut.x :=  x;
    PointOut.y :=  y;
    PointOut.z :=  z;
end;

{We are using a cube which has 8 point. This is where we setup the }
{coordinates for each point. The middle of the cube is at (0,0,0)   }
procedure InitCube;
begin
  Pnts[1].X := -50;
  Pnts[1].Y := -50;
  Pnts[1].Z := -50;
  Pnts[2].X := 50;
  Pnts[2].Y := -50;
  Pnts[2].Z := -50;
  Pnts[3].X := 50;
  Pnts[3].Y := 50;
  Pnts[3].Z := -50;
  Pnts[4].X := -50;
  Pnts[4].Y := 50;
  Pnts[4].Z := -50;
  Pnts[5].X := -50;
  Pnts[5].Y := -50;
  Pnts[5].Z := 50;
  Pnts[6].X := 50;
  Pnts[6].Y := -50;
  Pnts[6].Z := 50;
  Pnts[7].X := 50;
  Pnts[7].Y := 50;
  Pnts[7].Z := 50;
  Pnts[8].X := -50;
  Pnts[8].Y := 50;
  Pnts[8].Z := 50;
end;

{The following function returns true if the sum of the  }
{parameters is greater then zero and false if it is     }
{less then zero. We will use this function to determine }
{Which sides of the cube to hide and which to show      }
function ShowSide(V1,V2,V3,V4 : Extended) : Boolean;
begin
  if (V1+V2+V3+V4) > 0 then
    ShowSide := TRUE
  else
    ShowSide := FALSE;
end;

{We are using a double buffer. This function determines if a side}
{is visible. If it is, it draws the 2D representation on our      }
```

10

```
{bitmap buffer with the fill set to the color passed          }
procedure AddSide(P1,P2,P3,P4:Integer;SideColor : TColor);
begin
 if ShowSide(PntsOut[P1].Z,PntsOut[P2].Z,
              PntsOut[P3].Z,PntsOut[P4].Z) then
   begin
     DoubleBuffer.Canvas.Brush.Color := SideColor;
     DoubleBuffer.Canvas.Polygon([TPPnts[P1],TPPnts[P2],
                        TPPnts[P3],TPPnts[P4],TPPnts[P1]]);
   end;
end;

procedure TForm1.FormCreate(Sender: TObject);
{When the form loads, create and initialize our background bitmap}
{and initialize our double buffer bitmap.                    }
begin
    DoubleBuffer := TBitmap.Create;
    DoubleBuffer.Height := 200;
    DoubleBuffer.Width := 200;
    BlankBuffer := TBitmap.Create;
    BlankBuffer.Height := 200;
    BlankBuffer.Width  := 200;
    BlankBuffer.Canvas.Brush.Color := clWhite;
    BlankBuffer.Canvas.rectangle(0,0,200,200);
    InitCube();
    XAng := 0;
    YAng := 0;
    ZAng := 0;
end;

procedure TForm1.FormClose(Sender: TObject; var Action: TCloseAction);
{When we are done we need to clean up by freeing out bitmaps}
begin
    BlankBuffer.Free;
    DoubleBuffer.Free;
end;

procedure TForm1.Timer1Timer(Sender: TObject);
{The main procedure which draws the cube. This procedure is called  }
{by a timer that executes its OnTimer function every 20 milliseconds}

var
  M : Matrix;              {The matrix used to rotate the cube}
  Count2 : Integer; {Used to loop through points         }

begin
    XAng := XAng + XRot.Position;  {adjust the rotation angle}
    YAng := YAng + YRot.Position;  {by pulling out of the    }
    ZAng := ZAng + ZRot.Position;  {scroll bars              }
    {Adjust for degrees and build the rotation matrix}
    matrixRotate(M,(PI*XAng)/180,(PI*YAng)/180,(PI*ZAng)/180);
    {Loop through all of the points and rotate,}
    {the get 2D representation                 }
    for Count2:= 1 to 8 do
    begin
```

continues

Listing 10.10. continued

```
              ApplyMatToPoint(Pnts[Count2],PntsOut[Count2],M);
              TPPnts[Count2] := Point(trunc(PntsOut[Count2].X+100),
                                      trunc(PntsOut[Count2].Y+100));
          end;
          {Clear the double buffer by copyrect[ing] the Background}
          DoubleBuffer.Canvas.CopyRect(RECT(0,0,200,200),
                                    BlankBuffer.Canvas,RECT(0,0,200,200));
          {Build the cube by calling AddSide for each of the 6 sides}
          AddSide(1,2,3,4,clBlue);
          AddSide(5,6,7,8,clRed);
          AddSide(1,2,6,5,clYellow);
          AddSide(2,3,7,6,clGreen);
          AddSide(3,4,8,7,clPurple);
          AddSide(4,1,5,8,clSilver);
          {Copy the double buffer to the form}
          Form1.Canvas.CopyRect(RECT(0,0,200,200),
                              DoubleBuffer.Canvas,RECT(0,0,200,200));
      end;

      procedure TForm1.ResetCubeClick(Sender: TObject);
      begin
        XAng := 0;
        YAng := 0;
        ZAng := 0;
      end;
      end.
```

ANALYSIS The points are initialized in the InitCube procedure. This needs to occur only once because theses values never change. At each frame, you determine how the cube is situated and figure a new set of points reflecting the coordinates of the rotated cube. This is calculated by creating a rotation matrix and then calling ApplyMatToPoint for each of the eight points. This leaves you with a new set of three-dimensional points. Now you can simply drop the Z value, and you have X and Y coordinates for the eight corners.

You can play a little trick to determine which faces on the cube are hidden. If a cube is situated at (0,0,0), a face is showing if the sum of its Z values is greater than 0. This works only with certain types of objects, so usually hidden surface removal is more complex, but you can do it in the simple function, ShowSide.

Now you know what to draw and at which coordinates it needs to be drawn. The final task is to make the animation smooth. Each frame is triggered by an OnTimer event. The procedure reads the slider components to determine how much to increment each angle of rotation. To draw the frame, you use a memory bitmap and clear it by copying another bitmap. The second bitmap is used rather than a Rectangle method because Copyrect operates quicker then Rectangle. You next determine which sides need to be displayed and draw them on the memory bitmap with a polygon method. Each side is drawn with a unique color so that the final result is even more impressive. Finally, you use a copyrect to copy the memory bitmap onto the main form. This is an interesting example and can be easily modified to include more functionality.

The Next Level of Performance DirectX and OpenGL

The previous example shows how three-dimensional graphics can be created using standard Delphi components. One of the problems with using this technique is that it is not possible to take advantage of hardware that is specifically designed to perform 3D rendering (as many newer graphics cards are). It also forces you to do all of the hard work that a 3D graphics engine can automatically perform, such as hidden surface removal and shading.

OpenGl and Direct3D (one of the components of DirectX) are specifically designed to perform highly optimized graphics rendering that can take advantage of 3D hardware. Direct3D is based on the component object model and provides the highest performance available. OpenGL sets up a graphics pipeline where commands can be sent to the graphics hardware. In both OpenGL and Direct3D, software is used to emulate features that are not supported in hardware. OpenGL and Direct3D are beyond the scope of this book, but they deserved a mention here. If you need highest performance available in your graphics application, you should research these topics farther.

10

Summary

Graphics development is one of the hottest and most exciting topics in the computer industry. Delphi is an excellent development language for using the graphical features in Windows 95 and Windows NT. The primary drawing surface in Delphi is the canvas. The canvas enables an application to draw on a form, a paintbox, or a bitmap. Today you learned different ways to manipulate a canvas. You also learned about specific aspects of working with images and bitmaps, as well as underlying graphics theory.

Today also covered multimedia and animation techniques. You learned how to use the PlaySound API call to add sound effects to an application. You also learned about the media player visual component, which can play all sorts of multimedia files, including video. It's highly configurable and can be used many different ways.

Finally, you learned about animation. It's clear that the media player is ideal for pre-recorded video files, but there are times when you need to create smooth, on-the-fly animation. You saw how to improve performance and take advantage of certain methods that can be executed quickly. You concluded with an example of a three-dimensional rotating cube that illustrates the power of using simple methods in Delphi to create animation.

Q&A

Q **How can my application use Win32 graphics APIs with graphical components in Delphi?**

A Most Delphi components and objects have properties that you can use to link to their underlying handles. For example, the TBitmap class has a Handle property that you can access to perform bitmap APIs. Also, the canvas's device context (DC) is available through its Handle property.

Q **What are some of the advantages of drawing a bitmap off screen and then copying it to the display?**

A When you're drawing to an off-screen bitmap, the image does not experience any flicker. Also, you can maintain multiple images and swap them rapidly to a section of the screen.

Q **Can I use the MCI (media control interface) without using the media player component?**

A Yes, all the multimedia API calls are available. If you have the source code for the media player component, you will see that the component itself uses the MCI API.

Q **I used the Copyrect to move quickly a rectangular portion of a canvas. Are there any other ways to move parts of a canvas quickly?**

A Yes, you can access the Handle property of a canvas, which is a handle to its device context. You then can use any of the Win32 GDI calls you operate on the picture. For example, there is a call to move data to a parallelogram, and you can perform various masking operations.

Q **Can multiple threads write to the same canvas?**

A Yes, you must call the Lock method on the canvas before you manipulate it and the UnLock method when you are done with any individual operation.

Workshop

The Workshop provides two ways for you to affirm what you've learned in this chapter. The Quiz section poses questions to help you solidify your understanding of the material covered. You can find answers to the quiz questions in Appendix A, "Answers to the Quiz Questions." The Exercises section provides you with experience in using what you have learned. Please try to work through all these before continuing to the next day.

10

Quiz

1. In the simple animation example, what happens if `pmCopy` is used for the pen mode instead of `pmNotXor`?

2. Clipping is useful to confine a drawing to a particular portion of a form. What Delphi components could you use to automatically clip a drawing to a region of the screen?

3. How can an application use a method to load a bitmap into an image? How could an application copy a piece of the bitmap to a paintbox?

4. How does `Playsound` know to wait until the sound has completed before executing the next instruction or to execute the next instruction while the sound is playing?

5. What does the effect of the following call have on a media player component?

   ```
   MediaPlayer1.DisplayRect := RECT(50,50,200,200);
   ```

   Hint: It doesn't mean to play the video between coordinates (`50,50` and `200,200`).

6. When performing animation, what is the problem with drawing a frame, erasing it, and then drawing the next frame?

Exercises

1. Confirm that when a window containing a graphic object does not redraw itself after being covered, the image in that portion of the window is erased.

2. Modify the MIXUP program so that the newly created bitmap has the pieces arranged in a specific order, instead of being random (for example, so the X and Y pieces are transposed).

3. Write a program that continuously plays music in the background.

4. Use the media player component to play a video file. Give the user a set of choices as to where the video should be played (in its own windows or on the main form). Add scroll bars that let the user determine how big the picture should be.

5. Modify the rotating cube program so that the cube is rotating on a background that is a bitmap. Hint: Replace the blank bitmap used to clear the frame with a real bitmap.

10

Day 11

Delphi's Database Architecture

Programmers often come to a point where they ask:

"I have a large amount of data that my application needs to access and manipulate. Is there an easy way to do this?"

The answer is yes. Databases provide a generic means to store data. A database engine provides the mechanism to manipulate and view the data in the database. Without databases, programmers would be forced to write complex routines to do file manipulation whenever there was a need to store and access data efficiently. In essence, programmers would be responsible for creating the database and database engine.

Delphi has powerful database support built in. There are visual components that enable access to tables and methods to manipulate records. This chapter explains how to create your own databases with the tools provided with Delphi and how to integrate the database into your application. Delphi has the capability to perform powerful complex database manipulation or act as a simple front end.

A database *front end* is a program that provides an easy-to-use interface to access and manipulate the data in a database. Delphi includes a tool that makes front-end development almost effortless by doing almost all the development for you. This tool is called the Form Wizard. The Form Wizard creates a completely functional database front end without a single line of code.

The Relational Database Model

 Most new databases today are relational databases. A *relational database* stores information in logical tables made up of rows and columns. As expected, the tables are called database tables. Take a look at a simple table.

Suppose RAD University (RADU) wants to keep records on its student population. To do this, RADU organizes its data into a table, which is shown in Table 11.1.

Table 11.1. Data in relational form.

SSN	Name	Class	Phone	GPA
185-34-2345	Ada Smith	Freshman	423-3456	3.4
123-43-2233	Joe Brown	Freshman	213-2343	2.1
432-45-2345	Ashlyn Kelly	Freshman	213-2222	4.0
234-54-2345	Ron Beagle	Sophomore	423-1234	1.9

The columns in a table are called fields, and the rows are called records. For every record in the table, there must be related information in each field.

Jumping in with the Form Wizard

Delphi comes with a powerful tool that creates a form that maps fields in a table to entry/edit fields on a form. This section presents an example of how to build an application using the Form Wizard. This example uses one of the sample databases included with Delphi.

Using the Form Wizard

Using the Form Wizard is easy and fun. You make choices, and the wizard generates the code and screens for you. Follow these steps to create your first database screen:

1. Start Delphi.
2. Choose Database | Form Wizard from the main menu, and the Database Form Wizard dialog box appears, as shown in Figure 11.1.

Figure 11.1.

Selecting Form and DataSet options in the Form Wizard.

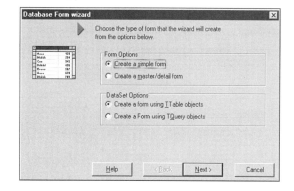

3. In the Form Options group, select `Create a simple form`. In the DataSet Options group, select `Create a form using TTable objects`. Click the Next button, and the next page of the wizard appears.

4. Choose `DBDEMOS` in the Drive or Alias name section. This brings up a list of tables in the left pane of the window, as shown in Figure 11.2.

Figure 11.2.

Choosing which tables to use in the Form Wizard.

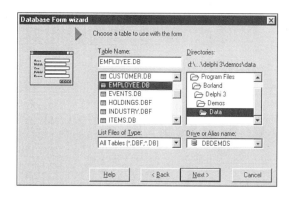

5. Choose `EMPLOYEE.DB`, and then click Next.

6. Press the >> button (between the two list boxes). This tells the wizard that you would like to build a form showing all fields. The result is shown in Figure 11.3. Click Next.

7. Click Next for all remaining pages until the form is created. You can do this because the defaults offered by the wizard are fine for this exercise.

8. Choose Run | Run from the menu.

Congratulations! You have just created your first Delphi database application. Figure 11.4 shows the application at work.

Figure 11.3.

Choosing which fields to use in the Form Wizard.

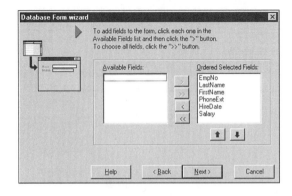

Figure 11.4.

Application built using the Form Wizard.

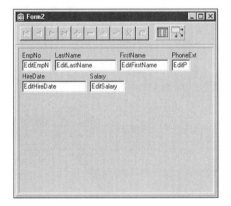

How Does It Work?

This sample application gives the user full control over a table containing information about employees. A database navigation toolbar is located at the top of the application so users can manipulate the records. Each button on the toolbar executes a different database function. The button functions are described in Table 11.2.

Run the application and spend some time playing with this simple front end. Choose Close to terminate the application when you're done.

Table 11.2. Database navigator buttons.

Icon	Function	Description
	Move First	Moves to the first record in the table.
	Move Previous	Moves to the previous record in the table.
	Move Next	Moves to the next record.
	Move Last	Moves to the last record.
	Insert	Inserts a new record at the current position.
	Delete	Deletes the record that is displayed.
	Edit	Enables users to modify fields in the current record.
	Post Edit	Saves changes to a record.
	Cancel Edit	Cancels changes to a record.
	Refresh Data	Reloads the current record. This is useful when multiple applications have access to a database and the current record may have changed.

Database Choices

One of the most powerful features of Delphi's database engine access is that Delphi provides a layer of abstraction between the underlying database and the database functionality. This brings up an interesting question, "What database should I use with Delphi?" There is no right answer, and choosing a database now does not mean that later a different database cannot be installed in its place.

Database Models

There are many applications that use databases. It wouldn't make sense for the IRS to use the same type of database as Joe's Garage and Service Center. Both of these obviously need to track vastly different amounts of data and are accessed by different numbers of applications. Also, there are issues that need to be addressed by databases that are accessed by more than one application or person. For example, what happens when two processes try to modify the same record at one time? Which types of security can be implemented to allow only partial data to be accessed by certain applications? These two issues are concurrence problems and security.

NEW TERM The process of determining what type of database is appropriate for an application is known as *scaling*. The power, complexity, and functionality of a database system often is related to its physical layout and infrastructure. In this section, you explore the three main classes of database layouts: stand-alone, file-share, and client/server. You also learn a bit about the multi-tier database structure that is included with Delphi Client/Server Edition.

The following sections describe the different types of database models:

- ☐ Stand-alone
- ☐ File-share
- ☐ Client/server
- ☐ Multi-tier

Stand-Alone Databases

Stand-alone databases are the simplest to deal with because you can ignore a lot of issues. A stand-alone database has its database stored in a local file system and a database engine to access it residing on the same machine. With a pure stand-alone database, you don't need to handle concurrence—the condition where two people try to change the same record at one time—because this never happens. In general, a stand-alone database is not used for an application that needs excessive computing power because processing time is spent doing data manipulation and is not totally available to the application.

Stand-alone databases are useful in development of applications that are distributed to many users, where each user maintains a separate database. For example, an application that tracks miles driven to determine fuel reimbursement could be developed using a stand-alone database. Each person using the application would store and manipulate his or her own gas data on their local machine. It is not necessary for a user of this application to access any other person's data, so a local database is well suited.

There are many powerful stand-alone databases. You can create and manipulate Paradox and dBASE databases with the Database Desktop that comes with Delphi. These can act as either stand-alone or file-share databases.

NOTE

> It is important to understand one of the most useful database features included in Delphi 3: native database drivers. Delphi now supports Microsoft Access and FoxPro, as well as dBASE native access. This means that you (the developer) gain faster access to these data sources than if you use ODBC drivers (which are discussed later in this chapter in the section "Why Use ODBC?"). This feature makes Delphi viable as a tool for migration of VB applications to Delphi.

File-Share Databases

A file-share database is almost exactly like a stand-alone database except that it can be accessed by multiple clients across a network. This provides a greater deal of accessibility because the database can be accessed and manipulated by different machines. For example, take the employee database used in the stand-alone database example. If an administrator changes an employee's salary, a payroll application printing checks could see the change immediately. However, the machine that accesses the database is running the database engine locally. Another advantage of a file-share database is that there are no pre-conceived notions of the network. The database engine does not care if Novell, Banyan, Microsoft NT, or any other network operating system is running because it simply sees the database as a file. A situation in which a file-share database may not be suitable is when a great deal of computation and simultaneous access needs to be performed on a database. For this, a client/server database is the solution.

Client/Server Databases

The high-end solution for database access is solved through the client/server model. In this case, a dedicated machine, or server, is tasked to perform database access for a group of clients. Consider the example of the IRS's database. The IRS may want to know all Social Security numbers for persons who made over $100,000 and paid less than $2,000 in taxes. In a file-share system, this would bring the requesting machine to a halt while it cranked through the data. However, in a client/server model, the client asks the server to perform the specified task. It is then up to the client to decide whether it wants to wait for the result or go on to do something more interesting. Meanwhile, the server has been optimized to handle requests in the fastest possible manner.

Although there are many performance and flexibility advantages to a client/server architecture, there also are many disadvantages. Client/server solutions are often much more expensive than a file-share solution. Also, client/server software needs a protocol, such as TCP/IP, in which to carry on a conversation. Although this is often flexible, it is an additional configuration and administrative function.

A New Paradigm: Multi-Tier Databases

There is a new and exciting way to handle data on a network. This new way is called a multi-tier system. This involves a combination of "thin" clients, application servers, and database servers in the back end. The result here is a system that allows for fail-over and data replication. This option won't be discussed in detail here because it comes only in the Delphi C/S Edition. If you have that version, you will get documentation for this anyway.

When developing Delphi applications that do not require backward compatibility to a database currently in use, you most likely will choose Paradox, Access, or dBASE because they are tightly integrated with Delphi. Also, database objects for dBASE and Delphi can be easily created and managed with the Database Desktop. Table 11.3 shows some statistics pertaining to the capacities of dBASE, Access, and Paradox.

Table 11.3. Comparison of Paradox, dBASE, and Access tables.

Attribute	Paradox	dBASE	Access
Maximum records	2 billion	1 billion	2 billion
Fields per table	255	1,024	1,024
Characters per field	Not applicable	256	Not applicable
Bytes per record	32,750	32,767	32,767

As you can see, all three databases are extremely powerful and capable of holding more data than most applications ever will need. Paradox and Access offer quite a bit more flexibility at the database level. This means that the tables can contain information other than just the raw data. For example, Paradox allows data validation to occur at the database level. Also, password security is integrated into Paradox. These features are very useful especially if the Delphi application will not be the only application accessing the data.

Choosing which database model is right for an application is often a difficult task. Luckily, Borland's database engine is flexible enough to change databases with little effort. If this doesn't provide enough flexibility, the database engine can communicate with ODBC, which can communicate with almost any database on the market today. ODBC is discussed in the section "Why Use ODBC?" later in this chapter, but now let's see how to create a new table using the Database Desktop.

Aliases

Databases can be arranged in many different ways. In Microsoft Access, multiple tables are stored in one file. Paradox and dBASE use a separate file for each table. A client/server-based system, such as Sybase or Microsoft SQL Server, stores all data on a separate machine and communicates with clients through a special language called SQL.

In addition to the method each type of database uses to store its data, some databases require additional information. This is a very complex task for the Borland database engine to handle if it wants to communicate transparently with many different types of databases because each seems to want slightly different information. For example, a Paradox database will want to know what directory represents the database, whereas a Sybase database may need a network address for the server, database name, user ID, and password. The solution to this problem is the use of aliases. An *alias* contains all the information that needs to be supplied to access a database. Therefore, when creating a Paradox alias, all that needs to be supplied is the directory containing the database objects. However, when more complicated data sources are needed, additional information will be provided.

Using the Database Desktop to Create a New Table

Now that you understand the basic elements of a table, it's time to create a new sample table. The Borland Database Desktop, shown in Figure 11.5, can be accessed by choosing Tools | Database Desktop in the Delphi IDE.

Figure 11.5.
The Borland Database Desktop.

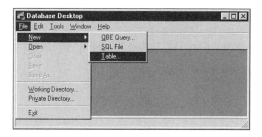

Creating a New Table

The creation of tables in Delphi is easy using the Borland Database Desktop. Follow these instructions to create the tables and the fields:

1. Choose File | New | Table, and the Create Table dialog box appears asking what type of table you want to create. For new applications, the Paradox database is most

likely the easiest to work with; therefore, choose Paradox 7. Click OK, and the
Create Paradox 7 Table dialog box appears, as shown in Figure 11.6.

Figure 11.6.

Defining the fields using the Database Desktop.

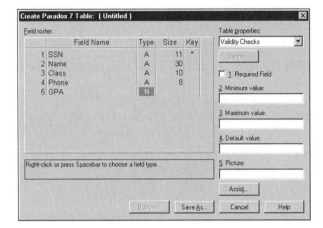

2. The first thing that you need to decide is what data you want to store in your table, and what type of data it is. For this example, consider the RADU student information table described earlier. Each field needs to be added in the Field roster portion of the dialog box. To add the first field, type SSN in the Field Name field. This says that you want to add a new field called SSN.

3. The next piece of information needed is what type of data will be stored in the field. Social Security numbers are stored as a string of characters. Right-click on the Type field (in the Field roster) to show the data types available. For a string, the Paradox type Alpha is used. Choose Alpha from the Type list being displayed.

4. For some data types, you need to supply a size. This tells the database the largest amount of data that can be stored in a field. For SSN, you know that all Social Security numbers are 11 characters, so type 11 in the Size field. Some data types, such as Number, do not use the Size field, and the Database Desktop disables the Size field for entries that do not use size.

5. The final piece of information you need to supply to the database is whether a field is a key. A key simply means that the field is guaranteed to be unique for every record. Using keys in databases is extremely important. For now, mark the SSN field as a key (by pressing the space bar or clicking on the Key field) because you know that there will be only one entry for every student and that every student will have a unique Social Security number.

6. To define the next field in the table, press Enter. Continue to define fields using the information in Table 11.4.

11

Table 11.4. Sample table field definition and attributes.

Field Name	Type	Size	Key
SSN	A	11	*
Name	A	30	
Class	A	10	
Phone	A	8	
GPA	N		

7. Click the Save As button to save the information about the table.

8. In the Save Table As dialog box, change the Drive (or alias) list box to **DBDEMOS**. Type **Studinfo.DB** in the New file name text box. Click OK. This saves the table. That's it! You created a new table.

Why Use Keys?

Why did you set the SSN number as a key? Keys help the database engine work efficiently. It helps if there is a definitive way to distinguish every record from all other records in a table. Paradox has a requirement that all fields that are keys should be placed at the top of the definition list. Although most databases do not force tables to have a key, it's always a good practice to key each table. However, what if the table you are working on does not have a natural key? This means that there is no field in the table guaranteed to be unique for every record. Consider Table 11.5, which might be used in a cooking database.

Table 11.5. Ingredients in the cooking database.

Recipe	Ingredient
Macaroni and Cheese	Macaroni
Macaroni and Cheese	Cheddar Cheese
Macaroni and Cheese	Milk
Tuna Melt	Tuna
Tuna Melt	Cheddar Cheese

You can't use Recipe as a key because there are multiple ingredients for each recipe. Ingredient can't be used either because the same ingredient can be used in many different recipes. Luckily, most databases have a way to work around this through special data types that are administered automatically by the database engine, and the database engine guarantees that the field will be unique. In Paradox, this data type is called the Auto-Increment data type. By defining a field as Auto-Increment, each time a record is added to the table an internal counter increases and sets the field value to that number. Table 11.6 is how you could set up the table layout for your recipe example using Auto-Increment to create a key.

Table 11.6. Cooking database field attributed with an automatic key.

Field Name	Type	Size	Key
CookBookKey	+		*
Recipe	A	30	
Ingredient	A	30	

When data is added to this table, each record automatically is assigned a unique value. The table looks like Table 11.7 after data has been added.

Table 11.7. Cooking data with the key added.

CookBookKey	Recipe	Ingredient
1	Macaroni and Cheese	Macaroni
2	Macaroni and Cheese	Cheddar Cheese
3	Macaroni and Cheese	Milk
4	Tuna Melt	Tuna
5	Tuna Melt	Cheddar Cheese

There is quite a bit more information that should be provided when creating a table, but this gives a model that can be worked with for now. Details will be provided later in this chapter in the section "Controlling Input into a Table," on how to increase performance of the database and how to ensure that only valid information is entered.

Now That I Have a Table, How Do I Access It From Delphi?

You've seen the easiest way to create an application that has access to a table in Delphi: the Delphi Form Wizard. Now take a closer look at what is happening behind the scenes and what steps are necessary to build an application from scratch.

The easiest way to access and manipulate databases in Delphi is by using the database visual components provided. Database visual components are stored on two tabs of the Visual Component Library: the Data Access and Data Control tabs. The components on the Data

Access tab are used to give Delphi information about what database tables and functions should be used, whereas the Data Control tab lists visual components that can display data in a database or provide an interface to manipulate the data (such as insert, delete, and modify).

Making Delphi Aware of a Table—The `TTable` Component

In order to use a table, the first step is to let Delphi know that you intend to interact with the table. To do this, you need to place on the form a `Table` object that accesses the data. Examining the properties sheet shows that there are two properties called `DatabaseName` and `TableName`. These are the two minimal properties that need to be set in order for Delphi to access the table. The `DatabaseName` property corresponds to the database aliases that are available. The `TableName` specifies which table in a database should be used.

Accessing the Student Information Table

The first steps in creating an application to access the student information database that you created earlier in this chapter are to place a `TTable` component on your form and then configure the `DatabaseName` and `TableName` properties. Follow this procedure:

1. Create a new application.

2. Place a `TTable` component on the form. You can find the `TTable` component on the Data Access tab of the Visual Component Library.

3. In the Properties tab of the Object Inspector, set `DatabaseName` to `DBDEMOS`. `DBDEMOS` is the alias in which the `Studinfo.DB` table was saved.

4. After you set the `DatabaseName` property, the `TableName` property should indicate a list box of all the available tables in the database. Choose `Studinfo.DB` for the database name.

5. Set the `Active` property to `True`. This immediately opens the table when the application is run. If this is set to `False`, the application will not be able to access any data in the table until the active property is set to `True` during runtime.

6. Set the `Name` property to `StudInfo`.

Two other properties that can be modified at runtime are `Readonly` and `Exclusive`. Setting `Readonly` to `True` enables the application to view only the data in the database; however, it will not be able modify that data. The `Exclusive` option ensures that the application is the only one accessing the data. At this point, the application has the information it needs to attach to a table. However, there is no way to manipulate the data until the `Table` object is associated with a `DataSource`.

Providing the Link—The TDataSource **Component**

Delphi has the ability to access database information from a series of components known as DataSets, one of which is the TTable component. Data-aware controls are controls that display and manipulate data in a database that is accessed through Delphi. To provide a layer of abstraction for controls that navigate through data and display information, the TDataSource was developed. The DataSource also provides a way to detect when changes are made to data and to detect what state the DataSet, or source of data, is in.

Adding the DataSource

Now that the TTable component is on your form, you need to connect a DataSource to it. This will enables data-aware components to use the TTable component you have defined. Follow these steps:

1. Choose a DataSource component from the Data Access tab, and add it to the form.
2. Set the DataSet property to StudInfo. This links the data source to the TTable component StudInfo, which in turn is accessing the StudInfo.DB table in the DBDEMOS database.
3. Set the name for the DataSource to dsStudent.

Data-Aware Controls—Seeing and Modifying the Data

At this point, you have set up everything Delphi needs to communicate with a table. However, it is now necessary to decide how the data should be displayed and how it should be manipulated. The easiest way to do this is with the data-aware controls. Most of the data-aware controls are for binding a database field to a visual component. For example, it is often necessary to have a text-edit field contain the value of a field in a table. The standard data-aware controls are extremely powerful and easy to use, and Delphi comes with many to choose from. Other than the DBNavigator, all the controls on the Data Control tab are used for displaying database data. To start with, add the DBGrid control to your example.

Adding a Data-Aware Control—The DBGrid

Now that the DataSource component is ready for us, let's hook some data-aware controls to it. Execute the following steps:

1. Place the DBGrid control on your form. This is the first control that is added that is actually seen at runtime; therefore, change the size so that it takes up a large part of the form.

2. Set the `DataSource` property to `dsStudent`; this links the control to the data source.

3. What happened? As soon as the `DataSource` property is set, notice that the field names automatically appear in the grid. If there was data in the `Studinfo.DB` table, this would also be displayed even at design time. However, if the `Active` property had been set to `False`, nothing would be seen until it was set to `True`.

4. Run the application. At this point, you actually can enter data into the grid. Type a Social Security number, press Tab, and type a name. Continue tabbing through the fields until a record is entered. On completion of the first record, the `DBGrid` control automatically puts the cursor on the next line. Continue to add a few sample records into the table. Note that if two records are entered with the same SSN, an error occurs. You will handle this gracefully a little later.

5. End the application, and add one more control: the `DBEdit` control. The `DBEdit` control displays one field of a table. Unlike the grid control that can display multiple records, the `DBEdit` control displays a field of the current record. The current record is simply the record that is being accessed by the database engine at a particular moment. The `DBGrid` control specifies the current record by placing a triangle next to it.

6. Add a `DBEdit` control to the form, and set the `DataSource` property to `dsStudent`. Now a field needs to be specified so the control knows what to display. To set the field, set the `DataField` property to `SSN`.

7. Run the application. Figure 11.7 shows this application executing.

Figure 11.7.

Application using `TTable`, `DataSource`, *and data-aware components.*

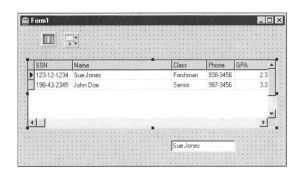

Notice that when a record is moved to or clicked on in the grid, this changes the current record. This application gives some control to the user, but it would be difficult to move around in a large database. Delphi has a powerful control that enables navigation through a table: the `DBNavigator`. The `DBNavigator` is a toolbar all by itself that allows easy navigation through a table.

Adding the DBNavigator

Now that the database is working, you need a way to navigate through the records. You could do this in code, but there is an easier way. Let's use the DBNavigator component as our navigation tool. Follow these steps to place and activate the DBNavigator control:

1. Select the DBNavigator control and place it on the form. Set the DataSource property to dsStudent.

2. Set the ShowHint property to True. This causes a hint to appear whenever the cursor is placed over one of the buttons on the toolbar.

3. Run the application. Notice how easy it is to move between records, jump to the beginning or end of the database, and to edit records. Figure 11.8 shows the new application with the addition of the DBNavigator.

Figure 11.8.

Adding the database navigator.

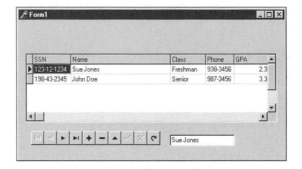

You have created a fully functional application using absolutely no code. Next, you learn how database controls can be manipulated with object Pascal from within Delphi.

Accessing Databases with Code

Now that we have examined how to access databases by manipulating visual components through the IDE, you will learn how to manipulate the components using Object Pascal. The database components offer a powerful set of events, properties, and methods that can be called from within a Delphi unit.

DataSet State

A dataset can be in one of six possible states: dsEdit, dsBrowse, dsInsert, dsInactive, dsSetKey, or dsCalcFields. The state gives information about the current interaction the application has with the dataset. To view records, the state should be in dsBrowse mode. If an application needs to modify a record, then the DataSet must be put into dsEdit mode.

Checking what state a DataSet is in can be done only at runtime by checking the State property. To change the state of the DataSet, the Insert, Edit, Post, Cancel, or Append method can be used. The Insert method causes a new record to be inserted and that record to be put into edit mode. To edit the current record, the Edit method can be used.

One of the powerful features of the Delphi database engine is that it provides support to commit or roll back changes when editing a record. When a dataset is in edit mode, changes can be made to many fields. When the changes are complete, a Post method can be applied to the dataset to keep and record the changes. However, if for some reason the application needs to restore a record's initial value, the Cancel method can be used. Listing 11.1 demonstrates how to save or roll back changes made to a record.

TYPE   **Listing 11.1. Confirming a change.**

```
Var
  Save:integer;

begin
  Save :=Application.MessageBox('Save Changes?', 'CONFIRM!',mb_yesno);
  if Save = IDYES then
      Studinfo.Post {Commit Transaction}
  else
      StudInfo.Cancel {Roll back Transaction};
end; {Procedure}
```

ANALYSIS   In this program, a message box is displayed in which the user is asked to confirm changes to the record that is being edited. If the user clicks Yes, the Post method is executed on the dataset, thus saving the changes. If the user clicks No, the Cancel method is used to undo any changes made during the edit. There is one flaw in this code. If the DataSet is not in dsEdit mode, and a Post or Cancel method is executed, an exception will occur. Therefore, the question is how can you check to confirm you are in edit mode? As mentioned earlier, the State property tells you what mode the DataSet is in. A safer example of this code is shown in Listing 11.2.

TYPE   **Listing 11.2. Confirming changes to a record, with validation of state property.**

```
Var
  Save:integer;

begin
  if Studinfo.State = dsEdit then
  begin
```

continues

Listing 11.2. continued

```
        Save :=Application.MessageBox('Save Changes?,'CONFIRM!',mb_yesno);
        if Save = IDYES then
            Studinfo.Post {Commit Transaction}
        else
            StudInfo.Cancel; {Roll back Transaction}
    end
  else
    Application.MessageBox('Not in Edit Mode!','Error',mb_ok);
end; {Procedure}
```

 These two examples have shown how control over records can be accessed from code. Your application can make a logical decision of whether changes should be saved or aborted. Next, you take a look at how to access the data fields.

Accessing the Fields

It often is necessary for a program to access and modify database fields. Fortunately, Delphi makes this very easy. The Fields property of a DataSet describes more than the values contained in the fields. The property also contains information about the structure of the table. For example, the Fields property can give the name of the fields, what data type they are, the size of data, and values for the current record. TTable objects have an array of fields. This array actually can be modified using the field editor to add, delete, and modify field definitions.

To start with the simplest case, if the application knows what the table definition is, fields can be accessed directly without having to determine what they represent or the data type. For example, in your Studinfo table, SSN is the first column; therefore, StudInfo.Fields[0].AsString equals the value of the SSN field for the currently selected record. Note that the array starts at offset 0. Also note that the data type must be known to access the data correctly. If you wanted to put in a text box, SSN=<Current Record's Social Security Number>, you could do it by having a statement like this one:

```
SSN.Text := 'SSN='+Studinfo.Fields[0].AsString;
```

Suppose that you incorrectly assumed that SSN would be stored as an integer, so you tried the following:

```
SSN.Text :='SSN='+IntToStr(Studinfo.Fields[0].AsInteger);
```

This compiles without any errors, but when the statement is executed, an exception occurs. How can you safeguard against this? It is possible to confirm the field name and data type of each column. This might be necessary if a generic database manipulation program is written, and the field types are unknown. Listing 11.3 checks the data type and field name against what is expected before accessing the data.

TYPE **Listing 11.3. Confirming field name and data type.**

```
begin
 if not(StudInfo.Fields[0].DataType=ftString) then
  begin
   Application.MessageBox('Error - Wrong Data type on
                          ➥Field 0','DB Error',mb_ok);
   exit;
  end; {if}
 if not(comparetext(StudInfo.Fields[0].FieldName,'SSN')=0) then
  begin
   Application.MessageBox('Error - Wrong Field Name on Field 0',
                          'DB Table Error',mb_ok);
   exit;
  end; {if}
 Application.MessageBox('Field 0 Checks out: Type=ftString Name=SSN',
                        'Information',mb_ok);
end; {procedure}
```

ANALYSIS In this example, the field type is confirmed. If the routine encounters anything other than an ftString, it displays an error message box and exits the procedure. Similarly, if the field name does not equal SSN, an error is displayed, and the routine exits. If the procedure can get past both conditionals, it is true that the field type and field name are valid.

Often it is difficult to access a field by the column position in a table. Therefore, Delphi enables you to access a column by its field name. To do this, address the control name followed by the FieldByName method and the data type. For example, to access the Class field for the current record and set the text of a list box, you could use a statement such as the following:

```
Edit1.Text:=Studinfo.FieldByName('Class').AsString;
```

Modifying the Fields in a Table

By default, a TTable component uses all the fields in the table it is linked to. However, Delphi enables you to modify which fields are used, assign new fields based on calculations, and set attributes about each field. To access the field editor for the TTable component, double-click on an instance of a TTable. This brings up a dialog box that enables you to add, delete, and define new fields. Notice that the dialog uses the form name and the table name as the dialog box's title.

This dialog box also gives easy access to the TFields components. The field is based on a type inherited for TField with any specific information about the data type. For example, if one of the fields is a string, the field would be of TStringField type. Just like other components, the fields have properties and events. One advantage of this is that different fields in a table can have different properties. A good example is the case in which you want to protect one field from changes yet allow a user to modify other fields. To do this, the ReadOnly property for the field you want to protect could be set to True. A large number of the field properties determine how data-aware controls display the data in the fields. For example there is an Alignment property, which determines if the data should be placed in the left, right, or center of the display field. Also, for floating-point numbers a precision value can be set to indicate what digit should be rounded.

Navigation of Records

You already have seen how to use the DBNavigator component to move through the table. The component provides the functionality to move forward or backward one record, or to jump to the beginning or end of the table. This can be done within your code as well. To change the current record, five methods are available on the TTable component, as described in Table 11.8.

Table 11.8. Dataset methods for navigation.

Method	Action
Next	Moves to the next record in the dataset.
Prior	Moves to the previous record in the dataset.
First	Moves to the first record in the dataset.
Last	Moves to the last record in the dataset.
MoveBy(I)	Moves by increments. For example MoveBy(3) moves three records forward. MoveBy(-2) moves two records backward.

Here's an important note about moving when a record is in edit mode. The move causes an implicit Post method to occur, and the record changes are saved. There will be no way to execute a Cancel method for the changes. While navigating through a table, it is often necessary to know if you have reached the beginning or end of a dataset. The EOF (end-of-file) and BOF (beginning-of-file) properties indicate if these conditions are true, as follows:

BOF   This is true whenever an application first starts, a call to the First method was executed, or a Prior call fails because the current record is the first one in the dataset.

EOF   This is true whenever there is no data in a dataset, a call to the Last method was executed, or a Next call fails because there are no more records.

One of the typical things done to a dataset is to perform some action on every record. In the next example, the procedure moves to the first record then loops through all the records until the EOF property is True. With each record, the Edit method is executed so that the value of the record can be changed. In the example, a random dorm room is being assigned to students. To do this, a random number is generated between 0 and 1. If the number is less than .5, a certain dorm is assigned (StudInfo.Fields[6]). Otherwise, the other dorm is assigned. After changes to the fields are made, a Post method is executed to save the change. This is not really necessary because a Next method will do the post as well. The source code for this example is shown in Listing 11.4.

TYPE

Listing 11.4. Moving through a `DataSet` and modifying every record.

```
procedure TForm1.AssnDormsClick(Sender: TObject);
begin
  Studinfo.First; {Move to beginning of DataSet}
  StudInfo.DisableControls; { Will increase performance }
  while Not(Studinfo.EOF) do {Check for end of dataset}
    begin
     StudInfo.Edit;
     {Generate a random number, assign 50% to QUAD, 50% to Hall}
     {Access Fields Directly by "Fields" Property }
     if random > 0.5 then
       StudInfo.Fields[6].AsString := 'QUAD'
      else
       StudInfo.Fields[6].AsString := 'HALL';
     StudInfo.Post; {Explicit Post (Not Really Needed)}
     StudInfo.Next; { Move to the next record }
    end; {end Loop}
    StudInfo.EnableControls; { Will increase performance }
end; {end Procedure}
```

ANALYSIS

Note that the controls can be disabled during the loop and then enabled when the loop is complete. This increases performance because the controls do not update after each iteration.

Calculated Fields

There are many circumstances in which you want to derive data from a database, but it doesn't make sense to actually store all the data. For example, if a warehouse keeps track of its inventory using a relational database where each item is a record, the number of units in stock are stored in one field, and the weight per unit is stored in another field. It doesn't make sense to store the total weight of the item because the total weight can be derived by multiplying the number of units by their weight. Therefore, if there are 120 CD-ROM drives, and each weighs two pounds, you know that there are 240 pounds of CD-ROMs stocked (it might be necessary to know this for shipping purposes).

You may say, "This should be simple; every time the user wants to know the total weight, my Delphi application can do the multiplication and display the result." True, but what if the application requires the result to be on the form at all times just like the rest of the fields? This immediately gets more complicated because your application now has to update the field whenever navigation through the dataset occurs, and it needs to know how to handle inserts, deletes, and all other database events. Fortunately there is an easier way.

NEW TERM Delphi provides an easy method to define additional fields in tables. These fields are called *calculated fields* because they are based on other fields in the table. The advantage of a calculated field is that the calculated value is not stored in the database; however, it is derived each time a record changes and needs to access or display the field.

To add calculated fields, use the fields editor, which you can access by double-clicking the `TTable` component. Click the Define button. You will need to supply a new field name and the data type of the field. By default, a component name is created; however, this can be modified if you desire. By defining the fields, you are only setting up placeholders and letting Delphi know what type of fields they are. The next step is to insert the code to calculate the fields. Delphi executes the procedure in the `OnCalcFields` event handler whenever there is a need to recalculate a field. While in the `OnCalcFields` event handler, the dataset will be in the `dsCalcFields` state. Only the calculated fields can be modified when in this state. It's your job to ensure that all calculated fields are derived correctly in this procedure.

Consider a sample application in which Joe's landscaping supply company requests a database to keep inventory of the landscape supplies (topsoil, bark chips, mulch, and so on). Joe's requirements lead us to form a table with the attributes shown in Table 11.9.

Table 11.9. Table attributes for landscaping supply example.

Name	Description
ProductCode	Key defining the product
CubicYards	The number of yards Joe has in stock
CostPerYard	The market price per yard
LbsPerYard	How much one yard weighs
MarketValue	The total market value of an item in stock
LbsInStock	The total weight of an item in stock

One way you could do this is by creating a table with the attributes listed in Table 11.9, and creating an application to access and update the data. However, there are relationships between the fields. Whenever the `CubicYards` field changes, the total market value and pounds in stock changes. Also, if the price changes, so will the market value. Therefore, if you wanted to keep this information in a standard table, the application would have to be sure to update all the relevant fields when changes are made. By using calculated fields, almost all this work is eliminated. All you need to do is design the table and omit the `MarketValue` and `LbsInStock` fields from the table structure.

In your application, bring up the field editor and add the MarketValue and LbsInStock fields as calculated fields. Figure 11.9 displays the field editor creating a new field MarketValue, which is a currency data type.

Figure 11.9.

The field editor.

The final step is to place the code behind the OnCalcFields event to process the calculation. This procedure is shown in Listing 11.5.

TYPE Listing 11.5. Code to calculate fields.

```
procedure TForm1.InventoryCalcFields(DataSet: TDataset);

Var
    CurrentPrice : double; { Convert integer to float
                        ➡to prevent overflow}
    LbsPerYard   : double;
    YardsInStock : double;

begin
    {Put field values into local variables }
    {just to make the code a little neater}
    CurrentPrice := Inventory.FieldByName('CostPerYard').AsFloat;
    LbsPerYard   := Inventory.FieldByName('LbsPerYard').AsFloat;
    YardsInStock := Inventory.FieldByName('CubicYards').AsFloat;

    {Assign Values to the fields that are calculated}
    Inventory.FieldByName('MarketValue').AsFloat :=
        CurrentPrice * YardsInStock;
    Inventory.FieldByName('LBSInStock').AsFloat :=
        LbsPerYard    * YardsInStock;
end; {Procedure}
```

ANALYSIS In this event handler, you set the local variables, CurrentPrice, LbsPerYard, and YardsInStock equal to their respective values in the record. The MarketValue and LBSInStock calculated fields are set based on multiplying the correct set of local variables.

Indexes

An index is a presorted order for the records in your table based on a particular field or fields. In the classic relational-database sense, you can have a key without an index. However, in Paradox and dBASE, defining a key automatically creates an index on that field. The main advantage of an index is that it significantly speeds searching and sorting by indexed columns. Consider a database with 10,000 records. To find the record with its Last Name field equal to Smith could take searching up to 10,000 records. Nonetheless, on average it would search about 5,000 before it could find a match. In this sample database, if an index existed on the name field, you would be guaranteed to find the record with a Last Name of Smith in about 14 comparisons. This is a remarkable increase in performance.

Most relational databases allow multiple indexes on tables. Before seeing how to create extra indexes using the Database Desktop, look at why indexes are not always good. It appears that by creating an index there is a huge boost in performance, true? Yes, as far as searching and sorting are concerned. However, creating an index slows update and insert transactions, and increases the size of a table. Therefore, when creating a table and planning the indexes, try to index columns that will be searched or sorted frequently. An advantage of the database being separate from the application is that if an index needs to be added to increase performance, it can be done at any time.

You may be thinking, "I know that an index was created for the key, but if I create other indexes, do all the values in the field need to be unique?" No, the key needs to be unique, but other indexes do not. How do you create indexes other than the primary key? The easiest way is with the Database Desktop. You can learn to do this by using the sample Studinfo.DB table and adding an index on Name.

Adding an Index

Now that you know about indexes and their uses, let's add one to the database. Follow these steps:

1. Open the Database Desktop by choosing Tools | Database Desktop option on the Main menu.
2. In the Database Desktop, choose File | Open | Table.
3. In the Drive (or Alias) box, choose DBDEMOS.
4. Choose Studinfo.DB, and click OK.

NOTE

If Delphi is running and the application is accessing the table, the Active property needs to be set to False in the TTable object, or Paradox will not let you modify the table.

5. Choose Table | Restructure Table. This shows all the fields in the Studinfo table.

6. In the Table Properties drop-down combo box, choose Secondary Indexes.

7. Click Define, and the Define Secondary Index dialog box appears.

8. Choose the Name field, and click the button with the right arrow in it. This moves the Name field into the Indexed Fields box. Click OK.

9. You are prompted to name the index. Call it NameInd, and click OK. Figure 11.10 shows the new secondary index added to the table.

10. That's all! Choose Save from the bottom of the restructure window, and choose then File | Exit to leave the Database Desktop.

Figure 11.10.

Defining a secondary index on a field.

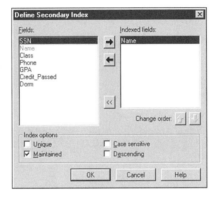

Now that a table can have multiple indices, how is a search in the table for a record done? The answer is simple. You can determine which index you want Delphi to use. The following sections explain the ordering of and searching for records.

Ordering Records

When cycling through a record set, the records are ordered by the current index. The IndexName property in the TTable object determines which index is in use. If no index is specified, the primary index is used to sort the records. Another way to tell Delphi what index should be used is with the IndexFieldNames property. Note that these two properties cannot both be set at the same time. When one is set, Delphi automatically clears the other. Consider a situation in which you want to add a menu item that changes the sort order of your student database from Social Security number to name. This could be accomplished by changing the IndexFieldNames property. Listing 11.6 shows how this is done.

Listing 11.6. Changing the sort order using a menu selection.

```
procedure TForm1.Order_By_NameClick(Sender: TObject);
begin
  Order_By_Name.Checked := True;
  Order_By_SSN.Checked := False;
  StudInfo.IndexFieldNames := 'Name';
end;
```

ANALYSIS First, the Order_By_SSN menu item is unchecked. Next, the Order_By_Name menu item is checked to indicate what index is being used. Finally the IndexFieldNames property is changed to sort the records in a different order.

Searching for Records

Up to this point, you've learned simple ways to navigate and modify records. However, suppose you wanted to access a particular record in a table. One thought that may come to mind is "Why don't I set up a loop and cycle through all the records until I find the one I want?" This would work, but you would forfeit a great deal of the power that the database engine provides. Using the tools provided in the TTable component, you can perform powerful searches. However, there is a major limitation in that only indexed fields can be searched.

Two techniques exist to search for records: the SetKey approach and FindKey approach. The procedure to search for values using TTable methods may seem somewhat non-intuitive. First, you have to put the table in a searchable state. To do this, you use the SetKey method. Once the SetKey method is executed, the table is in dsSetKey state. For example, to place the Studinfo table in dsSetKey state, you would execute this code:

```
Studinfo.SetKey;
```

Once a table is in a search state, set the Search field equal to a lookup value. Delphi uses this information to search for a specified value. Note that the Search field must be indexed. This is a little strange because in your code it looks like you're setting the value of the current record. However, you're in dsSetKey mode as opposed to dsEdit mode. This tells the database engine that you want to search. To take the simplest case first, search on the primary key. To find a record matching the key, set the value of the field equal to the search criteria. For example, in Studinfo, to search for the student whose Social Security number is 432-23-2121, you would execute this line of code:

```
Studinfo.FieldByName('SSN').AsString:='432-23-2121';
```

To move to the record that you are searching for, you need to complete the search by executing the GotoKey method. Therefore, to conclude the search, execute this line:

```
StudInfo.GotoKey;
```

What happens if the key is not found? The current record remains the same, and the function returns False. If the record is located, it becomes the current record, and the GotoKey method returns True.

This works well if you know the exact value you are trying to match. What if only part of the field is known? In that case, you would use the GotoNearest method. GotoNearest takes the information that is given and finds the nearest match. Suppose you want to implement a function that will ask for part of a student's Social Security number and find the student's record. This could be implemented as in Listing 11.7.

TYPE **Listing 11.7. Searching for a Social Security number.**

```
procedure TForm1.SearchSSNClick(Sender: TObject);
begin
  StudInfo.SetKey;
  Studinfo.FieldByName('SSN').AsString := teSSNSearch.text;
  Studinfo.GotoNearest;
end;
```

ANALYSIS This procedure puts the StudInfo table into SetKey state, and then sets the Social Security number equal to the one in the teSSNSearch text box. When the GotoNearest method is executed, the record set points to the record with the closest match to the Social Security number in the teSSNSearch textbox.

Delphi provides two shortcuts for searching on the key: FindKey and FindNearest. When executing a FindKey, or FindNearest, Delphi encapsulates the SetKey, Search Criteria (in this case, the FieldByName statement), and Goto statements into one function. Pass the FindKey or FindNext method an array of parameters corresponding to the key. For example, you can compress Listing 11.7 by changing the three statements into one, as shown in Listing 11.8.

TYPE **Listing 11.8. Search using less code but is harder to read.**

```
procedure TForm1.SearchSSNClick(Sender: TObject);
begin
    Studinfo.FindNearest([teSSNSearch.text]);
end;
```

ANALYSIS One advantage of the SetKey method is that it's not necessary to know the order of the indexed fields. For example, if there is a table with an index on First Name and Last Name, you could use a SetKey method along with the FieldByName method to set the LastName field to one value and then the FirstName field to another value. This would be followed by a GotoKey or GotoNearest, and it works every time. On the other hand, if you use the FindKey method, both search values are passed as an array. For example,

```
IRS.FindKey(['John','Smith']);
```

Or is it the following?

```
IRS.FindKey(['Smith','John']);
```

You can see the dilemma. If you do not know exactly what order Delphi is expecting arguments, you will not locate the records you are searching for.

Searching on Secondary Indexes

To search on an index other than the primary index, you set the IndexName property or the IndexFieldNames property exactly like you did to change the records' order. Therefore, to search for the closest name in your Studinfo table, you would execute the code in Listing 11.9.

TYPE

Listing 11.9. Searching by something other than the primary key.

```
procedure TForm1.SearchNameClick(Sender: TObject);
begin
  StudInfo.SetKey;
  StudInfo.IndexName := 'NameInd';
  Studinfo.FieldByName('Name').AsString := teNameSearch.text;
  Studinfo.GotoNearest;
end;
```

ANALYSIS This program does the same search as Listing 11.7, but here you have added the StudInfo.IndexName := 'NameInd'; line to specify an index other than the primary one (in this case, NameInd).

Setting a Range of Records

It is often advantageous to limit the records in your dataset by using some criteria. For example, you might want to show only the Freshman class in the Studinfo table. Or, you might want to show all the students with a grade-point average above 3.6 to compose the Dean's list. These operations are range limiting because they enable you to work with a smaller subset of the data. Once a range is in place, you can assume that the rest of the records do not exist. One way to gather a range is with the SetRange method.

Listing 11.10 shows how to choose an index by name, and set a range. The last procedure shows how to remove a range condition by using the CancelRange method.

TYPE

Listing 11.10. Displaying a subset of a dataset by using the `SetRange` method.

```
procedure TForm1.RangeFreshClick(Sender: TObject);
begin
  Studinfo.IndexName := 'ClassInd';
  StudInfo.SetRange(['Freshman'],['Freshman']);
end;

procedure TForm1.RangeDeansClick(Sender: TObject);
begin
  Studinfo.IndexName := 'GpaInd';
  StudInfo.SetRange([3.6],[5]);
end;

procedure TForm1.All1Click(Sender: TObject);
begin
  StudInfo.CancelRange;
end;
```

ANALYSIS   This program illustrates several ways to use the `SetRange` method to limit the amount of information that is returned. The first procedure sets the index to `ClassInd` and then sets the range to Freshman only. The second procedure uses the `GPAInd` as the primary index and then sets the range of values to `3.6` to `5`. And finally, the third procedure does a `CancelRange` to allow all records to be found in a search.

11

Controlling Input into a Table

In a perfect world, users would do everything you expected them to do. Unfortunately, this never happens. End users seem always to find a way to use an application in a way that was never intended. Although you never will be able to control everything that a user will do, there are some techniques you can use to stabilize an application and force the user to enter data and conform to the process flow that you engineered. This section discusses methods you can use to control the data that is entered into a database:

- [ ] Pick components
- [ ] Input masks
- [ ] Database-level constraints
- [ ] The `Cancel` method
- [ ] The `Validation` property on `TFields` and `TTables`

Use Pick Components as Opposed to Open Components

To make an application as user friendly as possible, don't let the user make mistakes. Design forms with pick components such as combo boxes, radio buttons, and list boxes wherever appropriate. The most dangerous data-aware controls to use are open components such as text-edit boxes and memo boxes. These allow the user to enter any data he or she wishes. Good form design can go a long way to having happy customers or users.

Input Masks

NEW TERM The first way you can force the user to enter what you are looking for is by using input masks. An *input mask* is a property on each field component. An input mask forces a control to accept input only in a certain format. For example, if you would like the user to enter a phone number into a field on your form, some people might use (916) 873-3454, whereas others may use 9168733454. These are both valid numbers, but it would be beneficial if all entries were consistent.

To enforce consistency, you can build an input mask using rules for what values can be placed in which field locations. For example, you could use an input mask of `000\-00\-0000;1;_` to enforce the form of a Social Security number. This would allow `183-34-9829` to be entered, but it would not allow `A34-34-2345` because the mask states that all characters must be numbers, and they must be in the form of `xxx-xx-xxxx`.

Great, this sounds powerful, but that string looks awfully confusing. Is there an easy way to create input masks? Yes, Delphi comes with a dialog box that helps you build the masks. To bring up the Mask Editor, double-click on the `EditMask` property of a `TField` object. The Input Mask Editor, shown in Figure 11.11, has a list of common masks as well as a field to enter a new mask and test it on-the-fly. To see all the capabilities of masks, refer to Delphi's online help for the `MaskEdit` property.

Figure 11.11.

The Input Mask Editor.

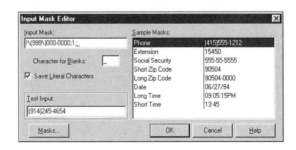

Database-Level Constraints

The MaskEdit property works well at an application level. However, if a database is going to be accessed by many applications, wouldn't it be nice if some rules could be put in place so that the data was somewhat consistent? Every database is different, but most have some way to enforce rules on the values that can be put into fields. For simplicity, the example in this section shows how to set validation criteria in Paradox. The rules are set in the database, and so if more than one application uses the database, the integrity will be maintained.

The data validation that can be performed in a Paradox table is as follows:

☐ Force a value to be entered for a field.

☐ Set the maximum value that a field can be.

☐ Set the minimum value that a field can be.

☐ Give a default value to a field if no value is supplied.

To set these criteria in a table, you use the Database Desktop. Remember that if an application that is accessing a table is opened, the Active property needs to be set to False, or the project should be closed. The steps to add validation criteria are as follows:

1. Open the Database Desktop by choosing Tools | Database Desktop from the Delphi main menu.

2. Choose File | Open | Table, and select the table on which you wish to put a constraint.

3. Choose Table | Restructure Table. This brings up the list of fields in the table and each one's associated data type.

4. Be sure the table properties box is set to Validity Checks.

5. Click on the field that you wish to put a constraint on, and type the details in the dialog box. For example, if you wanted to put a constraint on the GPA field of your Studinfo table, you would type **0** in the minimum box and **4.0** in the maximum box.

NOTE

> Just because you develop an application doesn't mean that you'll always own the database it relies on. Therefore, a constraint may have been placed on the data outside of the application. If a Delphi application violates the validation criteria, an exception will occur.

11

The Cancel Method

You can use the Cancel method as a last line of attack to control the user's input. In some cases, data validation is complex enough that it cannot be formulated into an input mask or database-level constraint. For example, Joe Mathimatica would like to develop a database to store his favorite prime numbers. To do this, he asks a you to create an application that enables a user to enter a prime number and has the computer validate that the input number is prime before it is stored in a database. You provide a solution that uses a dbTextEdit box to prompts users to enter their favorite prime numbers, a DBNavigator to move through the database, and a Save Changes button to commit inserts and modifications.

Your main task is to validate that the number actually is prime before you save it to the database. One way to do this is to execute the Edit method on entering the data field. Also, disable the navigator, which forces the user to click on the Save Changes button to save changes. You place the validation code in the OnClick event of a button.

NOTE

> To refresh your memory, a prime number is a number that cannot be divided by any number other than itself and 1. For example, 5 is prime because there are no two numbers that can be multiplied to equal 5. Six is not prime because 2*3=6.

In the validation code, you loop through all numbers from 2 through $n-1$ and check to see if the remainder is 0. If it is, you know that it is not a prime number, and you will jump out of the loop. Just so you'll know, this is not an efficient algorithm for checking primes because it can iterate as many times as the number. Listing 11.11 demonstrates using the Cancel method to confirm that a number is prime.

TYPE

Listing 11.11. Confirming a number is prime using the Cancel method.

```
procedure TForm1.EntPrimeEnter(Sender: TObject);
begin
  Nav.Enabled := False;    {Disable the navigator}
  Primes.Edit;             {place table into edit mode}
end;

procedure TForm1.SaveChangesClick(Sender: TObject);

Var
  IsPrime : Boolean;
  Count : Integer;
  NumToTest : Integer;
```

11

```
begin
   IsPrime := True;
   Count := 2;
   NumToTest := StrToInt(EntPrime.Text);
   While (Count < NumToTest) and (IsPrime) do
     begin
       if NumToTest mod Count = 0
         then IsPrime := False; { once we find one, we are done!}
       inc(Count); { Increment the Counter}
     end; {while}
   {If the number is Prime save the number to the database}
   {otherwise roll it back using the Cancel method }
   if (IsPrime) then
      Primes.Post
    else
      begin
        Application.MessageBox('Number is not Prime!','Invalid',MB_OK);
        Primes.Cancel;
      end; {else}
   Nav.enabled := TRUE; {Renable the Navigator}
end; {Procedure}
```

ANALYSIS This program validates that a number is prime before it is put into Joe Mathimatica's database of his favorite prime numbers. If you find that the number is not prime, a `Primes.Cancel` is called canceling the database update. If the number is prime, a `Primes.Post` is called, and the data is placed in the database.

Validation **Property on** TFields **and** TTables

So far you've seen three techniques to make data entry more valid: controlling what the user can enter, using database-level data constraints, and forcing the user to follow a process that enables the application to check the validity of data. The final method presented in this section involves the use of events and exceptions. By using procedures attached to On events in the field and table objects, an application can validate the data before it is stored. This is often advantageous because it gives users slightly more freedom as to how they want to enter and edit data.

Why would you need to validate at the table and field level? Because in some situations a field can be validated only with knowledge of itself. An example of this is the prime number database. The application can determine that the number is prime without knowledge of any other data. However, if you had an application that cashiers used to log their registers when they check in and out, your validation check may be that the amount coming in is greater than the amount going out. This validation cannot be done until knowledge of both amounts is present.

To validate at the field level, you need to place an event handler in the OnValidate event. This event is called just before data is written to the database. If you want to allow the data to be written, allow the procedure to execute. Use an exception to block processing. Listing 11.12 contains a revised version of the prime number validation that uses an OnValidate event.

Listing 11.12. Validation using the OnValidate event.

```
type
   EInvalidPrime = class(Exception);
{...}
procedure TForm1.PrimesFavPrimesValidate(Sender: TField);

Var
 IsPrime : Boolean;
 Count : Integer;
 NumToTest : Integer;

begin
 try
   IsPrime := True;
   Count := 2;
   NumToTest := StrToInt(EntPrime.Text);
   While (Count < NumToTest) and (IsPrime) do
     begin
       if NumToTest mod Count = 0
         then IsPrime := False; { once we find one, we are done!}
       inc(Count); { Increment the Counter}
     end; {while}
   {If the number is Prime save the number to the database}
   {otherwise roll it back using the Cancel method }
   if not(IsPrime) then
     begin
       raise EInvalidPrime.Create('Number is not prime!');
     end; {else}
  except
   on EInvalidPrime do
     begin
       Application.Messagebox('Number is not prime!','Invalid',MB_OK);
       EntPrime.Text :='';
       if (Primes.State = dsInsert) or (primes.State=dsEdit)
        then Primes.cancel;
     end;
 end;
end;
```

ANALYSIS Something to note is that the try and except clauses are used to catch your exception if you detect that a number is not prime. Also, the procedure uses the Exception.Create method to cause a custom exception to occur. To perform record validation, the procedure would be the same, but the code would be placed in the BeforePost event.

Exception Handling

It now should be apparent that your application must be aware of invalid data. Unfortunately, the application also should know what to do when errors or exceptions occur. If data can be validated, what would cause an exception? Many things. Here are a few of the most common:

☐ **Duplicate keys**—Although validation can be done to determine if a field meets criteria, it is an extra step to be sure that the key doesn't already exist. In the Studinfo table, if two records are added with the same Social Security number, an exception occurs. This goes back to the very definition of a key. A key must be unique for every record. The database engine uses the key as a hook to know what record it is operating on. In addition, if a key is violated, your data would be corrupt. You know that it is impossible for two people to have the same Social Security number; therefore, if two appeared in the database, it is due to human error. To keep the data meaningful, keys must be enforced.

☐ **Database validation error**—As mentioned earlier, constraints can be put on fields at the database level. However, what happens when one of these constrains is violated? You guessed it: an exception. Therefore, your application needs to be able to recover from invalid data exceptions gracefully, and it must contain procedures to enable the user to fix the data.

☐ **Invalid state for operation**—One final error that occurs frequently is a procedure executing code based on the assumption that a table is in a particular state. This is a very dangerous assumption in an event-driven environment. Tables can be in one of six possible states: dsInactive, dsBrowse, dsEdit, dsInsert, dsSetKey, and dsCalcFields. While in each state, the table behaves differently. For example, if the table is in the dsEdit state, the following statement would set the current record's class field to that of a freshman:

```
Studinfo.FieldByName('Class') .AsString:='Freshman';
```

However, the same statement executed when in a dsSetKey state would indicate that you want to search for the first freshman. These operations are actually the most difficult to debug because they do not cause exceptions. Some operations *will* cause exceptions. For example, trying to execute the Post or Cancel method when in a dsBrowse state causes an exception.

ODBC—A Further Layer of Abstraction

Borland's database engine can communicate with many different databases. This is useful if you want to change the underlying database structure at any time. For full flexibility and compatibility with almost *any* database, ODBC is available.

NEW TERM ODBC stands for *open database connectivity*. ODBC enables you to communicate with any database through a common interface by using what is known as an ODBC driver. The ODBC driver contains code that understands the specifics of a particular database and provides access to it through a standard set of API calls.

Using ODBC gives an application the greatest amount of flexibility because, in theory, switching the type of database that an application uses is as simple as switching ODBC drivers. In reality, there are other minor changes in the language passed to ODBC to communicate correctly with different database engines. If an application ever needs the highest level of performance with ODBC, the application can communicate directly with the ODBC API. I warn you that this is not straightforward, and it provides an additional layer of complexity. However, for optimal ODBC performance, it can be done.

Why Use ODBC?

Often you'll want to create an application, but can't scale it initially. ODBC enables you to use a file-based stand-alone database for development and switch to a client/server model later without a great deal of changes to the source code. This also is useful in creating a Delphi application that needs to be compatible with existing data. For example, if the current payroll system is on a Sybase SQL Server and you need to develop a front end to access the data, Delphi can use ODBC to connect and communicate with the database. Another example of backward compatibility is if you are trying to port some applications written in a different language to Delphi. ODBC enables you to migrate applications over to Delphi in an instance where Delphi does not have a native driver. In this case, the database can be accessed using an ODBC driver. For example, suppose you had a VB application that used an Excel spreadsheet to store data. You could use the Excel ODBC driver to access the Excel data from within Delphi, allowing you to migrate the application from VB to Delphi.

In ODBC terminology, an ODBC driver is the library that understands how to communicate with the underlying database. ODBC drivers often are available from the database vendor or third-party software companies. An ODBC data source is an instance of an ODBC object that uses a driver. For example, you might have a Sybase SQL Server ODBC driver, and HRDATA is an ODBC data source that is a SQL server with the human resource data. There can be a second data source using the same driver. Therefore, there might be an additional data source, INVENT, that points to a SQL server containing information on inventory.

The ODBCAD32 utility is used to create and configure ODBC data sources. Different configuration information will be needed for each ODBC data source. For example, an Access ODBC data source will need to be configured with the location of the .mdb file, whereas a SQL data source will need to be configured with the network address of the server and the network interface library to access the server.

To use an ODBC driver and communicate through ODBC in Delphi, you need to create a new Borland Database Engine (BDE) driver. Note that this may seem confusing because ODBC has ODBC drivers that are data drivers, and the BDE has internal drivers. A Borland database driver must be configured to access an ODBC driver. Therefore, to create a Borland database driver, follow these steps:

1. Enter the BDE Administrator by choosing Start | Programs | Borland 3.0 | BDE Administrator from the Windows taskbar.
2. Click on the Configure tab. Select Configuration | Drivers | ODBC. Right-click on ODBC, and select New from the pop-up menu.

3. Set the SQL link driver name to ODBC_XXXX where XXXX is the name of the BDE driver you wish to create, as shown in Figure 11.12.

4. Select the ODBC driver to be used to access the data and a data source to create an ODBC alias from, and press OK. Select Object | Exit to close the BDE Administrator.

That is all for creating the drive. To access the data, the easiest way in Delphi is to set up an alias using the Database Desktop.

Figure 11.12.

The Borland Database Engine Administrator.

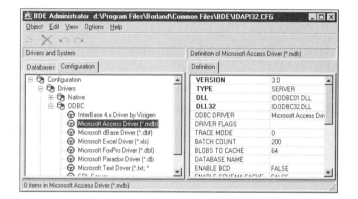

Using a Microsoft Access Database Through ODBC

Now you're going to create a sample ODBC database connection for use in Delphi. Although you are using Microsoft Access as the sample database, it is important to note that Delphi now provides native Access drivers. As a developer, you normally would use the native driver for the improvement in speed. Now let's define the ODBC data source by following these steps:

1. Run ODBCAD32.

2. On the System DSN tab, click Add. This displays a list of installed ODBC data drivers.

3. Choose Access Data *.mdb, and click Finish.

4. Type a name and description for the Access data source. For this example, use TestAccess for the data source name.

5. Click on the Select button. This brings up a list of .mdb files.

6. Use the dialog to select the file to access.

7. Click OK. Then click OK again to exit the ODBCAD32 program.

Before you can use the ODBC data source you have just defined, you must run the BDE Administrator. This application is installed in your Borland Delphi menu during the Delphi installation process. When the BDE Administrator runs, it automatically picks up any new

ODBC data sources and adds them to the BDE driver list. All you have to do now to make the ODBC data source work with Delphi is to leave the BDE Administrator, which saves the changes.

NOTE

> The BDE Administrator picks up only ODBC drivers automagically if the AUTO ODBC setting is set to True in the BDE Admininistrator. You can check the setting by following this procedure:
>
> 1. Run the BDE Administrator
> 2. Select the Configuration tab.
> 3. Select Configuration | Drivers | System | INIT.
> 4. The INIT definition appears in the right pane. The AUTO ODBC property is the first item on the list.

To use the ODBC alias in Delphi, follow these steps:

1. Create a new project, and add a TTable component.
2. Set the DatabaseName property to TstAccess.
3. When the TableName property is set, a dialog box may appear requesting a user ID and password. Just click OK.
4. Notice that the tables in the Access database are now available in the TableName property. Choose a table to work with, and continue as if you were working with any other table in Delphi.

NOTE

> If you can choose the ODBC data source in the TableName property, but when you set the Active property for the TTable component to TRUE, you get an "object not found" error, you forgot to run the BDE Administrator to update the BDE configuration.

Database Security and Passwords

You have heard of computer hackers and stories of top-secret data falling into the hands of the KGB after secret agents tap into data lines and decrypt the data with Cray supercomputers. These stories may seem like something out of a James Bond movie, but data security in real-world applications is nothing to be taken lightly.

Data security is the process that allows certain users, groups, or processes to read or manipulate data. Consider a simple example. At the Department of Motor Vehicles, it is advantageous to allow all clerks to view driving records. However, only a select few should be granted the power to modify them (or pretty soon friends and families of workers would have their tickets wiped clean).

Data security can also be linked to an application. In the prime number database example, the application does a powerful computation to prevent non-primes from being entered into the database. Suppose the user awakens in the middle of the night and says, "I have a favorite number that I must add to my database: 513!" The user starts the computer, bypasses the Delphi front end, goes directly to the Database Desktop, and adds 513. Because the value is added outside the application, no validation is done (513 is not a prime number, so you now have corrupted data). However, if there were some way to allow only certain users, applications, and groups to manipulate data, it would solve a lot of problems. This is why many database platforms integrate security into the database.

Security Levels

Depending on the database you are using, different levels of security are available. Although groups, users, and applications can be given access to databases, the discussion in this section is limited to individual users. The most common levels of security a database will use are as follows:

- [ ] **None**—It is very possible that anyone with physical access to the data can view it and modify it.

- [ ] **All or nothing**—This is the case where some technique will be needed to get access to the data. However, once the user is granted access, all database data is available, and full manipulation is possible.

- [ ] **Multi-user, table-level access**—This allows different users to access tables in either read, update, or insert mode. Therefore, Joe may have total control over his database, but Sam would be able only to read the data.

- [ ] **Multi-user, field-level access**—Field-level access is the most flexible type of data security. In field-level access, users are granted a level of access to each field in the table. Therefore, in the DMV example given earlier, a clerk could be granted update access on the Last Name field so that he could process name changes but would be granted read-only access on the Driving Points field. Additionally, some users may not even be given read access on certain fields. For example, if a small company keeps a database of its employees, it could make the name, mail stop, and extension public information, but keep the salary and home address omitted from public access.

Authentication

NEW TERM Now that you understand how different users can be given different levels of access, the question becomes "How do you know what user is trying to access your data?" The answer is authentication. *Authentication* is the process used to confirm that an entity is actually who it claims to be. When a user proves her identity, she has been authenticated.

In order to complete the security cycle, the database engine needs to authenticate a user and then determine what access that user has. The most common way to implement authentication is with some type of password scheme. Paradox uses a master password that defines the table owner. Secondary passwords can be defined by the table owner and given field-level access. Another common method used by databases to perform authentication is a user ID/ password combination. This is a better approach because the user's identification is not associated with his or her password. This also is more secure from an administration approach because the database owner doesn't need to know each user's password.

Working with More Than One Table

One of the primary reasons that relational databases are used is because the database format is easy to understand and can be easily manipulated. In the examples that you have examined up to this point, only one table has been used, and all the needed information has been contained in that one table. However, it would be very inefficient and difficult to manage databases if data was always stored in one table. Consider the example of a university that wants to keep records on its students and the courses the students have taken. To do this with only one table, it might look like Table 11.10.

Table 11.10. Inefficient data representation for student data.

Student Number	Name	Phone	Course	Grade
12345	Jeff Smith	234-3445	CH101	C
12345	Jeff Smith	234-3445	EN333	A
12345	Jeff Smith	234-3445	NP343	A
34343	Jim Brown	543-2345	BI333	C
34343	Jim Brown	543-2345	NP343	B

This is inefficient database design because data is repeated in multiple records and is difficult to manage. There are quite a few problems with this approach. First of all, when a student changes phone numbers, every record identifying the student must be found and modified.

11

Also, the same data is repeated many places in the database, which is a very inefficient use of space. Take this one step further, and add the course descriptions to each record. Before you know it, the table is extremely large and difficult to manage. The reason the information is represented inefficiently is because the design does not take into account that there is a relationship between the students and the classes they take. Note that Tables 11.11 and 11.12 represent exactly the same information but take up much less space.

Table 11.11. Student information table.

Student Number	Name	Phone Number
12345	Jeff Smith	234-3445
34343	Jim Brown	543-2345

Table 11.12. Grade table.

Student Number	Course	Grade
12345	CH101	C
12345	EN333	A
12345	NP343	A
34343	BI333	C
34343	NP343	B

These tables have a better design because the data is broken into multiple tables.

This is possible because there is a logical relationship between the data in the two tables. Note that although nothing technically would stop you from implementing this database with only one table, that would be poor database design because you wouldn't be taking full advantage of a relational model.

Foreign Keys

NEW TERM   You already know that a key is a field or combination of fields in a table that makes each record unique. This is known as a *primary key*. There are also fields in tables called *foreign keys*. A foreign key means that the value is a key in a different table. An example of a foreign key would be the Student Number field in the course information table (the course information table would be a table listing the students enrolled in each course). The field is not unique in this table, but it always will be unique in the student information table.

Relationships

There are three main ways that tables can relate to one another. There can be a one-to-one relationship, a many-to-one relationship, or a many-to-many relationship. Let's look at each of these. Tables with true one-to-one relationships are rare because the information often can be included in the original table. However, in some cases where certain information is rarely needed, it may make sense to keep the detail in one table and the frequently used data in another. One of the most powerful types of a relationship is a many-to-one. This means that there can be multiple references to data in a detail table. This is extremely useful because data is not repeated, and changing it in one place affects all references.

The following is an example of a many-to-one relationship:

> The DMV keeps data on drivers and automobiles. Driver data is kept in the DRIVER table that includes a driver's license number, name, address, and points. Information on vehicles is stored in the AUTO table. This table tracks the vehicle identification number, model, year, and the owner's driver's license number. The driver's license number in the AUTO table is a foreign key. The VIN (vehicle identification number) in the AUTO table is a primary key, and the driver's license number in the DRIVER table is a primary key. Drivers can own more than one car, but cars cannot have more than one owner. Therefore, there are many cars to one owner, or a many-to-one relationship.

There are also many-to-many relationships. Many-to-many relationships often are implemented with an intermediate table containing foreign keys associated with each of the tables containing the relationship. Here's an example:

> Students take classes; therefore, each student can take more than one class (many classes). Classes also have many students enrolled; therefore, there is a many-to-many relationship between students and classes. One of the tables in this database contains information on students such as ID numbers, names, and addresses. Another table describes the courses with information such as course number, description, number of credits, and prerequisites. To indicate which students are taking what classes, there should be a third table added containing one field that is a student number and another field that is the class. Note that from this table, you can generate either a class schedule for every student, or a student enrollment list for each course.

The primary objective in database design should be that information exists in only one place and that each table represents one logically related piece of the database. One final note is that there are no rules. This is not like writing a program in which, if the syntax is not exact, the compiler gives an error. Data can be effectively represented in many different ways, as long as you don't forget that a database is simply a representation of data. Next, you look at linked cursors, which provide an easy way to manipulate tables that are related in a many-to-one relationship.

The Importance of Using Data Modules

From now on, you'll place non-visual database visual components on a data module so that you can access them in multiple applications. Remember that you need to use the File | Use Unit command from the main menu to use components on a data module.

MasterSource **and** MasterField **Properties**

One of the most common reasons to use a many-to-one relationship is to provide detailed information in one table that is accessed from a foreign key in another table. Delphi provides an easy method to exploit this relationship by using the MasterSource and MasterField properties on TTable objects.

The MasterSource and MasterField properties allow one table to control which record is accessible in a detail table. For example, consider a table containing student grades. This could be displayed using a DBGrid component. There also could be a set of fields that would display information about the student referenced in the current record, such as name, phone number, and dorm. To link the tables together, the student information table uses its MasterSource and MasterField properties to determine what record is being accessed in the grades table. In this instance, the student table would be considered the detail table, and the grades table would be considered the master table.

To implement the master/detail relationship, a data source needs to be associated with the master table. This component name is then specified on the MasterSource property of the detail component. One final piece of information is needed to make the association work: the field that is common to both tables needs to be specified. There are some important issues about the fields that need to be addressed. The field to which the master joins in the detail table must have an index on that field in the detail table. The association is made in the MasterField property of the detail table. To create this association, perform the following steps:

1. Add TTable and DataSource components for both the master and the detail tables. You can use the ORDERS.DB table for the master and CUSTOMER.DB for the detail. Both of these are in the DBDEMOS database.

2. Bring up the properties sheet for the detail table (CUSTOMER).

3. Set the MasterSource property to the data source component that accesses the master table.

4. Double-click the MasterFields property; this brings up the Field Link Designer dialog box. You need to pick which detail field maps to which master field. The fields must be exactly the same data type. After the fields are linked, click OK. This action is shown in Figure 11.13.

The sample application in Figure 11.14 uses a field link to display order information in one grid and customer information in another. For whichever order is selected, the customer detail for that order is displayed.

Figure 11.13.
The Field Link Designer.

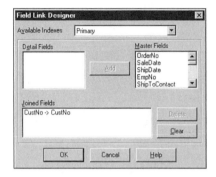

Figure 11.14.
Order application using linked fields.

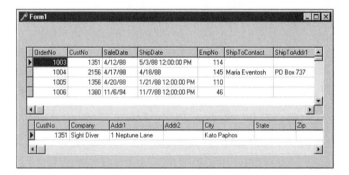

Delphi enables applications to manipulate tables using the TTable component. With this component, methods exist to search for records, sort records, link tables, and move through a record set. The shortcoming of the TTable component is that each of these tasks requires a separate method, or property definition, and it is difficult to combine operations. To solve this problem, Delphi also provides a secondary method, the TQuery visual component, to interact with a database. The TQuery visual component enables an application to communicate with the database through a language called Structured Query Language (SQL). SQL (pronounced sequel) is extremely powerful, and if used properly can make many complex tasks simple.

11

Summary

Today you learned basic database concepts and how to manipulate tables in Delphi, particularly how to use the TTable component to gain database access. The DataSource component acts as an intermediate layer between the TTable and data-aware components. Data-aware components are a powerful set of components that can access a dataset and enable the application to view and manipulate data. Relational database design and performance issues were presented. Some of the information included keys and indexes. Keys are used to maintain uniqueness, and indexes are primarily for performance. You also were introduced to the issue of data security and how different databases implement it. And finally, you finished out this day learning about using multiple tables and foreign keys in your application.

Q&A

Q In the Studinfo table, if I wanted to allow the user to edit all fields except Social Security number, how could I do it?

A Use the Readonly property in the StudInfoSSN component. Fields are attached to datatables and manipulated as components. By setting the Readonly property to True, this field cannot be modified.

Q What happens when an application attempts to violate a validity check in an application?

A An exception occurs. It is up to you to handle this condition gracefully. Use try and except blocks of code to handle database exceptions.

Q What if I need to store information with a many-to-one relationship—for example, if I wanted to store information about each class a student takes?

A The correct way to do this is with multiple tables. A field in your detail table will have the key to the master table. In Studinfo example, the COURSE table would have a field called SSN that would link back to the main Studinfo table.

Q I have a stand-alone file that absolutely needs security but does not have integrated security features. What can I do?

A The answer is to implement security at a different level. Either encrypt the entire database file, or save the sensitive data in encrypted form. Another method would be to store the data on a network that implements its own security. Remember that your data is only as secure as your weakest link.

Workshop

The Workshop provides two ways for you to affirm what you've learned in this chapter. The Quiz section poses questions to help you solidify your understanding of the material covered. You can find answers to the quiz questions in Appendix A, "Answers to the Quiz Questions." The Exercises section provides you with experience in using what you have learned. Please try to work through all these before continuing to the next day.

Quiz

1. If a table is in dsBrowse state and a method such as Post is executed, what happens?
2. How can an application determine what type of data is stored in a field?
3. If an application needs to change how records are ordered, what property needs to be changed?
4. Which database models can be accessed by multiple people or applications simultaneously? Which cannot?
5. If a dataset is in dsCalcFields state, what cannot be done to non-calculated fields?
6. In a many-to-one relationship, what type of key is the column in the "many" table that indicates the key in the "one" table. (Hint: It is a type of key but not in the table in which it is listed. Some would say, "It has an accent.")

Exercises

1. Create a database application that uses all the data-aware controls.
2. Modify the example that stores favorite prime numbers to also display the number squared by using calculated fields.
3. Use database-level constraints to limit the maximum value of numbers stored in the prime number database. Add code to the application to display a message when a too-large number is entered.

Day 12

Reports and Charts

After you have learned to develop Delphi database applications as well as other applications that might process data, you might need to output that data to the printer in some type of report, graph, or chart. Today's lesson focuses on the QuickReport and TeeChart components with a brief mention of the Decision Cube components to wrap up the lesson. Keep in mind that the goal here is not to teach these tools in any great depth; it is to familiarize you with them and get you started. These are third-party tools that are included with Delphi in a fully functional form, which you can upgrade to later versions if you have the need or desire. As you'll see, these are very functional and useful tools. You are not required to register them to use them in your Delphi applications unless you want the upgraded versions. Because both are Delphi component sets, they'll become part of your application eliminating the need for third-party add-on products that require you to ship extra DLLs, OCX or ActiveX controls, and so on. So, let's take a look at what's available and how these tools can be of use to you.

QuickReport

So what exactly is QuickReport? QuickReport for Delphi is a set of components that enable you to visually design your reports and easily connect them to your code. The finished product enables your users to generate quality formatted reports that contain text and graphics. QuickReport is a banded report generator that has many features, which you'll learn about shortly.

Here is a list of some of the features in QuickReport.

- ☐ Visual report design
- ☐ Native Delphi VCL written in 100 percent Object Pascal
- ☐ Compatible with Delphi 1.0, 2.0, and 3.0
- ☐ Multithreaded
- ☐ Instant preview
- ☐ Unlimited-length reports
- ☐ Unlimited-length memo fields
- ☐ Report from any BDE-compatible data source, including ODBC
- ☐ End-user report design component
- ☐ Customizable preview
- ☐ Expandable with new printable components such as charts, bar codes, advanced graphics formats, and more
- ☐ Advanced expression evaluator with expression builder
- ☐ Report expert
- ☐ Export reports to ASCII text, comma delimited, or HTML; write your own add-on export filters

This information was extracted from the QuickReport documentation found on the Delphi CD-ROM. These are just some highlights. Because it is beyond the scope of this book to cover all the features and components, or even provide great detail for the features that are covered here, you should study the QuickReport documentation file after completing today's lesson, it is wonderfully written. You will, however, have a good start and the information necessary to create simple reports by the end of this lesson.

QuickReport Templates

Delphi includes some templates and a wizard to simplify creating basic reports. Rather than spending time on these templates here, you'll learn about some of the components they contain and put together some simple reports from scratch so you can get a feel for how it all works. Once you have an understanding of QuickReport, you'll be able to make use of the templates and the wizard with no difficulty just by setting some properties and adding some very simple code.

From the Delphi IDE, choose File | New. From the New Items dialog box, select the Forms tab, and you see the QuickReport Labels, QuickReport List, and QuickReport Master/ Detail icons (among others), as shown in Figure 12.1.

Figure 12.1.

The QuickReport templates.

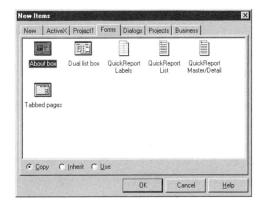

These are templates that will help you quickly start creating common reports. You simply add these to your project, and make the appropriate changes to fit your needs.

The Business tab of the New Items dialog box contains business-related form wizards, as shown in Figure 12.2. Here you can access the QuickReport Wizard to quickly create a report and tie it to an existing database. After completing today's lesson, you will have enough information to use these templates and the wizard. For now, let's move on and take a look at some of the QuickReport components.

The QuickReport Components

On Day 8, "The Visual Component Library," you briefly looked at all the components in the VCL, including the QuickReport components. The QuickReport components provide everything you need to quickly add reporting capability to your Delphi applications. Let's take a look at some of these components in a little more detail and then put them to use by writing a small application that prints a report from one of Delphi's sample database files.

NEW TERM Because QuickReport uses a banded report generator, you need to understand what bands are and how they work for you as you build reports. *Bands* are areas on a report that enable you to visually design your report by creating sections that contain text, images, graphs, charts, and so on. The bands become containers for other components that bring the information or graphics into the report. Some of these bands are enabled or disabled by setting properties in the TQuickRep component, and some are added by dropping one of the band components onto the TQuickRep component. In either case, they are key elements in designing your form layout.

Figure 12.2.

The New Items Business tab.

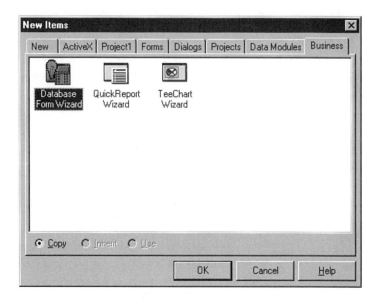

The TQuickRep Component

The TQuickRep component is used to connect to a dataset through the Table property. It also provides quite a few properties that provide great control in creating your reports, including the report title, bands, fonts, printer settings, and more. The TQuickRep component is also a visual component, and once it is connected to the database, it will be used as a container for the bands that make up the report.

The Band Components

The QRSubDetail, QRBand, QRChildBand, and QRGroup components are all QuickReport components that you can add to reports as needed providing functionality such as titles, headers, footers, detail areas for report data, and so on. By connecting these bands to a database and laying them out on the report where you want the information printed, you can quickly design your reports (see Delphi's online Help file for QuickReport for more information).

Other QuickReport Components

The rest of the components are divided into basically two categories: Those that are data aware and those that are not. These components are used to place text, images, charts, and so on, into bands on the report. You learn more about these as you move on to build a report.

Creating a Simple Report

Let's build a simple report that displays some text and an image so you can see just how powerful QuickReport is. Start up Delphi, create a new application project, and do the following:

1. Change the form's Caption property to Database Report Generator and its Name property to RepGen.

2. Add a second form and change its Caption property to Report Form - Hidden From User and its Name property to RepForm. Ensure that the Visible property is set to False (the default setting) because this form is not intended to be seen by the user; it acts as a container for the QuickReport components.

3. From the VCL Data Access tab in Delphi, drop a TTable component named RepForm on the form.

4. Use one of the database demos included with Delphi by setting the DatabaseName property for the TTable component to DBDEMOS.

5. Set the TTable TableName property to ANIMALS.DBF.

6. Set the TTable Active property to True.

7. From the VCL QReport tab, drop a QuickRep component on the form named RepForm.

8. Set the QuickRep component's DataSet property to Table1.

9. Double-click on the QuickRep component's Bands property to show its subproperties, and set the HasDetail property to True. At this point, you'll see the detail band on the report.

10. Drop a QRLabel component in to the detail band of the QuickRep component, and set its Caption property to Animal Name:. Position it to the left in the detail band.

11. Drop a QRDBText component just to the right of the QRLabel, and set its DataSet property to Table1 and its DataField property to Name.

12. Click on the detail band to select it, and then size the band down a bit to give you room to place an image on it.

13. Drop a QRDBImage component on the detail band, and position it to the left making sure to size it into a square that fits inside the band. Resize the band and QRDBImage as needed to get the size and proportions you want.

14. Set the QRDBImage component's DataSet property to Table1 and its DataField property to BMP.

12

If all went well, you should be able to preview your report by right-clicking in the QuickRep component area and selecting Preview. This brings up a Print Preview window showing what the report will look like with actual data on-screen for you to review, as shown in Figure 12.3.

Figure 12.3.

The QuickReport preview window.

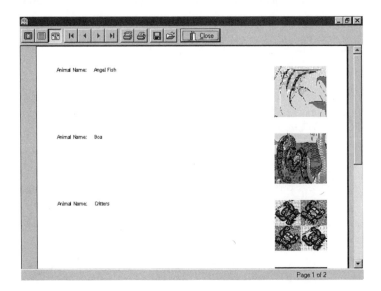

Congratulations—you have just created your first report with out a single line of code! If you like, you can print a sample report from the preview screen by clicking the printer button on the toolbar.

You can use what you have learned here to add more fields to a report by adding additional components. Now let's add some runtime functionality for the user.

Adding a Preview Window

The process of adding a preview function to your application is so simple it's almost embarrassing. You simply drop a button component on one of the user's forms; in this case, it is the main form called RepGen. Then, double-click on the button, and add the following line to its OnClick event:

```
RepForm.QuickRep1.Preview
```

When you try to run, compile, or do a syntax check, Delphi will detect that you need a second unit in the first unit's uses clause and will ask if you want to add it. Answer yes, and the uses clause will be updated for you.

12

That's it! Now when you run the application and click on the Preview button, the preview screen appears. Now you can see why I say it's almost embarrassing. Your boss and users will think you have slaved over the code adding all this functionality when it actually took a couple of minutes! Don't worry, I won't tell if you won't.

Printing Reports

If you haven't guessed by now, printing a report at runtime is no more work than adding a preview button. Add another button to the main form, and set its caption to Print. Double-click on the button, and add the following code to its OnClick event:

```
RepForm.QuickRep1.Print
```

Your application's main form should look something like Figure 12.4, and the code like Listing 12.1. You will, of course, have source for the hidden form (QREP.PAS) built by Delphi (it's not listed here).

Figure 12.4.

The Report applica-tion.

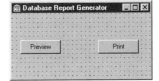

TYPE **Listing 12.1. The Report application's main form.**

```
unit main;

interface

uses
  Windows, Messages, SysUtils, Classes, Graphics, Controls,
  Forms, Dialogs,
  StdCtrls;

type
  TRepGen = class(TForm)
    Button1: TButton;
    Button2: TButton;
    procedure Button1Click(Sender: TObject);
    procedure Button2Click(Sender: TObject);
    procedure FormCreate(Sender: TObject);
  private
    { Private declarations }
  public
    { Public declarations }
  end;
```

continues

12

Listing 12.1. continued

```
var
  RepGen: TRepGen;

implementation

uses qrep;

{$R *.DFM}

procedure TRepGen.Button1Click(Sender: TObject);
begin
    RepForm.QuickRep1.Preview;
end;

procedure TRepGen.Button2Click(Sender: TObject);
begin
    RepForm.QuickRep1.Print;
end;
end.
```

ANALYSIS If you haven't done so already, run the application and test it out. Pressing the Preview button will show the report in the preview window, and the Print button will cause it to print. The database you used in this example has only a few records in it, so you will get about two pages if you print it. Some of the nice things about the preview feature, besides the fact that it shows you live data in the preview, are that it displays the number of pages, enables you to page through the data, and more. So, users will be able to take advantage of all the nice features—and you did it all with two lines of code.

TeeChart

As with the QuickReport components, the TeeChart components provide a lot of power and features with a minimum of work on your part. The coverage here will be brief. TeeChart ships with Delphi 3, but you can purchase TeeChart Pro version 3 for extended functionality and features. TeeChart Pro runs on all versions of Delphi.

For more information about an upgrade or details not covered in this lesson, refer to Delphi's online help and manuals that weigh in at well over 100 pages and are very nicely done.

Here's are some of the features of TeeChart:

☐ 32-bit version for Delphi 3
☐ Standard series types
☐ Statistical functions
☐ Data aware

☐ Series gallery

☐ 2D, 3D chart capabilities

☐ QuickReport integration

☐ Zoom, scroll, and real-time viewing

☐ Custom drawing

☐ Custom printing

☐ Design-time integrated chart and series editor

Let's take a quick look at TeeChart and build an application to test it out.

The TeeChart Components

The TeeChart components come in several flavors. Although the features are similar, they are spread out through the IDE on various tabs. On the Additional tab, you find the Chart, which enables you to create charts from data on-the-fly and display those charts on-screen. A data-aware version appears on the Data Controls tab. There also are versions that appear on the Decision Cube and QReport tabs. This gives the flexibility to chart your data and present it using several different methods.

The TeeChart Wizard

TeeChart provides a wizard to simplify setting up a project to use TeeChart by walking you through the process. In Delphi, select File | New to bring up the New Items dialog box. Select the Business tab, and you'll see the TeeChart Wizard icon, as shown in Figure 12.5.

Double-click on the icon, and the wizard will start up asking you to select a chart style, as shown in Figure 12.6. The two styles are database and non-database. You'll be led through a series of questions to choose the chart type, database to connect the chart to, and so on. When completed, the chart will appear on the form. At that point, you only need to add your code or make changes necessary for your application.

Creating a Chart

Let's build a simple application so you can see how to create a chart without a wizard. As you go through the remainder of the TeeChart section, you'll create the simple chart, enable the user to input data to be graphed, and display it on the form when the data has been input. Start by adding a chart to a form by following these steps:

Figure 12.5.

The Business tab contains the TeeChart Wizard icon.

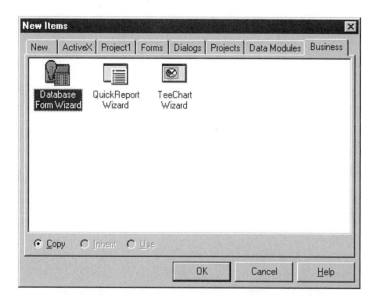

Figure 12.6.

TeeChart Wizard.

1. Start a new Delphi project.
2. From the Additional tab, drop a TChart component on the form. Resize the TChart to take up most of the top portion of the form leaving enough room at the bottom to place a button and some edit boxes, as shown in Figure 12.7.
3. Drop a button component, three label components, and three edit components on the form.
4. Set the button caption to Update.
5. Set the Label caption for Label1, Label2, and Label3 to Data1, Data2, and Data3, respectively.

6. Place the edit components 1, 2, and 3 below the label components of the same number, respectively, as shown in Figure 12.7.

7. Finally, change the form caption to TeeChart Demo.

Figure 12.7.
The TeeChart demo.

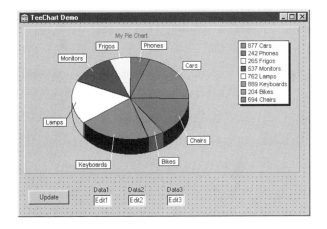

Now you need to make some changes to the chart. You can make changes to the properties at design time or at runtime, but in this example, you'll make most of the changes using the Chart Editor, as described in the following section.

Using the Chart Editor

Making changes to the chart's type and appearance can be done through the Chart Editor, which is shown in Figure 12.8. To bring up the Chart Editor, right-click on the TChart, which displays the a pop-up menu, and then select Edit Chart. The editor starts up displaying the Chart tab, which has several tabs underneath it. The Series tab should be selected by default.

Figure 12.8.
The Chart Editor.

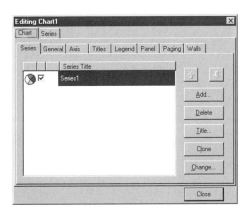

12

Do the following to set up the chart:

1. In the Series tab, click the Add button, which brings up a dialog enabling you to choose the chart type. Select the pie chart and click OK.

2. You can change the chart's title by selecting the Chart tab and then the Titles tab under that. Change the title from TChart to My Pie Chart, as shown in Figure 12.9.

3. When you are done, close the Chart Editor by clicking on the Close button.

Figure 12.9.

*The Chart Editor's
Titles tab.*

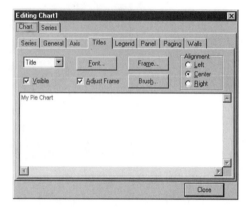

You should see a pie chart that is populated with random data. This enables you to position and size the chart on the screen to get a feel for what the chart will look like. Now, let's add some code to put data into the chart.

Setting Up a TeeChart Data Series

In this section, you add code to the button you placed on the form earlier to enable user input of data. Double-click on the button, and change its OnClick event to be as follows:

```
procedure TForm1.Button1Click(Sender: TObject);
begin
With Series1 do
Begin
    Add(  StrToInt(Edit1.Text),  'Data1'  ,  clRed  ) ;
    Add(  StrToInt(Edit2.Text),  'Data2',   clBlue  ) ;
    Add(  StrToInt(Edit3.Text),  'Data3',  clGreen  ) ;
end;
end;
```

After you have typed everything in, your finished program should look like Listing 12.2.

TYPE **Listing 12.2. TeeChart demo.**

```pascal
unit piechart;

interface

uses
  Windows, Messages, SysUtils, Classes, Graphics, Controls,
  Forms, Dialogs,
  ExtCtrls, TeeProcs, TeEngine, Chart, StdCtrls, Series;

type
  TForm1 = class(TForm)
    Chart1: TChart;
    Series1: TPieSeries;
    Button1: TButton;
    Label1: TLabel;
    Label2: TLabel;
    Label3: TLabel;
    Edit1: TEdit;
    Edit2: TEdit;
    Edit3: TEdit;
    procedure Button1Click(Sender: TObject);
  private
    { Private declarations }
  public
    { Public declarations }
  end;

var
  Form1: TForm1;

implementation

{$R *.DFM}

procedure TForm1.Button1Click(Sender: TObject);
begin
With Series1 do
Begin
    Add(  StrToInt(Edit1.Text), 'Data1' , clRed ) ;
    Add(  StrToInt(Edit2.Text), 'Data2', clBlue ) ;
    Add(  StrToInt(Edit3.Text), 'Data3', clGreen ) ;
end;
end;

end.
```

12

ANALYSIS This code populates the chart with data entered by the user and sets the color for slice of the pie chart. Data is retrieved from the edit boxes, converted to integer format, and then fed to the TeeChart when the user clicks on the Update button to display the chart.

Save the project. Name the unit PIECHART.PAS and the project TEECHART.DPR. Run the project, and you should get a form on the screen showing the chart. Because the chart has no data in it by default, you'll see the chart component area as you laid it out, but it will be blank. To test the chart, enter three numbers into the data edit boxes (for example, 10, 20, and 70) and click on the Update button. A nice 3D chart should appear on the screen, as shown in Figure 12.10).

Figure 12.10.

The TeeChart demo application.

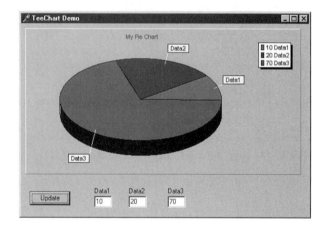

It's not covered here, but you also can provide the capability to print your charts (see the TeeChart documentation for more details on printing). And, as mentioned earlier, you can use one of the TChart components such as TDBChart or QRChart for database and QuickReport enhancements. You now should have a basic idea of what TeeChart components are used for and how to implement them in your applications.

Decision Cube

If you have the Client/Server Edition of Delphi, Decision Cube is a set of components that will allow you to build multidimensional data-analysis capability into your applications.

The Decision Cube Components

Decision Cube consists of six components. Three of them provide the ability to communicate with Delphi's database engine (DecisionCube, DecisionQuery, and DecisionSource), and three are visual components that enable you to work with and display your data (DecisionPivot, DecisionGrid, and DecisionGraph).

Decision Cube Overview

By using the components in the Decision Cube package, you can create applications that enable users (organizations and management) to create complex reports. These can be provided within an application or can be distributed over the network such as to a Web page. Because Decision Cube ships only with the Client/Server Edition of Delphi, no further coverage is provided here. Refer to the Decision Cube online help and documentation for further information.

Summary

Today you learned about QuickReport and the power it adds to Delphi. It's a very powerful tool that can save many hours of work in creating professional reports. You touched on some basics as you built a simple report that pulled data from the sample database table called ANIMALS.DBF. You also built a small application using only two lines of code to enable you to preview the report on-screen or send to the printer.

Next, you learned about the TeeChart components and found that, like the QuickReport components, they greatly simplify the work involved in creating charts and graphs. You built a simple application that enabled you to take input from the user and generate a pie chart. This application required you to write only three lines of code.

Although this chapter only scratched the surface of these two groups of components, you should have enough information to get started using them and have an idea of what is available. Both QuickReport and TeeChart are third-party products that ship with Delphi in fully functional versions. Both products also have upgrade options to get more features. You should read the documentation for each of these products because they both are very well done and contain all the information you should need.

You also learned a bit about Decision Cube, a set of tools that enables you to create tools and reports for multi-dimensional data analysis. Decision Cube is included only with the Client/Server Edition of Delphi 3.

Q&A

Q How do I add charts or graphs to my QuickReports?

A Use the TeeChart component QRChart.

Q Will QuickReport do labels?

A In fact, one of the QuickReport templates in the New Items dialog box is for this purpose. Because of the banded design, you can do quite a bit with QuickReports with some practice.

Workshop

The Workshop provides two ways for you to affirm what you've learned in this chapter. The Quiz section poses questions to help you solidify your understanding of the material covered. You can find answers to the quiz questions in Appendix A, "Answers to the Quiz Questions." The Exercises section provides you with experience in using what you have learned. Please try to work through all these before continuing to the next day.

Quiz

1. What type of report generator is QuickReport?
2. What are the bands used for in QuickReport?
3. Does the user see the QuickReport component?
4. When you build an application using QuickReport, how do you connect to your database—in other words, what components are used?
5. How do you set the type of chart you wish to use in a TeeChart?
6. How do you set the title of a TeeChart?
7. How do you invoke the Chart Editor for a TeeChart?
8. Can a TeeChart be printed?

Exercises

1. Build an application that prints a report for each field in the Animals table that you worked with earlier. (Use the QuickReport documentation if you need additional help.)
2. Build an application that pulls data from a database to populate a TeeChart. (Use the TeeChart documentation if you need additional help.)

12

Day 13

Creating Your Own Visual and ActiveX Components

As software becomes more sophisticated and complex, using components will become the preferred method for developing applications. Delphi is a wonderful development tool for creating components to be used in any software application that can use components. It can be used to develop both native Delphi visual components and ActiveX components. Visual components can be built and installed into the Delphi IDE without your needing to worry about some of the complexity of ActiveX. ActiveX components can be imported into Delphi, Visual Basic, Web pages, and any other product that supports the hosting of an ActiveX component.

Today, you start by looking at some of the reasons you may want to write components, and then you walk through what it takes to create visual components in Delphi, starting from a component that does nothing and ending with very useful and powerful components. You then learn about what ActiveX is and how Delphi can convert visual components into ActiveX components. You conclude by taking a visual component that you develop, turning it into an ActiveX component, and then using it in a scriptable Web application.

Why Write Components?

Components are powerful because they hide all the implementation details from you. Just as a driver does not have to understand how rack-and-pinion steering works in order to drive a car, an application or Web developer does not have to know how a visual component works in order to use it. He simply needs to know how to communicate with it. There are several reasons why you might want to write your own visual and ActiveX components.

Reuse Code

The interface to a component is built into the Delphi development environment. Therefore, if you use an object frequently, you can turn it into a visual component and add it to the toolbar. This makes using the component easier and hides the implementation in the library.

Modify Current Visual Components

Because Delphi is an object-oriented language and a visual component is an object, you can create a visual component that is a subclass of an existing one. Suppose, for example, that you love to use blue circles in your applications. You also want to take advantage of all the properties, events, and methods of the TShape component, but you always change the shape parameter to a circle and the color of the brush to blue. One shortcut to make development easier is to create a subclass of TShape called TBlueCircle. The TBlueCircle class would default to having the shape property set to circle and the color property set to Blue.

Sell Your Components

If you have to add specialized functionality to your application, you can buy a third-party component. This is one of the biggest advantages of a component-based system. For example, if you need networking capabilities, you either can write the networking routines yourself or buy a set of components that provide network capability. Likewise, you can create a component that provides additional functionality and sell it to other application developers. When you sell the library, you provide a compiled version of the product. Therefore, your customer does not see the source code or the implementation details of the product. When the component is added to a form, however, the developer can use the friendly interface to communicate with the component through the IDE.

See Changes in Behavior During Development

If you compile a piece of code into a visual component, you can see changes in its appearance during development. For example, when you set the value of the Shape property to a circle on the TShape component, the shape on the form changes into a circle. This happens before the component is compiled. This is extremely useful in components that are visible. During development, you can get a sense of how the application will look at runtime.

The Precursor to Components—A Quick Look at DLLs

Before you jump into creating components, here's a quick look at what it takes to build dynamic link libraries (DLLs) using Delphi. DLLs are not object oriented; they simply enable you to develop a procedure library in one language that can be used in any other. Another powerful feature of DLLs is that they are loaded at runtime as opposed to being statically linked into the application. This enables you to divide development and distribution into components instead of developing and statically linking one large application.

To demonstrate how to build DLLs in Delphi, you'll create a simple DLL and then call it from a C program. This DLL has one procedure that is passed one parameter, which is a PChar and reverses the string. For example, if you called ReverseStr(X) and X = "CATFOOD", X would equal "DOOFTAC" when the procedure returned.

To create a new dynamic link library, follow these steps:

1. Choose File | New from the main menu bar and then choose DLL. This creates a skeleton DLL.

2. Add functions or procedures that you want to implement. In this example, you are adding the implementation code for the ReverseStr procedure. Listing 13.1 shows the implementation of ReverseStr.

TYPE **Listing 13.1. ReverseStr, a DLL that reverses strings.**

```
library DelphiReverse;

{ Important note about DLL memory management: ShareMem must be the
  first unit in your library's USES clause AND your project's (select
  View-Project Source) USES clause if your DLL exports any procedures or
  functions that pass strings as parameters or function results. This
  applies to all strings passed to and from your DLL—even those that
  are nested in records and classes. ShareMem is the interface unit to
```

continues

Listing 13.1. continued

```
    the DELPHIMM.DLL shared memory manager, which must be deployed along
    with your DLL. To avoid using DELPHIMM.DLL, pass string information
    using PChar or ShortString parameters. }

uses
  SysUtils,
  Classes;

procedure ReverseStr(strToReverse : PChar);export;stdcall;

var
   BFLen : integer;
   Temp  : char;
   Count : integer;

begin
   BFLen := StrLen(strToReverse);
   for Count := 0 to (BFLen div 2)-1 do
   begin
      Temp := strToReverse[Count];
      strToReverse[Count]    := strToReverse[BFLen - Count - 1];
      strToReverse[BFLen - Count - 1] := Temp;
   end;
end;

exports
  ReverseStr;
end.
```

ANALYSIS This program implements the functions that you want the DLL to contain. Note that the options `export` and `stdcall` need to be placed after the procedure declaration. These options specify that the function should be made available and that a standard calling convention should be used to pass parameters. The only other thing that needs to be in the library source is the `exports` section that is placed at the bottom of the unit. This specifies that the `ReverseStr` procedure should be exported. Exporting a function enables it to be made visible to the outside world. If you don't export it, for all intents and purposes, it is a internal function. Much as the interface section of a unit enables functions to be used from outside the unit, the `exports` clause enables the function to be called from outside the DLL.

After the project is complied, you have a DLL that can be called from almost any language, such as C, C++, Visual Basic, and of course, Delphi. Listing 13.2 demonstrates how a C program could dynamically load the `DelphiReverse` library procedure you just wrote and then call the `ReverseStr` procedure.

TYPE   **Listing 13.2. C code that calls the Delphi DLL.**

```c
#include <stdio.h>
#include <windows.h>

void main()
{
HANDLE   TheLib;
FARPROC  ReverseStr;
char     TheStr[] = "Beagles Sleep and Play!";
  TheLib = LoadLibrary("DelphiReverse");
  ReverseStr = GetProcAddress(TheLib,"ReverseStr");
  printf("Original String:%s\n",TheStr);
  ReverseStr(TheStr);
  printf("Reversed String :%s\n",TheStr);
  FreeLibrary(TheLib);
};
```

ANALYSIS   This program declares a string and sets it to `"Beagles Sleep and Play!"`. It then loads the `DelphiReverse` DLL into memory and gets the address of the `ReverseStr` procedure. The programs prints the original string, reverses it, and then prints the reversed string.

OUTPUT   The output from the program is as follows:

```
D:\BBTD30\Samples\CH14\CallDll\Debug>calldll
Original String:Beagles Sleep and Play!
Reversed String :!yalP dna peelS selgaeB
```

Building and Installing a Component

Building DLLs is simple, but they don't seamlessly integrate into the Delphi IDE. They're powerful, but they are not object oriented. Visual components solve both of these shortcomings. The first component that you build in this section just compiles and installs on the toolbar. You can add this `TDoNothing` component to a form even though it does not do anything. You can, of course, remove the component from the toolbar.

Components in Delphi are compiled into packages; therefore, the first thing you need to do in this example is to create a new package. Choose File | New to bring up the New Items dialog and then choose the "package" icon. This will then prompt you for a filename. For these examples, use a filename of `tdcomps`. You should now see a blank Package Manager dialog box, as shown in Figure 13.1.

13

Figure 13.1.

The blank Package Manager ready to add a new component.

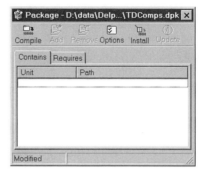

Adding the TDoNothing Component to the Package

In this example, you use the Component Expert to generate the code needed to build a bare-bones component. All components must be inherited from other components. If you want to start from scratch, you must create a subclass of the TComponent class, as follows:

1. Click the Add icon in the Package Manager dialog box, and the Add dialog box appears.

2. Select the New Component tab.

3. Specify TComponent for Ancestor type, TDoNothing for Class Name, and Samples for Palette Page. For Unit file name, choose a new .pas file to be used for the source code; leave Search path set to its default. Your dialog box should look like the one shown in Figure 13.2.

4. Click OK to save the settings.

Figure 13.2.

The Component Expert for TDoNothing.

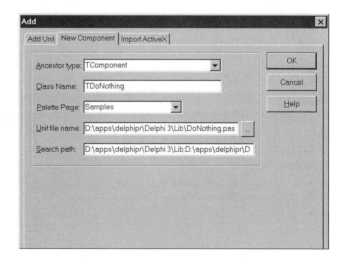

13

Delphi creates the shell of a unit that compiles to a visual component. Double-clicking on the unit in the Package Manager brings up the source code. Listing 13.3 shows the code that the expert produces for the TDoNothing component.

TYPE | **Listing 13.3. The shell of a visual component.**

```
unit DoNothing;

interface

uses
  Windows, Messages, SysUtils, Classes, Graphics, Controls,
  Forms, Dialogs;

type
  TDoNothing = class(TComponent)
  private
    { Private declarations }
  protected
    { Protected declarations }
  public
    { Public declarations }
  published
    { Published declarations }
  end;

procedure Register;

implementation

procedure Register;
begin
  RegisterComponents('Samples', [TDoNothing]);
end;

end.
```

ANALYSIS Usually, you would modify the shell to add custom functionality to the component. There are two parts to the component library: the TDoNothing class and the Register procedure. Delphi uses all the code associated with the class to determine how the component functions. It also calls the Register procedure to place the component on the toolbar. In this case, it simply installs the component on the Samples tab of the IDE.

13

Compiling and Installing the Package and Components

To compile and install the component, follow these steps:

1. In the Package Manager, click the Compile icon. This compiles the unit into the Package DPK file.

2. In the Package Manager, click the Install icon. This installs the package. If the package successfully installs, you see a dialog box informing you that the operation was successful, as shown in Figure 13.3.

Figure 13.3.

The package success-fully installed.

Look at the Samples toolbar. Notice that a new component appears on it. Put the mouse pointer over the component so that the hint shows. The new component is a DoNothing component. Create a new application and add the component to the form. When you click the component to view the properties and events pages, you see that there are two properties, as shown in Figure 13.4. The Name property defaults to DoNothing1, and the Tag property defaults to 0. There are no events on the events page. This is a fully functional visual component even though it does not do anything.

Figure 13.4.

The application and properties page with the DoNothing component.

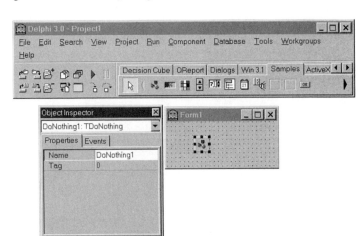

Removing the Component

You sometimes need to remove a component from the toolbar or uninstall it from Delphi. For example, an upgraded version of a visual component might become available, or you might want to remove a component that you do not use. The TDoNothing component that you just created is essentially useless. To remove it, follow these steps:

1. Select Project | Options from the menu and then select the Packages tab.
2. On the Packages tab, click on the package you just installed, and then click on Remove. The TDoNothing component is removed from the toolbar.

Writing a Visual Component

You, as a developer, use components by placing them on a form or by using the Create method. After you create a component, you can manipulate it by setting properties, calling methods, and responding events. You do not have to worry about how properties and methods work. The component calls its event handler when a particular event occurs. When you write a component, you must write the implementation details for properties and methods and call event handlers when the event should occur. The way this is done is to define a class that becomes the component and then fill in the necessary details.

Private, Protected, Public, and Published

Delphi uses object classes to create visual components. Different parts of the object class definition are declared in different protected regions. Variables, procedures, and functions can have four types of access:

Private	Only procedures and functions defined within the class definition have access, and only routines in the same unit have access.
Protected	Procedures and functions defined in the class definition have access, and so do procedures and functions in descendant classes.
Public	All procedures and functions have access.
Published	As with Public, all procedures and functions have access but with a hook into the Delphi IDE to display the information in the properties and events pages.

13

Properties

A developer in Delphi uses the properties of a component to read or set certain attributes—similar to the data fields stored in a class. Properties, however, can trigger code to be executed. For example, when you change the Shape property on the TShape component, the component actually changes shape. There must be a mechanism that tells the component to change shape when the property is changed. In other words, a property can take on two personalities: It can be a piece of data that affects how a component works, or it can trigger an action.

Methods

Methods are procedures and functions that a class has made public. Although you can use properties to call a function or a procedure, use them only if it is logical to do so. Methods, on the other hand, can be used any time. Another difference is that properties usually are set with one piece of data. Methods can take multiple parameters and can return multiple pieces of data through VAR variable declarations.

Events

Events enable developers or users to enhance the component when something happens—that is, when an event occurs. For example, the OnClick event means in effect, "If you want to do something when the user clicks this, tell me what procedure to execute." It is the job of the component designer to call the component user's events when necessary.

Building a (Somewhat) Useful Component—TMult

In this section, you create a visual component, TMult, that performs a task and includes at least one property, method, and event. Think of it as the "Hello, World!" of component design. It is impractical to use this component in real applications, but it demonstrates the basic concepts of component design. It also is an example of deriving a component from the top of the component hierarchy. All components have TComponent in their family tree. TMult is a direct descendant of TComponent.

Creating TMult

The TMult component has two properties of type integer that can be set at design time or runtime. The component has one method, DoMult. When it is executed, the two values in the properties are multiplied, and the result is placed in a third property called Res. One event in the TMult component, OnTooBig, is also implemented. If either number is set greater than 100, when the DoMult method is called, the component calls the code to which the user has pointed in the event page. TMult is an example of a purely functional component—it has no graphical parts. Examples of standard components that are purely functional include the TTimer, TDatabase, and TTable components.

TMult contains the following properties:

Val1   The first value to multiply. It is available at design time and runtime.

Val2   The second value to multiply. It is available at design time and runtime.

Res   The value obtained by multiplying Val1 and Val2. It is available only at runtime.

TMult contains one method, DoMult, which implements the multiplication of Val1 and Val2. TMult's event, OnTooBig, calls the user's event handler (if one exists) whenever Val1 is multiplied by Val2 and either value is greater than 100.

Building TMult

The first step is to create a unit that has the standard shell for all components. To do this, use the Component Expert as before, and name the file Tmultiply. Figure 13.5 shows how you should fill in the Component Expert for TMult.

Figure 13.5.

Component Expert parameters for TMult.

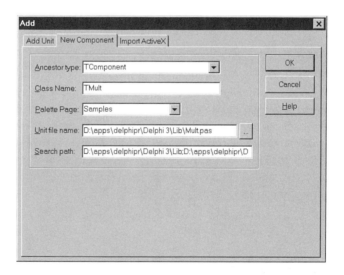

The code generated includes a shell for the TMult class declaration and one procedure for registering the function. To develop the component's properties, method, and event, you must modify the class definition and provide the corresponding procedures and functions. Double-click on the Tmultiply unit in the Package Manager to bring up the source code.

Adding Properties to TMult

TMult has three properties: Val1, Val2, and Res. Val1 and Val2 are available at design time and runtime, whereas Res is available only at runtime. Because each property holds data, you must define variables in the TMult class to hold data. Users do not access the variables directly but, instead, through a specialized call. Therefore, the variables that hold data for the three properties are declared in the Private section of the class definition—which means that only functions and procedures within the class can access the data. By convention, the names of the variables begin with F (which stands for "field"), followed by the name of the property. In this case, all the properties are integers, so they are declared as type integer. The class declaration is as follows:

```
type
  TMult = class(TComponent)
Private
    FVal1 : integer;
    FVal2 : integer;
    FRes  : integer;
Protected
Public
Published
end;
```

Now you must declare the properties themselves. Use the property key word in the class definition. The property definition typically appears in one of two places. If a property will be available at design time, it must be declared in the published section of the declaration. If it is available only at runtime, it is placed in the public section. In this case, the properties are stored as simple data types, and no special action is performed when the data is read or written. Therefore, it is possible to use direct access to read and write the property. With direct access, you tell Delphi to set or return data from a variable when a property is read or written. The read and write methods define the variables. Here are the property definitions for the three properties:

```
type
  TMult = class(TComponent)
Private
    FVal1 : integer;
    FVal2 : integer;
    FRes  : integer;
protected
public
    Property Res:integer read FRes;      {Property to Obtain Result}
published
    property Val1:integer read FVal1 Write FVal1 default 1; {Operand 1}
    property Val2:integer read FVal2 Write FVal2 default 1; {Operand 2}
end;   {TMult}
```

Because the Res property is read-only, you do not need a direct access method to write to the FRes variable.

Val1 and Val2 are set by default to 1, which is misleading. The default that a property shows is actually set in another step of creating the component—adding a constructor. Delphi uses the default value on the property line to determine whether it should save the value when a user saves a form file. When a user adds this component to a form and leaves Val1 set to 1, the value is not saved in the .dfm file. If the value is anything else, though, it is saved.

You have declared the properties for the component. If you installed the component now, Val1 and Val2 would appear in the Properties dialog box. You have a few more steps to follow to make the component function.

Adding the Constructor

A constructor is called when a class is created. It is often responsible for the dynamic memory allocation or resource gathering that a class needs. The constructor also sets defaults for the variables in a class. When a component is added to a form at design time or runtime, the constructor is called. To declare the constructor in the class definition, add a constructor line in the public portion of the class declaration. By convention, Create is used as the name of the constructor procedure, as shown in this example:

```
{...}
public
constructor Create(AOwner : TComponent); override;{Main Constructor}
{...}
```

The constructor is passed one parameter—the component that owns it. It is different from the parent property. You must specify that you want to override the default constructor for the ancestor class, TComponent. In the implementation portion of the unit, you add the associated code for the constructor, as in this example:

```
constructor TMult.Create(AOwner: TComponent);
BEGIN
  inherited Create(AOwner); {Call constructor for parent class}
  FVal1 := 1;                      {Set Default for Value1}
  FVal2 := 1;                      {Set Default for Value2}
END; {End constructor}
```

For any parent-specific construction to be performed, you must first call the inherited Create procedure. In this case, the only additional step is to set default values for Val1 and Val2 that correspond to the default section of the property declaration.

Adding a Method

A method is simpler to implement than a property. To declare a method, place a procedure or function in the public portion of the class definition, and write the associated procedure or function. In this case, you add the DoMult method, as follows:

13

```
{...}

public
  procedure DoMult; {Method to multiply}

{...}

procedure TMult.DoMult;
Begin
  FRes := FVal1 * FVal2
End;
```

Your component now works, so a user can add it to a form, and set values for Val1 and Val2 at design time and runtime. During execution, the DoMult method can be called to perform the multiplication.

Adding an Event

An event enables a user to have specialized code executed when something happens. For your component, you can add an event that is triggered whenever Val1 or Val2 is greater than 100 and DoMult is executed. You can modify that code so that the Res property remains unchanged when this happens.

In Delphi, an event is simply a specialized property—a property that is a pointer to a function. Everything else that applies to properties applies to functions.

One final piece of information that the component needs to provide is when to call the user's event handler. This is simple. Whenever it is time to trigger an event, test whether the user has defined an event handler. If she has, call the event. You must add the declarations to the class definition, as follows:

```
{...}
Private
   FTooBig : TNotifyEvent;
   {...}
published
   Property OnTooBig:TNotifyEvent read FTooBig write FTooBig;   {Event}
   {...}
end;   {TMult}
 {...}
```

The TNotifyEvent type, which is used to define FTooBig and OnTooBig, is a generic function pointer type that passes one parameter of type component—usually Self. The final step is to modify the TMult.DoMult procedure so that it calls the event handler if either number is too large. Before you call the event handler, you check whether an event is defined. To do this, you use the assigned function, which returns True if an event is defined for the event handler and False if it is not.

Listing 13.4 shows all the code for the component.

TYPE **Listing 13.4. The completed TMult component.**

```
unit TMultiply;

interface

uses
  SysUtils, WinTypes, WinProcs, Messages, Classes, Graphics, Controls,
  Forms, Dialogs, StdCtrls;

type
  TMult = class(TComponent)
Private
  FTooBig : TNotifyEvent;
  FVal1 : integer;
  FVal2 : integer;
  FRes  : integer;
protected
public
  {Main Constructor}
  constructor Create(AOwner : TComponent); override;
  {Method to multiply}
  procedure DoMult;
  {Property to Obtain Result}
  Property Res:integer read FRes;
published
  property Val1:integer read FVal1 Write FVal1 default 1; {Operand 1}
  property Val2:integer read FVal2 Write FVal2 default 1; {Operand 2}
  Property OnTooBig:TNotifyEvent read FTooBig write FTooBig;  {Event}
end;  {TMult}

procedure Register;

implementation

constructor TMult.Create(AOwner: TComponent);
BEGIN
  inherited Create(AOwner);
  FVal1 := 1;
  FVal2 := 1;
End;

procedure TMult.DoMult;
Begin
 if (Val1 < 100) and (Val2  < 100) then
  FRes := FVal1 * FVal2
 else
  if assigned(FTooBig) then OnTooBig(Self);
End;

procedure Register;
begin
  RegisterComponents('Samples', [TMult]);
end;

end.
```

13

Testing the Component

You can install this component by following the procedure described earlier in the chapter. After the component has been installed, you can test it by creating an application that uses it.

Figure 13.6 displays the component layout for the test application, and Listing 13.5 shows the code.

Figure 13.6.

Component layout for TMult *test application.*

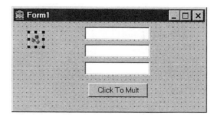

TYPE **Listing 13.5. Main unit for testing** TMult.

```
unit main;

interface

uses
  SysUtils, Windows, Messages, Classes, Graphics, Controls,
  Forms, Dialogs,
  StdCtrls, TMultiply;

type
  TForm1 = class(TForm)
    Mult1: TMult;
    EdVal1: TEdit;
    EdVal2: TEdit;
    EdResult: TEdit;
    Button1: TButton;
    procedure Button1Click(Sender: TObject);
    procedure Mult1TooBig(Sender: TObject);
  private
    { Private declarations }
  public
    { Public declarations }
  end;

var
  Form1: TForm1;

implementation

{$R *.DFM}
```

```
procedure TForm1.Button1Click(Sender: TObject);
begin
   { Set Properties }
   Mult1.Val1 := StrToInt(EdVal1.Text);
   Mult1.Val2 := StrToInt(EdVal2.Text);
   { Execute The Method}
   Mult1.DoMult;
   { Capture the result }
   EdResult.Text := IntToStr(Mult1.Res);
end;

procedure TForm1.Mult1TooBig(Sender: TObject);
begin
   Application.MessageBox('Boy What a Wimpy Component!',
                          'Component Says It Is Too Big',
                          MB_OK);
end;
end.
```

ANALYSIS The test application for this component consists of three edit boxes and one button. A user can place numbers in the first two edit boxes. When she clicks the button, the numbers are multiplied using the component, and the result is placed in the third edit box. You can add an event handler that displays a dialog box stating that at least one of the numbers is too large if the OnTooBig event is triggered.

As Figure 13.7 shows, the event handler is called when a number greater than 100 is multiplied in the TMult component.

Figure 13.7.

The TMult *test application event handler.*

Using Procedures To Get and Set Property Values

The TMult component relies on an awkward two-step process for obtaining the product of two numbers. Whenever you change the value of Val1 or Val2, Res should be recalculated automatically. To do this, you can call a procedure whenever the property is set. Likewise, you can call a function that returns the value of the property whenever it is read.

NEW TERM An *access method* is the process of calling a procedure or function when a property is accessed. To use access methods, you replace the direct-storage variable name with the name of the function used to manipulate the data on the property declaration. To implement access methods in the TMult method, you must make the following changes to the class declaration:

```
{...}
type
  TMult = class(TComponent)
Private
   FTooBig : TNotifyEvent;
   FVal1 : integer;
   FVal2 : integer;
   FRes  : integer;
   {**********  Move DoMult to Private Area *******}
   procedure DoMult;
   {**********  Add SetVal1 and SetVal2 Definition *******}

   procedure SetVal1(InVal : Integer);    {To Set Value1}
   procedure SetVal2(InVal : Integer);    {To Set Value2}
protected
public
   {Property to Obtain Result}
   Property Res:integer read FRes;
   constructor Create(AOwner : TComponent); override;{Main Constructor}

published
   {**********  Set access methods *******}
   property Val1:integer read FVal1 Write SetVal1 default 1; {Operand 1}
   property Val2:integer read FVal2 Write SetVal2 default 1; {Operand 2}
   Property OnTooBig:TNotifyEvent read FTooBig write FTooBig;  {Event}
end;   {TMult}
{...}

procedure TMult.SetVal1(InVal : Integer);
Begin
  FVal1 := InVal;
  DoMult;
End;
procedure TMult.SetVal2(InVal : Integer);
Begin
  FVal2 := InVal;
  DoMult;
End;
{...}
end.
```

In the test program, you no longer need to call the DoMult method. In fact, if you attempt to call DoMult, the application does not compile because it has been moved to the private region. The functionality otherwise remains the same.

Modifying an Existing Component—
TButClock

TMult demonstrates many of the issues involved in writing components, but it does not demonstrate how a component can be derived from an existing component. One of the key advantages of an object-oriented programming language is that an object can be derived from a parent class. For example, if you want a component that is a green button, you do not have to write all the code that makes a button look like a button and that provides hooks for all the possible user interactions. A generic button already exists.

With inheritance, you can derive a new class that has all the functionality of a parent class with the addition of a customized feature or enhancement. In this section, you create a component called TButClock. It acts exactly like a standard button except that the Caption property is overwritten automatically with the current time.

To build a component from an existing component, you use the Component Expert to create the shell of the component and override any functionality that should be added. For the example in this section, you use a worker thread that is put into a loop until the component is destroyed. The worker thread sleeps for one second, and then calls a callback function in the component to update the caption with the current time. The code for the TButClock component is shown in Listing 13.6.

TYPE **Listing 13.6. The TButClock component.**

```
unit unitTBC;

interface

uses
  Windows, Messages, SysUtils, Classes, Graphics, Controls,
  Forms, Dialogs,
  StdCtrls,extctrls;
type
  {Callback Type so Thread can Update Clock}
  TCaptionCallbackProc = procedure(X : String) of object;

  {Thread Object}
  TUpdateClock = class(TThread)
  private
    procedure UpdateCaption;
  protected
    procedure Execute; override;
```

continues

13

Listing 13.6. continued

```
    public
      UpdateClockProc : TCaptionCallbackProc;
    end;

    {Main Component}
    TButClock = class(TButton)
    private
      { Private declarations }
      MainThread  : TUpdateClock;
      procedure UpdateCaption(X : String);
    protected
      { Protected declarations }
    public
      { Public declarations }
      constructor Create(AOwner : TComponent);override;
      destructor  destroy; override;
    published
      { Published declarations }
    end;

procedure Register;

implementation

procedure TUpdateClock.UpdateCaption;
{This Routine Calls The UpdateClockProc with the }
{accurate time                                   }
begin
    UpdateClockProc(TimeToStr(Now));
end;

procedure TUpdateClock.Execute;
{ Loop until we are told to terminate and then exit}
begin
 while (not Terminated) do
 begin
  Synchronize(UpdateCaption);
  Sleep(1000);
 end
end;

constructor TButClock.Create(AOwner : TComponent);
begin
    inherited Create(AOwner);
    {Create the Worker thread in suspended mode}
    MainThread := TUpdateClock.Create(True);
    {Set the callback pointer}
    MainThread.UpdateClockProc := UpdateCaption;
    {Release the thread from suspended mode}
    MainThread.Resume;
end;

destructor TButClock.Destroy;
{Called when the component is destroyed}
```

13

```
begin
   { tell the thread to terminate}
   MainThread.Terminate;
   { Wait for termination }
   MainThread.WaitFor;
   { Cleanup TButClock}
   inherited Destroy;
end;

procedure TButClock.UpdateCaption(X : String);
{Set the caption when told to do so}
begin
   Caption := X;
end;

procedure Register;
begin
  RegisterComponents('Samples', [TButClock]);
end;

end.
```

ANALYSIS   The analysis of this code is presented in the following sections.

The Constructor

The constructor first executes any necessary code from its parent. In this case, the object is a descendent of TButton, so it is important that the button does whatever allocation or initialization is necessary for it to function properly. After you call the inherited constructor, you create an instance of the TUpdateClock worker thread class by calling its create method. The create method is passed True to indicate that the thread should be suspended when it is created. After the thread is created, you need to do the following:

1. Set the thread's UpdateClockProc property to the UpdateCaption procedure. This tells the thread what to do when it is time to update the button's caption.

2. Release the thread from suspended mode by calling Resume, as shown in the following code:

```
constructor TButClock.Create(AOwner : TComponent);
begin
    inherited Create(AOwner);
    {Create the Worker thread in suspended mode}
    MainThread := TUpdateClock.Create(True);
    {Set the callback pointer}
    MainThread.UpdateClockProc := UpdateCaption;
    {Release the thread from suspended mode}
    MainThread.Resume;
end;
```

13

The Destructor

For the destructor, you need to tell the thread to terminate and then wait for termination before the TButClock component can be safely destroyed, as shown here:

```
destructor TButClock.Destroy;
{Called when the component is destroyed}
begin
   { Tell the thread to terminate}
   MainThread.Terminate;
   { Wait for termination }
   MainThread.WaitFor;
   { Cleanup TButClock}
   inherited Destroy;
end;
```

The UpdateCaption Procedure

The worker thread calls UpdateCaption and passes it the Time to update the caption with, as shown in the following code (you could have put the time logic in this procedure, and it would work just as well).

```
procedure TButClock.UpdateCaption(X : String);
{Set the caption when told to do so}
begin
   Caption := X;
end;
```

The Register Procedure

You finish the component with the Register procedure, which states that the TButClock component should be placed on the Samples page of the visual component library, as shown in this code:

```
procedure Register;
begin
  RegisterComponents('Samples', [TButClock]);
end;
end.
```

Using the Button Clock

After you build the button clock component, it is ready for use. When you add the component to a form at design time, it actually keeps time even before the program is compiled. You did not modify the functionality of the Caption property so that it can be read; it indicates the current time. You have not prevented the user from writing to the Caption field. Whatever he writes to the Caption property is overwritten with the current time the next time that the worker thread writes the new time. Figure 13.8 shows an application using the button clock component.

Figure 13.8.

Using the button clock.

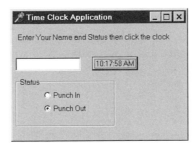

Declaring a New Event—`UserPlot`

When you worked with `TMult`, you saw how to add an event to a component. You made some assumptions, though. You declared the property as a `TNotifyEvent` type. For passing other parameters to or from an event, Delphi declared `TNotify` as a pointer to a function that is passed a `TObject` as a parameter. If an event must use other parameters, you can declare the appropriate type. The following example shows how to declare a new event type. It is used to create an event that passes a real number to the event handler and returns a different real number by using a `var` parameter.

Depending on the types of applications that you design, the component you write in this section might be useful. It is often necessary to plot a mathematical function graphically. Many components enable you to create a graph by supplying a set of points, but few enable you to simply supply the function that you want to plot. This component does exactly that. An event called `OnUserFunc` is defined. It passes an X value and wants a Y value returned. The range and scale factors are set as properties. Therefore, if you want to plot the function $Y=X^2$, you add the component to your form and the following code to the `OnUserFunc` event:

```
procedure TForm1.FuncGraph1UserFunc(X: Real; var Y: Real);
begin
  Y := X * X;
end;
```

The `TFuncGraph` component handles all the scaling and transforms the coordinates. Essentially, you need to type only one line of code. The other examples in this chapter showed you how to implement most of this component. The entire code for `TFuncGraph` appears in Listing 13.7. The following sections focus on how to define a new event type and how to create an event based on the new type.

13

TYPE   **Listing 13.7. The** `TFuncGraph` **component.**

```
unit PlotChart;

interface

uses
  Windows, Messages, SysUtils, Classes, Graphics, Controls,
  Forms, Dialogs;

type
  TUserPlotFunc = procedure(X : real ; var Y : real) of object;
  TFuncGraph = class(TGraphicControl)
  private
     { Private declarations }
     FRangeMinX : integer;
     FRangeMaxX : integer;
     FRangeMinY : integer;
     FRangeMaxY : integer;
     FUserFunc  : TUserPlotFunc;
  protected
     { Protected declarations }
     procedure paint; override;
  public
     { Public declarations }
     constructor Create(Aowner : TComponent); override;
  published
     { Published declarations }
     property RangeMinX : integer read FRangeMinX write FRangeMinX;
     property RangeMaxX : integer read FRangeMaxX write FRangeMaxX;
     property RangeMinY : integer read FRangeMinY write FRangeMinY;
     property RangeMaxY : integer read FRangeMaxY write FRangeMaxY;
     property OnUserFunc : TUserPlotFunc read FUserFunc write FUserFunc;
     property Width default 50;
     property Height default 50;
  end;

procedure Register;

implementation

constructor TFuncGraph.Create(Aowner : TComponent);
begin
{simply set default width and height and range}
   inherited Create(AOwner);
   Height := 50;
   Width  := 50;
   FRangeMaxX := 1;
   FRangeMaxY := 1;
end;

procedure TFuncGraph.Paint;
var
  X,Y  : integer; {Real Pixels}
  RX,RY : real;    {Users Coordinates}
```

```
begin
  inherited Paint;
  Canvas.Rectangle(0,0,Width,Height);
  For X := 1 to Width do
    begin
      {convert X into user's X     }
      {Note the Width cannot be 0 }
      RX := FRangeMinX + (((FRangeMaxX - FRangeMinX)/Width)*X);

      {If the component user has assigned a plot function}
      {call the function, otherwise set RY = 0            }
      if assigned(FUserFunc) then
        FUserFunc(RX,RY)
       else
        RY := 0;

      {Now convert RY back into pixel coordinates}
      Y := round((1-((RY-FRangeMinY)/(FRangeMaxY-FRangeMinY)))* Height);
      if X = 1 then
        Canvas.MoveTo(X,Y)
       else
        Canvas.LineTo(X,Y);
    end;

end;

procedure Register;
begin
  RegisterComponents('Additional', [TFuncGraph]);
end;

end.
```

ANALYSIS   The analysis of this listing is presented in the following sections.

Creating a New Event Type

The key to this component is to enable the user to define an arbitrary function to plot. You do this by implementing a new event type, TUserPlotFunc, whose definition is as follows:

```
TUserPlotFunc = procedure(X : real ; var Y : real) of object;
```

This type is declared in the type section of the unit. Note that TUserPlotFunc is a procedure—which looks strange in the type section. This means that you can declare a variable that is a pointer to a procedure that takes the arguments defined in the type declaration. Once the type is set up, you define a published property of TUserPlotFunc to create an event that uses the defined parameters, as shown here:

```
published
   property OnUserFunc : TUserPlotFunc read FUserFunc write FUserFunc;
```

13

When the component is installed, a new event called OnUserFunc is listed, as shown in the following code snippet. If the user double-clicks the event, Delphi creates a new procedure with the correct parameters.

```
procedure TForm1.FuncGraph1UserFunc(X: Real; var Y: Real);
begin

end;
```

Calling the Event

To call the user's event handler from your component, call the variable that points to the procedure and pass the necessary parameters. Make sure that a valid event is defined. To check whether an event is defined, call the assigned function. Here is an example of calling the user's function:

```
if assigned(FUserFunc) then
        FUserFunc(RX,RY)
```

Using TFuncGraph

Figure 13.9 shows how powerful a custom event can be. By typing only eight lines of code, as you can see in Listing 13.8, you can graph four mathematical functions. This is truly rapid application development.

Figure 13.9.

Using the TFuncGraph *component to graph four mathematical functions.*

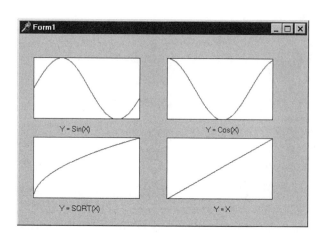

13

Type | **Listing 13.8. Test program for** TFuncGraph.

```
unit unitPlotApp;

interface

uses
  Windows, Messages, SysUtils, Classes, Graphics, Controls,
  Forms, Dialogs,
  StdCtrls, PlotChart;

type
  TForm1 = class(TForm)
    FuncGraph4: TFuncGraph;
    FuncGraph1: TFuncGraph;
    FuncGraph2: TFuncGraph;
    FuncGraph3: TFuncGraph;
    Label1: TLabel;
    Label2: TLabel;
    Label3: TLabel;
    Label4: TLabel;
    procedure FuncGraph1UserFunc(X: Real; var Y: Real);
    procedure FuncGraph3UserFunc(X: Real; var Y: Real);
    procedure FuncGraph4UserFunc(X: Real; var Y: Real);
    procedure FuncGraph2UserFunc(X: Real; var Y: Real);
  private
    { Private declarations }
  public
    { Public declarations }
  end;

var
  Form1: TForm1;

implementation

{$R *.DFM}

procedure TForm1.FuncGraph1UserFunc(X: Real; var Y: Real);
begin
  Y := X;
end;

procedure TForm1.FuncGraph3UserFunc(X: Real; var Y: Real);
begin
  Y := Cos(X);
end;

procedure TForm1.FuncGraph4UserFunc(X: Real; var Y: Real);
begin
  Y := Sin(X);
end;
```

continues

13

Listing 13.8. continued

```
procedure TForm1.FuncGraph2UserFunc(X: Real; var Y: Real);
begin
  Y := sqrt(X);
end;

end.
```

ANALYSIS This simple test application plots four functions, Y=X, Y=sin(X), Y=cos(X), and y=√(x). The scale for the Y coordinates as well as the range of X are set by the properties of each of the four coordinates. The TLabel components are simply used to write a caption under each graph.

An Overview of ActiveX and ActiveX Components

Microsoft originally introduced OLE (object linking and embedding) in order to provide a standard that enabled objects to communicate with a host application. The original specification was aimed at a way to enable an application, such as Excel, to embed a spreadsheet into any other application that supported the OLE standard. OLE 1.*x* was missing some critical functionality, and an OLE 2.0 specification was written and implemented. At that point, it became clear that OLE supported the foundations for a technology that enabled generic objects to be shared, the component object model (COM). This concept was used to create a component specification for OCX components. OLE was a quite misleading acronym because COM can be used for much more than embedding and linking objects. This brings us to the current standard ActiveX and ActiveX components, the outgrowth of OLE and OCXs built on top of COM.

COM can be thought of as the binary standard for sharing components between two pieces of code. COM abstracts the implementation of an object from the functions that the object can perform. The functions that an object can perform are described in its interfaces. An interface is an access method to a set of logically related functions that an object can implement. Each object class has a unique class ID (CLSID) that supports an arbitrary set of interfaces. All classes must support the IUnknown interface that can then be used to access any other interfaces that the class supports. This is done through the QueryInterface function, which is always supplied in the IUnknown interface. The QueryInterface function allows an application to ask the question, "Hey object, do you support functions that enable me to *xxxx*?" The object either will reply, "Yes, and here is where these functions can be accessed," or, "No, I do not support those functions." This is an extremely powerful object model because it enables an application at runtime to determine if an arbitrary object can perform a task.

COM objects are implemented through several methods. The COM object can be compiled into a DLL or an OCX that runs in the same process space as the calling application. A COM object also can run in its own process space as a compiled executable. With distributed COM (DCOM), the object can run on a different machine, anywhere in the world. The COM system services remove the complexity of calling COM objects even though the implementation code may be in a different process or on a different machine. ActiveX components are COM objects that implement a base set of interfaces that enable the component to be embedded into applications that can host ActiveX components.

Here is the good news: Delphi makes creating ActiveX components painless. You can take an existing Delphi visual component and turn it into an ActiveX component. The host application then will be able to manipulate properties and respond to events just as a Delphi application can with visual components. You also can add new properties, methods, and events to the ActiveX component to provide additional functionality.

Turning a Visual Component into an ActiveX Component

The first step in creating a new ActiveX component is to create a new ActiveX library. To create the library, choose File | New from the Delphi menu bar, select the ActiveX tab, and then choose ActiveX Library. This creates a new project that will compile to a .OCX file (the actual module that stores the ActiveX components). Next, choose File | New from the Delphi menu. In the resulting dialog box, choose ActiveX Control. The ActiveX Control Wizard appears. This wizard will generate the code needed to create an ActiveX control from an existing visual component.

The wizard requires three key pieces of information: what visual component the ActiveX component should be based on, the class for the new ActiveX component, and what the location of the implementation file should be. There are also options that enable you to use design licenses, versioning, and an About box. In the sample application you create in this section, you take the button clock visual component and turn it into an ActiveX control. Figure 13.10 shows how this looks in the ActiveX Control Wizard.

This wizard generates all the code necessary to compile the component to an ActiveX component. To compile the control, simply choose Project | Compile from the Delphi menu.

There are two methods of development that you can use to add functionality to an ActiveX control. The first is to add functionality to the visual component that the ActiveX control is based on and rebuild the ActiveX component. The other way is to add functionality directly to the ActiveX component. Let's take a look at what was actually generated by the ActiveX Control Wizard. First, examine the source code generated by the wizard; it's shown in Listing 13.9.

13

Figure 13.10.

*The ActiveX Control
Wizard.*

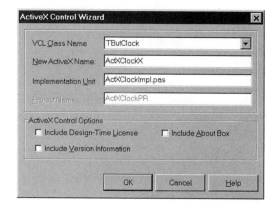

**Listing 13.9. ActiveX control source code generated by the
ActiveX Control Wizard for the button clock control.**

TYPE

```
unit ActXClockImpl;

interface

uses
  Windows, ActiveX, Classes, Controls, Graphics, Menus, Forms,
  ➥StdCtrls,
  ComServ, StdVCL, AXCtrls, ActXClockPR_TLB, unitTBC;

type
  TActXClockX = class(TActiveXControl, IActXClockX)
  private
    { Private declarations }
    FDelphiControl: TButClock;
    FEvents: IActXClockXEvents;
  protected
    { Protected declarations }
    procedure InitializeControl; override;
    procedure EventSinkChanged(const EventSink: IUnknown); override;
    procedure DefinePropertyPages(DefinePropertyPage:
      ➥TDefinePropertyPage); override;
    function Get_Cancel: WordBool; safecall;
    function Get_Caption: WideString; safecall;
    function Get_Cursor: Smallint; safecall;
    function Get_Default: WordBool; safecall;
    function Get_DragCursor: Smallint; safecall;
    function Get_DragMode: TxDragMode; safecall;
    function Get_Enabled: WordBool; safecall;
    function Get_Font: Font; safecall;
    function Get_Visible: WordBool; safecall;
    procedure Click; safecall;
    procedure Set_Cancel(Value: WordBool); safecall;
    procedure Set_Caption(const Value: WideString); safecall;
    procedure Set_Cursor(Value: Smallint); safecall;
```

13

```
      procedure Set_Default(Value: WordBool); safecall;
      procedure Set_DragCursor(Value: Smallint); safecall;
      procedure Set_DragMode(Value: TxDragMode); safecall;
      procedure Set_Enabled(Value: WordBool); safecall;
      procedure Set_Font(const Value: Font); safecall;
      procedure Set_Visible(Value: WordBool); safecall;
  end;

implementation

{ TActXClockX }

procedure TActXClockX.InitializeControl;
begin
  FDelphiControl := Control as TButClock;
end;

procedure TActXClockX.EventSinkChanged(const EventSink: IUnknown);
begin
  FEvents := EventSink as IActXClockXEvents;
end;

procedure TActXClockX.DefinePropertyPages(DefinePropertyPage:
  ➥TDefinePropertyPage);
begin
  { Define property pages here.  Property pages are defined by calling
    DefinePropertyPage with the class id of the page.  For example,
      DefinePropertyPage(Class_ActXClockXPage); }
end;

function TActXClockX.Get_Cancel: WordBool;
begin
  Result := FDelphiControl.Cancel;
end;

function TActXClockX.Get_Caption: WideString;
begin
  Result := WideString(FDelphiControl.Caption);
end;

function TActXClockX.Get_Cursor: Smallint;
begin
  Result := Smallint(FDelphiControl.Cursor);
end;

function TActXClockX.Get_Default: WordBool;
begin
  Result := FDelphiControl.Default;
end;

function TActXClockX.Get_DragCursor: Smallint;
begin
  Result := Smallint(FDelphiControl.DragCursor);
end;
```

13

continues

Listing 13.9. continued

```
function TActXClockX.Get_DragMode: TxDragMode;
begin
  Result := Ord(FDelphiControl.DragMode);
end;

function TActXClockX.Get_Enabled: WordBool;
begin
  Result := FDelphiControl.Enabled;
end;

function TActXClockX.Get_Font: Font;
begin
  GetOleFont(FDelphiControl.Font, Result);
end;

function TActXClockX.Get_Visible: WordBool;
begin
  Result := FDelphiControl.Visible;
end;

procedure TActXClockX.Click;
begin

end;

procedure TActXClockX.Set_Cancel(Value: WordBool);
begin
  FDelphiControl.Cancel := Value;
end;

procedure TActXClockX.Set_Caption(const Value: WideString);
begin
  FDelphiControl.Caption := TCaption(Value);
end;

procedure TActXClockX.Set_Cursor(Value: Smallint);
begin
  FDelphiControl.Cursor := TCursor(Value);
end;

procedure TActXClockX.Set_Default(Value: WordBool);
begin
  FDelphiControl.Default := Value;
end;

procedure TActXClockX.Set_DragCursor(Value: Smallint);
begin
  FDelphiControl.DragCursor := TCursor(Value);
end;
```

```
procedure TActXClockX.Set_DragMode(Value: TxDragMode);
begin
  FDelphiControl.DragMode := TDragMode(Value);
end;

procedure TActXClockX.Set_Enabled(Value: WordBool);
begin
  FDelphiControl.Enabled := Value;
end;

procedure TActXClockX.Set_Font(const Value: Font);
begin
  SetOleFont(FDelphiControl.Font, Value);
end;

procedure TActXClockX.Set_Visible(Value: WordBool);
begin
  FDelphiControl.Visible := Value;
end;

initialization
  TActiveXControlFactory.Create(
    ComServer,
    TActXClockX,
    TButClock,
    Class_ActXClockX,
    1,
    '',
    0);
end.
```

ANALYSIS   The way that the implementation works is that a new class is generated, TActXClockX, which has a TButClock visual component in the private section of the class definition. All the properties and methods for the ActiveX component are defined as procedures and functions in the ActiveX declaration. For example, the Cursor property is implemented with the function Get_Cursor, and the procedure Set_Cursor. These procedures are called when the Cursor property is set or read. Their implementation is generated automatically by the ActiveX Control Wizard.

In addition to the ActiveX implementation file that is generated, the ActiveX Control Wizard also builds a type library. A type library defines the interfaces and the properties for the components in an ActiveX library. Delphi includes a special type library editor that enables you to modify (and view) the type library information for an ActiveX control. To view the type library, choose View | Type Library, and you'll see what controls, interfaces, and property pages are in the project, along with their properties, events, and methods, as shown in Figure 13.11.

13

Figure 13.11.

The type library for the button clock ActiveX component.

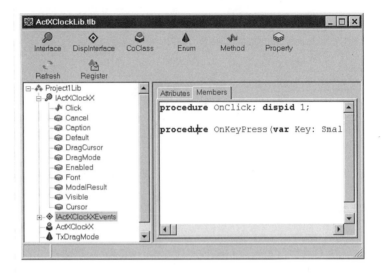

Adding a Method Directly to an ActiveX Component

It is also very easy to add properties, events, and methods directly to an ActiveX control. To demonstrate this, the sample application in this section has you add a new method called MakeBold that just sets the font of the caption to bold. To add the method, choose Edit | Add to Interface from the Delphi menu to bring up the Add To Interface dialog box. Make sure that Interface is set to Properties/Methods, and for Declaration, type **procedure MakeBold;**, as shown in Figure 13.12.

Figure 13.12.

Adding a method to the component.

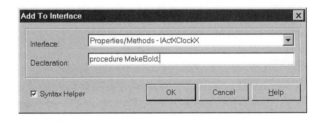

This did three things; it added the MakeBold method to the interface definition in the type library, added the MakeBold method to the class definition, and created a skeleton for the MakeBold procedure, which is shown in the following example:

```
procedure TActXClockX.MakeBold;
begin

end;
```

It is your job to finish the implementation code by adding the code to change the font. The final procedure reads as follows:

```
procedure TActXClockX.MakeBold;
begin
   FDelphiControl.Font.Style := [fsBold];
end;
```

The FDelphiControl referenced in this procedure is an instance of the TButClock component that is encapsulated in the ActiveX control. When the MakeBold method is called on the TActXClockX ActiveX component, the procedure sets the Font.Style property to fsBold in the encapsulated component. You can see the declaration of FDelphiControl in the class definition.

When you compile the project, you have an OCX containing the implementation for the ActiveX component. ActiveX components need to be registered on a system before they can be used. The ActiveX library is able to self-register if the host application is capable of calling the registration procedure. It also is possible to register the component within the Delphi IDE by choosing Run | Register ActiveX Server. For your sample component, register it now by using the Run | Register ActiveX Server menu option.

You also can use the Unregister ActiveX Server option to uninstall a control from your machine. One of the easiest ways to test your component is to use the Web Deploy command to have Delphi generate a test Web page with your component in it. You'll take this one step farther in the next section by embedding the clock component in a Web page that is scripted so that it interacts with other components on the page.

Using an ActiveX Component in a Scriptable Web Page

The real beauty in using ActiveX components is that they are language and application independent. In the sample application presented in this section, you create a Web page that has two ActiveX components: the all-too-familiar button clock, and Microsoft's standard command push button. You add some VBScript to the Web page so that, when the standard push button is clicked, the font on the button clock becomes bold. This Web page is shown in Figure 13.13.

The HTML to create this page is presented in Listing 13.10.

13

Figure 13.13.

*ActiveX components
in a Web page linked
together with
VBScript.*

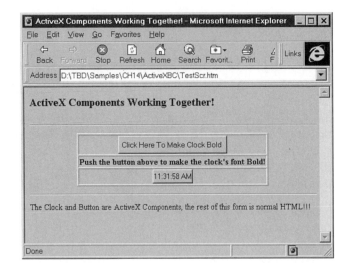

TYPE **Listing 13.10. HTML to create an ActiveX component page.**

```
<HTML>
<HEAD>
<TITLE>ActiveX Components Working Together!</TITLE>
</HEAD>
<BODY>
<H2>ActiveX Components Working Together! </H2>
<HR>
<CENTER><Table Border=1>
<TR><TD ALIGN=CENTER>
 <OBJECT ID="PushForBold" WIDTH=203 HEIGHT=32
 CLASSID="CLSID:D7053240-CE69-11CD-A777-00DD01143C57">
    <PARAM NAME="VariousPropertyBits" VALUE="268435483">
    <PARAM NAME="Caption" VALUE="Click Here To Make Clock Bold">
    <PARAM NAME="Size" VALUE="4313;678">
</OBJECT>
</TD></TR>
<TR><TH>Push the button above to make the clock's font Bold!</TH></TR>
<TR><TD ALIGN=CENTER>
 <OBJECT ID="ClockButton" WIDTH=75 HEIGHT=25
    CLASSID="CLSID:C8EE0B43-8C8F-11D0-9FB3-444553540000">
    </OBJECT>
</TD></TR></TABLE></CENTER><HR>
The Clock and Button are ActiveX Components,
the rest of this form is normal HTML!!!

<SCRIPT LANGUAGE="VBScript">
   Sub PushForBold_Click()
      call ClockButton.MakeBold()
   end sub
</SCRIPT>
</BODY>
</HTML>
```

ANALYSIS Each of the ActiveX components is marked by an <OBJECT> tag that includes an ID of what the component should be known as within the page. Within the object tag, information about the component is specified. The key piece of information is in the CLASSID property. This actually specifies what ActiveX component should be placed on the page for the object. Note that the class ID matches that of the CoClass GUID displayed in Delphi's type library viewer. The other parameters on the object tag specify any additional startup or initial parameters that should be used for the object. For example, on the normal command button, you set the caption to Click Here To Make Clock Bold. You specify an event handler by using VBScript to invoke the MakeBold method when the regular push button is clicked. You could have used JScript or any other scripting language that is supported.

Summary

Delphi is a premier product for writing applications. It also is a premier application for creating components that can be used both within Delphi and in other applications. You examined how components work and what is necessary to create, install, and use your own components. One of the most powerful features of Delphi's object model is that it is object oriented, which means you can take an existing component and enhance it. You also examined how to create and use ActiveX components. These components can be used within Delphi and in many other applications. The bottom line is that if you write your code as reusable components, the next time you need to perform a similar task, the component already will exist and be ready for use. This will save you immeasurable time.

Q&A

Q Can I create a visual component and not inherit any ancestor class?

A No. Every component must be a descendent of a class—even the most basic class, TComponent.

Q Can I integrate help into my component?

A Yes. Delphi gives many hooks for help. Review the component writer's guide for details.

Q Can I create custom property pages for my ActiveX components?

A Yes. You can choose File | New to access the New Items dialog box, select the ActiveX tab, and choose "property page." This page can then be linked to the component.

Q Can I turn an ActiveX component into a visual component?

A Yes. Delphi gives you the ability to create a visual component wrapper around an existing ActiveX component.

13

Workshop

The Workshop provides two ways for you to affirm what you've learned in this chapter. The Quiz section poses questions to help you solidify your understanding of the material covered. You can find answers to the quiz questions in Appendix A, "Answers to the Quiz Questions." The Exercises section provides you with experience in using what you have learned. Please try to work through all these before continuing to the next day.

Quiz

1. Are properties in components simply variables, or is it possible to link code to properties in a component?

2. What is the difference between properties that are available during development and those that are available only at runtime?

3. What is the difference between `published` and `public`?

4. What is the difference between how an event is defined and how a property is defined?

5. What are a class ID, a type library, and an interface used for?

6. Can ActiveX components be used outside of Delphi?

Exercises

1. Add a property to the `TButClock` component that enables a user to specify an alarm time. Also, add an `OnAlarm` event that is called when the specified time is reached.

2. Add the same functionality that Exercise 1 describes to the button clock ActiveX component.

3. Turn the `TPanel` component into an ActiveX control, and add functionality so it displays a message that an application can set using a property.

Day 14

Building Internet Applications with Delphi

In the last few years, one of the biggest buzzwords has been "Internet." What makes the Internet so powerful? One reason is protocols (the language that network applications use to communicate), which enable an average user to access information and applications from anywhere in the world. The same concept enables companies to make information and applications accessible to employees throughout a company using its intranet. An intranet is a private network that can have resources similar to those on the Internet, but they are accessible only to individuals who are granted access.

Many people think that "The Internet" and "The World Wide Web" are synonymous. They are not. The World Wide Web (WWW) is only one application, or set of protocols, that uses the Internet as a delivery mechanism. The Internet is the physical and logical network that connects all computers which are attached to it. The network protocol through which machines on the

Internet communicate is TCP/IP (transmission control protocol/internet protocol). WWW servers and browsers communicate through higher level protocols—mainly HyperText Transfer Protocol (HTTP) and File Transfer Protocol (FTP)—to communicate content and information between the client and server.

Note that applications now can be built to use any protocol that sits on top of TCP/IP and use the Internet to communicate. Similarly, you should not limit yourself to using the HTTP protocol only for browsing the Web because it can be used to enable any application to communicate with any other application. For example, if you wanted to develop a race car game where one driver could race against another, the data could be shared between the two programs using HTTP.

This chapter introduces you to basic World Wide Web concepts and how to use Delphi to produce robust server and client WWW applications. Delphi is an extremely powerful tool for creating Web-based applications. This chapter exposes only the tip of the iceberg of what can be developed with Delphi. Be sure to consult Delphi's online Help and manuals to fully comprehend the limitless power of the Web!

The Power of the HTTP and HTML Protocols

The two most influential protocols the Web uses are HTTP and HyperText Markup Language (HTML). Considering HTML a protocol is slightly misleading. HTML is simply a standard that describes the format of the content. This means that if you state that a document is based on the HTML standard, readers can interpret certain "tags" to have meaning. For example, consider a document that has the following content:

```
<HTML>
<B> This is Bold </B> <BR>This is not!
</HTML>
```

This would be interpreted as two lines of text with the first one stating "This is Bold" in a bold font and the second line stating "This is not!" in the standard font. The <B> tag turns bold on, the </B> tag turns bold off, and the <BR> tag indicates a line break. I won't go into any details of HTML here; however, there are many books on HTML syntax and many programs that generate HTML.

HTTP is one of the most powerful client/server network protocols. One reason it is so powerful is that it enables a client and server to communicate without having to maintain a persistent network connection. A URL is a universal resource location, such as http://www.borland.com, that represents an object on the Internet. If you use a Web browser to go to the URL http://www.borland.com, for example, the Web page is transferred to the browser and the user can read it. However, by the time the page has finished loading, the connection has been terminated. Think of the server as delivering a burst of data. For an application that has a large amount of time where the network is idle (such as when a user is reading a Web page), using bursts of data is powerful because the server can handle other requests for information and does not need to maintain the resources associated with maintaining idle connections.

So what is actually going on within the HTTP protocol? It is basically a transaction-oriented protocol where the client asks for a piece of data, and the server honors the request and then terminates the connection. The requested content can be almost anything such as HTML documents, images, applications, or other items that both the client and server "understand."

One final bit of commentary on the power of Web technology deals with universal resource locators, or URLs. A URL is just a string that is a universal key to content on the Internet. The real power of URLs is that they enable many different technologies to be used together with seamless integration. One Web server application written in Delphi can be transparently integrated with another Web application written in Perl on a different machine running a different operating system. An example of this scenario could involve a Delphi Web server application that returns product information to a Web browser. When users decide to purchase the product, they submit the product number to a Perl application on a UNIX server that is tied into the corporate shipping and distribution system.

The Hardware and Software You Need for the Examples in This Chapter

To use the server-based samples presented in this chapter, you need a Web server that supports CGI, ISAPI, NSAPI, or WIN-CGI (or any combination of these). Microsoft Internet Information Server or Personal Web Server (which ships with Windows NT 4.0) handle both CGI and ISAPI. There also are other servers that will run on Windows 95, such as the personal Web server that ships with Front Page 97. The difference between these different types of server applications is explained later in the chapter.

To use Active Forms, you need a browser that supports ActiveX, such as Microsoft Internet Explorer 3.0.

Static Content on the Internet

14

When the World Wide Web emerged, it contained almost exclusively static Web pages. This meant that when a Web browser selected a URL, the Web server would return the HTML document that corresponded to the URL. HTML could also contain hyperlinks to other

Web pages. From a server administration standpoint, the Web administrator (or Webmaster) simply would save HTML files in a logically mapped drive structure. This paradigm was fine for delivering static information, but it could not be used for anything interactive or for delivering Web content that was built on-the-fly.

Listing 14.1 presents an example of a simple static Web page.

TYPE | **Listing 14.1. A simple static Web page.**

```
<HTML>
<TITLE> Joe's Landscaping Supply Store </TITLE>
<BODY>
<H1> Joe's Landscaping Supply Store </H1>
<HR>
We specialize in making your yard look its best!
<BR>
<B> Call 1-800-FOR-JOES  </B> for more information!
<HR>
<A HREF="http://www.joes.com/prices">
Click Here For Price Information </A>
</BODY>
</HTML>
```

When the client (or browser) asks for `http:\\www.joes.com\default.htm`, the Web server sends back the contents of the file `default.htm`, with some additional bookkeeping information to the client. This may suit Joe's needs just fine, but it is rather dull and always will be the same every time a customer visits the page. Suppose Joe would like to enhance his page by having a random slogan presented every time his page is visited. How could you do that? The answer is with dynamic HTML.

Creating Dynamic Web Content with Delphi

One key point to remember with dynamically generated HTML is that *all* processing is done on the server. The server can no longer return just the contents of a file (because that would be static). Instead, if a dynamic request is made, the server will process custom code on the server to determine what to send back to the client. The server can process this code using several techniques. The two most common methods to process customized code are either to spawn an executable that tells the server what to return, or to invoke a DLL that executes custom code and tells the server what to return.

Delphi supports four types of server-side processes to produce dynamic HTML, including the following:

Process	DLL or EXE
ISAPI	DLL
NSAPI	DLL
CGI	EXE
WIN-CGI	EXE

This chapter focuses mainly on ISAPI processes and CGI applications; however, NSAPI processes are very similar to ISAPI, and WIN-CGI is very similar to CGI. So what is a CGI application, and what is an ISAPI DLL? Why should you use one or the other? These questions are answered in the next section.

Differences Between ISAPI, NSAPI, CGI, and WIN-CGI

Executable server processes, such as CGI and WIN-CGI, and in-process DLLs, such as ISAPI and NSAPI, both have advantages and disadvantages.

Common gateway interface (CGI) applications were the first type of application that produced dynamic HTML. When a Web server receives a request to process a CGI, it passes all information from the client to the CGI application in environment variables and standard input. The CGI application basically returns the HTML that should be sent to the client through standard output. It actually is more complex than this in the sense that headers and commands can be transferred, but this is the general idea.

To demonstrate how a CGI application works, you'll write a standard console executable that functions as a simple CGI application (this is not the best way to write Web applications in Delphi, but it is important to understand what is happening). Listing 14.2 says hello and displays the current time. Once the program has been compiled, you simply need to place the executable in a directory that has Web-execute privileges on your Web server. The user then simply accesses the URL that points to the application, as shown in Figure 14.1.

14

Listing 14.2. A simple CGI executable using a console application.

TYPE

```
program consolecgi;

uses
  SysUtils;

begin
  writeln('Content-Type:text/html');
  writeln;
  writeln('<H1> Hello </H1> <HR>');
  writeln('The Current Time is '+TimeToStr(Time));
end.
```

Figure 14.1.

A Web client accessing the simple console CGI application.

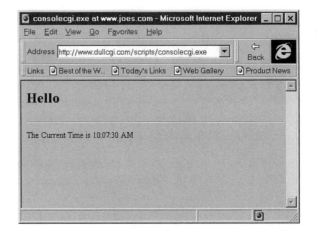

ANALYSIS   This application works by simply sending the data that needs to be sent to the client to standard output by using a series of Writeln statements. You might be thinking that was so easy you'd like to write all your Web applications as console CGI applications. You could do this, but you would not be able to use the common framework that Delphi provides for developing server-side applications. Delphi's Web server framework, which you'll hear about shortly, can be used to keep a common code base for both executable and in-process Web processes. It also provides routines for doing a lot of the grunt work associated with developing CGI and ISAPI/NSAPI applications.

One of the best reasons to develop CGI applications over ISAPI (Internet server API) or NSAPI (Netscape server API) applications is that almost every Windows-based Web server can use the same compiled executable. The best situation in which not to choose CGI is when performance is a major concern. Every time a client application calls a CGI program, the Web server needs to create a new process, execute the CGI executable, return results to the client,

14

and finally clean up any resources. That is a lot of work for the Web server to perform if it is being bombarded by many requests. Wouldn't it be nice if the Web server could execute your custom logic within its own process space and not need to spawn a new executable each time a dynamic request is made? You bet. This is exactly what ISAPI (and NSAPI) applications do. ISAPI is Microsoft's version of their Web server API, and NSAPI is Netscape's version.

NEW TERM An ISAPI application is a thread-safe DLL that runs in the process space of the Web server. When an HTTP request is made that calls the ISAPI DLL, the Web server takes a thread from its thread pool and starts the thread executing in the DLL. A *thread pool* is a set of worker threads that the Web server manages. This pool can dynamically grow or shrink depending on the server's load. After results have been returned to the client, the thread can be returned to the thread pool. This is a much more efficient use of system resources than spawning a new process. One disadvantage of using ISAPI is that thread-safe code can be difficult to write and test. Another is that with an ISAPI application, once the DLL is loaded by the server, you need to stop the server if you want to replace the DLL.

The Delphi Web Server Framework

It seems like a difficult decision to choose between CGI applications and in-process DLLs (ISAPI and NSAPI). The good news is that with Delphi you can maintain a common code base and compile the project to a CGI, WIN-CGI, ISAPI, and NSAPI application.

Rewrite your simple time CGI application using the Delphi Web framework, as follows:

1. Start Delphi.
2. Choose File | New to bring up the New Items dialog.
3. In the New tab, choose the Web server application and click OK.
4. You will be prompted for the type of server you want to build. For now, choose CGI Stand alone executable, and click OK.

This creates a new project with one Web module and the correct settings to build the CGI executable. The next step is to add custom logic to the application. Follow these steps:

1. Set the Name property on the WebModule to **CurrentTimeDisp**.
2. Double-click the Actions property of the CurrentTimeDisp Web module form. This brings up a new dialog box entitled Editing CurrentTimeDisp.Actions. The dialog box has four columns: Name, PathInfo, Enabled, and Default.
3. Click on the Add button. This adds a new line to the actions table.
4. Click on the new line and use the Object Inspector to change the name of the new object to **DefaultAction**.

14

5. Double-click on the OnAction event in the Object Inspector to build the prototype for the event handler. This is the code that should execute when the Web server is called.

6. Edit this event handler so that it looks as follows:

```
procedure TCurrentTimeDisp.CurrentTimeDispDefaultActionAction(
  Sender: TObject;
  Request: TWebRequest;
  Response: TWebResponse;
  var Handled: Boolean);
begin
   Response.Content :=  '<H1> Hello </H1> <HR>' +
                        'The Current Time is '+
                        TimeToStr(SysUtils.Time);
end;
```

7. Save and compile the project to WEBTIME.EXE.

8. Place the executable file in an "executable directory" on your Web server. You should now be able to call this CGI application just as before. The client simply needs to specify the correct URL to execute the CGI application on the server, as shown in Figure 14.2.

Figure 14.2.

Hello CGI application built using Delphi's Web server framework.

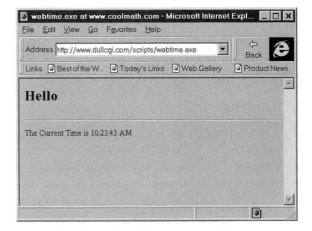

Converting the CGI Application to an ISAPI DLL

It is trivial to convert the CGI application to an ISAPI DLL (and maintain a common code base). Here are all the steps necessary to convert your Webtime sample to an ISAPI DLL.

1. Close any open projects.

2. Create a new Web server application, and choose (ISAPI/NSAPI) for the type of applications.

3. Use the Project Manager to remove the default unit and to add the unit that was created in the last example.

4. Compile the application to a DLL. That's it.

NOTE

> Remember when testing an ISAPI DLL that if you make any changes to the DLL, you will not be able to recopy the DLL to the Web server share until you stop and restart the Web service. This is not necessary for CGI applications because the new process is called each time a request is made. To execute the application, the user simply needs to specify the DLL in the URL. Here's an example:
>
> ```
> http://www.mysite.com/scripts/webtime.dll
> ```

Building "Real" Web Applications

Now that you know it's basically the same process to build any type of Web application with Delphi, you can concentrate on the core issue of Web application development: choosing whether you want to use CGI, WIN-CGI, ISAPI, or NSAPI.

The Web Transaction Model versus Event-Driven Programming

In Win32 GUI applications, the application is event-driven. There are components and forms that have event handlers which respond to different things that the user does. With a Web application, the user is not maintaining a constant connection with the Web server; therefore, every transaction must be considered an independent event. One of the challenges to this paradigm is that there is no inherent persistent storage. Each Web transaction is unaware of anything that has happened previously.

Think of what it would take to write a simple puzzle game in Delphi that runs as a Windows application. The configuration of the board could be kept in a structure, and every time the user made a move, the puzzle's configuration could be updated. This is somewhat more difficult in a Web server application because you need to "fake" persistent storage. In the sample application presented in the next section, you fake persistent storage by sending all information that the server needs every time the client makes a new request.

14

The Puzzle Sample

Consider a simple puzzle game you might have played at some time. There is a three-by-three grid that contains eight tiles—one slot is empty. The tiles can slide such that any tile next to the empty slot can slide into that spot. The object of the game is to arrange the tiles so they are in consecutive order with the empty slot in the lower-right corner, as shown in the following example:

```
3  2  6       3  2  6                      1  2  3
1  8  4  →    1  8  X    Eventually  →     4  5  6
7  5  X       7  5  4                      7  8  X
```

This example demonstrates three key concepts that are useful in developing Delphi Web server applications:

- [ ] How to enable a single application to perform multiple tasks using path information to trigger multiple events in the Action property on a Web form.
- [ ] How to read information passed from the client to the server using the TWebRequest object.
- [ ] How to simulate persistent storage by passing information from the client.

To build this sample application, follow these steps:

1. Create a new Web server application.
2. In the Actions property of the Web form, set up two Action objects, one with the Path property set to /**BOARD**, and the other left blank, as shown in Figure 14.3.

Figure 14.3.

The Action *editor for the Web module showing the two* Action *objects.*

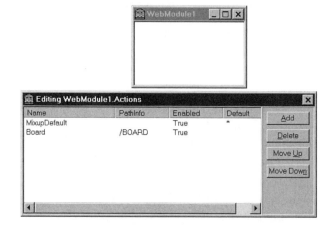

Listing 14.3 shows the source code needed for the rest of the implementation. The CanMove, BuildRef, and DrawBoard functions are stand-alone helper functions that you can enter into

the unit manually. The two Action events can be added by double-clicking on the OnAction event item for both actions. The current implementation assumes that the executable will be in the virtual directory scripts and the executable will be called TileGame.EXE.

TYPE Listing 14.3. A Web-based tile puzzle.

```
unit tgUnit;

interface

uses
  Windows, Messages, SysUtils, Classes, HTTPApp;

type
  TWebModule1 = class(TWebModule)
    procedure WebModule1BoardAction(Sender: TObject;
      Request: TWebRequest;
      Response: TWebResponse; var Handled: Boolean);
    procedure WebModule1WebActionItem1Action(Sender: TObject;
      Request: TWebRequest; Response: TWebResponse;
      var Handled: Boolean);
  private
    { Private declarations }
  public
    { Public declarations }
  end;

var
  WebModule1: TWebModule1;

implementation

{$R *.DFM}
function CanMove(X,Y:integer):boolean;
Var
   PossibleMoves : Array[0..8,0..8] of boolean;
   CountX,CountY : integer;
{Given that X is the missing Tile, this function answers the question}
{Can Position Y move to the Blank Space X?                          }
begin
  {Set All Moves to not Possible}
  For CountX := 0 to 8 do
    For CountY := 0 to 8 do
      PossibleMoves[CountX,CountY] := False;
  {Allow Adjacent tiles to Slide}
  {Tile 0 Missing} PossibleMoves[0,1] := True;
                   PossibleMoves[0,3] := True;
  {Tile 1 Missing} PossibleMoves[1,0] := True;
                   PossibleMoves[1,2] := True;
                   PossibleMoves[1,4] := True;
  {Tile 2 Missing} PossibleMoves[2,1] := True;
                   PossibleMoves[2,5] := True;
```

14

continues

Listing 14.3. continued

```
            {Tile 3 Missing} PossibleMoves[3,0] := True;
                             PossibleMoves[3,4] := True;
                             PossibleMoves[3,6] := True;
            {Tile 4 Missing} PossibleMoves[4,1] := True;
                             PossibleMoves[4,3] := True;
                             PossibleMoves[4,5] := True;
                             PossibleMoves[4,7] := True;
            {Tile 5 Missing} PossibleMoves[5,2] := True;
                             PossibleMoves[5,4] := True;
                             PossibleMoves[5,8] := True;
            {Tile 6 Missing} PossibleMoves[6,3] := True;
                             PossibleMoves[6,7] := True;
            {Tile 7 Missing} PossibleMoves[7,4] := True;
                             PossibleMoves[7,6] := True;
                             PossibleMoves[7,8] := True;
            {Tile 8 Missing} PossibleMoves[8,5] := True;
                             PossibleMoves[8,7] := True;
          CanMove := PossibleMoves[X,Y];
        end;

        function BuildRef(Tiles : Array of integer;Tile1,Tile2:integer):string;
        {This procedure builds the reference for the selected piece         }
        {It Needs to Swap the tile that was clicked on with the blank space}
        Var
          Count    : integer;
          RefBuilt : string;

        begin
          {The following line would refer to a .DLL if ISAPI}
          RefBuilt:= '/scripts/TILEGAME.EXE/BOARD?';
          for Count := 0 to 8 do
          begin
             if Tiles[Count]=Tile1 then
              RefBuilt := RefBuilt + IntToStr(Tile2)
             else if Tiles[Count]=Tile2 then
              RefBuilt := RefBuilt + IntToStr(Tile1)
             else
              RefBuilt := RefBuilt + IntToStr(Tiles[Count]);
          end;
          BuildRef := RefBuilt;
        end;

        procedure DrawBoard(Tiles : Array of integer;Response: TWebResponse);
        { Here we actually Draw the Board. Note that we are passed a }
        {TWebResponse Object and then set its content property to the}
        {corresponding HTML                                         }
        Var
            BlankSpace : Integer;
            Count      : Integer;

        begin
         { Place Heading HTML }
```

14

```
Response.content:='<TITLE> Tile Puzzle Game </TITLE>';
Response.content:=Response.content+'<H1> Tile Puzzle Game </H1><HR>';
Response.content:=Response.content+'<CENTER><TABLE BORDER = 1><TR>';
BlankSpace := 9;

{Figure out which tile is missing (tile 0)}
For Count := 0 to 8 do
 if Tiles[Count] = 0 then BlankSpace := Count;

{Loop through all 9 squares}
For Count := 0 to 8 do
begin
  {Check to see if current tile is the missing tile}
  if Tiles[Count] = 0 then
    Response.content := Response.content +'<TD>X<TD>'
  {Check to see if we can slide the current tile into the blank space}
  else if CanMove(BlankSpace,Count) then
          begin
            Response.content := Response.content +'<TD> <A HREF="'+
                                BuildRef(Tiles,0,Tiles[Count])+'">'+
                                IntToStr(Tiles[Count])+' </A><TD>'
          end
        else
          Response.content := Response.content +'<TD>'+
                              IntToStr(Tiles[Count])+'<TD>';
  { At the end of every row, terminate the row and start a new one}
  if Count Mod 3 = 2 then
    Response.content := Response.content + '</TR><TR>';
end;
{close the table}
Response.content := Response.content +
                    '</TR></TABLE></CENTER><HR> Tilegame V.1.0';
end;

procedure TWebModule1.WebModule1BoardAction(Sender: TObject;
  Request: TWebRequest; Response: TWebResponse; var Handled: Boolean);
{When the user moves, the Board Path is invoked, this simple      }
{pulls the new board configuration out of the query string,       }
{checks to see if the user has won and if not redraws the board }
var
  Tiles : array[0..8] of integer;
  Count : integer;
  TempTile : string;

begin
    {Check to see if we have a winner}
    if Request.Query = '123456780' THEN
     begin
      Response.Content := '<H1> You Win! </H1> <HR>';
      Response.Content := Response.Content+
                          '<A HREF="/scripts/tilegame.exe">'+
                          'Click Here To Play Again </A> <HR>';
     end
    else
```

14

continues

Listing 14.3. continued

```
              {If not, pull board config out of Request.Query and redraw board}
              begin
               for Count := 0 to 8 do
               begin
                 TempTile :=  copy(Request.Query,Count+1,1);
                 Tiles[Count] := StrToInt(TempTile);
               end;
               DrawBoard(Tiles,Response);
              end;
end;

procedure TWebModule1.WebModule1WebActionItem1Action(Sender: TObject;
  Request: TWebRequest; Response: TWebResponse; var Handled: Boolean);
{This procedure is called when a new game is requested (NO BOARD path}
var
    Count       : integer;
    BlankCount : integer;
    BlankTile  : integer;
    TryMove     : integer;
    Tiles       : Array[0..8] of Integer;

begin
 Randomize;
 { Set Board to Initial State  }
 For Count := 0 to 7 do
    Tiles[Count] := Count +1;
 { Last Tile is missing (represented by 0)}
 Tiles[8] := 0;

 {Mix up board by randomly sliding tiles 100 times}
 For Count := 0 to 100 do
 begin
    {Find the Blank Tile}
    BlankTile := 0;
    for BlankCount := 0 to 8 do
      if Tiles[BlankCount] = 0 then
        BlankTile := BlankCount;
    repeat
      TryMove := Random(9);
    until CanMove(BlankTile,TryMove);
    Tiles[BlankTile] := Tiles[TryMove];
    Tiles[TryMove]    := 0;
 end;

 {Draw the Initial Board}
 DrawBoard(Tiles,Response);
end;

end.
```

14

 The Web module can support multiple Paths. A path is the portion of the HTTP request URL following the application, but before the query string. For example, the following HTTP URL:

```
http://www.dogfood.com/showdogs.exe/LOOKUP_BREED?DOGTYPE=Beagle
```

would contain a path of Path="/LOOKUP_BREED" and a query string of DOGTYPE=Beagle. Therefore, by passing a Web application multiple paths, you can cause it to implement multiple functions. You use two paths in this application. The first one is blank, which means that if the application is invoked without a path, the OnAction event handler will be invoked. In the tile game, this randomizes the board and starts a new game. You use the BuildRef function to place anchors behind any tiles that can be moved to the empty slot (the logic for this is in the CanMove function). The anchor contains a /BOARD path and a query string equal to what the board would look like if that tile were chosen. Note that an HTML Anchor is the set of tags that enable it to act as a hot link. You are basically looking one move ahead for all the possible moves the user may choose. When a /BOARD path request is entered, the application invokes the OnAction event handler associated with this path. The /BOARD path event handler checks to see if the game has been won. If the user has won the game, a message is displayed. Otherwise, the board is simply redrawn in the configuration passed in by the query string.

An example of this application at work is shown in Figure 14.4.

Figure 14.4.

Web server tile game.

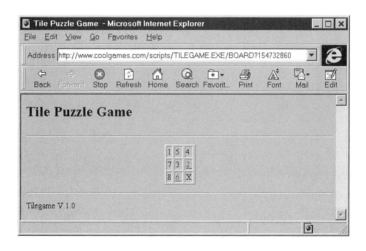

The Query string comes from the TWebRequest object, which is passed to the PathInfo event handler. This object contains all the information that the client (likely a Web browser) has sent the server. The application's job is to take any information needed from the client from this object, execute its logic, and send information back to the client through the TWebResponse object.

Obtaining Information from the Client Using Forms

You've seen server applications that execute without any client input, such as the Webtime application, and applications that examine the query string for customized input, such as the tile game application. In this section, you look at how your application can use forms in order to receive and process data from the WWW browsers.

Forms use standard input components such as buttons, drop-down list boxes, check boxes, and other components to get data from a user and send it to the Web server. Figure 14.5 shows a simple page with a form used to get a customer's phone number.

Figure 14.5.

A Web page with a simple Form.

The client takes all the input typed into the form, encodes it into a special format, and sends it to the server. Listing 14.4 shows the source code for the HTML page that is shown in Figure 14.5.

TYPE Listing 14.4. HTML to produce simple form's page.

```
<html>
<head>
<meta http-equiv="Content-Type"
content="text/html; charset=iso-8859-1">
<title>Joe'</title>
</head>
```

14

```
<body bgcolor="#FFFFFF">

<h2>Joe's Landscape and Supply</h2>

<hr>

<h4>To have a sales representative contact you please enter your
name and phone number below:</h4>

<form action="http://www.joeslandscape.com/scripts/maillist.exe"
method="GET" name="Mailing List">
    <div align="center"><center><table border="0">
        <tr>
            <td>Name: </td>
            <td><input type="text" size="20" name="Name"></td>
        </tr>
        <tr>
            <td>Phone</td>
            <td><input type="text" size="20" name="Phone"
            value="(XXX)-XXX-XXXX"></td>
        </tr>
        <tr>
            <td align="center" colspan="2"><input type="submit"
            name="B1" value="Submit"></td>
        </tr>
    </table>
    </center></div>
</form>

<p> </p>
</body>
</html>
```

ANALYSIS   This listing contains three input tags. These tags correspond to the two input boxes and one push button on the form. Think of the input components as being variables that will be set to some values when the form is submitted. In this case, the Name and Phone variables will be returned to the Web server with information that was typed. The information is passed to the Web server application specified in the action section; in this case, the data will be sent to the following URL:

```
http://www.joeslandscape.com/scripts/maillist.exe
```

One important part of the form is the method section of the form tag. This specifies that the data from the form either should be included in the application's URL as a query string or passed independently from the query string. A method of Get sends the data in the URL, a method of Post sends the data from the form as content (such as through standard input for a CGI application). This is important because there are different properties that need to be accessed in the TWebRequest object depending on whether a GET or POST request is issued.

14

What actually is passed to the Web application? You can find out by creating a simple Web application that displays the Query string from a form. This application only needs a default path handler with the following OnAction event handler:

```
procedure TWebModule1.WebModule1WebActionItem1Action(Sender: TObject;
  Request: TWebRequest; Response: TWebResponse; var Handled: Boolean);
begin
  Response.Content := Request.Query;
end;
```

Compile this to MAILLIST.EXE and place it on the Web server in the scripts (or any executable) directory. What happens when you type a name of **Steve O'Donohue** and a phone number of **(919)-123-4567** into the sample form generated by Listing 14.4? The Web server processes the request and displays the following string:

```
Name=Steve+O%92Donohue&Phone=%28919%29-123-4567&B1=Submit
```

It looks something like Steve O'Donohue and the phone number you typed, but there sure is a lot of other weird stuff in there. This is the encoded string returned from the form. The encoding scheme is as follows:

- [ ] All fields (variables) are separated by &s.
- [ ] Field names precede data with an equal sign (=).
- [ ] Spaces are converted to plus signs (+).
- [ ] Any non-alphanumeric character is converted to a percent sign followed by the ASCII value in hex. An example is %2D.

To work this backwards and decode an encoded string, you would need to follow this procedure. First break the string at the &:

```
VARIABLE 1: Name=Steve+O%92Donohue
VARIABLE 2: Phone=%28919%29-123-4567
VARIABLE 3: B1=Submit
```

Next, you would break each variable at the = sign:

```
VARIABLE(Name) : Steve+O%92Donohue
VARIABLE(Phone): %28919%29-123-4567
VARIABLE(B1):    Submit
```

Any + becomes a space:

```
VARIABLE(Name) : Steve O%92Donohue
VARIABLE(Phone): %28919%29-123-4567
VARIABLE(B1):    Submit
```

Any %xx is converted back to a character:

```
VARIABLE(Name) : Steve O'Donohue
VARIABLE(Phone): (919)-123-4567
VARIABLE(B1):    Submit
```

I bet you're hoping that you don't need to write code to perform all of these steps yourself in order to pull the data stored in a form out into a usable format. The good news is that you don't.

Let's change the OnAction event handler to the following to demonstrate how methods can be used to decode form-encoded strings for you:

```
procedure TWebModule1.WebModule1WebActionItem1Action(Sender: TObject;
  Request: TWebRequest; Response: TWebResponse; var Handled: Boolean);
begin
  Response.Content := '<HTML>Var1:'+Request.QueryFields.Strings[0];
  Response.Content := Response.Content +'<br>Var2:'+
                      Request.QueryFields.Strings[1];
  Response.Content := Response.Content +'<br>Var3:'+
                      Request.QueryFields.Strings[2];
  Response.Content := Response.Content +'</HTML>';
end;
```

Now the response from the Web application is this:

```
Var1:Name=Steve O'Donohue
Var2:Phone=(919)-123-4567
Var3:B1=Submit
```

Delphi does all the hard work for you by decoding the query string. It did this because you used the TStrings collection QueryFields. Therefore, to access the raw query string, use the Request.Query property, and to access the decoded fields, use the Request.QueryFields property. If the form were submitted with a POST method as opposed to a GET, the application would need to use the Request.Content property and the Request.ContentFields property.

To finish your phone contact application, add code to log the customer's name and phone number to a file and respond back with a confirmation and a positive message. The final application's code is shown in Listing 14.5.

Listing 14.5. Application that logs customer name and phone number.

TYPE

```
unit unitMailList;

interface

uses
  Windows, Messages, SysUtils, Classes, HTTPApp;

type
  TWebModule1 = class(TWebModule)
    procedure WebModule1WebActionItem1Action(Sender: TObject;
```

continues

14

Listing 14.5. continued

```
      Request: TWebRequest; Response: TWebResponse;
      var Handled: Boolean);
  private
    { Private declarations }
  public
    { Public declarations }
  end;

var
  WebModule1: TWebModule1;

implementation

{$R *.DFM}

procedure TWebModule1.WebModule1WebActionItem1Action(Sender: TObject;
  Request: TWebRequest; Response: TWebResponse; var Handled: Boolean);

var
  F        : TextFile;
  Callline : string;

begin
  AssignFile(F,'calllist.txt');
  if FileExists('calllist.txt') then
    Append(F)
   else
    ReWrite(F);
  callline := copy(Request.QueryFields.Strings[0],6,
                 length(Request.QueryFields.Strings[0])-5);
  callline := callline +' will be contacted at '+copy(
             Request.QueryFields.Strings[1],7,
             length(Request.QueryFields.Strings[1])-6);
  Response.Content := '<HTML>'+callline+'<br> Have a Nice Day!';
  Response.Content := Response.Content +'</HTML>';
  writeln(F,callline);
  Close(F);
end;

end.
```

ANALYSIS   When the Web client submits the form, the `WebModule1WebActionItem1Action` procedure is called. It decodes the input from the form and writes the input to a file. The `FileExists` call is used to determine if the file already exists. If the file does exist, it appends to the file by calling `Append(F)`; otherwise, it writes a new file by calling the `ReWrite(F)` procedure. Because the filenames are a constant length, you can pull the data out of the `QueryString` property by using the `copy` function and specifying a fixed value for the second parameter. Figure 14.6 shows the response from the Web application after the form has been submitted.

Figure 14.6.

Confirmation that the customer will be called.

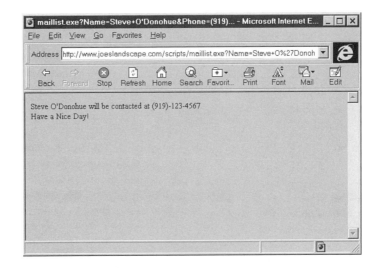

Using Active Forms on the Client

Many Web browsers now allow the client to execute code on the client machine as opposed to leaving the server responsible for all processing. The two major technologies that allow this are Java and ActiveX. It is advantageous to use server processing when you want to reach the largest audience. There are many browsers in the world that either do not have client features or do not have their client features enabled. You might want to think about using client browser technology if there is constant interaction between the user and the application, or if you already have a Windows application that you want to port as a Web tool. Delphi enables you to create ActiveX components for use in scriptable Web forms, and it also offers Active forms. This is a very powerful tool because it enables you to create a form as an ActiveX component. You can then embed this form in a Web page that supports ActiveX. Let's walk through creating an active form and then creating a Web page with the form embedded in it.

First, create an active form by following these steps:

1. Close any open projects, and then choose File | New.

2. In the New Items dialog box, select the ActiveX tab, and then choose ActiveX Library.

3. Choose File | New again, select the ActiveX tab, and then choose Active Form. The Active Form Wizard will appear and prompt you for a new ActiveX name and what the implementation unit should be called. For this example, use MathForm for the ActiveX name and MathFormImpl.pas for the implementation file. You can leave all of the ActiveX control options unchecked.

14

4. This creates what appears to be a new application, but the form displayed is actually the beginning of an ActiveX component. You now can place components and add code to the form just as if you were writing a Windows application.

For this example, suppose a Math teacher is using the WWW to post his lessons and supply additional information. The current lesson plan is dealing with the area of circles and squares. It would be nice if the Web page could have a circle and square on it. It also would be nice to have a slider bar that would adjust the volume of the circle and square so their volumes always were equal, as shown in Figure 14.7. This requirement would be very difficult to meet using a Web server application but is trivial using active forms.

Figure 14.7.

The Math lesson Web page using an active form.

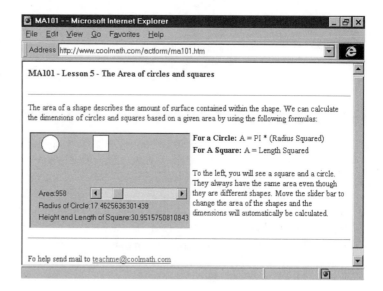

Continue creating the application by following these steps:

1. Place six components on the form: two shape components, three label components, and one slider component.

2. Name one of the shape components **Circle**, and name the other shape component **Square**.

3. Set the shape property on the Circle object to **stCircle** and the square's shape property to **stRectangle**. Set the name property of the ScrollBar to **Area** and the min and max properties to **100** and **5000**, respectively.

4. Implement the OnChange event on the scrollbar and the OnCreate event of the form as shown in Listing 14.6. Note that these are the only procedures you need to add. Delphi auto-generates the rest of the source code for this listing.

14

Listing 14.6. The Math application using active forms.

```
unit MathFormImpl;

interface

uses
  Windows, Messages, SysUtils, Classes, Graphics, Controls, Forms,
  Dialogs,
  ActiveX, AxCtrls, MathLib_TLB, ExtCtrls, StdCtrls;

type
  TMathForm = class(TActiveForm, IMathForm)
    Area: TScrollBar;
    Label1: TLabel;
    Label2: TLabel;
    Label3: TLabel;
    Square: TShape;
    Circle: TShape;
    procedure FormCreate(Sender: TObject);
    procedure AreaChange(Sender: TObject);
  private
    { Private declarations }
    FEvents: IMathFormEvents;
    procedure ActivateEvent(Sender: TObject);
    procedure ClickEvent(Sender: TObject);
    procedure CreateEvent(Sender: TObject);
    procedure DblClickEvent(Sender: TObject);
    procedure DeactivateEvent(Sender: TObject);
    procedure DestroyEvent(Sender: TObject);
    procedure KeyPressEvent(Sender: TObject; var Key: Char);
    procedure PaintEvent(Sender: TObject);
  protected
    { Protected declarations }
    procedure EventSinkChanged(const EventSink: IUnknown); override;
    procedure Initialize; override;
    function CloseQuery: WordBool; safecall;
    function Get_Active: WordBool; safecall;
    function Get_AutoScroll: WordBool; safecall;
    function Get_AxBorderStyle: TxActiveFormBorderStyle; safecall;
    function Get_Caption: WideString; safecall;
    function Get_Color: TColor; safecall;
    function Get_Cursor: Smallint; safecall;
    function Get_DropTarget: WordBool; safecall;
    function Get_Enabled: WordBool; safecall;
    function Get_Font: Font; safecall;
    function Get_HelpFile: WideString; safecall;
    function Get_KeyPreview: WordBool; safecall;
    function Get_ModalResult: Integer; safecall;
    function Get_PixelsPerInch: Integer; safecall;
    function Get_PrintScale: TxPrintScale; safecall;
    function Get_Scaled: WordBool; safecall;
    function Get_Visible: WordBool; safecall;
    function Get_WindowState: TxWindowState; safecall;
    function ShowModal: Integer; safecall;
```

continues

Listing 14.6. continued

```
          procedure Close; safecall;
          procedure DisableAutoRange; safecall;
          procedure EnableAutoRange; safecall;
          procedure Print; safecall;
          procedure Set_AutoScroll(Value: WordBool); safecall;
          procedure Set_AxBorderStyle(Value: TxActiveFormBorderStyle);
            safecall;
          procedure Set_Caption(const Value: WideString); safecall;
          procedure Set_Color(Value: TColor); safecall;
          procedure Set_Cursor(Value: Smallint); safecall;
          procedure Set_DropTarget(Value: WordBool); safecall;
          procedure Set_Enabled(Value: WordBool); safecall;
          procedure Set_Font(const Value: Font); safecall;
          procedure Set_HelpFile(const Value: WideString); safecall;
          procedure Set_KeyPreview(Value: WordBool); safecall;
          procedure Set_ModalResult(Value: Integer); safecall;
          procedure Set_PixelsPerInch(Value: Integer); safecall;
          procedure Set_PrintScale(Value: TxPrintScale); safecall;
          procedure Set_Scaled(Value: WordBool); safecall;
          procedure Set_Visible(Value: WordBool); safecall;
          procedure Set_WindowState(Value: TxWindowState); safecall;
        public
          { Public declarations }
        end;

    implementation

    uses ComServ;

    {$R *.DFM}

    { TMathForm }

    procedure TMathForm.EventSinkChanged(const EventSink: IUnknown);
    begin
      FEvents := EventSink as IMathFormEvents;
    end;

    procedure TMathForm.Initialize;
    begin
      OnActivate := ActivateEvent;
      OnClick := ClickEvent;
      OnCreate := CreateEvent;
      OnDblClick := DblClickEvent;
      OnDeactivate := DeactivateEvent;
      OnDestroy := DestroyEvent;
      OnKeyPress := KeyPressEvent;
      OnPaint := PaintEvent;
    end;

    function TMathForm.CloseQuery: WordBool;
    begin

    end;
```

14

```
function TMathForm.Get_Active: WordBool;
begin
  Result := Active;
end;

function TMathForm.Get_AutoScroll: WordBool;
begin
  Result := AutoScroll;
end;

function TMathForm.Get_AxBorderStyle: TxActiveFormBorderStyle;
begin
  Result := Ord(AxBorderStyle);
end;

function TMathForm.Get_Caption: WideString;
begin
  Result := WideString(Caption);
end;

function TMathForm.Get_Color: TColor;
begin
  Result := Color;
end;

function TMathForm.Get_Cursor: Smallint;
begin
  Result := Smallint(Cursor);
end;

function TMathForm.Get_DropTarget: WordBool;
begin
  Result := DropTarget;
end;

function TMathForm.Get_Enabled: WordBool;
begin
  Result := Enabled;
end;

function TMathForm.Get_Font: Font;
begin
  GetOleFont(Font, Result);
end;

function TMathForm.Get_HelpFile: WideString;
begin
  Result := WideString(HelpFile);
end;

function TMathForm.Get_KeyPreview: WordBool;
begin
  Result := KeyPreview;
end;
```

14

continues

Listing 14.6. continued

```
function TMathForm.Get_ModalResult: Integer;
begin
  Result := Integer(ModalResult);
end;

function TMathForm.Get_PixelsPerInch: Integer;
begin
  Result := PixelsPerInch;
end;

function TMathForm.Get_PrintScale: TxPrintScale;
begin
  Result := Ord(PrintScale);
end;

function TMathForm.Get_Scaled: WordBool;
begin
  Result := Scaled;
end;

function TMathForm.Get_Visible: WordBool;
begin
  Result := Visible;
end;

function TMathForm.Get_WindowState: TxWindowState;
begin
  Result := Ord(WindowState);
end;

function TMathForm.ShowModal: Integer;
begin

end;

procedure TMathForm.Close;
begin

end;

procedure TMathForm.DisableAutoRange;
begin

end;

procedure TMathForm.EnableAutoRange;
begin

end;

procedure TMathForm.Print;
begin

end;
```

```
procedure TMathForm.Set_AutoScroll(Value: WordBool);
begin
  AutoScroll := Value;
end;

procedure TMathForm.Set_AxBorderStyle(Value: TxActiveFormBorderStyle);
begin
  AxBorderStyle := TActiveFormBorderStyle(Value);
end;

procedure TMathForm.Set_Caption(const Value: WideString);
begin
  Caption := TCaption(Value);
end;

procedure TMathForm.Set_Color(Value: TColor);
begin
  Color := Value;
end;

procedure TMathForm.Set_Cursor(Value: Smallint);
begin
  Cursor := TCursor(Value);
end;

procedure TMathForm.Set_DropTarget(Value: WordBool);
begin
  DropTarget := Value;
end;

procedure TMathForm.Set_Enabled(Value: WordBool);
begin
  Enabled := Value;
end;

procedure TMathForm.Set_Font(const Value: Font);
begin
  SetOleFont(Font, Value);
end;

procedure TMathForm.Set_HelpFile(const Value: WideString);
begin
  HelpFile := String(Value);
end;

procedure TMathForm.Set_KeyPreview(Value: WordBool);
begin
  KeyPreview := Value;
end;

procedure TMathForm.Set_ModalResult(Value: Integer);
begin
  ModalResult := TModalResult(Value);
end;
```

14

continues

Listing 14.6. continued

```
procedure TMathForm.Set_PixelsPerInch(Value: Integer);
begin
  PixelsPerInch := Value;
end;

procedure TMathForm.Set_PrintScale(Value: TxPrintScale);
begin
  PrintScale := TPrintScale(Value);
end;

procedure TMathForm.Set_Scaled(Value: WordBool);
begin
  Scaled := Value;
end;

procedure TMathForm.Set_Visible(Value: WordBool);
begin
  Visible := Value;
end;

procedure TMathForm.Set_WindowState(Value: TxWindowState);
begin
  WindowState := TWindowState(Value);
end;

procedure TMathForm.ActivateEvent(Sender: TObject);
begin
  if FEvents <> nil then FEvents.OnActivate;
end;

procedure TMathForm.ClickEvent(Sender: TObject);
begin
  if FEvents <> nil then FEvents.OnClick;
end;

procedure TMathForm.CreateEvent(Sender: TObject);
begin
  if FEvents <> nil then FEvents.OnCreate;
end;

procedure TMathForm.DblClickEvent(Sender: TObject);
begin
  if FEvents <> nil then FEvents.OnDblClick;
end;

procedure TMathForm.DeactivateEvent(Sender: TObject);
begin
  if FEvents <> nil then FEvents.OnDeactivate;
end;

procedure TMathForm.DestroyEvent(Sender: TObject);
begin
  if FEvents <> nil then FEvents.OnDestroy;
end;
```

14

```
procedure TMathForm.KeyPressEvent(Sender: TObject; var Key: Char);
var
  TempKey: Smallint;
begin
  TempKey := Smallint(Key);
  if FEvents <> nil then FEvents.OnKeyPress(TempKey);
  Key := Char(TempKey);
end;

procedure TMathForm.PaintEvent(Sender: TObject);
begin
  if FEvents <> nil then FEvents.OnPaint;
end;


procedure TMathForm.FormCreate(Sender: TObject);
begin
  Area.Position := 2500;
end;

procedure TMathForm.AreaChange(Sender: TObject);
begin
    Circle.Width  :=trunc(2.0 *(sqrt(Area.Position/3.14159)));
    Circle.Height :=trunc(2.0 *(sqrt(Area.Position/3.14159)));
    Square.Width  :=trunc(sqrt(Area.Position));
    Square.Height :=trunc(sqrt(Area.Position));
    Label1.Caption :=  'Area:'+
                       IntToStr(Area.Position);
    Label2.Caption :=  'Radius of Circle:'+
                       FloatToStr(2.0 *
                              (sqrt(Area.Position/3.14159))/2);
    Label3.Caption := 'Height and Length of Square:'+
                       FloatToStr(sqrt(Area.Position));
end;

initialization
  TActiveFormFactory.Create(
    ComServer,
    TActiveFormControl,
    TMathForm,
    Class_MathForm,
    1,
    '',
    OLEMISC_SIMPLEFRAME or OLEMISC_ACTSLIKELABEL);
end.
```

ANALYSIS This application will compile to an ActiveX OCX. The ActiveX OCX will be used as the code base for the form as an ActiveX component. When a Web application references the class ID (CLSID) for the component, that you created, it will embed the active form into the client's Web page. It is important to note that the ActiveX component can be used in any application that can embed ActiveX components and not just Web-based clients. After the client embeds the component, it executes as any Delphi form would in an application. When the user moves the slider bar, the resulting area for the square and circle is calculated, and the corresponding shape component's dimensions are updated. The application also displays the area and the dimensions of the shapes using the label components.

Delphi offers a powerful feature called "Web deploy" which enables you to quickly build a Web page to test the component and also to place the ActiveX OCX on your Web server. Before you can use this option, you must configure the Web Deployment options by selecting Project | Web Deployment Options from the main menu. These options should be filled in as depicted in Figure 14.8. In addition to deploying the application, this feature also can digitally sign the active form. You should consult Delphi's online manuals for further information regarding the use of Microsoft's *authenticode* technology to sign your software.

Figure 14.8.

Web Deployment Options dialog box.

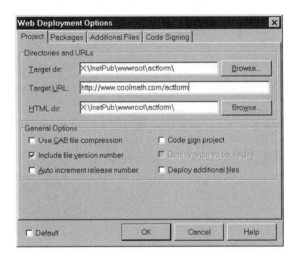

The three mandatory fields on the Web Deployment Options dialog box that need to be filled in are Target dir, Target URL, and HTML dir. The target directory is where the ActiveX OCX will be placed. This file location corresponds to the URL directory in the Target URL field. For example, if on your Web server the D:\InetPub\WWWROOT directory corresponds to http://www.joes-farm-supply.com/, you could specify D:\InetPub\WWWROOT for Target dir and http://www.joes-farm-supply.com for Target URL. Note that in this example, the virtual root directory for the Web server resides at the physical location D:\InetPub\WWWROOT. The HTML Dir field is used to specify where a sample document that will embed the Active form should be placed. You can use this sample document as a starting point to build your Web page that uses the active form. To actually have Delphi place the files on a Web server, choose Project | Web Deploy.

Listing 14.7 shows the default Web page that Delphi builds and places it in the "HTML directory."

14

**Listing 14.7. The Web page generated by Delphi's Web
Deploy option.**

`TYPE`

```
<HTML>
<H1> Delphi ActiveX Test Page </H1><p>
You should see your Delphi forms or controls embedded in the
form below.
<HR><center><P>
<OBJECT
  classid="clsid:E1C4AE03-5B32-11D0-9FB3-444553540000"
  codebase="http://www.coolmath.com/actform/cmproj.ocx#version=1,0,0,0"
  width=350
  height=250
  align=center
  hspace=0
  vspace=0
>
</OBJECT>
</HTML>
```

`ANALYSIS` The generated object tag is what signifies that an object should be embedded in the HTML page. The `width`, `height`, `align`, `hspace`, and `vspace` attributes define the placement, size, and position of the component in the form, respectively. The `classid` attribute defines what component should be inserted. If the machine has the ActiveX component that corresponds to the class ID already installed, it simply embeds the component in the form. If the component is not registered in the system, then it uses the `codebase` tag to download the component. The version information ensures that the user has a current version of the OCX registered on their system. The Web page that Delphi creates is shown in Figure 14.9.

Figure 14.9.

*Sample Web Page
built by Web deploy.*

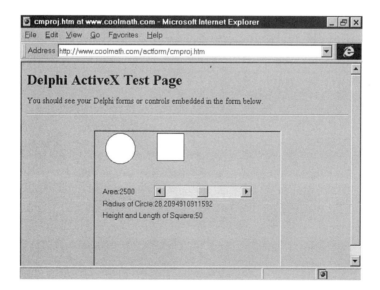

14

NOTE

> If your Web browser refuses to accept the component because it is not digitally signed, you may need to alter your browser's security settings to enable non-authenticated ActiveX components. In Microsoft Internet Explorer, you can do this by setting the "safety level" to "medium." Be sure to read Explorer's documentation on what the different safety levels mean.
>
> If you update the version of the OCX and try to have your browser re-install the component, you will need to close the browser and restart it. You can use a version of -1,-1,-1,-1 to always download the component. For example, the following lines:
>
> ```
> codebase=
> "http://www.coolmath.com/actform/CMPROJ.ocx#version=1,2,0,0"
> ```
>
> will download the DLL and reinstall the component if the user is currently running version 1.1.0.0 or earlier.

The final step to get your Web page to look like the one in Figure 14.7 is to modify the HTML. You can do this by hand, or you can use your favorite HTML editor. Listing 14.8 shows the HTML used to build the Web page displayed earlier in Figure 14.7.

TYPE

Listing 14.8. HTML for the completed Math lesson Web page using an active form.

```
<!DOCTYPE HTML PUBLIC "-//IETF//DTD HTML//EN">
<html>

<head>
<meta http-equiv="Content-Type"
content="text/html; charset=iso-8859-1">
<meta name="GENERATOR" content="Microsoft FrontPage 2.0">
<title>MA101 -</title>
</head>

<body bgcolor="#FFFFFF">

<h3>MA101 - Lesson 5 - The Area of circles and squares</h3>

<hr>

<p>The area of a shape describes the amount of surface contained
within the shape. We can calculate the dimensions of circles and
squares based on a given area by using the following formulas:</p>

<table border="0">
    <tr>
```

```
    <td rowspan="3"><!--webbot bot="HTMLMarkup" startspan -->
    <OBJECT
    classid="clsid:E1C4AE03-5B32-11D0-9FB3-444553540000"
    codebase="http://www.coolmath.com/actform/
    ➡CMPROJ.ocx#version=-1,-1,-1,-1"
    width=300
    height=175
    align=center
    hspace=0
    vspace=0
    >
</OBJECT><!--webbot
    bot="HTMLMarkup" endspan --></td>
    <td><strong>For a Circle:</strong> A = PI * (Radius
    Squared) </td>
  </tr>
  <tr>
    <td><strong>For A Square:</strong> A = Length Squared</td>
  </tr>
  <tr>
    <td>To the left, you will see a square and a circle. They
    always have the same area even though they are different
    shapes. Move the slider bar to change the area of the
    shapes and the dimensions will automatically be
    calculated.</td>
  </tr>
</table>

<hr>

<p>For help send mail to <a href="mailto:teachme@coolmath.com">
teachme@coolmath.com</a></p>
</body>
</html>
```

Summary

Today you learned how to create client- and server-based Web applications with Delphi. Delphi offers a powerful Web server framework that enables you to concentrate on the application's core logic instead of worrying about the details of interacting with the Web server. You saw how to create a basic CGI application and then use the same code base to build an ISAPI application. The tile game example demonstrates the use of multiple dispatch paths to allow the same application to perform multiple tasks. This example also demonstrated what is required to develop a somewhat complex server-side application where information about a previous state needs to be used.

Web forms are used to collect information from users, and you learned about the built-in features Delphi offers to decode and read information passed to a server application through forms. When a Web application wants to take full advantage of the machine's system services

14

or has a high degree of interaction, a server-based application is not suitable. In this case, ActiveX fills a large void by allowing a component to be embedded in the Web page that can do anything a native Win32 application can do.

One of the easiest ways to create self-contained complex ActiveX components is to use the active forms features of Delphi. Our final example builds a math tutorial application that embeds an active form to allow the area of shapes to be varied using a slider bar.

The bottom line is that Delphi is one of the best tools available for developing both client and server Web applications.

Q&A

Q Can I use specific features of ISAPI or any of the other supported server targets using Delphi's Web server framework?

A Yes, each target has a set of classes that inherit the mandatory features from the general code base but provide specific functionality.

Q Is there an easy way to register the ActiveX components when I am testing?

A Yes, you can use the Run | Register ActiveX server and Run | Unregister ActiveX Server menu options to install and un-install the active forms from within the development environment.

Q Is it possible to run a Web server application in the debugger?

A Yes, you need to run the debugger on your server machine and actually debug the Web server process. Consult Delphi's online documentation for details.

Workshop

The Workshop provides two ways for you to affirm what you've learned in this chapter. The Quiz section poses questions to help you solidify your understanding of the material covered. You can find answers to the quiz questions in Appendix A, "Answers to the Quiz Questions." The Exercises section provides you with experience in using what you have learned. Please try to work through all these before continuing to the next day.

Quiz

1. Do CGI applications run in the process space of the Web server? What about ISAPI applications?

2. When using forms to get information from a Web client, what property can be accessed to automatically decode the data sent by the user?

3. When a user accesses a Web page that contains an ActiveX form that they do not have registered on their system, how does their browser know where to get the component?

Exercises

1. Create a Web server application that receives input from a form that contains radio buttons, drop-down boxes, and check boxes.

2. Create a Web server application that uses the database HTML generation components.

3. Port the tile game Web server application to an active form.

14

Day 15

Deploying Applications

When you have completed development on an application, you may need to ship it to other users or customers. Today's lesson presents some topics that should be of interest to most developers. First, you learn about Delphi's new package feature. Packages give you the option to build thin applications through the use of runtime libraries known as Packages. You also learn about the Windows 95 Logo requirements and the Windows 95 Registry, and how to build a simple installer. Finally, you learn a bit about InstallShield, which comes with Delphi and provides a quick and simple method of building professional-quality installers.

Packages—An Overview

If you came to Delphi 1.*x* or 2.*x* from a Visual Basic background, you know that Delphi creates stand-alone executables (meaning that your application and all its resources can reside in one executable file). When compared to Visual Basic executables, Delphi executables can seem quite large. But, Delphi executables are stand-alone, and you don't have to ship a bunch of files with them. They also run faster. Although this is all true, and Delphi always has had the speed and power, the executables were kind of big if you planned to have a bunch of them on one system. I used to wonder why Delphi didn't give you the option to use runtime DLLs or to compile to stand-alone executables. Borland to the rescue with packages in Delphi 3!

NEW TERM *Packages* are special DLLs that contain the entire Visual Component Library as well as other objects, functions, procedures, and so on. These DLLs enable you to create very small executables when you turn on support for packages. You even can compile your own components and libraries into packages. Packages have the file extension `.DPL` to distinguish them from regular DLLs.

But what if your memory and hard disk space aren't a concern—why use packages? Suppose you are developing applications that must be distributed to users over a network or the Internet. Without packages, every time you ship a new executable, you also are shipping the VCL code inside each executable. With packages, a 180KB executable shrinks to about 9KB or 10KB. You ship all the packages and get them installed on the client once. Then, when you make updates or come out with new applications, you ship small executables.

Let's take a look at some of the different ways packages are used in Delphi.

Runtime Packages

Runtime packages contain the Delphi VCL, which are divided into four DPLs (`VCL30.DPL`, `VCLX30.DPL`, `VCLDB30.DPL`, and `VCLDBX30.DPL`). `VCL30.DPL`, for example, contains most of the common objects, components, and so on, used in most applications such as forms, buttons, controls, printers, and so on. You also will find other packages for things such as QuickReport (`QRPT30.DPL`), DecisionCube (`DSS30.DPL`), and TeeChart (`TEE30.DPL`). For a more detailed account of objects and components contained in each of the DPLs, refer to Delphi's online help or manuals.

Custom Packages

You can add custom packages to Delphi—packages that you have created yourself or purchased from a third-party vendor. Custom packages are used just like runtime packages and must be shipped and installed on the user's computer.

Design-Time Packages

Delphi uses a package type called design-time packages, which have a special purpose. These packages are used for installing components on Delphi 3's IDE Component Palette or to create special property editors for use in custom components. Design-time packages are not used by applications; they are used by Delphi. The design-time package DPLs are DCLSTD30.DPL, DCLDB30.DPL, DCL31W30.DPL, DCLQRT30.DPL, DCLNET30.DPL,, DCLSMP30.DPL, and DCLOCX30.DPL. These DPLs do not need to ship with your applications, they are strictly for design-time use.

Component Packages

In Delphi 3, all components are installed as packages in the IDE when you install Delphi on your system. When you write a component to add to Delphi 3, you must now compile a package that contains your component and add it to the IDE before you can use it.

Using Packages

Rather than presenting all there is to know about packages here, which is beyond the scope of this book, this section describes the most common use of packages to get you started using the packages that ship with Delphi 3. If you need more advanced information regarding creating packages, refer to Delphi's online help and manuals.

Support for Packages

To use packages in your application, you must turn on the support for packages and then compile and build your application. Let's walk through a simple example of building an application with and without packages and compare the results.

Start by building the simplest of Delphi applications, a blank form.

1. If Delphi is not running, start it up.
2. Create a temp directory to store your project.
3. When the blank form appears on the screen, choose File | Save Project As, select the temp directory you just created, and save the project and unit files as their default names of project1.dpr and unit1.pas.
4. Choose Project | Build All. This builds an executable without support for packages, and it's called project.exe.
5. Check the size of project1.exe in your temp directory. The file should be slightly less then 200KB, which includes all the VCL code compiled into the executable.

6. Choose View | Project Manager. Click on the Project Options button when the Project Manager dialog box appears to bring up the Project Options dialog box.

7. To turn on support for packages in the Projects Option dialog box, select the Packages tab, check the option named Build with runtime packages, and click OK.

8. Rebuild your executable by choosing Project | Build All (as you did in step 4).

9. Recheck the file size of project1.exe in your temp directory. It should now be approximately 9KB.

To use the packages that ship with Delphi 3 with your applications, all you need to do is to turn on support as you did here. Keep in mind that if you use packages, you must ship the DPLs used by your applications, VCL30.DPL at a minimum. Check Delphi's online help and manuals to make sure that you include all necessary package DPLs for the components, objects, and libraries that your application uses.

Other Considerations for Using Packages

You also will want to keep in mind that the packages make use of the Windows API that is contained in various DLLs. If any of these DLLs are missing or out of date, you could have problems. Testing your application on a target system, possibly one with a clean install of Windows 95 or NT, and then insuring that it runs without errors can prevent this. Error dialogs will occur for any files that are required but are missing so that you can determine what the requirements are for your application to run properly. You then can make sure you ship the required files, or you can require the user to have a specified OS release, patch set, and so on.

If you do decide to ship DLL files that are not provided with Delphi or are not found on a standard Windows 95 or NT load, you need to understand and work out any licensing issues with the vendor, such as Microsoft.

One other thing you should consider if you are marketing your product or distributing it for use by someone that you may not directly support is to include one version of your application that uses packages and another that does not. This gives users the option to use the configuration that best suits their needs.

Setting Package Options

Let's take a quick look at the Packages tab in the Project Options dialog box, as shown in Figure 15.1. The first group is labeled Design packages. Here you find a list box that enables you to select the design-time packages. Clicking on a design-time package in this list shows the associated path and DLL filename in the status area below the list. This group also

15

contains Add, Remove, and Edit buttons that enable you to add, remove, and edit packages in the IDE for design-time use. The Components button displays the components contained in the selected design-time DLL.

Figure 15.1.

The Packages tab in the Project Options dialog box.

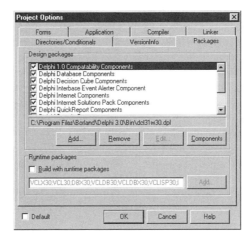

The Runtime packages group in this tab enables you to toggle the check box to turn on or off support for packages, as you already have done. You also can use the edit box to specify the names of the packages to be used in the project (the filenames do not use an extension here). By default, all the Delphi packages are turned on in the Design packages section, and the package names appear in the edit box in the Runtime packages section. If you write or obtain new design packages, you can add them using the Add button.

Regardless of your decision to use or not to use packages, you will need to understand a few other topics to deploy commercial-quality, industry-standard applications that carry the Windows 95 logo. So, let's move on to the basics regarding these topics.

Windows 95 Logo Requirements, the Registry, and Installers

In 1981, IBM introduced the IBM PC and PC-DOS; clones followed shortly afterward. Installing a program usually involved nothing more than copying files to a disk or a subdirectory and running the executable or batch file. In those days, some programs had install programs that simply copied the files for you into a subdirectory. As time went on, users could select options, which were added to configuration files—.dat, .cfg, and so on. There was no standard for setting up and installing programs. Every programmer had her own way of keeping track of user settings and other information needed by the program.

When you wanted to clean your hard disk, you often had a difficult time determining which files were needed. The AUTOEXEC.BAT and CONFIG.SYS files contained lines that applied to particular programs.

Windows brought .ini files and SETUP.EXE programs—not a bad idea at the time. Windows even provided API functions that you could use to create, read, and write .ini files easily. This development helped standardize naming conventions, access methods, formatting, and even the location of files, but it still was not enough. The .ini files had their own problems. Some programmers used the win.ini and system.ini files, whereas others used their own application-specific .ini files. Some used combinations thereof.

All those .ini files and Windows applications made cleaning a hard disk even more complex. In DOS, you had to delete the application directory and its contents, and maybe a few lines in the config.sys and autoexec.bat files. In Windows, if you delete an application's files and directories, remnants often remain in the win.ini and system.ini files from the application's installer. This causes clutter, confusion, and unpredictable effects in Windows. Applications are available that monitor your software installs and enable you to completely uninstall programs and all their files, but you cannot always trust them to work. Many Windows programs share DLLs and other resources. To work properly, uninstall programs must be installed *before* other applications. Because they can't possibly have a complete database of every Windows program, they cannot uninstall every program properly unless they monitored its installation.

Windows NT and Windows 95 use the Registry rather than .ini files to store system settings and information. Microsoft requires developers to use the Registry to store configuration information, follow a given set of standards, and provide complete install and uninstall programs—otherwise, they are not permitted to display the Windows 95 logo on their software. This is good for developers because they have standards to follow. It is good for end users because they now have an easy, orderly method for installing and uninstalling their software.

NEW TERM The *Registry* is a hierarchical database used by Windows to store system hardware and software settings, and program and user settings. Windows 95 and Windows NT store information in the Registry that would be stored in .ini files in Windows 3.1.

The remainder of this section covers the requirements that an application must satisfy to earn the Windows 95 logo. You learn about what the Registry is and how to use it. You write your own install and uninstall program using the Registry. You also learn about using a third-party product to create applications that meet the Windows 95 logo requirements, regardless of the method that you used to create your installer and uninstaller.

15

Meeting the Windows 95 Logo Requirements

15

The Windows 95 logo requirements are technical requirements that developers must follow when they create software or hardware. This section introduces you to the some of the important concepts. To help you design applications, you should consult *Programmer's Guide to Microsoft Windows 95* and *Windows Interface Guidelines for Software Design* from Microsoft Press. The requirements are occasionally updated, so be sure to obtain the latest information from Microsoft. When you write an application that meets the requirements, you need to apply to Microsoft before it can display the logo.

Obviously, you do not have to write applications that satisfy all the Windows 95 logo requirements. If you are writing freeware, shareware, or your own personal software, it might not be worth the effort. Even so, it does not hurt to follow the standards as much as possible. That way, if you decide to market your application later, you won't have as much work to do to earn the logo.

Microsoft looks at applications in four main categories:

- [ ] File-based applications
- [ ] Non-file-based applications that run exclusively in full mode—not windowed
- [ ] Utilities, including file and disk utilities and virus-scanning and cleaning programs
- [ ] Development tools

The following requirements apply to applications in all categories:

- [ ] The application must use the Win32 API.
- [ ] The application must follow the Windows 95 look and feel for the user interface.
- [ ] The application must be tested, must successfully run on both Windows 95 and Windows NT, and must be adjusted as necessary to compensate for differences in features between the two.
- [ ] The application must support long filenames and display them appropriately in dialog boxes, controls, and so on.
- [ ] The application must support plug and play.

There are more requirements regarding the use of OLE, MAPI (messaging application programming interface), and UNC (universal naming convention). In addition, an application must provide install and uninstall programs, and it must use the Registry rather than the WIN.INI and SYSTEM.INI files. When you do obtain a complete list of the current requirements and start designing your application, you will find that Delphi's VCL makes most of the work a breeze because many of the tasks are already done.

The Registry

The Registry is a database that stores information about system hardware configuration, Windows, and Windows applications. Almost everything that is found in an .ini file in Windows 3.1 goes in the Windows 95 or Windows NT Registry. The Registry is organized in a hierarchical format. It is quite complex, containing many levels of keys, subkeys, and values. This section focuses on the Registry and the install and uninstall program that you will write.

 NOTE

> You should acquire a copy of the Windows 95 Resource Kit and a good reference book on the Win32 API. The Microsoft Developer's Network CD-ROMs also contain information about the Registry.

The Registry divides its data into two categories: computer-specific and user-specific. Computer-specific information includes anything related to the hardware and its settings and to the installed applications and their settings. User-specific information includes desktop preferences, user profiles, user-selected printers, and network settings.

Six main registry keys contain all the subkeys and entries—many entries are nested several levels deep. The four computer-specific top-level keys are as follows:

Hkey_Local_Machine	Information about the computer, including installed hardware and software settings
HKey_Current_Config	Information about current hardware
HKey_Dyn_Data	Dynamic status information used by plug-and-play routines
Hkey_Classes_Root	Information about OLE, drag and drop, shortcuts, and the Windows 95 user interface

The two user-specific top-level keys are as follows:

Hkey_Users	User information, including desktop settings and application settings
Hkey_Current_User	Information for the user who is currently logged in

To work with the Registry, you need to know how to view it, change it manually, and verify that changes are recorded properly. Here's how easy it is.

1. Choose Run from the menu bar in Windows 95 or Windows NT to open the Run dialog box.
2. Enter REGEDIT.EXE. This brings up the Registry Editor, as shown in Figure 15.2, which enables you to view and edit the Registry.

Figure 15.2.

The Registry Editor.

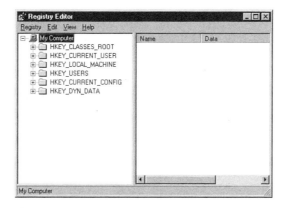

15

WARNING

You never should make changes to the Registry unless you know what you are doing. Make sure that you back up the Registry and your data before you test your application or give it to other users.

TIP

To back up the Registry, copy SYSTEM.DAT in the Windows subdirectory to a safe place. This is a hidden file, so you need something that can see it, such as Windows Explorer in Windows 95.

In the Registry Editor, you move through the Registry just as you do through the directory structure with Windows Explorer. Look at the Registry menu options. Notice that you can export and import the entire Registry or just portions of it between text files. The Registry's Edit menu shows the editing functions relating to the highlighted entry. To highlight different selections, just click the desired entry. If you need more information on the Registry Editor, refer to Delphi's online help or manuals.

Today, you'll use REGEDIT to verify that your program is working correctly. If you make a typing error, you can use REGEDIT to fix the mistake.

The following information, for example, was exported from the hardware section with REGEDIT:

```
[HKEY_LOCAL_MACHINE\hardware]

[HKEY_LOCAL_MACHINE\hardware\devicemap]

[HKEY_LOCAL_MACHINE\hardware\devicemap\serialcomm]
"COM1"="COM1"
"COM2"="COM2"
```

```
[HKEY_LOCAL_MACHINE\hardware\DESCRIPTION]
```

```
[HKEY_LOCAL_MACHINE\hardware\DESCRIPTION\System]
```

```
[HKEY_LOCAL_MACHINE\hardware\DESCRIPTION\System\FloatingPointProcessor]
```

```
[HKEY_LOCAL_MACHINE\hardware\DESCRIPTION\System\FloatingPointProcessor\0]
```

Some information is stored as a subkey, whereas other information is stored in the values within a subkey, as in this example:

```
[HKEY_LOCAL_MACHINE\hardware\devicemap\serialcomm]
"COM1"="COM1"
"COM2"="COM2"
```

Make sure that you are comfortable with the Registry before you attempt to write code that modifies the Registry.

Writing the Install and Uninstall Program

Before you write your simple installer, take a look at what Microsoft recommends to satisfy the Windows 95 logo requirements. An installer should do the following:

- [ ] Provide a standard Windows GUI.
- [ ] Provide the ability to uninstall the application and related files safely.
- [ ] Check the hardware and software configuration.
- [ ] Check available space on the hard disk.
- [ ] Copy the application and required files to the hard disk, creating subdirectories as needed.
- [ ] Modify the Registry and files as needed to make the application function properly.
- [ ] Provide users with installation options, such as typical, compact, custom, and silent (unattended).
- [ ] Provide common default settings.
- [ ] Ask for a disk only once during the installation.
- [ ] Beep and prompt for the next disk when ready.
- [ ] Display a progress indicator that shows the user how much has been done in the installation process.
- [ ] Provide a user with the ability to cancel the installation before completion.
- [ ] Keep a log of all the installed files and changes to the user's system.
- [ ] Clean up when an install is canceled or when the uninstall program is run.
- [ ] Remove any files, Registry entries, shortcuts, and other changes made during the installation.

15

These are most of the important requirements. Check with Microsoft for the latest requirements and information.

The simple installer that you write in this section does not meet all these requirements—only a few, such as copying a file to disk and making a Registry entry. The purpose here is to introduce you to some of the details behind installers. After seeing all that, you might want to obtain a third-party install program generator.

With Delphi, you can easily make updates to the Registry using the Tregistry object. The Tregistry object makes use of the Windows API and does all the hard work for you. All you need to do is pass the appropriate information to the properties of the object, and your Registry updates are done. Let's look at how you set this up in code. Let's first look at the key code and what it does, and then use Listing 15.1 to build the application. The first thing you must do is create a Tregistry object. You can do this by first defining a variable of type Tregistry, as follows:

```
Var
    MyRegistry : Tregistry;
```

You will need to add a reference to the Registry unit in the uses clause because it is not included by default. Next, you need code to create the object. By using the create method for the Tregistry object, you create an object called MyRegistry.

```
MyRegistry:=TRegistry.Create;
```

Now that you've created the object, it is ready for use by the code that follows. This code will be used by the setup program you are creating. Create a key in the Registry that will contain a value where the application name and version will be stored. You will store this in the standard location used by many applications, under KEY_LOCAL_MACHINE\SOFTWARE.

The first thing you need to do is to set the Root Key Location in the Registry because it defaults to HKEY\CURRENT_USER. Add the following line of code:

```
MyRegistry.RootKey:=HKEY_LOCAL_MACHINE;
```

The value that is passed to the RootKey property is of type integer. The Windows unit has all the Standard Key Values defined as constants with the appropriate names, and so you can simply put the name of the key when assigning the value to RootKey.

With the Root Key Location set, all you need to do is open the key, stuff the value, and close the key to make the changes to the Registry. You can do this with the following code:

```
If MyRegistry.OpenKey('SOFTWARE\MyCompany\MyApp',True) then
begin
   MyRegistry.WriteString('MyAppVer','My Application Version 1.0');
   MyRegistry.CloseKey;
   MyRegistry.Free;
end;
```

If a key already exists with the same name, it is opened. If you pass a subkey that contains subkeys, some of which exist and some of which do not exist, the subkeys that exist are opened and the subkeys that do not exist are created and opened.

The SOFTWARE subkey exists, but the MyCompany and MyApp subkeys do not. SOFTWARE is opened, and the others are created and opened.

NOTE

> Although you can read and change most of the Registry information, the Hkey_Dyn_Data keys and values contain Plug-and-Play status information about system devices. This is read-only information.

Now you can build a simple program that checks available disk space, creates a subdirectory, copies a file from a floppy to the new subdirectory, and adds Registry entries about the program. The program also contains an uninstall option, which you can activate by passing /U on the command line.

1. Create a new project.
2. Name the project MYSETUP.DPR and the unit INSTALL.PAS.
3. Use Figure 15.3 as an example of how to lay out the form.
4. Set the form's properties so that it is centered on startup and is not sizable.

Figure 15.3.

The MYSETUP *form.*

WARNING

> Make sure that you have a backup of your Registry file before you run code that will modify its contents.

Use Listing 15.1 to create your program. Make sure the code is identical.

15

TYPE Listing 15.1. Complete code for the MySetup application.

```
unit install;

interface

uses
  Windows, Messages, SysUtils, Classes, Graphics,
  Controls, Forms, Dialogs,
  StdCtrls, FileCtrl,Registry;

type
  TForm1 = class(TForm)
    Button1: TButton;
    Label1: TLabel;
    Edit1: TEdit;
    Button2: TButton;
    procedure Button2Click(Sender: TObject);
    procedure Button1Click(Sender: TObject);
    procedure FormCreate(Sender: TObject);
  private
    { Private declarations }
  public
    { Public declarations }
  end;

var
  Form1: TForm1;

implementation

{$R *.DFM}
Var
    MySubKey : PChar;
    MyRegistry : TRegistry;
procedure TForm1.Button2Click(Sender: TObject);
begin
     Application.Terminate;
end;

procedure TForm1.Button1Click(Sender: TObject);
Var
    {storage for free disk space value}
    DskSpc : Longint;
    {Predefined disk space minimum}
    MinDSpace : Longint;
    {File Variables to use in copy routine}
    InFile,OutFile : File;
    {variable to keep track of records read and written}
    NumRecsRead : integer;
    {Buffer used to copy file}
    Buf : array[1..4096] of Byte;
```

continues

Listing 15.1. continued

```
begin
    {Check Disk space of drive c:}
    MinDSpace:=1024000; {1 meg minimum disk space}
    DskSpc:=DiskFree(3);{get disk space on c}
    If DskSpc<MinDSpace then
    begin
        ShowMessage('Not enough Diskspace, setup aborting');
        Application.Terminate;
    end;
    {Create directory}
     mkdir('c:\myapp');
    {---------------Start Copy Routine-----------}

    AssignFile(InFile,'a:\myapp.exe');
    AssignFile(OutFile,'c:\myapp\myapp.exe');
    {Open files and Set record size to 1 byte}
    Reset(InFile,1);
    Rewrite(OutFile,1);
    While Not Eof(InFile) Do
    Begin
        {Read a 4K Byte Block into the buffer}
        BlockRead(InFile,Buf,SizeOf(Buf),NumRecsRead);
        {Write a 4K Byte Buffer to new file}
        BlockWrite(OutFile,Buf,NumRecsRead);
    end;
        {Flush buffers to disk and close the file}
        CloseFile(InFile);
        CloseFile(Outfile);
    {---------------End Copy Routine-------------}
    {Make Registry Entry using TRegistry Object}
    MyRegistry:=TRegistry.Create;
    MyRegistry.RootKey:=HKEY_LOCAL_MACHINE;
    If MyRegistry.OpenKey('SOFTWARE\MyCompany\MyApp',True) then
    begin
        MyRegistry.WriteString('MyAppVer','My Application Version 1.0');
        MyRegistry.CloseKey;
    end
    else
        begin
            ShowMessage('Registry Update Failed!');
            MyRegistry.Free;
            Application.Terminate;
        end;
    ShowMessage('Installation Complete');
    MyRegistry.Free;
    Application.Terminate;
    {Done making Registry Entry with TRegistry Object}
  end;
procedure TForm1.FormCreate(Sender: TObject);
Var
    F : File;
begin
    {Check for command line option /U, if so uninstall
     otherwise fall through and get ready to install}
```

15

```
If (ParamCount > 0) and ((ParamStr(1) = '/U') or (ParamStr(1) = '/u'))then
    begin
        AssignFile(F,'c:\myapp\myapp.exe');
        Erase(F);
        RmDir('c:\myapp');
        MyRegistry:=TRegistry.Create;
        MyRegistry.RootKey:=HKEY_LOCAL_MACHINE;
        MySubKey:='SOFTWARE\MyCompany';
        If MyRegistry.DeleteKey(MySubKey) then
        begin
            ShowMessage('MYAPP Successfully Uninstalled');
            MyRegistry.CloseKey;
            MyRegistry.Free;
            Application.Terminate;
        end;
end;
end;
end.
```

ANALYSIS The various sections of code are commented so that you can follow along this analysis easily. It concentrates on the code that affects the Registry, but you should look at each section of code.

The bulk of your program is contained in the code for Button1, the continue button. Button2 is the abort button and contains only a line of code to terminate the program. After declaring variables in Button1, you check the free disk space by setting a variable for 1MB and then checking the free disk space. If you have less than 1MB of free disk space, the program displays a message and aborts. If you have enough disk space, the program continues by first creating the application directory, C:\MYAPP in this case.

Next the program copies the application MYAPP.EXE to C:\MYAPP using knowledge gained about file I/O on Day 9, "Input, Output, and Printing."

Now you get into the meat of the program, updating the Registry. Take a close look at the code that makes your Registry entry. First, you create your Tregistry object, as discussed earlier, by creating a variable of type Tregistry called MyRegistry, in this case by putting MyRegistry : Tregistry; in the Var section. Next you use the create method to create the object, as shown here:

```
MyRegistry:=Tregistry.Create;
```

When opening the Registry key using the MyRegistry.OpenKey in an If statement, you check if the open key process was a success. If the code is successful, it drops through, updates the value in the new key using WriteString, and then continues. Otherwise, the program displays an error message and then terminates. The following line of code writes the application version number string to the Registry:

```
MyRegistry.WriteString('MyAppVer','My Application Version 1.0');
```

Finally, the program displays the success message and exits with these two lines of code:

```
ShowMessage('Installation Complete');
Application.Terminate;
```

That takes care of the install portion of the program. Remember that you need to have an uninstall option? Well, this program does. To activate the uninstall portion of the program, you must specify a /U as a command-line parameter. Do this by putting some code into the form create event because it executes when the program starts. Take a look.

The following If...then statement checks for parameters on the command line:

```
If (ParamCount > 0) and ((ParamStr(1) = '/U') or (ParamStr(1)) then
```

If the /U or /u is found, it erases the file myapp.exe from the c:\myapp directory as follows:

```
begin
    AssignFile(F,'c:\myapp\myapp.exe');
    Erase(F);
```

Next it removes the c:\myapp directory as follows:

```
RmDir('c:\myapp');
```

Here you remove the Registry entry that was added when myapp.exe was installed and check the return code of the Registry entry deletion process. You then display a success message when the process is complete and exit the application, as shown here:

```
MyRegistry:=TRegistry.Create;
            MyRegistry.RootKey:=HKEY_LOCAL_MACHINE;
            MySubKey:='SOFTWARE\MyCompany';
            If MyRegistry.DeleteKey(MySubKey) then
            begin
                ShowMessage('MYAPP Successfully Uninstalled');
                MyRegistry.CloseKey;
                Application.Terminate;
            end;
```

As you can see, writing a simple installer and updating the Registry is not a big deal, but you do have quite a bit more work to do than what you did here if you want a nice, user-friendly installer.

NOTE

In this example, you hard coded the drive and directory values. Therefore, you might have to change the code to fit your needs if you plan to use a drive other than drive A or a directory other than C:\MYAPP.

If you have taken all the precautions and saved your Registry file to a safe place, you can run the program and see it in action. To do this, follow these steps:

1. Copy a small executable that you are familiar with to a blank formatted floppy.
2. Rename the executable to `myapp.exe`.
3. Compile and run the program, and the application's form appears.
4. Press the Continue button. The floppy drive light should come on as the program copies the file to the new directory—`c:\myapp`. A message box should indicate that the installation was successful.

To test the installation, follow these steps:

1. Check whether the directory `c:\myapp` exists. It should contain the application `myapp.exe`.
2. Check whether the Registry was updated correctly by choosing the Windows 95 or Windows NT Run option, type `REGEDIT`, and click OK to bring up the Registry Editor.
3. When `REGEDIT` pops up, double-click on `HKEY_LOCAL_MACHINE`, then on `SOFTWARE`. In other words, open to the following in the tree list portion of the Registry Editor:

   `HKEY_LOCAL_MACHINE/SOFTWARE`

   You should see `MyCompany` as a subkey.
4. You can open each subkey as in step 3 until you get down to the `MyApp` subkey. The value that contains the version number (`MyAppVer`), as shown here, will appear on the right side of the Registry Editor under the Name and Data headings:

   `HKEY_LOCAL_MACHINE/SOFTWARE/MyCompany/MyApp/MyAppVer`

The above Registry information is displayed in a tree format in `REGEDIT`.

When you are satisfied that the installation works properly, you should test the uninstall portion of the code using these steps:

1. Run the program again but this time use the `/U` parameter on the command line. You also can run from Delphi by choosing Run | Parameters to access the Run Parameters dialog box, adding `/U` to the parameters, and then pressing F9 to run the program.
2. The file and directory are deleted, and the entries are removed from the Registry.
3. To verify this, search for the directory (`c:\myapp`) and use `REGEDIT` to view the Registry to ensure that the Registry entries added earlier have been removed.

To make this installer satisfy the Windows 95 logo requirements, you need to do much more work. This program falls severely short of a good installer. It doesn't compress files, store values such as a path in the Registry to make the entries useful, provide indicators of installation progress, or create a folder or group with shortcuts or icons. You now have, however, an idea of what creating an installer involves. Writing a decent installer actually warrants a book of its own.

For many people, creating an installer and uninstaller from scratch does not make sense. You should use a third-party install program generator to create your installers whenever possible. They help ensure that your applications have a consistent look and feel during the installation process. They also save you time and hassles. There is no need to reinvent the wheel, so to speak, unless you plan to write your own commercial installer.

Using a Commercial Install Program Generator

Several third-party tools are available that generate install programs for you—just scan the advertisements in any Delphi, Visual Basic, or Windows developer magazine. This section covers InstallShield, which many programs on the market use. You probably have installed programs that use InstallShield. It provides gauges on the screen that track the progress of the entire installation and the current disk. With InstallShield, you can build a simple script, create a list of files to be installed, add messages, and compile an installer in no time.

The version of InstallShield used for this section is version 3, which runs on Windows 3.1, Windows 95, and Windows NT 3.5 or higher. If you want to be more elaborate, you might need a Windows resource editor (such as Borland's Resource Workshop) and a C++ compiler (such as Borland's C++ 4.0 or higher).

InstallShield 3.0 offers the following features:

- [ ] A scripting language that enables you to customize the installer for your needs
- [ ] Sample scripts
- [ ] Support for user dialog boxes
- [ ] Bitmaps for displaying graphics and information for the user
- [ ] Updates to text files, including AUTOEXEC.BAT and CONFIG.SYS
- [ ] Registry updates
- [ ] Create and uninstall options
- [ ] The ability to access the Windows API or DLLs from a script

InstallShield's scripting language looks like a cross between C and Pascal, but you do not need to understand either one to use it. You should feel comfortable with InstallShield after you familiarize yourself with the commands and syntax of the scripting language. You can customize the sample scripts that come with the package to fit your needs. The manual is packed with all the information you need to get going quickly. The product also has a royalty-free license agreement, which means that you can ship your installers with as many programs as you like.

The beginning of an InstallShield script has a constant-declarations section, like the one in this example:

```
declare

// Constant declarations.
#define SPACE_REQUIRED          100000          // Disk space in bytes.
#define APP_NAME                "My Application"
#define PROGRAM_FOLDER_NAME     "My Application Folder"
#define APPBASE_PATH            "Program Files\\MyCompany\\Myapp1\\"
#define APPBASE_PATH_WIN32S     "Programf\\MyCompany\\Myapp1\\"
#define COMPANY_NAME            "MyCompany"
#define PRODUCT_NAME            "MyApp"
#define PRODUCT_VERSION         "1.0"
#define DEINSTALL_KEY           "Sample1DeinstKey"
#define UNINSTALL_NAME          "Sample1App"
#define PRODUCT_KEY             "myapp.exe"
```

By making changes that apply to your application in the declaration section of a sample script, you can create an installer quickly. Code for creating program groups and Registry entries, checking disk space, creating subdirectories, and decompressing and copying files is provided in the sample script. You use their constant names, but you set your own values. After you set up the constants, the sample scripts will compile. After you compile a list of files to be installed and move them to a floppy disk, your installer is ready for use.

You can make only small changes to the sample scripts at first. Then, as you become more familiar with the product and the scripting language, you can customize your installers as much as you want. The scripting language is powerful. It has a wealth of functions for doing just about anything you might need in an installer. You can run other DOS or Windows applications from the installer. The language is also extensible through its ability to call functions in DLLs and the Windows API. This means that you can write your own functions and routines in Delphi to extend its power and capability. InstallShield's manual is well written and has information on creating DLLs with Borland and Microsoft C++ compilers.

InstallShield 3.0 is useful in creating install programs for any Windows applications regardless of the languages they are written in. Stirling Software also has InstallShield Express Lite for Delphi, a Windows application for creating installers for Delphi applications. InstallShield Express Lite for Delphi presents you with what looks like a yellow notepad that has a checklist on it. You click each item and are presented with dialog boxes that ask for information. You point and click your way through the selections, enter application names, your company name, files to be installed, Registry entries, and so on. You can create a disk image and do a test run. When you are satisfied, the files are transferred to setup disks, and your application is ready to ship.

You literally can create an installer in about 10 minutes and not write a single line of code. That's right, no script to write as there is with InstallShield 3.0. And now for the best news of all, ISXpress for Delphi ships with Delphi 3.0! Whether you use the InstallShield Express or other InstallShield product, you easily will be able to produce high-quality installers that meet the Windows 95 logo requirements with little or no coding in a very short amount of time.

Summary

Today you learned about the Windows 95 logo requirements that applications and installers must meet. You saw how important the Registry is and how it eliminates the need for .ini files. You wrote a simple installer that checked available disk space, created a directory, copied files to the new directory, and made Registry entries. You enabled the program to uninstall the files and clean up the Registry entries.

You also learned about InstallShield, a third-party install program generator that simplifies the process of making professional installers. You are now ready to create your own installer and uninstaller package. What are you waiting for? Go make your first million!

Q&A

Q What if I need to update or create .ini files?

A You still can use the TIniFile object in Delphi to work with .ini files. It should be used only for backward compatibility or in cases where the Registry is not suitable for the task. Use of .ini files can disqualify your application for the Windows 95 logo. Refer to Delphi's online help and manuals for information on the topic.

Q What if I want my install program to update the Windows 95 Add/Remove Programs section in the Control Panel so that I can uninstall it easily later?

A This is simple, provided that your program has an uninstall feature or that you have written a separate uninstaller. Add the following entries to the Registry:

```
HKEY_LOCAL_MACHINE
\SOFTWARE\Microsoft\Windows\CurrentVersion\Uninstall\
  ➥Application Name
  DisplayName=Product Name
  UninstallString=path and filename with any necessary
  ➥command line parameters.
```

Your uninstall code must remove these entries from the Registry when it is done.

Workshop

The Workshop provides two ways for you to affirm what you've learned in this chapter. The Quiz section poses questions to help you solidify your understanding of the material covered. You can find answers to the quiz questions in Appendix A, "Answers to the Quiz Questions." The Exercises section provides you with experience in using what you have learned. Please try to work through all these before continuing to the next day.

15

Quiz

1. What are Packages, and why should you use them?
2. When Microsoft reviews requests to display the Windows 95 logo, what are the four main categories of programs that it considers?
3. List three requirements that fit programs in all four categories.
4. How do you add a Registry key?
5. How do you delete a Registry key?
6. Why should you use the Registry rather than .ini files?
7. How many main Registry keys are there?
8. What is the name of the Registry file in Windows 95? Does it show up in a normal directory listing?

Exercises

1. Modify the install program that you created in this chapter so that the name of the file, the directory, and the path information are not hard coded. Make the program get the necessary information from a file called SETUP.LST. The program should be able to install multiple files listed in SETUP.LST. Make the form go full screen, and give it a blue background. Make it look more professional.
2. Use REGEDIT to export a copy of the Registry. Consult Delphi's online help for information. Then export the contents of only one main key.

APPENDIX
A

Answers to the Quiz Questions

Day 1

1. The first benefit is that you can rapidly prototype front ends to show customers with a minimum amount of work. The second benefit is that you do not have to throw that work away as you would if you used one of those demo front-end builders. You can turn your demo into the end product. That means you don't waste time. Even another benefit is that a RAD environment offers a highly integrated, high-level tool set to maximize your productivity.

2. The visual components differ in many ways from ActiveX controls. One way is that VCs compile right into your executable because they are native Delphi code. ActiveX must be included separately with your finished product.

3. Delphi, of course! (Pascal)

4. Syntax highlighting is a feature offered in the Delphi development environment in which the editor understands the Delphi language. Through this understanding, the editor is able to color code different portions of your code (comments are gray; reserved words are blue). You can change the colors used to highlight the code. The benefit of this feature is to point out mistakes and make the code easier to read.

5. You would choose the Component | Install Component menu selection from the Delphi main menu to install a VC or ActiveX control. To install a Delphi package, choose Component | Install Package from Delphi's main menu.

Day 2

1. Constants cannot change their value during the execution of the application, whereas variables are designed to do exactly that.

2. Because our mathematical equations in code must act the same as the real world of math; otherwise, the computer would generate incorrect answers.

3. Typed constants are basically variables that are pre-initialized. The benefit here is that with pre-initialization your variable starts out life fulfilled!

Day 3

1. 100 times. The outer loop goes 10 times around, and for each one of those times, the inner loop runs through 10 iterations: $10 \times 10 = 100$.

2. `While...do` tests the condition prior to entering the loop.

3. A function is designed to return a single value, whereas a procedure is designed to returns no values. Use a `var` statement in the parameter list to effectively "return" values.

4. Passing around large data structures has a large overhead. It is more memory efficient to pass a pointer around.

Day 4

1. The goals are modifiability, efficiency, reliability, and understandability.
2. It supports information hiding by creating units. Units enable you to hide the implementation details of an application and present an interface to the data.
3. Because in the real world you have objects that are based on other objects. In Delphi, you can create a Car class, and then create child objects that inherit the Car class properties but add their own. The result could be a convertible class, a race car class, and so on.

Day 5

1. .PAS, .DPR, .DOF, .DFM, and .RES are created at design time, and .DCU and .EXE are created at compile time.
2. Unit heading, interface part, implementation part, initialization part, and finalization part.
3. To add a new form to your project, you can select the new form button from the SpeedMenu or choose File | New Form. To remove a form from the project, you can use the Project Manager user interface to select the form and then click on the remove-unit button. You also can select the form you wish to remove and use the Remove File From Project icon on the SpeedMenu, or you can use choose File | Remove From Project.
4. When you delete a form from a project, the associated .PAS or .DFM files are not deleted. Their references in the project source file are just removed.

Day 6

1. Default keymapping, IDE classic, Brief emulation, and Epsilon emulation.
2. Environment Options Editor tab.
3. The gutter is used to set breakpoints and show where they are set by displaying a red dot. The gutter also shows the current line of execution with a green arrow.
4. To trace into a DLL with Delphi 3's debugger, you must write or use a "host application" that will call the DLL. Choose Run | Parameters, and then select enter the Host Application name. Enter run parameters if applicable. Set breakpoints,

watches, and so on, as desired, and then click on Run. Delphi will use the host application to launch and call the DLL and then stop at the first breakpoint in the DLL.

5. WinSight32 is a tool known as a spy. WinSight32 enables you to monitor Windows processes, Windows, Windows messages, and so on.

6. Three features of CodeInsight include Code Templates, Code Completion, and Code Parameter Expert. Code Templates quickly display the syntax for code structures and statements such as `For` loops, `If...Then...Else` statements, and so on. Code Completion finishes code for you quickly on-the-fly by enabling you to select the desired method from a pop-up list box. The Code Parameter Expert shows the syntax for the procedure, function, or method so that you can see the proper parameters and their correct usage in the function or procedure.

7. Press Ctrl+F5 or choose Run | Add Watch to pull up the Watch Properties dialog box. Then just type the name item, such as a variable that you want to watch.

8. Besides setting a watch, you can use ToolTip expression evaluation by placing the cursor over a variable during a debug session. After a short pause, the value of the variable under the cursor will be displayed in a ToolTip.

9. False. The compiler stops on a breakpoint before executing it.

10. To resume normal execution after stepping through a program, remove breakpoints if necessary and press F9.

Day 7

1. Right-clicking on an object brings up context-sensitive menus that apply to that object. This helps you see what functions can be performed on this object at this time.

2. Those specific-sized windows are designed to go well with specific screen resolutions for maximum visibility and usefulness. Also, if we all use them, it helps reinforce the uniformity of the environment.

3. So that the user does not have to spend a lot of time learning how to navigate your application's menu bar, but instead can spend it learning the application itself.

Day 8

1. The user can view a visual component at runtime if the visible property is set to `True`. A nonvisual component is visible at design time but not at runtime.

2. Nested properties are properties within properties. You can spot a property with nested properties because it has a plus sign to the left of it. If you click the plus

sign, it expands to show the nested properties. Properties can be nested several levels.

3. A method is a function or procedure declared inside a component or object that can be called to affect the behavior or appearance of that object.

4. Components and objects have events associated with them that, when activated, execute associated event handlers (sections of code). An example of a common event would be a mouse click.

5. MaskEdit.

6. Timer.

Day 9

1. Typed files are files that are formatted a particular way and that store a particular type of data in specific fields.

2. Seek(var F; N: Longint);

3. Using an untyped file in Delphi enables you to work with any file. You can use EXE files as well as DLLs, text files, or others. As an untyped file, Delphi treats each file as just a stream of bits, and it is up to the programmer to handle the data once the file is opened.

4. No, you can assign a file variable to the Printer and print to it using commands such as Writeln();.

5. You must add Printers to the Uses clause.

6. BeginDoc and EndDoc.

7. True.

8. There is no code to execute the Properties dialog box. It is accessed from the Print dialog box.

9. CopyRect.

10. You simply draw the circle on the Printer canvas just as you would a screen-related canvas, such as a form.

```
begin
     {Start the print job}
     Printer.BeginDoc;
     {Set the width of the pen to be 5 pixels wide}
     Printer.Canvas.Pen.Width:=5;
     {Draw an ellipse with the upper left corner at 0,0
      and the lower right corner at 200,200}
     Printer.Canvas.Ellipse(0, 0, 200, 200);
     {complete and print the print job}
     Printer.EndDoc;
end;
```

Day 10

1. The triangle would not erase itself and would leave a trail as it moved across the window.

2. The easiest way to perform clipping in a rectangular region is to use a PaintBox visual component. The PaintBox visual component prevents anything from being drawn outside the paint box.

3. Image visual components can encapsulate a bitmap object. Bitmap objects have a LoadFromFile method that can be used to load a bitmap from a file into the bitmap, which in turn loads the image into the image component. The CopyRect method can be used to copy a portion of any canvas (including a canvas in a bitmap) to any other canvas (including the canvas of a PaintBox).

4. PlaySound accepts a set of parameters that determine how a sound is played and where the source of the sound is located. One of these parameters determines if the sound is played synchronously or asynchronously. If the sound is played synchronously, the application waits until the sound has been played. The asynchronous setting allows the sound to play while the application continues to execute.

5. It means to set the display region between pixels 50,50 and 250,250. The first set indicates the location (50,50), and the second set indicates the width and height (200,200).

6. Drawing directly on a canvas causes a flickering effect. To achieve smoother animation, draw on a bitmap and then copy the image to the visual canvas.

Day 11

1. An exception will occur if you attempt to execute a method that attempts to change data while a table is in a dsBrowse state.

2. Fields can be accessed as components. The TField component has a DataType property which indicates what type of data a particular field contains.

3. The IndexName property on a TTable component can be set to a secondary index to order the records by the index specified.

4. Both file share and client/server databases support multiple applications accessing the database simultaneously. Some true standalone databases allow only a single application to access it.

5. Regular fields cannot be updated when a data set is in a dsCalculate state. Only calculated fields can be updated while in this state; however, all fields can be read.

6. A field indicating a key in a different table is called a *foreign key*.

Day 12

1. QuickReport is a banded report generator.

2. Bands in QuickReport are used to display data and images as containers for QuickReport components used to visually build a report.

3. No. The QuickReport components are used to design and build reports, not to be viewed by the user.

4. A TTable connects to the database, and the TQuickRep component connects the QuickReport bands and components to the table.

5. To select Chart type, in the Object Inspector for the TChart, double-click on the SeriesList to bring up the Chart Editor. Next, select the Chart tab and then the Series tab under the Chart tab. Click on the Add button, select the desired chart type from the TeeChart Gallery, and then click OK.

6. Using the Chart Editor, select the Title tab under the Chart tab, and then enter the title.

7. Double-click on the SeriesList from the Object Inspector.

8. Yes.

Day 13

1. When a component user sets a property, it can trigger a procedure that processes all the applicable logic.

2. Properties available at development time can be set by using the Object Inspector. Properties available at runtime can be set only by using Object Pascal code.

3. A public property is available to any code at runtime. Specifying a property as published will make it appear in the Object Inspector and thus be available at development time.

4. Both properties and events are declared identically. However, events are defined as special event types that make the Object Inspector list them on the Events page.

5. A class ID is a unique identifier that distinguishes a class from every other class in the world. An application can create an instance of a class by specifying the class ID. A type library defines the sets of functions, or interfaces, that an object exposes. An application can use a type library to access functions in a COM object before the application is compiled or executed.

6. Yes, ActiveX components can be used in any application or language that understands how to create an instance of an ActiveX component. Some examples of applications that can use ActiveX components include Internet Explorer, Visual Basic, Visual C++, and Microsoft Word.

Day 14

1. CGI applications run in their own process space. Therefore, it is almost impossible for a misbehaved CGI application to take down a Web server. On the downside, it is rather expensive to spawn a new process for each application request. An ISAPI Web application runs in the same process space as the Web server, so there is an increase in performance, but it incurs extra concerns dealing with thread safety and stability.

2. The `TWebRequest.QueryFields` property can be accessed to read the decoded information passed from the client. This saves you a great deal of work in that you don't need to write the decode routines themselves.

3. The `codebase` tag is used to tell a Web client where an ActiveX component can be found if it is not installed on the user's system. Version information can be appended to the tag to ensure that the user has a current version of the component.

Day 15

1. Packages are special DLLs that contain all the Delphi components and libraries. When you turn on support for packages, you can ship the packages once and then ship "thin applications" (small executables), making distribution over a network or the Internet much quicker.

2. File-based applications, non-file-based applications that run exclusively in full mode not windowed, utilities including file and disk utilities, virus-scanning programs, virus-cleaning programs, and development tools.

3. The answers are as follows:

    a. The application must use the Win32 API.

    b. The application must follow the Windows 95 look and feel for the user interface.

    c. The application must be tested and successfully run on both Windows 95 and Windows NT and be adjusted as necessary to compensate for differences in features between the two.

4. Using the `Tregistry` object's `WriteString` method.

5. Using the `Tregistry` object's `DeleteKey` method.

6. One reason is that it is a requirement for the Windows 95 logo. Another reason is that it is a safer place to store your program's configuration information than `.ini` files because `.ini` files are easily deleted.

7. Six: `Hkey_Local_MACHINE`, `Hkey_Current_Config`, `Hkey_Dyn_Data`, `Hkey_Classes_Root`, `Hkey_Users`, and `Hkey_Current_User`.

8. The Registry filename is `SYSTEM.DAT`. It does not appear in a normal directory listing because it is a hidden file.

INDEX

V

MACMILLAN COMPUTER PUBLISHING USA

A VIACOM COMPANY

Technical ---- Support:

If you need assistance with the information in this book or with a CD/Disk accompanying the book, please access the Knowledge Base on our Web site at **http://www.superlibrary.com/general/support**. Our most Frequently Asked Questions are answered there. If you do not find the answer to your questions on our Web site, you may contact Macmillan Technical Support **(317) 581-3833** or e-mail us at **support@mcp.com**.